# Renewing American Industry

# Renewing American Industry

*Paul R. Lawrence*
*Davis Dyer*

**THE FREE PRESS**
*A Division of Macmillan, Inc.*
NEW YORK

Collier Macmillan Publishers
LONDON

The Free Press
A Division of Macmillan, Inc.
866 Third Avenue, New York, N.Y. 10022

Collier Macmillan Canada, Inc.

Printed in the United States of America

printing number
1 2 3 4 5 6 7 8 9 10

**Library of Congress Cataloging in Publication Data**

Lawrence, Paul R.
    Renewing American industry.

    Includes index.
    1. Industrial management — United States —
Case studies. 2. Organizational change — United
States — Case studies. 3. Organizational ef-
fectiveness — Case studies. 4. United States —
Industries — Case studies. I. Dyer, Davis.
II. Title.
HD70.U5L38   1983      338.0973      82-72096
ISBN 0-02-918170-4

To
Martha, Edward and Prudence

# Contents

# Preface

THIS STUDY has long roots into the past. As a young graduate student at the Harvard Business School in the early forties I was greatly influenced by Elton Mayo and his book, *The Human Problems of an Industrial Civilization*. Mayo's work identified the pivotal role of industrial organizations in influencing the quality of individual lives and the quality of civilization. I have been caught up ever since in the challenge of making industrial organizations more effective in these roles. Current industrial problems have not only strengthened my conviction that improving organizations is crucial, but have also provided a special timeliness for addressing these issues.

In the early stages of writing this book I realized that I needed the collaboration of a trained historian; in 1979 Davis Dyer joined the project. The project became a truly joint effort as the "I" changed to "we." Together we shared the challenge of finding a new and relevant way of understanding the problems of American industry.

In the late 1970s when work on this book began, U.S. industry was much less conspicuously in trouble than it is now. Since then the popular press has made sure that the public is aware, for instance, of the plight of the automobile industry with its fall from record profits to record losses in the face of foreign competition. While autos are the most dramatic example, all industry, including the service and financial sectors, high technology as well as heavy industry, is having serious problems. Critics, economists, and journalists agree on the symptoms of the trouble which besets the American industrial scene: declining productivity, unemployment, high interest rates, inflation, an aging workforce, a worsening trade balance. There is no agreement, however, on the causes of these difficulties. Some critics argue the improper use of macroeconomic tools of fiscal and monetary policy. Some lament the inconsistencies of government action and call for an explicit and coherent "industrial policy." Still others, pointing to the miracle of the Japanese economy, argue that American businessmen have been too focused on financial ratios and quarterly earnings to see the need for the long-term investments necessary to maintain a healthy, competitive position.

So the arguments go, an inconclusive debate attempting to diagnose—and by extension to suggest a cure for—the plight of American business. In spite of the breadth and intensity of the debate, the protagonists seem largely to ignore the internal capacities of business organizations that determine whether or not they can cope creatively with significant changes in their environment. What, one asks, are these internal features? Do some particular qualities characterize those American industrial organizations which have been able to sustain their initial success over a long period? Why do so many firms, as they mature, lose their capacity to adapt? Is there a readaptive process by which organizations can continually sustain both efficiency and innovation?

Adaptation is a powerful metaphor. Evolutionary biologists describe organisms as adapting to their environments when adjustments or accommodations take place which increase the likelihood of their survival. This is a slow, one-way process with organisms adapting to their environments over many generations. Business environments change much more rapidly than natural ones, however, so that in order to succeed business organizations must continually adapt and readapt to the ever-changing scene. This ongoing adaptation further differs from the process of biological adaptation in being a two-way process: a successful business organization not only adapts to its environment but, to a degree, can shape that environment. Organization and environment are, in effect, mutually adaptive.

The argument developed in this book will ask the reader to cope with certain abstract, perhaps unfamiliar, terms in the interest of seeing common patterns in diverse industries. Unfortunately, everyday vocabulary is surprisingly inadequate for discussing the adaptive interplay between organizations and their environments. This linguistic inadequacy was highlighted by the trouble we had in selecting a title for this book. "Change" was proposed as a key word but change can be for the better or the worse. Was "industrial health" a useful metaphor, or as we eventually decided, did it overextend the biological analogy? Even the word "organization" had a possible static connotation. We cite this seemingly petty problem of the difficulties encountered in choosing a title as a warning to the reader that, for the sake of ultimate clarity, we have felt the need to develop some of our own terminology; we saw this step as unavoidable.

A word about our procedure. We have drawn on a wide range of the professional literature on organizations and industrial history. We have examined in considerable depth the adaptive history of seven industries that address basic human needs: transport (automobiles), materials (steel), health (hospitals), food (agriculture), shelter (residential construction), energy (coal), and communication (telecommunications). While Chapters 2 through 8 are based largely on public information and archival sources, six doctoral students contributed to the project field work done in these industries, and we have both conducted many field interviews.

In each of these industries there is great diversity among firms; large and small, old and new, simple and complex, healthy and sick. As we have examined their histories we have looked for critical turning points, key acts of leadership, crucial governmental impacts, and important organizational practices and strategies. From this investigation we have found the building blocks with which to construct a model, piece by piece, of the readaptive process. The quest to understand this process framed the historical research: the historical research, in turn, provided new evidence and suggested new ways of thinking about the process.

We believe that this way of thinking about organizations has important implications for both business managers and government policy makers. It is relevant not only to the challenges currently facing the seven industries studied here, but, beyond that, to all business sectors. We hope our model will help business managers begin to think in new ways about the choice of appropriate organizational forms and strategies and public managers to think in new ways about gearing policies to the distinctive need of each essential industry.

By now our reasons for writing this book should be clear. We have studied the record of historical change in American industry looking for ways to improve the record of future change, for we believe that in America's industrial past lies a key to understanding its present and to achieving the full potential of its future. Our analysis, of course, will be open to question and change; in such a marvelously complex field of inquiry there can be no simple, final answer. Others will now, we hope, feel challenged to build on our evaluation of American industrial organizations.

Paul R. Lawrence
Davis Dyer

June 24, 1982
Cambridge, Massachusetts

# Acknowledgments

WE ARE DEEPLY INDEBTED to a great many people for their generous and constructive assistance in the development of this book.

This project from its inception to its conclusion has been encouraged and financially supported by the Division of Research at the Harvard Business School. In particular we are grateful to Richard Rosenbloom who, as Director of Research, helped launch the project and to Raymond Corey who, as the subsequent Director of Research, saw it through to a conclusion. We benefitted from the consistent support of Dean Lawrence Fouraker and later Dean John McArthur.

Individuals with special expertise contributed ideas and suggestions for the chapters on the seven basic industries: William Abernathy and Mark Fuller for autos; J. Ronald Fox and Paul Marshall for steel; Alan Sheldon, Barbara Rosenkrantz and Paul Starr for hospitals; Ray Goldberg for agriculture; Quinn Mills and Robert Eccles for housing; Robert Stobaugh, Balaji Chakravarthy and Gerald Drummond for coal; Anthony Oettinger, Calvin Pava, and George D. Smith for telecommunications. Thomas Lifson gave us the benefit of expert thinking on the section on Japanese industry. The doctoral students who helped dig out the basic facts about each industry were Victor Faux, Diana Barrett, Martin Charns, Thomas Clough, Robert Eccles and Balaji Chakravarthy.

Colleagues who were especially helpful in critiquing drafts of the entire manuscript were Andrew Pettigrew, John Kotter, Robert Miles, Renato Taguiri, Michael Beer, and Jeffrey Sonnenfeld.

Harrison White, Rodney Beddows, William Pounds, Lawrence Hrebniak, and Malcolm Knapp provided stimulating and useful ideas at the formative stage of the project.

Alfred D. Chandler, Jr., Susan Reverby, David Rosner and Molly Selvin were particularly helpful with bibliographic research and providing access to unpublished material.

Rita Perloff, with extraordinary skill, has guided the complex manuscript material through several versions. To her, and to Muriel Wallace, we express special appreciation. We are indebted to Jonathan Wylie, Nancy Jackson and Anne Stiles Wylie for their excellent editorial assistance.

In spite of all this help we, the authors, are entirely responsible for the accuracy of our material and the soundness of our conclusions.

# CHAPTER 1

# Dilemmas Facing American Industry

IN INDUSTRY AFTER INDUSTRY, U.S. firms are losing their competitive advantage to foreign firms. This loss is the underlying cause for the country's present, serious, economic distress and the many social problems closely related to it. Unemployment, adverse balance of payments, decline in the growth of the gross national product, low rate of productivity gain, and the high level of interest rates and inflation are but symptoms of a seriously weakened position industry by industry, firm by firm. Even a significant upswing in the entire economy would provide only temporary and partial relief from this general weakened condition.

The American public is well aware of the threat posed by the industrial strength of certain European countries and especially of Japan. In addition, firms in other countries have emerged as tough, international competitors: South Korea, Taiwan, Brazil, Hong Kong, Mexico, and Singapore are now serious challengers to U.S. firms. The list of industries in which leadership has migrated overseas is equally sobering: radios, cameras, television, watches, stereo equipment, shoes, steel, tires, motorcycles, memory chips, and machine tools. The recent addition of automobiles to this roster has proved particularly threatening and disruptive. Soon, moreover, the United States may well find the automobile industry in even greater trouble and the computer industry added to the list of industries in which it has failed to keep its number one position.

1

We do not make the chauvinistic presumption that the United States has a god-given right to dominate every world industry. To the contrary, it is healthy from an American as well as an international perspective that foreign economies be strong and assume leadership whenever they achieve a competitive advantage. The problem for the United States, moreover, must not be exaggerated to imply that America has suddenly become economically impotent, for by any standard its resources are still enormous.

America has always been particularly successful at developing new industries. Almost every important new industry over the past one hundred years had its initial success in the United States. This country's diversity, entrepreneurial spirit, risk capital, and potential markets continue to foster the development of new businesses. There is no reason to think it has lost this start-up strength. Rather, the problems appear later in an industry's history, as it reaches maturity: even seemingly healthy firms cannot be counted on to sustain their dynamic and competitive stance. Organizations have shown this tendency to stagnate as they grow older and bigger; soon they become vulnerable to foreign competition. Although the present symptoms of this condition may be particularly acute, the problem is by no means new. Over the last century the United States lost its world leadership in shipbuilding, ocean transport, railroading, and textile manufacturing.

It is generally recognized that our economy faces serious problems. Leaders of business, labor, and both political parties acknowledge that the problems are real and must be addressed. With increasing emphasis the press in the United States is focusing national attention on the weaknesses of many established industries. This attention is all to the good. The most disturbing aspect of the present situation, however, is that a lack of agreement on the underlying causes for the poor economic performance precludes any concerted remedial action.

The list of areas of disagreement seems endless. Contradictory remedies are touted by the supporters of contradictory explanations for the roots of the current industrial malaise. Arguments for direct government support in such forms as guaranteed loans are no less vigorous than arguments for indirect support such as tax incentives for business investment. A solution to this particular debate would lead to equally sharp disagreement over whether government support should flow to sick industries or strong ones. In the realm of international trade, key business and labor leaders call for import restrictions even as economist Milton Friedman and his followers champion increased free trade. During the same years that the Justice Department was trying to break up two of America's larger and healthier companies (unsuccessfully in the case of IBM, successfully in the case of AT&T), others were urging consolidation of all oil companies into a single state enterprise. The argument that the United States ought to copy Japan in managing business, government and union relations is countered with the argument that cultural differences between the two countries would prove an insurmountable barrier to the success of such an approach.

Countless theories are put forth about government regulation of industry in the United States. In the interest of lessening unemployment and coping with foreign competition, there are eloquent pleas to give industry relief from strict regulations concerning pollution, product safety, and equal opportunity. Meanwhile, there are regular reports that new instances of pollution, product hazards, work hazards, and employee inequities call for increased regulatory action. In a growing concern with the quality of business management, cogent arguments indentify plain bad management as the source of a significant number of economic problems. At first some agreement on this point seems possible, but further analysis quickly reveals a multitude of different definitions of good and bad management.

So the debates on the possible causes and cures for the condition of American industry go on. The diverse and conflicting ideas about causes are leading to piecemeal, inconsistent, and half-hearted remedies. What they ignore, almost without exception, is what would seem to be the critical question: *why do so many American firms and industries fail, in their maturity, to maintain their competitive vitality?* Inquiry and debate seldom address the dubious record of industrial organizations in responding to fundamental changes in their environment. This oversight grows increasingly hard to comprehend since environmental uncertainty is almost sure to increase. Changing environmental factors will continue to pose a challenge to industrial health in the United States as well as elsewhere in the industrial world: witness the volatility of world politics; the escalating changes generated by the new information technologies; the coming impact of new biological technologies; the continuing pressure of population growth; the industrial aspirations of the Third World countries; the finite nature of our natural resources; the fragility of our ecosystem. In the face of these challenges, ongoing organizational adaptation is clearly essential to the long-term well-being of all industrial societies.

In sum, there is agreement that American industry is beset by difficulties, but because there is so little agreement on the causes of these problems, there is no consensus about what effective remedial action there might be. Inquiry and debate consistently overlook not only the dynamic interplay between an industry and its changing environment but more importantly overlook the tendency in American firms for stagnation to follow closely on the heels of initial success. We propose that an historical overview of the way key organizations and industries have, in fact, adapted to changing conditions can provide significant clues to the fundamental causes of the difficulties and dilemmas American industry now faces. We believe that a more complete and comprehensive understanding of these causes can lead to workable solutions.

Before an analytic, historical overview can effectively be either presented or examined for those clues, however, we as authors and readers should agree on the framework in which our observations will be organized. Furthermore, we must establish a common vocabulary, specialized though it may be, so that we can describe in sufficient detail the operation of the framework. We assume, to this end, that industrial organizations are affected by changes in their environments and that, acting either singly or collectively, they can and do affect their environments. The quality of this process of *mutual adaptation* is of specific concern in our analytic approach. It is, therefore, a distinctive feature of our approach, unlike that taken by most economists and organization theorists, to examine both external conditions and internal organizational forms and to show how they interact to effect mutual adaptation.

To begin analyzing the process of mutual adaptation we first need a general way to characterize the immediately relevant environment of the firms to be studied. We take two points as given: (1) every organization must secure *resources* from its environment in order to survive; and (2) it must also utilize *information* from its environment to make some sense out of all the events going on around it. Building on these points, we have evolved a chart, a working analytic framework, which is a simple but powerful way of mapping the adaptational journey both of industries and of their key firms. With it as a guide, observations of complex and often seemingly contradictory events in the diversity of both past and present industrial development prove to contain logic and pattern as we shall see. But again a caveat: the chart can serve as a useful guide only after the ideas governing its structure and function have been carefully described. Beginning with Chapter 2 we can demonstrate, in the context of our industrial histories, how the model can actually be used to organize and interpret the complex material under consideration.

The two operational axes of the chart, *An Analytic Framework of Adaptation* (see Figure 1.1), represent the important analytical distinction we see between the two aspects on any organization's environment: its *information domain* (the vertical axis) and its *resource domain* (the horizontal axis).* In this way those parts of an organization's environment on which it relies for material supplies and those on which

*In developing our framework we have drawn on theories from economics, cybernetics, biology, and learning theory as well as from organization theory. In the Appendix there is a more technical statement of these ideas and an exposition of their roots in existing research and theory.

it relies for what one can think of as intellectual or factual raw material are clearly differentiated. Any firm will experience uncertainty and lack of stability in its resource domain as a *scarcity* of essential material resources. Uncertainty about information, on the other hand, is experienced as an excessive *complexity* in respect to competitors, customers, technological development, and any other area in which information is essential. High uncertainty in both or either domain makes existence difficult for organizations; certainty tends to assure survival.

The important central point to these observations about the two domains on which an organization depends can be stated as a proposition:

> The difficulty organizations experience in coping with their resource domain *and with their* information domain *depends on the degree of uncertainty in these areas.*

The sliding scale, from low to high, on the vertical axis of the information domain measures the complexity of its variable aspects, i.e. variations in competitors, in technology, in customers, in products, and finally the variations in government regulations. As the degree of complexity in these factors increases so does the amount of information an organization needs to consider in order to make wise choices in regard to the goods and services it provides. The definition of this process reads:

> The number of variations in an organization's immediate environment which directly influence its choice of which goods and services to supply is called its information complexity (IC).

By this definition IC would, for example, usually be lower under monopoly conditions since there are no competitors to develop strategies requiring analysis; IC would usually be higher when a large number of competitors using different strategies offer competitive goods and services. IC would be expected to be lower when only one technology exists for producing a given product or service. It would also be likely to be lower when a firm serves only a single type of customer rather than multiple market segments, each of whose special needs and preferences ought, ideally, to be considered. The number and complexity of product variations would increase IC as would the number and complexity of relevant government regulations. We will take all these sources of IC into consideration in characterizing the overall IC of any organization.

The sliding scale on the horizontal axis of the resource domain, again marked high, low, and intermediate, measures the degree of dif-

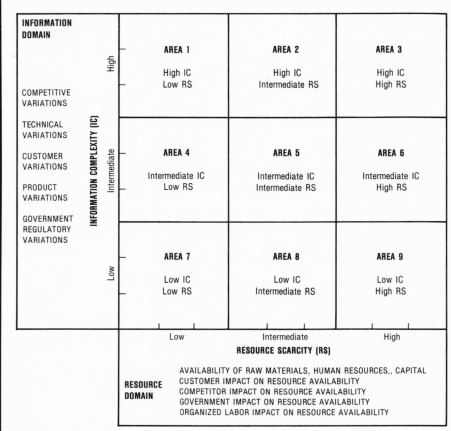

**Figure 1.1   Analytic Framework of Adaptation**

ficulty an organization has in securing the resources it needs to assure successful operation. In other words, it is concerned with scarcity of resources, whether raw material, capital, or people. Again, in the concise words of a definition:

> *The degree of difficulty an organization experiences in securing the resources it needs to survive and grow is called its* resource scarcity (RS).

The resources under consideration in judging an organization's RS are normally secured in exchange for the goods and services the organization offers. The result of the exchanges is a fluctuating balance of resource scarcity or abundance for the organization. The level of RS for an organization reflects changes in environmental factors such as customer demand for its particular goods and services, the actions of gov-

The Analytic Framework of Adaptation will be used repeatedly in the book to map the history of firms and to show the general tendencies of entire industries. Each of the nine areas shown represents a different type of organizational environment that is defined by the indicated combination of *information complexity* (IC) and *resource scarcity* (RS). Firms and industries can and do move from area to area at different historical periods as a result of their own actions or changes in the various environmental elements.

As an example, on the small replica of the Framework to the right, the simplest version of the history of the American automobile industry is used to give a feel for the way the shorthand of RS and IC can track the development of either a firm or an industry over many years of complex circumstances.

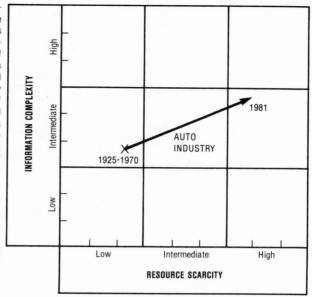

Beginning in 1925 the automobile industry was characterized for over 40 years by intermediate Information Complexity (IC) and low Resource Scarcity (RS). This fact is indicated by the X in Area 4. Significant evidence of the industry's fairly low RS was the very healthy profit margins the dominant firms enjoyed; the established "Big Three" pattern was an important diagnostic indicator of the intermediate range of the industry's IC.

During the 70's far-reaching changes occured in the industry's environment. The IC and especially the RS of the automobile industry were increasingly affected. These alterations in its position are reflected by the movement of the industry upward through Area 5. By 1981 its position was well into the upper left segment of Area 6 with its intermediate IC and high RS.

Chapter 2 analyzes the history of the automobile industry in detail.

ernment and labor, and the press of competitors for the same limited resources. Concomitantly, the organization influences the level of RS by means of the quality, cost, and quantity of goods and services it makes available for exchange. Long-term profit margins and the amount of a firm's assets are two of the more important indicators of RS that reflect the interplay among these variables.

We hope that by now the possibilities inherent in the Analytic Framework of Adaptation have begun to be apparent: by determining an organization's rank on its two intersecting axes, nine types of industrial environments can be distinguished. Labelled 1 to 9 on the chart, these nine "areas" are the shorthand we will use from now on to describe the environmental conditions faced by different firms and industries. We are now ready to define our key normative concept, *readaptation*, and the conditions that we posit as contributing to the *readaptive process*.

*An organization is defined as being in a state of* readaptation *when its performance is simultaneously efficient and innovative.*

In judging efficiency one asks: are resources being wasted? Is the quality of the output, its value to the ultimate consumer, commensurate with the costs of production? In judging innovation one asks: is a stream of ideas for relevant new goods and services and production techniques not only forthcoming but actually put to use in manufacture and distribution?

In industry after industry, competitors around the world are proving that organizations must be *both* efficient and innovative if they are to remain on the leading edge. It is self-evident that efficiency is necessary if an organization is to remain viable. It may be less obvious, but it is equally true, that there is a pressing need for innovative action when an organization is faced with a changing environment; simply being efficient is no longer enough.

Efficiency and innovation are difficult to reconcile. In the short run, these two performance targets can impede and block each other: innovations coming from the development laboratory are a hindrance to maintaining current production efficiency, while a drive, for instance, to cut costs in the name of efficiency is almost certain to reduce the budget for innovation. This tension is often expressed as a struggle between short-term and long-term policy, between the necessary looseness of creativity and the necessary rigidity of control. In every instance of such conflict, imaginative problem-solving is required if an either/or choice between innovation and efficiency is to be avoided. Over a long period, an organization can remain productively efficient only if it is actively and systematically on the look-out for new ideas and is regularly engaging in the problem-solving that resolves their conflicts with current efficiencies. We maintain that, if organizations are to be efficient production systems, they must also be innovative learning systems.

*The process by which organizations repeatedly reconcile efficiency and innovation is called the* readaptive process.

This concept of the readaptive process is central to our model. While other forms of mutual adaptation are possible — some industries and firms adapt only to the degree of achieving good records in just one of these two ways — we restrict the concept of readaptation to those cases in which the process of mutual adaptation leads to high levels of both efficiency and innovation. Adaptation of this sort is unique, we believe, in providing advantages for society as a whole as well as for the members of the organizational community at issue: the symbolism of the bottom line gives way to a test of authentic value, the creation of wealth.

We can speak in general terms about the need for organizations to be both innovative and efficient but, in the last analysis, individuals, the members of organizations, must do it. If innovation is to occur, individuals will need to observe and learn about their changing environment and come up with the fresh and suitable ideas that, step by step, are put into practice. Likewise, if efficiencies are to be maintained on a day by day basis, individuals have to invest the energy and exercise the discipline of making the best use of existing methods to produce the best quality of existing products. For a convenient summary we can say:

*For the readaptive process to be sustained, organizational members need to* learn *in order to be innovative and need to* strive *in order to be efficient.*

What conditions promote the needed learning process and the needed striving process? Drawing upon an extensive research literature,* we judge that organizations as represented by either group or individual efforts can have either too much or too little information complexity to foster the learning process. Too little IC cannot provide the diversity and variety that stimulate creative thinking. Too much IC can overload the cognitive capacity of the organizational membership working either individually or collectively. That is, the confusion of high IC discourages learning. Intermediate IC, on the other hand, induces the learning process. For similar reasons we hypothesize that either too much or too little resource scarcity can slow down the striving process in an organization. Too little RS reduces the motivation for seeking ways to be efficient, while too much RS means that the resources basic to achieving efficiency and innovation are lacking. Intermediate RS tends to induce the striving process. We consider these relationships between the organization and its environment as the governing dynamic central to readaptation. Thus:

*Readaptation, characterized by continuing efficiency and innovation, is most likely to occur when information complexity and resource scarcity both fall in the intermediate range of the Framework of Adaptation or in Area 5.*

Until now we have addressed the external conditions that foster or impede readaptation to the neglect of conditions internal to a given organization. An intermediate amount of RS and IC may well induce top

*See Appendix.

managers to learn and to strive, but other members of the organization may remain unaffected unless internal organizational arrangements spread similar inducements. In effect, the organization's internal practices need to disseminate the influence of intermediate IC and RS to organization members at all levels if they are to work toward high innovation and efficiency. Drawing again on prior research,* we believe that the underlying strategy and structure of an organization, its policies and practices in regard to human resources, and its distribution of power all contribute importantly to the readaptive process.

Certain internal conditions must be met if the total membership of an organization is to be involved in the learning and striving necessary for the readaptive process. In the first place, the organization must clearly and systematically communicate to the membership its goals and expectations. There must be as little ambiguity as possible regarding the principles underlying the organizational strategy, structure, and practices. Briefly:

> *The readaptive process depends on an organization's entire membership being made cognizant of the broad purpose, ethical standards, and operating principles of the firm with emphasis given throughout to the value of both efficiency and innovation.*

The second necessary internal condition involves the basic structure of an organization. If all the members of an organization are to direct their energies toward being efficient and innovative, the structure of the organization must reflect its external environment. This is accomplished by two processes; one we call *organizational differentiation*, the other *organizational integration*.

> *As information complexity increases, organizations must, within the limits of their resources, employ new kinds of specialists if they are to learn and innovate in regard to the new, incoming information. This is the process of organizational differentiation (D).*

As an example: as government regulations proliferate, firms need to add specialists in public affairs to their staffs.

> *As resource scarcity increases, organizations must increase the number of mechanisms available for coordinating their activities if they are to be efficient—up to the point, that is, that the*

*See Appendix.

*scarcity of resources itself acts as a constraint. This is the pro-cess of* organizational integration (I).

These extra integrative mechanisms take such forms as control systems, centralized planning staffs, and decentralized liaison staff and task forces.

Since, by and large, organizations foster innovation through differ-entiation, efficiency through integration, we can state that:

*Within a given firm readaptation will be most likely when both organizational differentiation and organizational integration are high.*

Because there are resource and size constraints with high levels of RS and IC, organizations with a high D and high I structure are most likely to appear in Area 5 of the adaptational framework (Figure 1.1). For any organization being analyzed on the basis of this model, the linkage between its differentiated organizational units (sales, finance, etc.) and environmental elements as well as the integrative linkages among all these organizational units are shown schematically in Fig-ure 1.2.

A third internal condition crucial to the readaptive process is the balanced use of three kinds of human resource practices that can help to draw employees into the affairs of a firm. The employees can be involved by such market-like financial devices as merit raises, bonus payments, and gain-sharing plans to supplement regular wages and salaries. In addition, they can be drawn into the affairs of the organi-zation by traditional bureaucratic mechanisms, the organization's chain of command and its rule book. Finally, certain mechanisms aimed more directly at an individual's membership needs (Ouchi uses the term "clan mechanisms"[1]) can be operative; e.g., provisions for employment security, use of work teams, job rotation, and practices re-flecting the organization's concern for the general well-being of the employee and his/her family. That is:

*The readaptive process depends on an organization making balanced use of three kinds of human resource practices affect-ing the involvement of their employees:* market mechanisms *of-fering tangible financial rewards* (M); bureaucratic mecha-nisms *encouraging stability in the organization* (B); *and* clan mechanisms *encouraging a sense of membership* (C).

A fourth internal condition needs to be met if the employees of an organization are to be involved in the process of readaptation: power

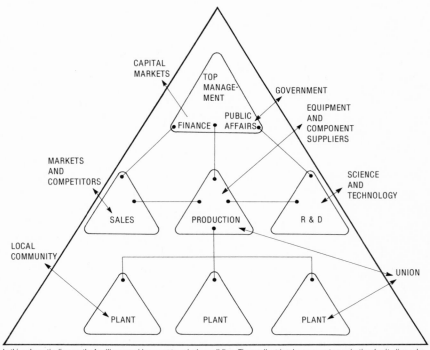

In this schematic diagram the familiar pyramid represents a single small firm. The smaller triangles represent organizational units (i.e. sales, R&D, plant, etc.) that are *differentiated* from one another so they can link (◄———►) effectively to specified elements of the firm's environment (i.e. markets, government, etc.). These differentiated units are also shown as linked to one another (●———●) to indicate their *integration*.

**Figure 1.2    A Schematic Description of Differentiation and Integration**

must be relatively evenly distributed. The temporary assignment of extra clout to a single department can sometimes be useful, for example in giving some extra weight to the sales department during a sudden downturn in orders. But a lasting and significant imbalance of power seriously impedes communication and complicates problem solving. This is a particular hazard in large organizations where concentration of power at the top is a usual feature of the organizational hierarchy. No one subgroup, not even top management, can dominate completely if the total membership is to be involved actively in learning and striving. Thus:

> *The readaptive process depends on the organization's structure reflecting over-all a relatively even distribution of power; there must be a reasonable balance in the vertical hierarchy as well as among the operating functions and/or divisions positioned horizontally throughout the organization.*

For convenience, we group these internal factors necessary for readaptation under the collective heading of *readaptive form and strategy*. Figure 1.3 shows the interplay we expect in the complete readaptive process among these internal factors and the environmental factors we discussed earlier.

For further help in understanding the dynamics of the readaptive process, the hypothetical development paths which might be expected for firms in a newly emerging industry with attractive prospects is traced in Figure 1.4.

The time has come to turn to the individual histories of seven American industries if the barebone analytic framework as it has been presented in the abstract is to be brought to life. The systematic analyses of the seven histories are challenging in themselves, but, in addition, we would point out that our ultimate goal goes well beyond simply organizing complex historical data. In brief: our goal is to provide both industrial management and government agencies with a new way of thinking so that they can replace conflicting and fragmented policies with wiser and more comprehensive ones. This goal is ambitious but consistent, we are convinced, with the severity of the threats posed by the current condition of American industry.

The accepted function of government is to establish the ground rules within which firms operate. In this regard, government can use-

**Figure 1.3  The Readaptive Process: Interaction Between the Environment and Readaptive Form and Strategy**

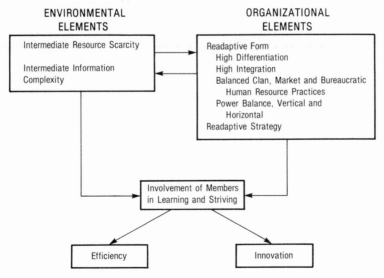

ENVIRONMENTAL ELEMENTS

ORGANIZATIONAL ELEMENTS

Intermediate Resource Scarcity

Intermediate Information Complexity

Readaptive Form
High Differentiation
High Integration
Balanced Clan, Market and Bureaucratic
    Human Resource Practices
Power Balance, Vertical and
    Horizontal
Readaptive Strategy

Involvement of Members in Learning and Striving

Efficiency

Innovation

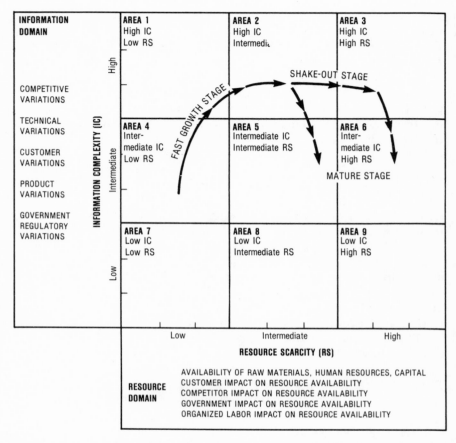

This figure charts the hypothetical paths of development of new firms with highly attractive technical or market innovations in a newly emerging industry. As the first new firm starts up, IC is probably intermediate since some variations in customers and technologies will need analysis. We assume that this firm will have no particular trouble acquiring the necessary resources for getting under way, given its attractive innovations, so RS will be low. These conditions will start the firm off in Area 4.

The first firm's early success can be expected to attract competitors that increase IC by introducing new complexities in the form of variations in products and technology. RS will not immediately increase and the firms will move into Area 1.

In time the increasing number of competitors and each firm's growth in production capacity result in the market's beginning to be saturated. With this development, the firms' RS will increase, resulting in a move into Area 2 or even, for some, into Area 3.

A "shake-out" stage now inevitably takes place with some failures and consolidations. Eventually the shake-out lowers IC and some of the surviving firms which went into Area 3 become stuck as organizations with tight margins and drop into Area 6. Others of the surviving firms, most likely those that were in Area 2, continue to have favorable resource exchanges and profit margins. This will put them in Area 5. To the extent these firms have a readaptive strategy and form, we expect them to continue on in Area 5 and achieve readaptive outcomes.

## Figure 1.4    The Possible Development Paths of Firms in a Typical New Industry

fully be thought of as a balancing factor in helping to keep RS and IC at the intermediate level; the dynamics of the marketplace and the technologies of an industry do not, by any means, always lead automatically to the desirable intermediate level of these variables. Since government policies affecting specific industries are currently determined more by the push and pull of special interest pressures rather than by a consistent, overall point of view, any steps government now takes to encourage innovation and efficiency are susceptible to costly errors. The list of current government policies that significantly influence competitive factors in industry is long and lacks coherence. Clearly it is too much to hope that a completely consistent and rational policy can be provided by uncoordinated government agencies, but certainly by being able to understand more fully, through a single method of analysis, the consequences of their actions, government officials ought to be significantly helped in making their contributions to the readaptive process more predictable and more creative.

Industry could similarly be helped to make wiser and more creative choices in determining organizational form and strategy. Management can be helped to rethink organizational goals, to focus on the creation of real value and wealth with less preoccupation with strictly short-term profits. The reasons for the success of international competitors, especially the Japanese, need not be so puzzling and debatable a phenomenon. The importance of involving the total organizational membership in learning and striving could be fully appreciated. The hazard of driving for current efficiencies at the expense of innovation could be avoided. As we see, our approach to problem-solving can help an individual firm as well as an entire industry develop a consistent set of actions leading to long-term industrial health.

The analytic framework we have proposed for thinking about industrial organizations promotes neither environmental determinism nor completely free enterprise, for *making choices* is at its center. Choices by business managers, choices by government, choices by labor leaders must all be made. Only when leadership in all these established institutions — management, government, labor — becomes committed to concerted action can American industry, faced with the most serious challenge in its history, be set on the road to readaptation and renewal.

As we examine the histories of our seven industries we will look not only for answers to general issues concerning readaptive behavior but will consider in depth particular questions affecting individual industries. For instance, why does steel have such a poor record of efficiency and innovation while American agriculture has had such an amazing record as an innovative and efficient industry? Why have hospital costs risen out of control? Can we expect a successful degree of readaptive practice in AT&T now that it is moving away from being a regulated monopoly? How does an industry, like coal, whose fortunes shift overnight from stagnation and depression cope with the changes of its new position? In sum: each of the seven industries has, and has had, its particular problems and opportunities; what choices have they made in the past, what options are open to them now?

We have chosen the deeply troubled United States automobile industry as the starting point for demonstrating in detail the way the Framework of Adaptation can be used.

# CHAPTER 2

# Autos: On the Thin Edge

THE SORRY CONDITION of the U.S. auto industry is news to no one. Chrysler's brush with bankruptcy, record losses and layoffs at Ford, the decision of the American Motors Corporation to sell controlling interest to a French company, staggering losses at once-mighty General Motors: all this has been front-page stuff for several years now. In a crisis of such magnitude, there is plenty of blame to go around, and there has been no shortage of critics (inside and outside the industry) offering opinions as to what went wrong. Some say government is at fault, exacting compliance with unreasonable and expensive safety, environmental, and fuel-efficiency standards too soon, and subsidizing the price of oil for too long. Others blame our trade partners, especially Japan, for a headlong drive to export autos in order to satisfy their domestic employment needs. Still others accuse leaders in industry management or labor of being short-sighted and greedy, sacrificing quality products, responsibility to the public, and productivity to fat margins or high wages and benefits.

There is truth in some of these analyses, but much of the current discussion is pointless because it is offered in an accusatory spirit and is seldom accompanied by useful recommendations for action. Nor has anyone (to date) attempted to view the current crisis against a broader understanding of the way our economy works and, in particular, of what conditions inside and outside the firm are most likely to promote

17

continued economic growth and social responsibility. In short, what is missing is some attention to the theory of how organizations function.

We believe economic growth and social responsibility are most likely to be realized when organizations face intermediate amounts of uncertainty about their environments, when these organizations adopt a particular form with particular human resource practices, and when these organizations fix as their long-term aim the reconciliation of two often contradictory goals—efficiency and innovation. In this chapter we shall show how and why the U.S. auto industry once produced these outcomes, no longer does so, but might once again.

## THE U.S. AUTOMOBILE INDUSTRY IN THE EARLY 1980s

In 1980, a memorable year for the industry, the major U.S. automakers—General Motors, Ford, Chrysler, and American Motors—collectively lost more than $4 billion, or about $12 million per day. Chrysler set a U.S. corporate record by losing $1.7 billion and was saved from bankruptcy only by the election-year beneficence of the government. Ford was scarcely in better shape, with losses totaling $1.5 billion; only its profitable operations overseas kept it from much worse results. By the end of 1980 one-fourth of the total industry labor force—more than 200,000 workers—had been laid off. Chrysler alone permanently closed ten manufacturing plants. 1981 brought little relief. Rather, the sales slump intensified and even the automakers' major efforts at retrenchment achieved only minor financial improvement, a collective loss of $1.3 billion.

The ripple effects of the auto crisis are enormous. It is estimated that about one-fifth of our gross national product springs from the automobile and related industries. Some 3,000 automobile dealers have gone out of business since 1979. Another 650,000 jobs were threatened in steel, rubber, and glass companies, machine toolmakers, and hundreds of small suppliers to the auto industry.

The American auto crisis has been easier to describe than to analyze. Several views have emerged in the popular press. First, industry managers have made an easy target. *Time* magazine, for instance, pronounced that "In the end . . . the auto industry's problems rest with Detroit's managers, who failed to plan for a new-car market after the 1974 oil embargo."[1] Joseph Kraft, writing in the *New Yorker*, espoused a similar view when he described the industry's "downsizing decision" after 1974. Kraft, who documented General Motors' lead over the other American firms in building small cars, implicitly suggested that if corporate leaders had made the decision to produce small cars in

1973 and had then acted swiftly on the decision, there would have been no crisis later on.[2] On the other hand, William Tucker, an editor of *Harper's*, argued cogently that the Big Three automakers were encouraged to build large cars by consumers, who spurned compacts between 1974 and 1979, and by the government, which refused to lift price controls on oil in the mid-1970s.[3]

A recent report from the government takes a more balanced view and even-handedly blames the industry, the labor force, and itself for the crisis. *The U.S. Automobile Industry, 1980*, an interagency study directed by Neil Goldschmidt, secretary of transportation in the Carter administration, pinpoints four major causes of the crisis: slowdown of demand, government mandated technological change, encroachment by imports, and high labor costs. First, the energy shocks of 1973–74 and 1978–79 have changed American taste in automobiles profoundly. Consumers of the 1980s are likely to prefer more fuel-efficient cars and to retain them longer than their earlier models. This behavior poses two problems for the industry: consumers are demanding a type of automobile that the American producers have never built in volume, while annual sales are growing much more slowly than in the past.

Federal regulation also has had a severe impact on the industry. Since the late 1960s, government has pressed strenuously for improvements in safety, pollution, and fuel efficiency, and the industry has been required to invest heavily in what some insiders consider "nonproductive innovation."* In addition, the changing design of the automobile requires new process and product technologies. Robotics will be used increasingly on assembly lines to handle materials and to weld and paint the chassis. The new car itself will have freshly designed engines and transmissions and make greater use of lightweight materials. At present, the automakers have used up most of their working capital and debt capacity to finance this innovation, with dire consequences for profitability and their ability to attract new investment. It is estimated that the U.S. industry will require a capital investment of some $80 billion in the 1980s to produce the new automobiles competitively. In view of its present financial condition, it is difficult to see where this money will come from.[4]

A third fundamental problem for the automakers is that increasing competition from abroad will prevent them from passing on their higher costs to consumers. The share of the American market captured by imports (especially Japanese) jumped from 15% in 1972 to 27% at the end of 1981 (Figure 2.1). Foreign automakers have been in a strong

---

*Such assertions ignore how the industry has been helped by U.S. fuel economy standards. It is clear that the current crisis would be much worse if the automakers had not been pushed to improve fuel economy in the 1970s.

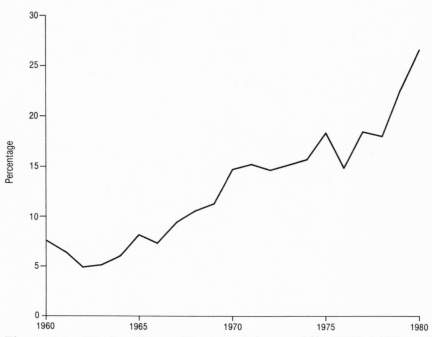

**Figure 2.1    Market Share of Imported Automobiles 1960–1980**

SOURCE: *Ward's Automotive Yearbook*, various years.

position to sell in the suddenly energy-conscious American market, because for years they have built small, light, fuel-efficient cars. Thus the
foreign companies already possess production skills that American
firms are now acquiring at great cost. Indeed, it is estimated that Japanese producers enjoy a cost advantage of some $1,500 to $2,000 per
car. Some of this cost differential derives from wage costs, which run
higher in the United States than in Japan, while American productivity
has improved more slowly (Figure 2.2). U.S. autoworkers earn about
twice the benefits of their Japanese counterparts, for example, while
the Japanese use approximately half the man-hours to build an automobile.[5] And, as Douglas Fraser, president of the United Auto Workers (UAW), points out, "the typical U.S. auto manager outearns his
Japanese colleague by some 700%."[6]

The federal government has taken various actions recently to coun-
teract the automobile crisis. Secretary Goldschmidt, in his letter of
transmittal accompanying the report, recommended that the government immediately negotiate trade restrictions with the Japanese and
adopt fiscal policies to help the industry attract capital. For the longer
term, Goldschmidt hoped that management, government, and labor

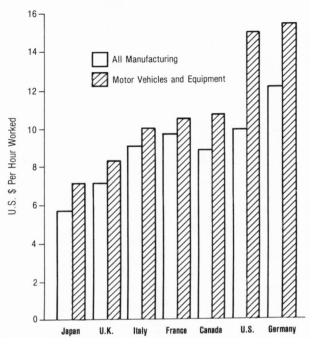

**Figure 2.2    Average Production Worker Compensation, Mid-Year 1980: All Manufacturing and Motor Vehicles and Equipment**

SOURCE: U.S. Department of Transportation, *The U.S. Automobile Industry, 1980* (Washington, D. C., 1981), p. 41.

might establish a new "compact" to work together for the common benefit of each.[7] The Reagan administration has pursued more traditional approaches. In 1981 the government negotiated a voluntary import restraint agreement with the Japanese; it also modified the tax laws to allow faster depreciation and removed or relaxed some safety and environmental regulations.

Such prescriptions are fine as far as they go. Amid all the verbiage on the auto crisis, however, there has been little analysis of the auto firms as *organizations* or of the automakers' ability to adapt to their changing environment. It is largely assumed that if the right public policy is found, or if the right business strategy is articulated and pursued, then the crisis will end. No one has asked whether the automakers have the kind of organization that can respond to the right public policies and internal strategies. Our analysis of organizational adaptation suggests that this is a crucial question indeed.

According to our model, the automakers currently face conditions of high resource scarcity (losses, lack of capital, regulatory compliance costs) and moderate to high information complexity (imports, demanding regulations, new technologies). The strategies and organizations that landed them in these circumstances are unlikely to get them out. While the automakers have clearly changed their strategies, it is less certain that their organizations will be able to respond effectively. Let us look then at the historical development of automobile firm and industry structure to see the changing organizational and environmental conditions that produced the present industry crisis. Along the way we shall generate some answers to the question of what went wrong and perhaps suggest some remedies to improve the auto industry's health.

## THE EVOLUTION OF THE AMERICAN AUTOMOBILE INDUSTRY

The history of the American auto industry can be divided into several distinct stages: a "start-up" period from the 1890s to about 1910; a "rapid growth phase" in the next decade; a "shakeout" or consolidation phase in the 1920s; and a "mature phase" from the 1930s to the 1970s.*

### START-UP

The notion of a self-propelled carriage vehicle is ancient, although its realization awaited the late nineteenth century. Scholars still debate about the nature of the technology and which European engineer invented what when. It is clear, however, that several preconditions had to be met before the isolated construction of "horseless carriages" could become an industry. At the least, there had to be opportunities for use and consumer demand in addition to the "right" technologies. These preconditions were partly satisfied in the 1880s by the development and popularity of the bicycle. It was the "safety bicycle," featuring chain drives and pneumatic tires, that first whetted the popular appetite for private transportation, encouraged communities to build suitable roads, and inspired mechanics and engineers to tinker with self-propelled vehicles.

It is generally agreed that the honor of manufacturing the first automobile belongs to two German engineers, Daimler and Benz, who built vehicles independently in 1885. The first Americans to construct

*This terminology will be familiar to readers who are aware of similar analyses of stages, or life cycles, in the evolution of organisms, products, organizations, industries, even whole economies and societies. Some of these life cycle theories are deterministic. In using these terms, however, we do not mean to suggest that the development of the auto industry followed an inevitable course. Rather, we employ this analysis as a descriptive tool.

a successful "horseless carriage" were the Duryea brothers of Springfield, Massachusetts, eight years later. The beginnings of the industry itself are less easy to pinpoint, although 1897 is a convenient date. In that year four promising ventures — the Pope Manufacturing Company, the Olds Motor Vehicle Company, the Winton Motor Carriage Company, and the Stanley Brothers — began business in earnest.[8] Vehicles only trickled from the factories in the 1890s, however. For instance, the largest of the early competitors, the Pope Manufacturing Company, built only five hundred electric and forty gasoline cars in the first two years of production.[9]

Entry to the automobile industry was easy in these early years, as the capital requirements to assemble a simple vehicle were low. All it took were some inexpensive parts, a garage or spare room, and time. Bicycle companies, carriage makers, machinists, engineers, electricians, and plumbers found it a simple matter to diversify into the automobile business. By 1900 there were some fifty-eight "firms" selling autos; in 1910 there were more than two hundred (Figure 2.3). A quarter to a third of these were relatively promising ventures.[10] There were some surprising entrants among these firms, including General Electric, Maytag, and Sears, Roebuck & Co. Customers faced a heady choice amid this variety. It was possible to buy, for example, an "Averageman's Car," an "Everybody's," a " Great Smith," an "Electrobat," a "Harvard," or two distinct "Yales," all with different shapes, sizes, power plants, and prices.[11]

If it was easy to get started in the business, survival was something else entirely. The typical automaker was a simple organization consisting of one or two owner-entrepreneurs and a handful of workers. The lives of these firms were precarious and often fleeting. Many vanished within a year or two. Short-term survival normally depended upon the ability to attract help (and credit) from suppliers and dealers. Survival in the long run turned on the ability to manufacture cars cheaply. As many hopeful automakers discovered, the market for novelty or luxury automobiles quickly became saturated. If the industry was to sustain rapid growth, costs and prices had to fall within reach of the wider public. This, in turn, entailed some standardization of technology and design, which favored larger producers.

RAPID GROWTH

The new century offered wonderful opportunities for the automobile business. In 1900 American manufacturers built 4,192 cars; by 1910 they produced some 180,000; by 1920 more than 1.9 million vehicles rolled out of the plants.[12] Despite this prodigious growth, however, the number of automakers dwindled as it became increasingly difficult for small firms to remain in business. The industry quickly became

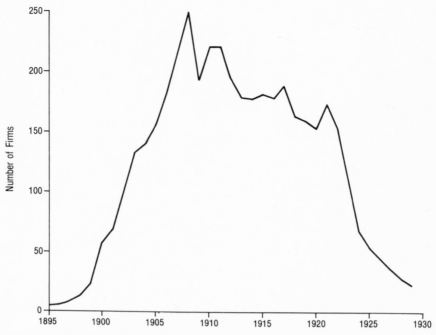

**Figure 2.3     Number of Firms Competing in the Automobile Industry 1895–1929**

SOURCE: Based on tabular material in Robert Paul Thomas, *An Analysis of the Pattern of Growth of the Automobile Industry 1895–1930* (New York: Arno Press, 1977), p. 324.

concentrated, with the top three producers—Ford, General Motors, and EMF (Studebaker)—accounting for about half of total national production in 1908.[13] Two different strategies, mass production and horizontal merger, encouraged this concentration.

The dominant automakers' success in building affordable cars for the masses produced the great burst of sales in the decade after 1910. Indeed, this was the great difference between European and American carmakers. In Europe the automobile remained an aristocratic toy for decades, while in the United States producers perceived the possibilities of enormous growth if a sturdy and reliable car could be produced cheaply enough. Thus, in the early years, many small, lightweight "buggies" and "runabouts" were built and sold for $500 or less. While a number of entrepreneurs glimpsed the opportunity to exploit the low-priced market, Henry Ford pursued it with monomaniacal intensity. As he later recalled (with the perfect confidence of hindsight), he had determined by 1907 that he would

> build a motor car for the great multitude. It will be large enough for the family but small enough for the individual to run and care for. It will be

constructed of the best materials, by the best men to be hired, after the simplest designs that modern engineering can devise. But it will be so low in price that no man making a good salary will be unable to own one — and enjoy with his family the blessing of hours of pleasure in God's great open spaces.[14]

The fruit of these efforts was the Model T, the "Tin Lizzie," the Ford Motor Company's single model in production for nearly two decades.

Ford's breakthrough in cost, of course, depended on revolutionary improvements in manufacturing. These included the creation of a final assembly process from finished parts as a distinct operation achieved at the Olds Motor Works in 1902, and, of course, the famous moving assembly line introduced by Ford in 1913.[15] Ford had been mulling over these ideas for some time, while techniques of mass production already existed in a number of industries, including firearms, sewing machines, and bicycles. The problem in the case of the automobile was to design a method of assembly for a much larger, heavier, and more complex product than had ever been attempted. The usual procedure was to give work teams or "gangs" a pile of about five thousand parts and have them build up the car from scratch. As Ford himself later described it, "In our first assembling we simply started to put a car together at a spot on the floor and workmen brought to it the parts as they were needed in exactly the same way that one builds a house." As demand increased, however, it became "necessary to devise plans of production that would avoid having the workers falling over one another." Thus, in 1913, came the assembly line and the notion of "taking the work to the men instead of the men to the work. We now have two general principles in all operations — that a man shall never have to take more than one step, if possibly it can be avoided, and that no man need ever stoop over."[16]

The effects of the new work system were little short of amazing. In 1912, the last year of traditional methods, the company built 78,611 vehicles; the next year, with the assembly line in place for magnetos and chassis, 182,809 vehicles were produced; in 1914, with the system more fully established, 260,720 Model Ts rolled off the assembly line. Costs and prices plummeted. When the Model T was introduced in 1908, it sold for $850. By 1916, when Ford built more than half a million cars, the price fell to $360.[17] Simultaneously, the company put together an extensive dealer network to sell these cars to an eager public.[18]

The second successful growth strategy in the automobile industry was merger and combination. This had been tried ineffectually in the late 1890s by the promoters of the Electric Vehicle Company, a dubious attempt to monopolize the market for electric taxicabs. A few years later, William C. "Billy" Durant resorted to the strategy once more when he established General Motors (GM) as a holding company in 1908. GM was formed in two periods of feverish combination, 1908–1910 and 1916–20. In the first of these, Durant put together about twenty-five firms into what a leading automotive historian has described as "a confused patchwork of companies."[19] In Durant's defense, it should be said that GM included four substantial firms with national sales networks — Buick, Oldsmobile, Cadillac, and Oakland (later Pontiac).[20]

Several motives underlay the formation of General Motors.[21] First, there was a clear intent to at least moderate, if not restrict, competition. Durant twice tried to buy out Ford but couldn't raise the cash; he also tried repeatedly to join with Benjamin Briscoe, another empire builder, to form a truly gigantic combination. Durant's second motive was — in contrast to Ford — to offer different products in different markets. Thus Buick sold vehicles in the middle price range, bracketed by Cadillac on the low end and Oldsmobile higher up.* The third merger motive was to insure a steady supply of materials to the car manufacturing units. Although General Motors was initially a merger of final assembly firms, Durant, in his freewheeling quest for companies, purchased some suppliers. In the first merger wave Durant included Champion Ignition (spark plugs), Northway Motor Manufacturing (engines), and the Weston-Mott Axle Company; in the second wave came Delco and Remy (electrical supplies), Fisher Body, Hyatt Roller Bearing, Frigidaire, and many others.[22] Durant's precarious financial schemes — he bought most of these companies by swapping stock rather than paying cash — eventually led to his separation from GM in 1920. By then, however, the disorganized nucleus of a very profitable company was in place.

GM's move to consolidation was mimicked by other firms, including Chrysler (Figures 2.4 to 2.6). Whatever the strategy of growth, the rewards for the established survivors were very great indeed. The nine firms that "came to be continually successful" by 1910 annually earned

**Figure 2.4    Corporate Genealogy: Ford Motor Company**

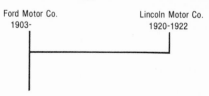

*This hierarchy changed in the next decade when Cadillac became a luxury vehicle and when Chevrolet, brought into General Motors in 1918, competed more directly with Ford.

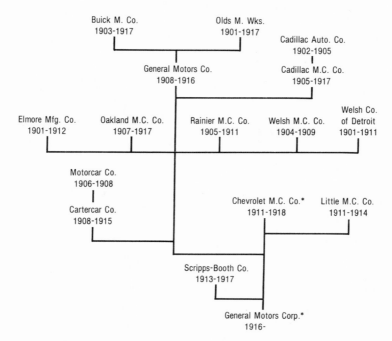

**Figure 2.5    Corporate Genealogy: General Motors Company**

SOURCE for Figures 2.4–2.6: Philip Hillyer Smith, *Wheels within Wheels* (New York: Funk & Wagnalls, 1968), pp. 280–281 and 283.

about 40% on net worth until 1917 and, with some fluctuations, about half that in the next decade.[23]

INDUSTRY CONSOLIDATION

By the end of World War I the automobile industry's rapid growth began to slow. The number of producers fell by half (from a high of 250) between 1908 and 1920. The next decade produced even more dramatic concentration. By the end of the 1920s there were fewer than twenty-five automakers left in the business while the seven largest firms accounted for more than 90% of the market.[24] (See Figure 2.3 and Figure 2.7).

It is generally agreed that several factors contributed to this shakeout.[25] First, a recession in 1920 and 1921 wiped out many small firms.

## Figure 2.6  Corporate Genealogy: Chrysler Corporation

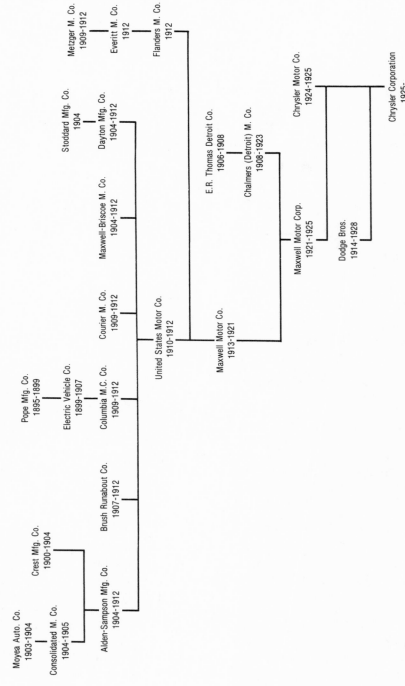

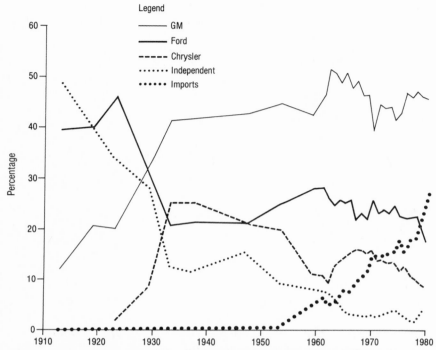

**Figure 2.7  Historical Trends in U.S. Market Share 1913–1980**
Sources: U.S. Federal Trade Commission, *Report on the Motor Vehicle Industry* (Washington, D. C., 1939), p. 29; Lawrence J. White, *The Automobile Industry since 1945* (Cambridge, Mass.: Harvard University Press, 1971), pp. 290–306; *Ward's Automotive Yearbook*, various years.

Second, overall demand tapered off in the 1920s so that for the first time automakers competed for the same pool of customers. Simultaneously, the used-car business took off, creating additional difficulties for marginal producers. Third, economies of scale in production and marketing favored the larger firms. Companies with standardized production and/or the capacity to offer a family line of cars achieved lower unit costs than companies without either advantage and could compete more effectively on price. Similarly, as competition increased in the 1920s, firms with national sales and dealer networks predominated. Fourth, the growing popularity of the closed car favored big producers. The capital investment in the machinery, stamping presses, and dies required to build closed-roof cars, and hence to sell to customers in northern climates, was very great.

The new automotive world of the 1920s, in which first-time buyers were becoming scarce, called for new business strategies. The evidence of the marketplace belied Henry Ford's belief that customers cared only about price. As a writer for *Fortune* put it, a "Model T was a wonderful car, but it certainly did not flatter your pride of ownership."[26] Under Durant's successors, Pierre S. Du Pont and Alfred P. Sloan, Jr., General Motors settled on a new way of doing business. In 1919, the Du Pont interests helped GM found a subsidiary, the General Motors Acceptance Corporation, to provide credit for dealers and consumers to buy new cars. In the mid-1920s Du Pont and Sloan rationalized GM's product line and offered cars in every price range, from Chevrolet at the low end, through Oakland, Buick, and Oldsmobile in the middle, to Cadillac on top. Thus GM divisions no longer competed extensively with each other. Moreover, Sloan set about making General Motors a more effective rival to Ford by competing on quality as well as price. As Sloan later recalled:

> We proposed in general that General Motors should place its cars at the top of each price range and make them of such a quality that they would attract sales from below that price, selling to those customers who might be willing to pay a little more for the additional quality, and attract sales also from above that price, selling to those customers who would see the price advantage in a car of close to the quality of higher-priced competition. This amounted to quality competition against cars below a given price tag, and price competition against cars above that price tag.[27]

In addition to this explicit strategy of "quality products sold at a fair price," General Motors pursued what might be called an "emergent strategy" of offering annual models differentiated by style and color changes.[28] In the mid-1920s GM fell into a pattern of introducing new models in the autumn of each year. Although this tactic was initially intended to highlight technological improvements, under the influence of Sloan and auto designer Harley Earl, changes in style and color scheme gradually became more prominent features of annual models.[29] This strategy of producing annual models differentiated by style quickly became a formidable competitive advantage for the larger automakers and deterred potential entrants to the industry.

General Motors reaped a financial bonanza almost immediately. In 1926 the company surpassed Ford in production and sales, and earned record profits. No other automaker, however, followed this strategic path until the formation of the modern Chrysler Corporation in the late 1920s. Walter Chrysler, himself a former GM executive, had pieced his company together from the bankrupt remains of several firms earlier in the decade. In 1928 Chrysler acquired the properties of the deceased Dodge brothers, thereby bringing to the Chrysler family a direct competitor to low-cost Fords and Chevrolets. By then, however, General Motors' competitive advantage was overwhelming. In 1931 the market shares of the Big Three (General Motors, Ford, and Chrysler) stood at 43.3%, 25%, and 19%, respectively.[30] Profits were high throughout the industry, although there were substantial disparities among the Big Three and a widening gap between them and the major independent producers.[31]

## MATURITY

The oligopoly market structure established in the automobile industry by the end of the 1920s proved to be remarkably enduring (Figure 2.7). For most of the next four decades, the Big Three shared about 90% of the market while the remaining independent companies dwindled and merged or disappeared in the face of increasing imports. No new entrants into the industry survived more than a few years.* Throughout this period General Motors' strategy and structure were models for its major competitors. General Motors, Ford, and Chrysler each offered a family line of automobiles and trucks and competed on the basis of style and marketing rather than on technology and manufacturing. Over the years the industry acquired some characteristics of a mature industry. Some economists, including Lawrence J. White, for instance, have recently criticized this oligopoly structure for breeding excess profits, a poor record of innovation, and (ironically) remoteness from consumer wishes.[32] To other observers, however, the American automobile industry satisfied broader social needs by providing inexpensive, reliable, and comfortable transportation for a people on the move.[33]

While the structure of the automobile industry did not change much in this period, the growth and character of total demand in the years after World War II greatly enlarged the scale of automotive production. In the 1930s the automakers produced on average between two and three million passenger cars per year. By the 1950s total annual production doubled, averaging between five and six million units per year.[34] Every family, it seems, wanted at least one car, if not more. In addition, consumers tended to keep their cars for shorter periods, perhaps swayed by heavy advertising (or planned obsolescence) to purchase the latest models. If there was little fundamental change in automotive technology, the product's appearance altered considerably. Consumers were transfixed by a greater diversity of models, which were larger and more powerful, and offered a dazzling variety of accessories.

These changes in the market and the product tended to magnify the disparity between the Big Three and the smaller producers. The Big Three averaged a return of 16.7% on net worth during the period 1946 to 1967, nearly twice the rate earned by all manufacturing corporations (Figure 2.8).[35] With an average return of 20.7% in these years,

---

*Even Henry J. Kaiser's heavily financed attempt after World War II ended in ignominious and expensive defeat in 1953.

General Motors was far and away the industry leader and among the most consistently profitable of all American companies. Economies of scale in production and marketing took their toll on the independents and many of them lost money in the 1940s and early 1950s. Because the independents had insufficient resources to match the leaders' technological innovations, such as the V-8 motor or the automatic transmission, and because their advertising budgets were insufficient to overcome a second-rate product image, their days were numbered. Indeed, as the national economy recovered after the Korean War, several independents — Kaiser and Willys, Studebaker and Packard, Nash/ Kelvinator and Hudson (American Motors) — were forced to merge in order to maintain volume. Even this was but a stopgap measure, however, and by the mid-1960s only American Motors remained a marginal independent automaker.[36]

The era of the stable oligopoly reinforced several trends under way in earlier periods. First, company size conferred considerable advantages in production, marketing, distribution, and profits. Second, General Motors' strategy of offering models in every price range, with

**Figure 2.8    Annual Rates of Return 1946–1967**

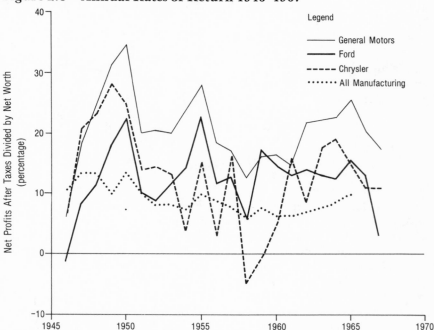

SOURCE: Based on tabular material in Lawrence J. White, *The Automobile Industry since 1945* (Cambridge, Mass.: Harvard University Press, 1970) p. 251.

annual models distinguished chiefly by changes in style, proved so powerful that Ford and Chrysler had to copy it to sustain rapid growth. Third, the American public apparently favored larger, faster, and better-appointed automobiles, as evidenced by trends in production. It is also true, however, that consumers were not given much choice until the late 1950s, when American Motors offered the diminutive Rambler and the first imports, Volkswagen and Renault, appeared.

## STRATEGY AND ORGANIZATION

The foregoing analysis of automobile industry structure is merely another way of talking about the auto companies' environment — the external economic conditions in which they competed. By about 1930 the modern industry was firmly established, competitive practices were well understood, and information complexity was therefore low to moderate. At the same time profits for the larger firms were good, and in the case of General Motors exceedingly good. Resource scarcity, therefore, was low to moderate, and we can say generally that the industry faced the conditions of Areas 4 and 5 during its long maturity. Different firms clearly experienced different conditions. General Motors occupied a more commanding position than Ford and, for most of the period, Ford a more commanding position than Chrysler.

In the evolution of the U.S. auto industry, organizational choice and internal structure were critical factors in determining not only the industry's shape but also the particular fate of each automaker. In the early years of competition, as we have seen, Ford's strategy of hard-driving production dominated all competitors. The company averaged better than 40% of the market between 1911 and 1925. By contrast, the combined market share of General Motors' auto assembly divisions oscillated between 12% and 20% in this period.[37] However, the effects of GM's reorganization in the early 1920s, under Du Pont and Sloan, combined with the articulation of a definite strategy of segmenting the market, proved more enduring than Ford's initial success. It was in the 1920s that General Motors permanently passed Ford in sales and production, as the two giant companies acted out one of the great morality tales of American management.[38]

Once automobiles became big business the advantages of good organization come to the fore. Henry Ford never understood this. In a famous essay entitled "Machines and Men," Ford observed:

> That which one has to fight hardest against in bringing together a large number of people to do work is excess organization and consequent red tape. To my mind there is no bent of mind more dangerous than that which is sometimes described as the "genius for organization."

"And so," he boasted proudly,

> the Ford factories and enterprises have no organization, no specific duties attaching to any position, no line of succession or of authority, very few titles, and no conferences. We have only the clerical help that is absolutely required; we have no elaborate records of any kind, and consequently no red tape.[39]

The Ford Motor Company was run just so. A brilliant organizer of production, Ford made no effort to conceal his contempt for organized management. He himself asserted leadership sporadically but always with finality. He sometimes left management of the company to his son Edsel or to his assistants for months at a time before returning suddenly, imperiously, to make critical decisions. Aside from Edsel and a few vice-presidents, executives in the Ford Motor Company carried no titles and only vaguely defined responsibilities.[40] Not surprisingly, turnover of top executives was high, especially among those in finance and sales.[41]

Henry Ford's attitude toward professional management accorded with his general strategy of vertical integration. Rather than purchasing parts suppliers, as Durant had done, Ford went a step further and decided to build his own parts from raw materials. He bought enormous reserves of iron ore and coal and built a steelworks adjacent to his Model T assembly plant at the River Rouge in Dearborn. He also added a sawmill (after buying timber reserves) and a glassworks to the plant in the 1920s. He even purchased 2.5 million acres of land in Brazil, an estate christened Fordlandia, to plant rubber trees in hopes of eventually including a rubber factory at the River Rouge. Ford's notion, evidently, was to create a single monumental assembly line from raw minerals to the finished Model T. In the 1920s the company's slogan read: "From Mine to Finished Cars, One Organization."[42] Management's task became essentially the first-line supervisor's task—to keep this assembly process moving at full speed.

The contrast between the Ford Motor Company and the General Motors of Du Pont and Sloan could hardly be greater. GM's head-to-head competition with Ford necessarily entailed some emulation of production techniques. All similarities ended there, however. GM shied away from full-scale vertical integration and concentrated instead upon weeding and sorting Durant's sprawling empire. It was Sloan's "genius for organization," so ridiculed by Henry Ford, that made GM a successful company in the 1920s.[43] Sloan's formal association with Durant had begun in 1916 when Durant purchased Sloan's firm, Hyatt Roller Bearing. Disturbed by General Motors' chaotic organization, Sloan first proposed a plan to coordinate production and distribution in the company in 1920. Implementation of this plan, however, awaited Durant's fall and replacement by Du Pont, whose own explosives and chemical firm was simultaneously wrestling with similar problems of large-scale organization. Sloan's achievement was to combine the advantages of Durant's decentralized organization, which, after all, provided GM some strength in different markets, with strong financial coordination and scheduling of supplies common to the separate automaking units.

The organization in place at GM by 1924 embodied these principles exactly (Figure 2.9). Sloan gathered General Motors' subsidiaries together according to product or market criteria and created the concept of the group executive. The five automakers, the truck-making subsidiary, and various suppliers were established as autonomous divisions and treated as profit centers. This recognition of decentralization was balanced by the creation of a large general staff at headquarters, formed to monitor information and coordinate policy for the corporation as a whole.[44] Other top executives, including John Lee Pratt and Donaldson Brown, supplemented Sloan's "organization plan" by inventing new management techniques at General Motors. Pratt worked out statistical procedures to provide accurate records and forecasts of inventories, while Brown developed "standards" and controls for production costs and anticipated sales. This organization and these refinements nicely supported GM's strategy, finally made explicit in 1921, of having "a car at every price position, just the same as a general conducting a campaign wants to have an army at every point he is likely to be attacked."[45]

GM has long been recognized as a pioneer in the introduction of the "decentralized," or the "multidivisional," organization. Whereas most large businesses were organized with departments of engineering, manufacturing, sales, and so on, the multidivisional structure subordinated these functions to a division or product general manager. As Alfred Chandler describes the new structure:

> A general office plans, coordinates, and appraises the work of a number of operating divisions and allocates to them the necessary personnel, facilities, funds, and other resources. The executives in charge of these divisions, in turn, have under their command most of the functions necessary for handling one major line of products or set of services over a wide geographical area, and each of these executives is responsible for the financial results of his division and for its success in the market place.[46]

Chandler's description and terminology have won wide acceptance in academic and management circles, yet it seems clear that GM's organization represents something more than simply a multidivisional form. Indeed, its central characteristic was not simply the balance between centralization and decentralization, as drawn on a chart, but also the

**Figure 2.9  General Motors Corporation Organization 1924**

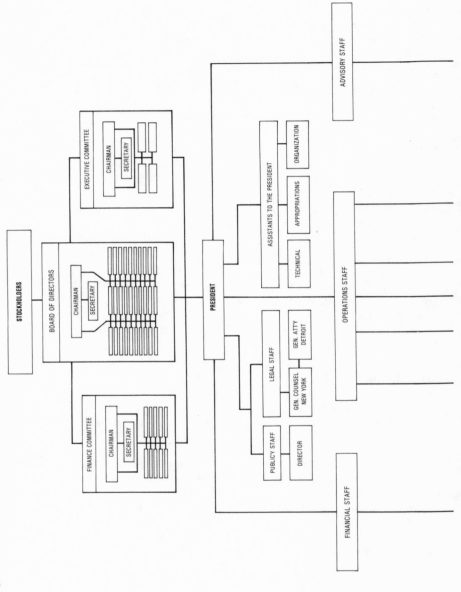

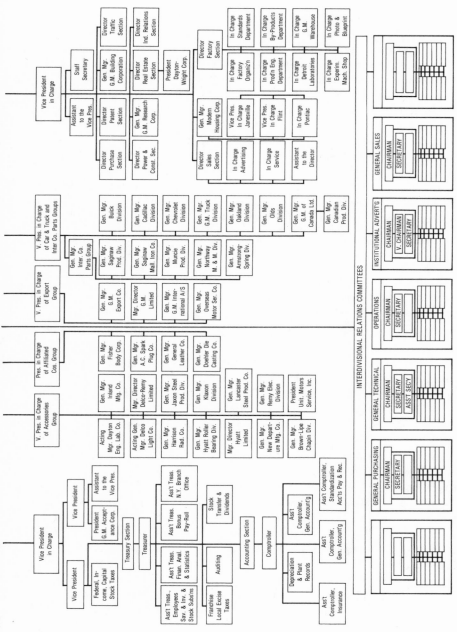

SOURCE: C. S. Mott, "Organizing a Great Industrial," *Management and Administration*, May 1924.

37

practical manner in which this balance was maintained. Sloan called this "decentralization with co-ordinated control," a concept that "evolved gradually at General Motors as we responded to the tangible problems of management."[47]

In addition to creating an active role for the central staff, Sloan grafted other coordinating mechanisms onto the multidivisional form, including committees at various levels. At the top two committees of the board of directors and senior managers focused on strategic policy and finance. Lower down — and here was a brilliant innovation — Sloan gradually introduced "interdivisional relations committees" to bridge the autonomous divisions on matters of common concern such as purchasing, advertising, technical engineering, operations, and so on. These committees served two principal purposes, education and persuasion. They were "not designed to function as administrative bodies," observed Donaldson Brown,

> but rather as a means of providing an opportunity for general discussion of problems of common interest. . . . Questions of policy are clarified; and through the operation of these several committees a means is provided of gaining a widely diffused knowledge and understanding of corporate policies, and a sympathetic compliance with them as they may bear upon the immediate problems of divisional management.[48]

The General Motors of 1924 therefore represented a new species of corporate organization. It managed "co-ordinated decentralization" by balancing a high degree of differentiation (high D) in its product/market divisions and a high degree of integration (high I) through various committees. In our terms, GM was not only one of the earliest multidivisional structures, but the first high D and I form.*

The strategic and organizational differences between GM and Ford were reflected in their respective profits in the 1920s. As per capita income grew, the American public shed its allegiance to the Model T for GM's more stylish models. Ford's market share fell from 56% in 1921 to less than 40% in 1926 and the company lost money for the first time. Despite prices slashed as low as $260, Model Ts would not move in sufficient volume to keep the River Rouge plant operating in the black. Indeed, in 1927 Ford closed the plant for nine months while he retooled for a new car, the Model A. This opportunity permitted General Motors to surpass Ford in production, a lead it has maintained in all but one year since.

Despite GM's great success in the 1920 and 1930s, it was some time before "Sloanism" crept over to Ford and Chrysler. The latter company, as we have seen, became a full-line producer after 1928; it be-

---

*This integration distinguishes the organization of GM from that of the classic multi-divisional structure established at Du Pont after World War I.

came more vertically integrated only after experiencing production and supply problems during World War II.[49] Ford finally added a middle-priced line of cars in 1938 with the Mercury. Thereafter, each of the Big Three competed directly in most markets, from inexpensive coupes to luxury sedans. Each wooed customers with new colors and styles and occasionally an innovation such as automatic transmissions or power accessories. They no longer competed explicitly on production costs.

Ford and Chrysler adopted GM's strategy more readily than its structure. At Ford the continuing dominance of the family owners hindered the full development of a decentralized organization. The elder Henry Ford remained a crabby and unconventional despot presiding over the company until shortly before his death in 1947. Because of his devotion to the days when selling cars meant producing them at the lowest cost, his contempt for modern management, and his senile infatuation with strong-arm personnel policies, his company performed erratically in the 1930s and 1940s. The company did not really recover from the depression until after World War II. It was then that Henry Ford II asserted control and brought in a group of General Motors executives and the famous "Whiz Kids," recasting the corporation into a multidivisional structure with tight financial controls but without other integrating mechanisms.*

In the 1950s Ford made a more determined attempt to copy General Motors' organization more directly when it created a separate division to manage a new car in the middle price range, the Edsel. The Edsel failed for many reasons — poor styling and quality, its introduction during a recession, and a confused marketing strategy. Its failure was also organizational. The Edsel division was not sufficiently integrated into the rest of the company and its managers failed to win the support and cooperation of executives in other auto divisions. The Edsel was discontinued after the 1960 model year.[50]

Ford's failure to replicate GM's system of decentralization and committee management happened partly because the Ford family was reluctant to relinquish power to outside managers. Henry Ford II's much publicized troubles in maintaining good relations with his chief operating officers and establishing a clear line of succession make a case in point. Between 1960, when Henry II asserted full control, and 1980, when Philip Caldwell succeeded him as chief executive officer, the company passed through a half-dozen presidents; in the entire postwar era, only four men have held the number-two position for more than

---

*The Whiz Kids were a group of ten young systems analysts and management control specialists from the army air force who arrived at Ford in 1946. Six of the ten later became vice-presidents in the company, while two (Robert S. McNamara and Arjay Miller) served as president of Ford.

two years. These periodic shake-ups at the top prevented a stable differentiated and integrated organization from taking root at Ford.

At Chrysler the centralized, functional organization endured until the 1970s. Walter Chrysler and his successor, K. T. Keller, kept close control over the company through the early 1950s. With centralization and traditional management styles deeply entrenched, the company resisted efforts to copy General Motors' structure when "Tex" Colbert (who followed Keller in the top job) tried to reorganize the company. The result was "sheer chaos," according to one company executive. "There were none of the mechanics for decision making and review, none of the accounting tools to support divisionalization."[51] It was only in the early 1970s that the company finally adopted the multidivisional form. Even then bizarre organizational arrangements remained. When Lee Iacocca joined Chrysler in 1978 he was startled to find some staff officers claiming wide powers and running their departments as independent fiefdoms. Reporting relationships were defined with more regard to tradition than to organizational rationality. Corporate staff reported to the chairman or president with no clear understanding of which functions belonged to operations and which did not. Iacocca fully reorganized the company along more conventional lines in 1979 and 1980.[52]

From the 1930s to at least the mid-1970s, then, there was remarkable continuity in strategy and performance among the Big Three automakers. Market shares and profitability held more or less constant, although there were significant organizational differences among the companies. GM took advantage of its larger size and more stable management to dominate the industry. All three companies, nonetheless, earned handsome rewards for their efforts. To all outward appearances, the Big Three possessed a sure formula for success.


## THE READAPTIVE RECORD

The U.S. automobile industry's long, stable tenure in Areas 4 and 5 produced some outcomes that generally pleased and rewarded both the industry and the public. For most of the period, the companies earned generous returns and offered excellent salaries and wages to attract and hold employees, while the consumer got a reasonably inexpensive and continually improving product. Over the years, however, the long equilibrium also reinforced some bad habits. Sloan's dominant strategy based on marketing and style subordinated technological innovation to production efficiency. There was little substantive innovation in the essential mechanics of autos after the 1920s. At the same time, as the business became better understood, managerial work became routine. The companies' concern for production efficiency also created tensions in the labor force, which erupted in a series of violent strikes in the 1930s and 1940s and culminated in the recognition of the United Automobile Workers (UAW) as a national bargaining agent. While unionization brought substantial material advancement to workers, the contracts struck between management and labor left control over production in the hands of the former. Over the years, management's implicit narrowing of focus on efficiency polarized its relationship to the work force.

Industry stability produced substantial material rewards for managers and workers. Sloan, the pioneer of so many innovations at General Motors, also developed a managerial compensation package that served as a model for the other automakers and for industry in general. General Motors started its annual bonus plan in 1918 in the belief

> that the interests of the corporation and its stockholders are best served by making key employees partners in the corporation's prosperity, and that each individual should be rewarded in proportion to his contribution to the profit of his own division and of the corporation as a whole.[53]

Sloan's aim in adding this market incentive was to create a group of "owner-managers" inside General Motors whose personal ambitions would dovetail with the continued prosperity of the company. On the basis of annual performance, key managers received handsome bonuses in cash or stock options, which, over the years, made them among the highest paid executives in all of American business. In our terms, Sloan added market incentives to supplement bureaucratic ones. On the other hand, the plan reinforced short-term strategic thinking in the company because it was in the managers' own interests to maximize profits year by year. There was little incentive, for example, to forego profits and bonuses for several years to make a long-term investment that would pay off only in the future. This was not such a critical problem while the business expanded or while Sloan and his immediate successors ran GM, but it became especially troublesome in the 1960s and 1970s.

A second unforeseen consequence of Sloan's managerial system also surfaced in the 1960s and 1970s. As the automobile business became more certain, it also became less challenging. The routinization of managerial work was compounded by the tendency of some of the companies to inbreed their managers. As a result the companies gradually lost some of the advantages of internal differentiation. This problem was particularly acute at GM, where many senior managers spent their entire careers with the company, starting with their undergraduate education. General Motors has been the only corporation in America with its own accredited college as a subsidiary — the General Motors

Institute (GMI). Although the company recently announced plans to divest GMI, most graduates traditionally received offers to join General Motors and most never worked anywhere else.[54]

John Z. DeLorean's partisan memoir of life at the top in General Motors offers abundant testimony to the dangers of corporate conformism and committee management gone mad. Senior executives, claims DeLorean, "spent little time looking at the big picture, instead occupying themselves with minuscule matters of operation which should have been considered and disposed of in the divisions or much farther down. . . ." To DeLorean, General Motors seemed to offer "a system which puts emphasis on form, style, and unwavering support for the decisions of the boss," and he blamed "system-men" for stifling initiative and creativity in the corporation. Once these system-men "get into power," said DeLorean, "they don't tamper with the system that promoted them. So a built-in method of perpetuating an imperfect management system is established." He also believed this explained why the company misread the market in the late 1960s and early 1970s.[55]

If managerial work in the auto industry became "stultifying" to people like DeLorean, then what of the actual work of production? The story is similar: As the industry expanded, higher and higher wages were traded for more and more boring and enervating jobs. Henry Ford, of course, established the nature of work in the plants when he introduced the moving assembly line in 1913. Ford also, in the next year, saw to it that labor would be well compensated for its efforts when he introduced the eight-hour shift for the unheard-of pay of five dollars per day. For these rewards workers in the plants committed themselves to routines and schedules determined by the speed of conveyor belts. It was a costly bargain. One worker told Edmund Wilson in the 1930s:

> Ye get the wages, but ye sell your soul at Ford's—ye're worked like a slave all day, and when ye get out ye're too tired to do anything—ye go to sleep on the car comin' home. . . . A man checks his brains and his freedom at the door when he goes to work at Ford's.[56]

The rise of the UAW in the 1930s and 1940s scarcely affected the nature of assembly line jobs. The establishment of the union solved the economic insecurity of the workers and provided a countervailing power to management. The UAW's great victories pertained chiefly to wages and benefits. In part, the union was deflected from addressing the enervating nature of the work itself by the very collective bargaining laws that gave it recognition and rights. The Wagner Act restricted negotiations between labor and management to "wages, hours, and other terms and conditions of employment." This clause was narrowly construed in the 1930s and 1940s and has opened up only gradually to include such items as supplementary unemployment benefits, work rules, and safe working conditions. The laws have seldom been read as permitting the labor force to achieve greater participation in the manufacturing process or more control over the substance of their own jobs.

The auto companies, moreover, severely resisted any proposals that threatened their "prerogatives" to manage and direct the work force. These issues came to a head in 1945–46 when the UAW struck GM for 113 days in a vain attempt to open the company's books in order to see how much of a wage hike the firm could afford without raising prices.* General Motors resisted this demand successfully but mollified the union at the next contract by offering to improve wages by an annual cost-of-living adjustment plus an "annual improvement factor" reflecting productivity gains in the U.S. economy in general. The 1948 contract thus formally institutionalized rising real incomes and expectations for UAW members. The autoworkers have been among the highest paid hourly workers in America ever since.

Even so, there were signs that the tradeoff of wages for control of the workplace sanctioned by the labor laws, management, and the UAW was no happy bargain. A famous survey conducted in the 1950s showed that autoworkers resented the time-discipline of the assembly line and that they derived little emotional satisfaction from their daily toil. "The work isn't hard," said a worker quoted in Walker and Guest's *The Man on the Assembly Line* (1952), "it's the never-ending pace. . . . The guys yell 'hurrah' whenever the line breaks down . . . you can hear it all over the plant."[57] At the time, however, the high wages and relative security of jobs in the plants were powerful incentives to preserve the status quo.

In the late 1960s and early 1970s, however, troubles in the workplace manifested themselves in disturbing ways. At General Motors, for instance, as a new generation of workers entered the plants, absenteeism rose 50% between 1965 and 1969, and ran as high as 20% on Mondays and Fridays. Over the same period employee turnover climbed 72%, the number of grievances lodged against supervisory personnel rose 38%, and disciplinary dismissals increased 44%.[58] The most widely publicized of these troubles occurred in 1972 when workers struck GM's assembly plant in Lordstown, Ohio where the Chevrolet Vega was being assembled. Media reporting glossed over some of the

---

*During the first round of contract negotiations between GM and the UAW in 1982, this position was seemingly reversed. The company and the union agreed "in principle" to pass on wage savings to consumers through lower prices. The UAW, moreover, would have had access to the company's books via an independent audit. However, the final contract approved in the spring of 1982 made no mention of this point.

principal causes of the strike including the reorganization of the plant, the merging of two local unions into one, and the elimination of hourly jobs. But working conditions were also at issue. Since the Vega was designed to be built with 43% fewer parts than most automobiles, Lordstown management planned to increase production from the normal rate of about sixty cars per hour to one hundred cars per hour. After several months of this frantic pace—some tasks had to be repeated every thirty-six seconds—some workers began sabotaging cars on the line while levels of absenteeism and grievances at the plant soared. Only after a three-week strike and the scrutiny of national attention did plant managers and workers redefine working conditions in the plant. By then, however, "the Lordstown syndrome" and "the blue-collar blues" had entered the language as symbols of the modern industrial worker's "alienation" from his daily labor.[59]

The automakers' internal structures, power relationships, and human resource practices led to an unbalanced record of managing efficiency and innovation. The companies were more successful with efficiency. Economist Lawrence White calculates that labor productivity in the auto industry improved at a rate of 4% per annum during the 1950s and 1960s, well above the rate of manufacturing generally. This is an impressive record that is sometimes lost in comparisons with foreign automakers' productivity. Yet in the 1970s productivity declined substantially—by 25% or more as labor troubles surfaced.[60]

At the same time, as discussed above, the automakers generated unusually high rates of return, which were paid out to stockholders rather than reinvested. Thus when lean times arrived the automakers were caught without the capital investment or the labor involvement to maintain historic improvements in productivity and efficiency.

The industry's record of efficiency came at the expense of innovation. While it is clear that automobiles improved steadily over the years, innovations (many of which originated at suppliers) tended to make driving simpler, faster, safer, and more comfortable. Automatic transmissions, for instance, came in the 1940s and 1950s, with power and disk brakes soon thereafter. However, American automakers did not spend much money on fundamental technology to change the power train until they were forced to do so by federal regulation and the energy crisis of the 1970s. Most of the pioneering efforts toward increased fuel efficiency, including advanced diesel engines, fuel injection, and stratified-charge engines, came from abroad.

Indeed, it has been argued that the auto industry achieved little substantive innovation after its earliest years. Writing from the vantage point of the early 1960s, Sloan admitted that "Great as have been the engineering advances since 1920, we have today basically the same kind of machine that was created in the first twenty years of the industry."[61] Certainly the most prominent features of today's automobile date from long ago: the internal combustion engine (the nineteenth century); shock absorbers, electric headlamps, asbestos drum brakes, steering wheels, standardized parts and designs (by 1910); the electric self-starter (1911); and the closed chassis, low-pressure pneumatic tires, and synchromesh transmissions (1920s). In this sense, Sloan was right: The product had matured by the 1920s.[62]

The readaptive record of the American automakers stands in marked contrast to that of their chief rivals in the 1980s, the Japanese. In the past two decades the Japanese have maintained astonishing levels of efficiency and innovation. It is generally agreed that Toyota is the low-cost auto producer in the world, as well as a leader in quality control. Fundamental product innovations originated at Honda and Toyo Kogyo (Mazda), although the Japanese have relatively small budgets for research and development. The Japanese are adept, moreover, at licensing and adopting technologies developed elsewhere when the market signals. Much of the Japanese automakers' success stems from their human resource practices, which involve workers in quality control and management of the workplace. These policies have been extremely successful in promoting a strong identity of purpose between workers and their employers.

## THE COMING OF THE AUTOMOBILE CRISIS

The U.S. automakers' failure to balance efficiency and innovation left them in an exposed position when a series of shocks disturbed the industry's competitive equilibrium. We shall do no more than note these problems here, as they are familiar to most readers.[63] In the first place, the social value of the automobile, so long unquestioned in America, suddenly became controversial in the 1960s. Consumers had registered disapproval of Detroit's products from time to time in earlier days. In the late 1950s, for instance, imports of small cars earned about a 10% market share, as city drivers apparently grew disgusted with congested freeways and scarce parking spaces. In the next decade, however, consumer disenchantment grew by orders of magnitude in three distinct ways: agitation for safer automobiles, promoted by Ralph Nader's indictment of the Chevrolet Corvair and given momentum by General Motors' underhanded attempt to discredit Nader; the clamor to reduce pollution caused by the automobile; and the cry to improve public transportation at the expense of the auto companies and the highway lobby. Small cars and foreign cars became more attractive and the imports' market share grew substantially in the late 1960s, well before the energy crisis sent their fortunes climbing still higher. The root of the foreign success, especially the Japanese, was an ability to deliver high-quality vehicles to the American market at low cost.

Although the energy crisis of 1973–74 rocked the industry, federal energy policy muffled that signal of continuing change. The 1975 Energy Policy and Conservation Act retained price controls on oil and shielded consumers from the effects of the energy crunch. As a result, small cars did not sell as well as predicted in the mid-1970s, and even the Japanese automakers watched their inventories pile up on the West Coast docks.[64] The market share of imports actually declined in 1975 and again in 1977–78 before the Iranian revolution reestablished the gravity of the energy crisis. (See Figure 2.1).

Twice then, in the late 1960s and in the late 1970s, Detroit was suddenly caught manufacturing the wrong product—overpowered and oversized vehicles with a growing reputation for low quality. Even when U.S. automakers attempted to compete directly with the imports the results were dismal. Indeed, the Ford Pinto and the Chevrolet Vega will be remembered in automotive history chiefly for the humiliations they caused their makers as objects of recalls and lawsuits, symbols of the blue-collar blues. The changing automotive reality of the late 1970s, born of trends in public policy, consumer attitudes, and demographics, now seems permanent. Pollster Daniel Yankelovich has captured the new mood:

> While Americans continue to cherish their cars, the psychocultural meaning of owning a car *is* changing. People feel that a car means freedom and independence and convenience—it takes you where you want to go when you want to. Our cars still make personal statements about us, but what they express is our taste, individuality, and autonomy, not our social status. Also, to increasing numbers of Americans a car is "just a car," a necessity of life that should be comfortable and styled to "suit me," but need not symbolize one's achievement in life.
>
> Therefore bigness, newness, excess power, and the other elements of conspicuous consumption are not as important as they once were—not worth endless sacrifice. Ninety percent of the public say they are willing to do without annual model changes in automobiles.[65]

Here in a nutshell is the backdrop to the automobile crisis of 1980. Caught between shifting public policies, especially with respect to energy, the industry compounded its troubles by misreading the American market. Indeed, the wonder is not that the auto crisis arrived, but that it was so long in coming.

## SENILITY OR REJUVENATION?
## THE CASE OF GENERAL MOTORS

Juxtaposing this gloomy portrait and our earlier developmental model of the auto industry's history, we might be tempted to conclude that the industry has entered a fifth era, or stage, one of senility and on-

rushing death. Yet the experience of General Motors in the recent crisis—it suffered market share and dollar losses much less than its domestic rivals—suggests a weakness in any deterministic life-cycle model
of industry evolution. GM has shown that the industry's decline may
not be inevitable or irreversible. In part, GM owes its relatively steady
performance to advantages of size. For example, it has absorbed regulatory compliance costs more easily than Ford or Chrysler. But GM was
also quicker to recognize its changing environment and to adopt a
long-term strategy which better balances innovation and efficiency.
Moreover, GM revived the high D and I form through the adoption of
project centers at the managerial level and Quality of Work Life
(QWL) programs for hourly employees. As a result, GM is the only
American auto company entering the 1980s with much reason for optimism.

GM's relative stability in the 1970s was a direct result of the company's ability to adapt to changing circumstances. After the humiliations
of the Nader incident, Lordstown, and the Vega, GM began to reeval-
uate some of its policies and practices. The company seemed to understand that its mistakes could be traced to a lack of internal differentiation. In the late 1960s and early 1970s GM took several steps to change
this. First, it began to proliferate internal committees to draw upon
specialized points of view. In 1965–66 the company created an automotive safety engineering group to act as a bridge between the operating divisions and government policymakers. Similarly, in 1970 GM
formed a research policy committee to study and consider the best
technological response to the demands of the Clean Air Act. These
steps were in keeping with a second change in GM's behavior—its decision to cooperate with government regulators on most issues rather
than to fight them. One manager recalled that key decision makers put
out the message in the early 1970s that "the [federal] standards are
here to stay. Find out what the regulators are doing. Help them out.
We have to learn to live with this."[66]

Third, GM began to listen to what critics and outsiders were saying. After the failure of Ralph Nader's 1970 "Campaign GM" to place
consumer representatives on the board of directors, the board itself
added outsiders and formed a public policy committee to examine and
oversee GM's public affairs positions. The outside directors were later
responsible for influencing the company's response to two critical issues
of the early 1970s, environmental policy and energy policy.* In 1971
General Motors took the unusual step of hiring two senior managers
from the outside: Ernest S. Starkman, an engineering professor at

---

*In 1970 the board created a Science Advisory Committee of outside experts to advise
the corporation on environmental issues. The board's action on energy policy will be
considered below.

Berkeley, became vice-president for environmental activities, and Harvard Business School professor Stephen H. Fuller was appointed vice-president for personnel administration.

In the early 1970s senior management and the board together sensed that big changes were coming.[67] In April 1973, the company switched from a five-year to a ten-year horizon in product planning.[68] This long-term perspective enabled the company to see, however dimly, that the U.S. market would eventually become a battleground for global competition and that foreign automakers enjoyed certain advantages. Accordingly, GM began investing about $1 billion annually on research and development, designing new ways to reduce automobile weight and increase engine efficiency without sacrificing the company's image as a builder of roomy cars for families. This approach paid off. Between 1972 and 1978 GM's fleet's average mileage per gallon rose from America's worst (12 mpg) to America's best (17.8 mpg).[69] After spending some $20 billion during the 1970s, GM has budgeted $80 billion for the 1980s, with plans to compete directly against imports and produce an electric-powered commuter vehicle by the end of the decade. Furthermore, GM became a more aggressive competitor in overseas markets. In 1972 it purchased a 34% interest in Isuzu, a Japanese firm.

In 1973 GM also committed itself to a new kind of organizational coordinating mechanism, the project center, to link corporate staff and line management in the car-making divisions. Traditionally, individual divisions, called "lead divisions," developed new products common to all of the corporation's models. For example, Pontiac was responsible for improvements in air conditioning, Chevrolet for frames, and Buick for brakes. Beginning in 1973 project centers took over some of the lead divisions' functions. The first center, formed to preside over the gradual shrinkage of the coming generation of autos, brought together representatives from each division as well as managers from the design, customer service, and marketing staffs. According to GM's president, this enabled the corporation "to get most of the advantages of divisionalization. . . . The development engineers were on a loan basis from all divisions. . . . We wanted a new design that would give each section of the car as much compatibility as possible across the full GM line."[70] The utility of the project centers became clear later, when GM established separate centers to manage the development of the X-body and J-body cars.

Finally, in 1972 the board ordered that a study of federal energy policy be undertaken. Completed in the spring of 1973, it predicted that energy policy "would have a profound effect" on the corporation's business.[71] When the first energy shock came that October, then, GM was strategically, organizationally, and psychologically prepared. GM rapidly committed itself to a new course by speeding up the development of the Chevette subcompact and the shrunken Cadillac Seville, as well as by "downsizing" its entire fleet in the later 1970s. As a result, GM brought its X-body, front-wheel-drive compacts to market more than a full year before Ford or Chrysler offered similar models.

In the later 1970s GM also strove to overcome the oppressive conformity that had alienated managers like DeLorean. It succeeded in restoring a comparatively high level of managerial commitment by its rejuvenation of the high D and I form and by its consensual decision making, although layoffs in 1974 and 1979–80 worked in the opposite direction. A writer for *Fortune* found it hard in 1978 "to find a top executive at GM who does not evidence enthusiasm for what he or the company is doing."[72] GM insiders attributed this change of mood to the company's ability to generate ideas and decisions without creating conflict. As a marketing executive put it:

> In this company there is a real competition of ideas. We thrive on the adversary process. Anyone with a good idea can get heard. The top people have been around a long time. They know each other and their way down in the organization very well. They have had many opportunities to appraise people's actions, their capabilities, their judgments. In this kind of organization, there are rarely single instants of decision. I frequently don't know precisely when a decision is made in General Motors. I don't remember being in a committee meeting when things came to a vote. Usually someone will simply summarize a developing position. Everyone else either nods or states his particular terms of consensus."[73]

The same *Fortune* writer, in an article written in 1981, described General Motors as "essentially a tribal organization," similar to its Japanese rivals. GM executives tended to agree. "Managers come to GM and somehow become part of it — and then it's like a religion," claimed erstwhile outsider Stephen Fuller. "We're more Japanese than we think."[74]

GM became the first of the Big Three to apply the remedies of "tribal organization" to the blue-collar blues. GM reasoned that one solution to low levels of productivity and high levels of absenteeism, turnover, alcoholism, grievances, and industrial sabotage would be to transform the nature of jobs on the assembly line. Beginning in 1968, various experiments in job improvement and enrichment were tried in several GM plants with encouraging results. At an assembly plant in Lakewood, Georgia, for instance, first-line supervisors were trained to be more open and less formal with their subordinates. As the number of grievances dropped, hourly employees were encouraged to help rearrange work areas in order to make their job tasks more interesting and productive. To accomplish this, a plant manager recalled, "It was necessary to push the decision-making process to the lowest level of the organization."[75]

In 1973 the UAW lent its formal support to what union vice-president Irving Bluestone dubbed GM's "Quality of Work Life" (QWL) efforts.* QWL proceeded in a decentralized fashion, with local plant managers and union representatives working together to define and implement the concept. The program has occasionally met opposition from local managers who see it as a surrender of their traditional prerogatives, and from suspicious workers who fear that it is a cover for speedups and heavier work loads. Nonetheless, participation in QWL programs has become mandatory for management and voluntary for labor, and the effort has become generally popular with both sides. Where QWL has won employee acceptance, the results have been impressive. An assembly plant in Tarrytown, New York, for instance, had a poor record of quality performance, as measured by inspection counts or dealer complaints. Quality performance improved so much under QWL that the plant went from being one of GM's worst to one of its best. At the same time, absenteeism and the filing of grievances dropped significantly.[76]

A diesel engine plant in Bay City, Michigan, produced an immediate payoff under QWL. Before the plant opened, the general manager calculated that with an investment of about $350,000 in machinery and equipment, engine push rods could be built for 29 cents apiece. Before this investment was made, however, the manager met with the employees who would be producing the rods and, as he recalled,

> One operator suggested that he could handle six cut-off machines instead of four by modifying our material handling system which simplified his job. Another operator stated that he could run *two* welders instead of one with a minor rearrangement. The jobsetter said that with the rebuilt equipment he could service this job along with his current assignment. Another operator noted that he could use a current welder for both service and the diesel rod, thus saving the purchase of new equipment. In addition, there were several other proposals to improve the efficiency of the operation. The final result of this effort is the elimination of [some] investment and piece cost reduction of five cents. This cost reduction will result in a savings to the corporation of sixteen cents per engine.[77]

QWL has gained the firm support of GM's top management and most of the directors of the UAW. At the end of 1980, 84 of 155 GM bargaining plants had some sort of QWL program in place. The program has not been an unqualified success, however. Several plants, including, ironically, Lakewood, Georgia, have moved away from QWL

---

*Ford and Chrysler lagged General Motors in QWL efforts. Ford formally established its Employe Involvement program as part of its contract with the UAW in 1979. Less is known about Chrysler's efforts, although the corporation has had a memorandum of agreement on QWL with the UAW since 1973.

back to the old way of doing business. Furthermore, serious obstacles must be overcome. The shrinkage of the industry in the coming decade will force economic trade-offs between management and labor which will be difficult to negotiate: cost control vs. wage growth, outsourcing vs. employment levels, productivity gains vs. job security. The 1982 contracts create some mechanisms for the two sides to discuss these sensitive issues, although it is much too early to predict confidently what will happen. Nonetheless, the general success of QWL gives reason for hope. Certainly, GM and the UAW remain committed to changing traditional authoritarian practices and adversarial positions. "It is morally right to involve people in the decision-making process," argued Stephen Fuller, "and it would be right even if it didn't lead to improved productivity, profits, and cost."[78]

In sum, while great storms shook the American automobile industry in the 1970s, GM's performance was relatively steady. The reason for this, we suggest, is that GM was better able than its rivals to satisfy the conditions for organizational adaptation and readaptation. It adopted a long-term strategy, supported by the high D and I form and flexible human resource policies from the top to the bottom of the organization. Among the other automakers, Ford appears to be managing more readaptively in the 1980s as well. The success of the Ford-UAW "Employe Involvement Program" (similar to QWL at GM) accounted partly for the company's ability to consummate the 1982 labor contract which increases communication and shares decision-making more evenly between labor and management. This new spirit of cooperation and the mechanisms which now support it portend well for the long term health of the auto industry once it emerges from its immediate crisis.

## CONCLUSION

Figure 2.10 encapsulates the history of the American auto industry in terms of the nine-area model introduced in Chapter 1. The first commercial sale of an American automobile took place in the mid-1890s. Early producers entered a rapidly growing market while the capital costs of making cars were very low (Area 4 conditions). Such favorable circumstances quickly attracted many competitors, among them Henry Ford. The industry first grew and then contracted, passing through Area 1 and 2 conditions as it grew more difficult to attract start-up capital and as production technology became standardized, favoring larger firms. The oligopoly that eventually emerged by the end of the 1920s resulted from two different kinds of strategies: Ford's emphasis on mass production targeted at a single market, the low-in-

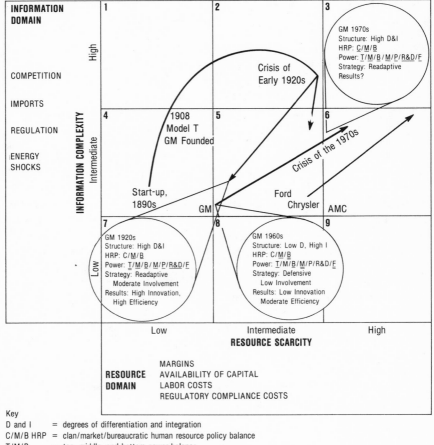

Key

D and I = degrees of differentiation and integration
C/M/B HRP = clan/market/bureaucratic human resource policy balance
T/M/B = top, middle, and bottom power balance
M/P/R&D/F = marketing, production, research and development, finance departmental
power balance

Underline indicates weight

**Figure 2.10   Evolution of the U.S. Auto Industry 1895–1980**

come buyer, and General Motors' strategy of consolidation, tight financial control, and a diversified product line aimed at different segments of the buying public. These two generic strategies, which one writer has dubbed "Fordism" and "Sloanism," were successful until recent events pushed the auto industry into Area 6 conditions.[79]

The Big Three automakers' long dominance of the American market in the four decades after 1930 might suggest that they were well adapted to their environment. Certainly, for most of that time, the business environment was supportive. The spectacular crisis of the late

1970s should give pause for further reflection, however. If the automakers were so well adapted to their environment, then why have their recent performances been so dismal? Admittedly, the business environment of the 1980s is dramatically different from that of the 1960s, yet this change—despite the suddenness of the energy crisis—did not take place overnight. Surely a truly adaptive organization ought to have responded better. What happened?

Our answer is that the internal conditions of the auto companies did not match the external conditions for readaptation during the industry's maturity. None of the companies pursued a readaptive strategy by attempting to balance innovation and efficiency. Only GM went into the 1930s with a high D and I structure. Even there, however, as DeLorean remarked, the integration maintained by the committee structure became stifling while internal differentiation withered. By the 1960s GM's high D and I organization was really low D and high I. Moreover, human resource practices typical of the auto industry did not engage the involvement of most employees in the larger purposes of the business. Bureaucratic and market incentives for managerial personnel were not balanced by clan mechanisms. In terms of power, the finance and, secondarily, the marketing groups overly dominated production and R&D. Finally, the standoff between management and labor did not reflect a working balance of power between the top and the bottom levels of the companies. Autoworkers were well paid, but were given little responsibility or opportunity to improve the production process.

It should not be surprising, then, that the auto industry was unable to sustain satisfactory levels of both efficiency and innovation over time. The great temptation for any organization, of course, is that when it achieves success in one of these areas the other suffers. While the automakers achieved production efficiency, product innovation slowed. Short-term success spawned short-term incentives, which bred more short-term success, a vicious circle until a series of shocks brought the entire automobile industry skidding toward a crash in 1980.

The history of the U.S. auto industry therefore contains an important lesson for managers, workers, and public policymakers: Stability and adaptation are not the same things and are not necessarily mutually supportive. Organizational readaptation involves both striving for resources and learning from experience. It is a difficult goal to achieve and maintain, even in favorable circumstances.

This lesson will become even clearer as we take up the story of the steel industry in the next chapter. As we shall see, there are many parallels between the auto and steel industries, but critical differences in the role of the dominant firm and in the nature of the product. One has to look to the last century to find a dominant steel firm that was clearly readaptive. As a result, the industry has no recent organizational models to learn from. Moreover, since steel companies were making more homogeneous products for more homogeneous customers, they faced a more stable environment with lower levels of IC than confronted the auto companies. Thus steel companies felt little pressure to innovate over the years and they were even less able to respond to the challenges of foreign competition. The crisis in steel has been building for a long time.

# CHAPTER 3

# Steel: The Slumping Giant

FOR MORE THAN SEVENTY YEARS the United States led the world in production of steel. The history of this first great American industry has been inextricably intertwined with our mythology about American engineering know-how, the sort of hard-driving capitalists who make it to the top, and our national character itself. Andrew Carnegie and J.P. Morgan created Big Steel; the steel business in return made Carnegie, in Morgan's words, "the richest man in the world" by 1901. In the early 1900s foreign visitors marveled at the gigantic scale and advanced technology of U.S. plants. Steel has provided the stuff of countless propaganda films ever since. Steel locomotives, fabricated on steel machines and running on steel rails spurred the economy a century ago; steel has girded skyscrapers, undergirded the automobile, and framed the airplane. Virtually every item American workers use, from hammers to sophisticated machines, from office typewriters and filing cabinets to computers, is made, at least in part, of steel. Steel is a metaphor for American toughness and durability, which extends even to our comic-book heroes: Superman is "the man of steel," "able to bend steel with his bare hands."

What a shock it is, then, to consider the present fortunes of the industry! Newspapers regularly carry stories of the superiority and lower cost of foreign steel, environmental hazards in the Mahoning Valley, low rates of return on investment, and the closings of steel plants. In

1980 Wisconsin Steel, the nation's thirteenth-largest steelmaker, ceased production, and McLouth Steel, the twelfth-largest, hovered on the brink of bankruptcy in 1982. Other major steel companies are involved in a headlong rush to flee the industry. U.S. Steel's acquisition of Marathon Oil is only the most spectacular of many examples of diversification. Clearly, the industry environment and the performance of leading firms are no longer mutually supportive. Steelmen are prone to trace their misfortunes to unfair foreign competition, government interference, and high labor costs. There is some justice in these charges, but the story of this slumping industry is far more complicated than steelmen will admit in public. It is a story of a mature industry with a tradition of adversarial relations with its work force, an industry that has lost its capacity for radical technological innovation, resisted administrative reform, fought government regulation bitterly, and surrendered foreign markets. Unlike the auto crisis, the steel industry's difficulties unfolded slowly. One cannot identify a single turning point or series of decisions leading to the present industry woes. Rather the current crisis in steel has built up gradually over a long period.

## THE U.S. STEEL INDUSTRY: THE FIRST HUNDRED YEARS, 1860–1960

The first century of the U.S. steel industry divides into three stages. In the first, from the 1860s to 1901 the Bessemer process, the growth of demand for steel products, and the managerial policies of Andrew Carnegie combined to transform the iron industry from fragmented and dispersed small businesses into giant, fully integrated steel firms. This period culminated in the forming of the U.S. Steel Corporation. The second period, 1901–30, witnessed the growth of U.S. Steel's major rivals and the establishment of the present market structure. Finally, from 1930 to 1960, American steel firms comfortably dominated the international market. Throughout these years the United States boasted it had the largest, most innovative, and most productive steel industry in the world, although, as time wore on, this boast acquired a hollow ring.

### BEGINNINGS (1860–1901)

At the time of the Civil War steel manufacturing was a minor business. Only thirteen small companies produced less then 12,000 tons of steel in 1860. Iron manufacturing, on the other hand, was thriving throughout the twenty-six states. Iron was produced in two stages: smelting, which transformed raw materials into pig iron; and refining, which turned pig iron into wrought iron, a more uniform and salable product (Figure 3.1). In 1860, 286 blast furnaces, some still located in the midst of forests ("iron plantations") furnishing charcoal for basic energy, produced nearly a million tons of pig iron. Hundreds of small establishments then refined it into bars, sheets, rails, wire, and other shapes. The processes of smelting and refining were seldom combined. An English visitor noted only six fully integrated ironworks in the country in 1854.[1] Railroads bought most of the wrought iron, although consumers ranged from makers of small machines and implements, to bridge contractors, to the builders of the *Monitor* and the *Merrimac*.

This fragmented industry had become a big business by the 1890s. Peter Temin, the historian of the nineteenth-century iron and steel industry, attributes this transformation to two factors: "an increasing sophistication in the use of heat," and "the growth of the American economy, which produced an ever-growing demand for iron and steel as well as a continuing demand for better quality iron and steel in more complex and heavier shapes."[2] To these factors we may add a third: Carnegie's application of rigorous cost control and centralized management.

Advances in technology made large-scale production of steel possible and revolutionized the structure of the iron industry. Henry Bessemer and William Kelly simultaneously discovered a completely new way to make steel in the 1850s. Technological advances that enabled engineers to work with higher temperatures were a necessary prerequisite to the new technique. The hot-blast process (1828) and the gradual replacement of charcoal by different grades of coal made it possible to smelt iron ore and fluxes in larger volume. Elsewhere higher temperatures enabled new processes, such as puddling and rolling, to turn pig iron into wrought iron and steel. Bessemer and Kelly then discovered that carbon could be removed from the pig iron easily by blowing hot air across the molten metal. This had two effects—the temperature of the metal continued to rise, making it still easier to handle; and the process could be stopped part way to yield steel. An English engineer, Robert Mushet, then found a way to ensure uniform quality in the steel by injecting a controlled amount of carbon back into the molten metal.

Just as the Bessemer-Kelly process inaugurated the age of steel, so the continued application of higher temperatures and better engineering wrought a second revolution in steel production with the introduction of the basic, or open-hearth, process on a commercial scale in the 1880s. Here the open-hearth furnaces, driven by still higher temperatures, replaced puddling and removed the need for workers to stir molten metal continuously. The new furnaces had two other key advantages. They handled still greater volumes of metal, and they could

Figure 3.1  Stages in the Production of Iron and Steel 1830–1980

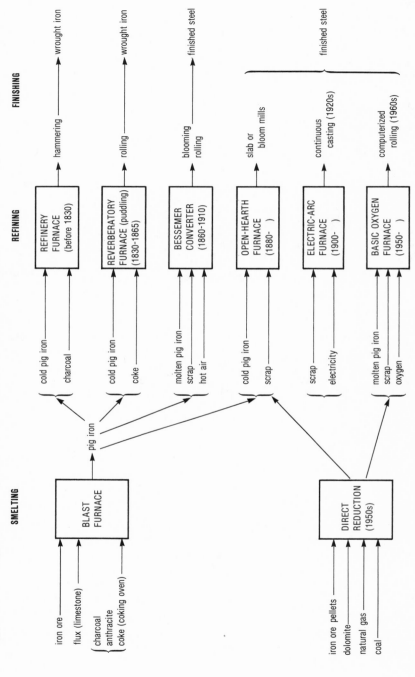

work with a lower grade of ore and a higher proportion of scrap. This reduced the cost of materials substantially.[3]

The discovery of cheap methods of making steel coincided with a sharp increase in its demand. For just at the time the Bessemer-Kelly process was patented, the railroads, in the quest to produce bigger and faster trains, required rails to be stronger, lighter, and less brittle than could be made from iron. Between 1860 and 1870 the volume of rail production in the U.S. tripled, with steel rails making up an increasing proportion. Indeed, in 1877 production of steel rails permanently overtook production of iron rails. The rapid spread of steel rails also spurred vertical integration of the manufacturing plants, since a large rolling mill running at capacity could require the output of three blast furnaces.[4] By the end of the nineteenth century, blast furnaces and steel mills were normally built on the same site.

The new technologies affected the structure of firms as well as the structure of the industry. Not only did demand for wrought iron wither, but the Bessemer process, because it required high temperatures and precise chemistry, also required careful engineering of a new order. Moreover, Bessemer plants produced greater volumes and realized economies of scale.[5] Technological change and expanding demand thus generated trends toward bigness and vertical integration, although these outcomes were also influenced by the new managerial skills Andrew Carnegie brought to the industry.

Carnegie had learned business as a protégé of J. Edgar Thomson and Thomas Scott on the Pennsylvania Railroad in the 1850s and 1860s. By the time he reached thirty, Carnegie had already made a small fortune through prudent investments in businesses connected with the railroad: Pullman sleeping cars, axles, and iron bridges. He struck it rich, however, when he left the railroad to concentrate on manufacturing steel rails. His success derived from his insight that the techniques of large-scale management pioneered on the railroad could be transferred to the manufacturing sector. He understood that plant design was important, that logistics was an essential part of the business, and, above all, that costs had to be constantly evaluated and controlled. And it did not hurt relations with his biggest customer that Carnegie named his first Bessemer plant after J. Edgar Thomson.

A detailed history of the development of Carnegie Steel is beyond the scope of this chapter, although we can enumerate some of the methods that made him "the richest man in the world" by the time he retired in 1901. In the first place, Carnegie adhered to a simple management philosophy, which he reduced to two essential maxims: "Cut the prices; scoop the market; run the mills fast;" and "Watch the costs and the profits will take care of themselves."[6] Carnegie imported centralized management and strict cost accounting from the railroads and applied them very successfully in the steel business.

Second, Carnegie was a master of "hard-driving," the ability to make furnaces produce far in excess of rated capacity. The Lucy furnace, for instance, produced 13,361 tons of steel in its first year of operation, but the improvements of Carnegie's engineers enabled it to exceed 100,000 tons annually within a few years. Carnegie also saw the importance of investing in the latest technology. Indeed, he was single-minded on this point. In 1885, for example, Carnegie began to phase out Bessemer steel production in favor of the open-hearth process, although much of his plant was less than ten years old. "Even though Carnegie had hundreds of thousands of dollars invested in Bessemer converters," writes his most authoritative biographer, Joseph Wall, "he was ready to scrap them in favor of a better and more economical process. Construction costs never bothered Carnegie. It was operational cost that mattered, and that simple truth was a major reason for his success."[7] In short, Carnegie's management emphasized both efficiency and innovation.

Third, Carnegie adopted a strategy of vertical integration early on. He built the Lucy furnace in 1870 to supply another of his companies which fabricated iron bridges. A few years later the Lucy furnace supplied iron to his steel plant at Homestead, Pennsylvania. In the 1880s Carnegie integrated backward into production of coke and in the 1890s he bought into the fabulous ore deposits of the Mesabi range in Minnesota. He announced the intention in 1900 to integrate forward into manufacture of finished steel products. Thus Carnegie gained control over his business from the mining of raw materials through the production of steel itself.

Not resting there, Carnegie also pursued a strategy of product diversification. As early as the 1870s he had expanded his product line beyond steel rails into structural shapes. In 1900, when his business was very big indeed, Carnegie announced plans to begin producing finished steel products such as tubes, wire, sheets, and nails in order to capture new markets. He gave particular care to marketing these products. He maintained personal contacts with railroad leaders and actively promoted the virtues of steel in the construction of America's burgeoning cities. Carnegie's attention to this end of the business was not matched by his competitors for decades.

Carnegie had an almost uncanny ability to spot capable people and promote them to the right jobs. The clearest examples are the plant designer Alexander Holley, the plant superintendent Captain William Jones, and executives Charles M. Schwab and William E. Corey, but thirty of his thirty-three superintendents rose from the ranks of labor to become major figures in the steel business.[8] While it would be ludicrous to hail him as an enlightened employer concerned about the quality of work life in his mills, Carnegie publicly supported the workers' right to unionize. His relentless drive to reduce costs led him to many confrontations with the work force, most severely and tragically at the Homestead strike of 1892. Nevertheless, among his peers, Carnegie stood out as an innovator in labor relations. Under the advice of Captain Jones, for example, the Carnegie mills led the nation in moving from two twelve-hour shifts to three eight-hour shifts, although this plan was opposed by the union and later scrapped by Henry Clay Frick, one of the company's top executives. At a higher level, Carnegie freely used incentive plans and the prospect of partnerships to motivate his managers and increase their involvement in the company.

Carnegie's business practices rewarded him handsomely. The Thomson works turned annual profits at a rate of 25% to 30% in its first three years, reaching more than $400,000 in 1878. Profits soared through the next two decades — $3 million by 1886, $6.7 million by 1896, $40 million by 1900. And through it all Carnegie kept dividends low as he plowed his earnings back into the business.[9]

The dizzying growth of Carnegie Steel put heavy pressure on competitors to keep up. Fortunately, from their points of view, Carnegie confined his activities to the area around Pittsburgh. Elsewhere his rivals and imitators built smaller steel empires. J. P. Morgan financed and Judge Elbert Gary managed a group of companies in Illinois and Minnesota under the umbrella of Federal Steel. Elsewhere, a notorious financier and speculator, "Judge" W. H. Moore, combined another set of companies into the National Steel Company centered in Youngstown. Small companies were swallowed up as the industry grew more concentrated. Barriers to entry grew higher by the year. Between 1869 and 1899 the number of "blast furnace establishments" declined from 386 to 223. The number of steel rolling mills remained constant at over 400, although the gaps between rich and poor, large and small widened considerably.[10]

The steel industry's increasing size and concentration exemplified trends occurring in American manufacturing as a whole. The opening of national networks of communication and transportation after the Civil War underlay the rise of "big business" in this period. U.S. enterprises generally grew in two stages: Changing technologies facilitated growth by vertical integration chiefly in the 1870s; and geographic spread and the desire to restrict competition spurred growth by horizontal merger in the 1880s and 1890s.[11] The late 1890s witnessed an especially large wave of mergers, the biggest of which occurred in the steel industry. In 1901 the nation's three largest steel firms — Carnegie, Federal, and National Steel — joined with some smaller companies to form the world's first billion-dollar corporation — U.S. Steel.

U.S. Steel was capitalized at $1.4 billion. At its founding it controlled "three-fifths of the steel business of the country" as well as "hundreds of millions of tons of desirable Lake ore in reserves, over 50,000 acres of the choicest coking-coal lands, over 1,000 miles of railroads, . . . a fleet of 112 Lake steamers and barges, not to mention large investments in docks, natural-gas and limestone properties, and other kindred branches of the industry." As the U.S. commissioner of corporations concluded in 1911, "It is clear that the United States Steel Corporation at its organization, in 1901, overshadowed not only any individual competitor in the industry in the United States but all competitors combined."[12]

There were several motives behind this gigantic combination beyond Carnegie's willingness to retire from the business. The merger climaxed a decade of fierce competition among the largest firms in the industry. In this sense the creation of U.S. Steel was merely the culmination of the wave of mergers and combinations that had swept American manufacturing generally in the period. More particularly, J. P. Morgan was especially afraid of ruinous competition if Carnegie proceeded to build his giant steel-finishing plant on the shores of Lake Erie. This venture represented not only a stage of forward integration and a threat to create excess capacity, but also suggested that Carnegie would no longer be confined to dominating business in the Pittsburgh area. Morgan's fears were lent urgency by rumors that Carnegie, upset by rising freight costs, was thinking about building his own railroad. All of these factors point up the defensive and reactive reasons for the merger.

Second, the merger reflected the industrywide evolution toward complete vertical integration. The companies that made up the new corporation had been moving in different directions in the 1890s. Some finished steel producers, such as the American Steel Hoop Company, were attempting to integrate backward into raw steel production, while others, like Carnegie, intended to move forward. The new corporation combined both tendencies and formed a completely integrated enterprise from ore and coal production to a wide range of finished products. The merger's advocates trumpeted the efficiencies to be gained when a single set of managers could control costs at every stage of the business. As the new firm and industry structure took shape, however, efficiency ceased to be an important concern.

Finally, the principal players took the opportunity to realize an immediate vast profit. Moore in particular had made his fortune by selling inflated securities at every chance, and the U.S. Steel merger offered him a bonanza. When the corporation issued its $1.4 billion in stock in 1901, the actual value of the constituent properties was estimated by the government to be less than $700 million. Clearly, enormous fortunes were realized. The syndicate that underwrote the merger received $62.5 million![13]

The great merger marked the end of one period of the industry's history and the beginning of another. For the next three decades the steel industry passed through an adolescence of rapid growth and attendant growing pains. These years witnessed growing demand from new customers, the establishment of a stable market structure in the industry, growth in the size of firms and the scale of operations, troubled labor relations, modest improvements in technology, and sharp increases in productivity. U.S. Steel deliberately chose to let its market share erode even while its capacity and profits grew and its chief competitors' market share rose through aggressive marketing and horizontal merger.

The new century offered steel companies a very favorable business environment. The railroads remained the largest single customer, although the growing automobile and truck industries consumed steel voraciously. (See Chapter 2.) Other major new customers included electrical equipment suppliers, appliance manufacturers, highway construction companies, oil and gas companies, and, of course, military suppliers during World War I. Foreign markets expanded as well. In 1900 the U.S. exported just over one million gross tons of iron and steel, in 1929 over three million tons. At the peak of the war, exports averaged over five million gross tons. These were great years for the steel business. Total U.S. production grew fourfold, from 13.5 million gross tons in 1901 to 56.4 million tons in 1929.

The modern industry structure took shape in these extremely favorable conditions. With high profits and increasing control over resources, the major steel companies faced the conditions of Areas 4 and 5 on our model: resource scarcity (RS) was low and information complexity (IC) moderate. Under Judge Gary's defensive strategy, U.S. Steel declined to press for more of the market than it had originally held. Sensing public hostility to big business as well as the likelihood of an antitrust suit, Gary declared in 1908, "We are perfectly satisfied to limit the amount of our business to our proportion of capacity and to do everything possible we can to promote the interests of our competitors."[14]

U.S. Steel grew slowly and steadily, content to sacrifice market share while its competitors grew more rapidly (Figure 3.2).[15] Although it brought its huge integrated works at Gary on stream by 1911, U.S. Steel generally confined itself to the slow modernization and rationalization of its far-flung activities.

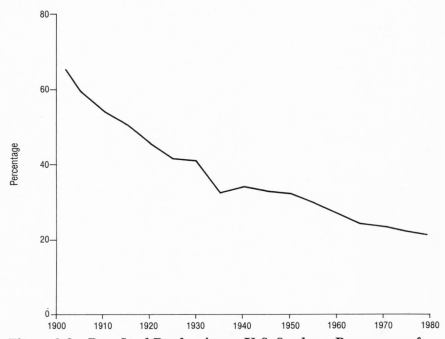

**Figure 3.2    Raw Steel Production at U.S. Steel as a Percentage of Total U.S. Production 1902–1979**

SOURCES: U.S. Steel, annual reports, American Iron and Steel Institute, *Annual Statistical Report*, 1980; Institute for Iron and Steel Studies, *The Steel Industry in Brief: Databook, U.S.A., 1979–80.*

U.S. Steel remained by far the largest single firm in the business — more than twice as big as its nearest competitor. Its chief rivals grew largely by the time-honored method of horizontal merger. Republic Steel and National Steel, two of the top five in 1930, were consolidations of firms gathered into fully integrated operations in the late 1920s. Bethlehem Steel, under the guidance of Charles M. Schwab, grew at first in atypical fashion. After leaving U.S. Steel, Schwab pulled together a small but thriving steel plant in eastern Pennsylvania and a bankrupt shipbuilding concern. Bethlehem capitalized on a new process for rolling structural shapes and began to look to new markets for business. It acquired rich ore deposits in Chile, while World War I created a boom for its ship-building and munitions interests. By the early 1920s Bethlehem had climbed from a marginal position to become the second largest firm in the industry. Schwab cemented his position by acquiring two other top-ten producers in 1922.[16] Other large firms grew by consolidation of family businesses (Jones & Laughlin), concentration on a single geographic market (Inland), or exploitation of new technology (Armco). By the end of World War I small producers were in eclipse. U.S. Steel and its major competitors, Bethlehem, Republic, National, Inland, Jones & Laughlin, and Armco, dominated the steel business.

What was good for the big steel firms was not necessarily good for the steelworkers. The big steel companies combined to resist unionization, while labor-saving technology imperiled jobs and sent wages tumbling. The Amalgamated Association of Iron, Steel, and Tin Workers, the dominant union in the industry, tried unsuccessfully to strike the industry in 1901, 1904, and 1909, but their hold on the work force was weakened by a fatal inconsistency. They were a union composed exclusively of skilled workmen, but advances in steelmaking increasingly stripped the industry of skilled jobs. Moreover, immigrants arriving in America flocked to the mills eager to work in almost any conditions. Steel industry managers understood these developments and gradually dislodged the union from their plants.[17] By 1910 the Amalgamated Association was all but dead and fresh efforts to organize and strike were greeted with firings, lockouts, and the hiring of scab labor. In the fall of 1919 thousands of workers joined more than seventy strikes hoping to establish a reasonable wage scale and restructure their hours. These strikes ended quietly in 1920, however, when Judge Gary refused to acknowledge worker demands and simply outwaited his opponents.

A more powerful stimulus to change in the workplace was the gradual buildup of public pressure on management in the steel companies. In the first two decades of this century, journalists, philanthropic organizations, religious commissions, and government investigations portrayed conditions in the mills as a national scandal.[18] Foremost in the public eye and chief among worker demands was the abolition of the 12-hour working day accompanied every two weeks by a 24-hour shift, "the long-turn," when the day and night shifts were transposed. A worker's day thus became a dreary round of toil: "A man works, comes home, eats and goes to bed, gets up, eats and goes to work."[19] Public pressure and strong words from President Harding eventually overcame industry reluctance to adopt the eight-hour shift in 1923. This was a significant victory, though it was earned independently of the movement to organize workers in the industry.

During the first three decades of the 20th century, there were few major technological innovations in the manufacture of steel. No firm, including U.S. Steel, made significant investments in research and development. Rather, existing equipment and procedures were steadily made more efficient. The switch to electricity as the main source of energy in the mills greatly improved the efficiency of rolling and handling. The electric furnace, capable of still higher temperatures, had been introduced on a commercial scale in France in 1900 but was adopted here only slowly because of the rudimentary state of knowledge about electricity and fixed investment in other technologies. Production of steel by the open-hearth method surpassed Bessemer production in 1908 and nearly all new plants featured the newer process. Plants also became larger, a trend symbolized by U.S. Steel's mammoth works on the south shore of Lake Michigan built between 1905 and 1911. This was a fully integrated plant boasting eight blast furnaces, 56 open-hearth furnaces, and complete facilities for rolling and blooming. Indeed, the plant was so large that the corporation had to build a city around it — Gary, Indiana — to accommodate its workers.

The most revolutionary innovation of the period came in steel processing. A small family-owned steel company in Ohio, the American Rolling Mill Company (Armco), introduced the continuous caster or cold strip mill in 1924. Actually invented in Germany in the nineteenth century, the continuous rolling process had been tried ineffectually several times in America before an Armco engineer, John B. Tytus, made it a success. Continuous casting, while hardly "one of the ten greatest inventions of man," as has been claimed, nevertheless permitted tremendous gains in productivity.[20] It has been estimated that one mechanized rolling mill could match the output of forty hand sheet mills. Productivity measured in tons per man-hour increased thirteen times. In contrast, mechanization and electrification improved productivity in blast furnaces by a factor of three between 1920 and 1930.[21]

### MATURITY (1930–1960)

By 1930, American steel firms, masters of their resources and certain of their competition, had reached maturity. The United States was the world's largest producer and exporter of steel. American steel could be found in products the world over, from the thinnest paper clip to the mightiest suspension bridge. Although the industry suffered heavily during the depression, its expansion during the war and postwar years rivaled that of the early part of the century. Profits ran high.[22] U.S. Steel continued to dominate the industry by wide margin. In 1936, according to *Fortune*, the corporation was bigger than its next six rivals combined, although Gary's successors continued his tolerance of smaller producers.[23] The oligopoly of U.S. Steel, Bethlehem, Armco, Republic, National, Inland, Jones & Laughlin, and Youngstown has proved remarkably stable. Indeed, the passing years have seen little change even in the ranking of firms in the industry (see Table 3.1). In 1937 U.S. Steel finally recognized the United Steel Workers of America (USWA) and other large firms followed within several

**Table 3.1    Eight Largest Steel Companies, Selected Years**

| RANK* | 1904 | 1938 | 1978 |
|---|---|---|---|
| 1 | United States Steel | United States Steel | United States Steel |
| 2 | Jones & Laughlin | Bethlehem Steel | Bethlehem Steel |
| 3 | Cambria Steel | Republic Steel | National Steel |
| 4 | Lackawanna Steel | Jones & Laughlin | LTV (includes Jones & Laughlin Steel and Youngstown Sheet and Tube) |
| 5 | Colorado Fuel and Iron | National Steel | Republic Steel |
| 6 | Pennsylvania Steel | Youngstown Sheet and Tube | Armco |
| 7 | Republic Iron and Steel | Inland Steel | Inland Steel |
| 8 | Maryland Steel | Armco Steel | Wheeling-Pittsburgh Steel |

SOURCES: Gertrude G. Schroeder, *The Growth of the Major Steel Companies, 1900–1950* (Baltimore: Johns Hopkins University Press, 1953), p. 199.
Robert W. Crandall, *The U.S. Steel Industry in Recurrent Crisis* (Washington, D.C.: The Brookings Institution, 1981), p. 12.

*Raw steel capacity

years, inaugurating a relatively peaceful phase of labor-management relations.

The industry's long stability stemmed partly from U.S. Steel's benevolence and partly from some informal agreements dating back to the early part of the century. Beginning in 1907 Gary sponsored a series of annual dinners at which, in his own words, "Steel people (came) together occasionally . . . to tell one to the others exactly what his business was. . . ."[24] What Gary did not say but clearly implied was that once U.S. Steel and others announced their prices it was understood that no one would attempt to undercut them. The Gary dinners broke up in 1911, but the spirit of cooperation lingered on. In 1908 Gary helped found the American Iron and Steel Institute, whose eventual semiannual meetings continued to serve some of the purposes of the earlier dinners. Although there is no conclusive evidence of formal collusion or price fixing, the pattern of pricing in the industry remained constant over many years. In practice U.S. Steel set or seconded price changes if they were to hold throughout the industry. This pricing behavior in large part accounts for the stability of the industry's market structure (although the relationship is obviously reciprocal) because high-cost producers were protected by the price leaders' conviction that nobody should go out of business. On the other hand, competitive forces never compelled firms to maximize efficiency.[25]

Steel's enduring market structure and pricing policies were matched by the characteristic organization of most firms in the industry. Most steel companies maintained "centralized, functionally departmentalized structures" with low levels of differentiation and integration.[26] An organization chart of the Atlantic Steel Company from about 1920, for instance, shows only three functional departments: sales, production, and finance. This simple structure, or only slightly grander versions in larger companies, typified most firms in the industry.[27] The functional structure was partly a response to the straightforward nature of the business. In the smooth functioning of an integrated steelworks, the essential managerial task is to coordinate the flow of materials from the mines through the mills to the distribution centers. Logistics and scheduling are paramount; hence centralization and large headquarters staffs. Thus the steel companies never copied the multidivisional forms of other large-scale manufacturers. Furthermore, observed Alfred Chandler in 1962,

> Neither have strategic decisions been numerous or complex enough to demand the building of a general administrative office with general executives and staff specialists. The selling of steel as well as the obtaining of ore and its production and fabrication followed a fairly long-established routine pattern. Decisions about the building of new plants, the opening of new markets, the development of new processes have been so few as to permit senior executives to concentrate on tactics.[28]

With so little pressure to stay abreast of the competition and with generally high profits, recruiting and advancement practices rigidified along with structures. With barriers to entry so high, no steelman could rise like Carnegie to dominate the industry by hard-driving. Rather, managerial advancement often reflected family connections in the steel business. Top executives normally hailed from generations of steel managers in steel-making communities; it was rare for a senior officer to spring from another background. For most of the twentieth century, at least, American steelmen have been a very homogeneous, ingrown group.[29]

The slow metamorphosis of U.S. Steel illustrates how little the industry's environment impinged on internal organization. Under Gary's leadership (1901–27), U.S. Steel remained essentially a holding company, or as a contemporary put it: "a federation of independent companies . . . each with its own distinct government, officers, sphere of influence, and particular products."[30] It was not until Myron C. Taylor succeeded Gary in the late 1920s that the corporation began to centralize around functional divisions and a large corporate staff.[31] This process took years to unfold. As late as World War II, the corporation largely remained a hodgepodge of units reflecting its scattered origins.

It comprised a parent holding company in New Jersey, a central management company in Delaware, corporate headquarters in Pittsburgh, and a host of subsidiary companies across the country. In 1951 the corporation consolidated its separate operations and reshaped its subsidiaries into divisions.

The next reorganization followed a dozen years later, when half of the general operating divisions were consolidated into larger steel-producing units. The new steel operations were then divided four ways, into heavy products, sheet and tin products, tubular shapes, and wire products (although wire was later dropped as a separate operating group). At the same time the commercial department (sales) was divided into five regions across the U.S., with area vice-presidents responsible for marketing all the products. In 1970 the corporation dropped this organization by operating groups in favor of an East-West geographical split in steel operations. It was only in the mid-1970s that the company finally broke away from its functional structure and reorganized into geographically defined divisions that combined operations and sales.[32]

The habits of the past affected investment decisions as well as pricing and organization. Throughout this century the biggest firms financed innovation with internal funds. While profits were high this practice presented no problem. However, because companies traditionally paid healthy dividends and because they were reluctant to seek outside funds, when profits thinned so did investment. Some of the more aggressive smaller firms occasionally resorted to long-term borrowing, but a study of investment patterns in the industry between 1900 and 1953 concludes that "capital expenditures have been closely related to profits, steel output, and current operating funds after dividends."[33] The range of investments, moreover, was limited. Firms tended to spend money on expansion of existing plants or on machinery to produce new products, such as sheet steel for autos, rather than on cost-saving innovations.[34]

While U.S. firms strove for ways to increase volume by building bigger plants, foreign firms without access to America's bountiful resources and markets pioneered the most revolutionary steel-making techniques. In Germany, Britain, Japan, and Canada firms invested heavily in electric arc furnaces and basic oxygen furnaces (BOFs). The key advantages offered by these technologies are the direct reduction of iron and an enormous saving in the time necessary to convert molten iron to steel. In the direct reduction process, iron ore is converted to sponge iron, a product suitable for conversion in electric furnaces, without passing through the molten state. In other words, this process precludes the need for coking coal and blast furnaces. In the BOF, first demonstrated in Austria after the war, molten metal is injected with "high-purity oxygen"—99.5% pure—which burns away impurities rapidly. BOF steel can be made much more quickly with lower capital investment and operating costs. Steel is ready to be poured after about thirty minutes in a BOF, as opposed to six hours or more for comparable volume in an open-hearth furnace.[35]

Although it would be unfair to characterize the major American firms as completely resistant to new technologies, they did not accept change readily. In part, this passivity was a matter of habit. In the 1930s the editors of *Fortune* asserted that "the chief energies of the men who guided [U.S. Steel] were directed to preventing deterioration of the investment value of the enormous properties confided in their care. To achieve this, they consistently tried to freeze the steel industry at present, or better yet, past levels."[36] The big producers did not begin to install basic oxygen furnaces until the mid-1960s, although McLouth Steel, a young producer in Detroit, had invested in a BOF a decade earlier.[37] It has been argued that "engineers and businessmen are more prone to regard progress as a smooth, continuous process of improving the old ways by small changes. In the industry's view these evolutionary improvements can sometimes make an old technique competitive with a new, to the point even of delaying displacement by the new."[38] Nonetheless, it remains beyond dispute that the largest U.S. firms fell behind foreign and smaller domestic companies in the development and diffusion of new technologies.

The recognition of the steelworkers' union by U.S. Steel in 1937 and by smaller rivals by 1941 spurred hopes for a new era of cooperation between labor and management. The Steel Workers Organizing Committee (SWOC), an arm of the CIO, dreamed of reaching a new level of industrial democracy. The leaders of the movement saw union history unfolding in stages. In the first, the union would struggle to win recognition by management. With that accomplished, individual companies would cooperate with the union in resolving particular grievances during the second stage. In the final "super-charged phase of collective bargaining," the two sides would form a partnership "directed toward increasing the productive efficiency of the industry."[39] In a 1942 manifesto entitled "Principles of Union-Management Relations," two leading figures in the SWOC argued:

> Management's assumption of sole responsibility for productive efficiency actually prevents the attainment of maximum output.
>
> The participation of organized workers in management provides an outlet for their creative desires, as it is essentially a creative and cooperative undertaking.
>
> Union-management co-operation to reduce costs, eliminate wastes, increase productive efficiency, and improve quality represents a practical

program that provides workers with effective direct participation in the creative phases of management.

Union-management co-operation tends to make management more efficient and unions more cost-conscious, thereby improving the competitive position of a business enterprise and increasing the earnings of both workers and owners.[40]

But it was not to be. Although the war brought industrial harmony, industrywide strikes followed in 1946, 1949, 1952, 1956, and 1959—five times out of ten contract settlements. The central issues seldom advanced beyond wage increases as the union backed down from its ambitious hopes and management continued its hard line. Moreover, government intervention frequently influenced the negotiations. The steelworkers demanded compensation comparable to that in other industries, while management was determined to control costs and the government wished to avoid both strikes and rising prices. The shortest of the postwar strikes lasted 26 days, the longest, in 1959, 116 days. Each fed on the long history of adversarial confrontations and each left behind a legacy of bitterness and mutual suspicion. The union generally won higher wages and, like the autoworkers, steelworkers enjoyed incomes and benefits that placed them at the forefront of American manufacturing labor. However, also like the autoworkers, the steelworkers failed to achieve much control over decision making in the workplace.

From all outward indications the largest firms in the American steel industry faced conditions typical of Area 4 or 5 during most of the twentieth century. Margins were high, competition and uncertainty manageable, vast sums of capital were reinvested in an expanding business, and managers and workers alike (after 1941) enjoyed high incomes and job security. As in 1901, the United States led world producers in steel by a wide, if diminishing, margin in 1960.

As the story of the steel industry makes clear, favorable environmental conditions are fleeting and mutable. Indeed, these very favorable circumstances—abundant resources, economies of scale, price stability, and increasing demand—also lulled U.S. companies into a false feeling of security. Following the lead of the industry's dominant firm, U.S. Steel, American steel companies pursued defensive, reactive strategies. As organizations, they did not evolve beyond moderately specialized, functional structures. Companies typically were managed in a top-down manner through well established bureaucracies. Senior managers showed little interest in involving the work force in the larger operation of the business, nor did the USWA pursue this goal after its earliest years. The U.S. steel companies' record of innovation was spotty, their record of efficiency suspect. The readaptive aspects of

Carnegie's management disappeared; most steel companies simply lost their competitive edge. It is not surprising, then, that the fortunes of the industry turned sharply downward in the 1960s.

## CRISIS IN THE STEEL INDUSTRY, 1960–1980

The 1960s opened ominously for the steel industry. The 1959 strike had been the longest and most bitter since 1919. In 1962 President Kennedy, worried by high inflation, marshaled every resource of the federal government against the major companies in order to force a rollback of prices. Even one hopeful sign in the same year proved chimerical. Bethlehem Steel began construction of a "greenfield mill," a brand-new fully integrated steel plant at Burns Harbor, Indiana, the first such built in America in more than ten years. But construction delays, cost overruns, and regulatory problems kept the plant from full operation for more than a decade. No greenfield mills have been constructed since then. Perhaps the most ominous sign of all occurred in 1959, when steel imports exceeded exports for the first time since the nineteenth century. At first only a trickle, this inward flow soon became a flood.

The last twenty years have seen unmitigated crisis in the U.S. steel industry. Foreign producers have captured increasing slices of the market. Substitute materials, aluminum and plastics, have eaten into the demand for steel. Some of steel's primary customers, such as the auto industry, have themselves fallen on hard times and have reduced their consumption of steel. Government safety and environmental regulation has increased costs in the mills dramatically. Steel management has bought the cooperation of labor by conceding very high wages, but has thereby added high labor costs to already high capital costs. The steelworkers themselves have paid for their wage gains with a loss of jobs since the companies have been forced to shut down old plants and marginal operations.

Steelmen attribute their misfortunes to unfair trade practices, heavy-handed government interference, and high labor costs. There is considerable justice in these charges. Western trade agreements have been slow to recognize that the Japanese and European economies are no longer significantly weaker than that of the United States. While foreign markets are often protected by tariffs or other less formal barriers, the American market remains the world's freest and most open. Thus foreign imports have made dramatic inroads into the domestic steel market since 1960, growing from 3.4 million short tons in that year to 15.5 million in 1980—a jump from less than 5% to more than 16% of total domestic supply (Figure 3.3).

**Figure 3.3    Imports as a Percentage of Apparent Steel Supply
1960–1980**

SOURCE: Based on tabular material in American Iron and Steel Institute, *Annual Statistical Report*, various numbers.

In the late 1970s industry spokesmen charged that foreign producers were dumping steel in the United States. A report prepared for the American Iron and Steel Institute (AISI) argued that both the Japanese and Europeans sold steel in the United States at prices not only lower than those charged in their own domestic markets but also significantly lower than the full cost of production. In 1976, for example, the six largest Japanese firms charged their domestic customers $9 more per ton than their American ones; by a second test, the study claimed that in 1976 the Japanese sold steel at $32 per ton below cost. European Economic Community (EEC) producers were even worse, according to the report. They sold at $50 per ton below cost in 1976, while in 1977 EEC domestic consumers paid an average of $35 per ton more than their American counterparts.[41]

In 1977 an interagency government committee headed by undersecretary of the treasury Anthony Solomon moved to counter these practices by recommending adoption of a "trigger price mechanism" (TPM). The new plan specified a "trigger price" based on estimates of Japanese production costs (presumed to be the world standard of efficiency) below which no foreign producer could sell in the United States. The TPM has brought some temporary relief to American companies since 1979, as the volume of imports has fallen. The trigger price policy has been a frequent subject of litigation, however, and its long-run viability remains questionable. There is little doubt that American producers will continue to have difficulty staving off foreign imports.

American steelmen have also complained about the U.S. government's environmental and safety regulations and its interference in setting prices. The Environmental Protection Agency (EPA) has ranked the steel industry only slightly below the coal industry and the automobile as a source of air pollution. In 1977 a government report estimated that the steel industry accounted for 20% of all particulate air pollution in the country, and steel plants also emit heat, hydrocarbons, and sulphur oxides to pollute both air and water.[42] The costs of cleanup have been high. David M. Roderick, chief executive officer of U.S. Steel, claimed that his firm spent nearly $2 billion through 1979 in compliance with environmental regulation. In 1980 U.S. Steel directed some 30% of all expenditures toward environmental costs.[43] The costs of clean air and water have been very high — $6 billion before 1978 and possibly another $4 billion by 1985. The industry similarly blames the Occupational Safety and Health Administration (OSHA) for increasing costs inside the mills.[44]

Government actions to hold steel prices down are a third source of the industry's irritation. Until 1945 the government either supported prices or left them alone, but since then it has actively sought to control them. The government acted in the belief that price increases in steel are a principal cause of overall inflation, since higher prices in this primary industry are multiplied throughout the economy as steel customers raise their own prices. In 1961 Otto Eckstein, an economic adviser to President Kennedy, argued that "rising steel prices accounted for 40% of the rise in the wholesale price index" between 1947 and 1958.[45] The AISI charges that the government has consistently held down prices while permitting inflationary cost increases: "The government has thus squeezed steel industry profits and hindered needed capital formation from both ends—i.e., by causing cost increases while holding down selling prices."[46]

Industry spokesmen have also spoken out on a related problem — the inconsistency of government policy. In 1976 there were some 5,600 federal regulations that affected the industry.[47] In the executive branch alone almost every cabinet department except agriculture and education was involved in policing the industry while such independent agencies as the Federal Trade Commission, Environmental Protection Agency, Council on Wage and Price Stability (COWPS), Coun-

cil of Economic Advisers (CEA), and the Office of the Special
Representative for Trade Negotiations monitored the industry as well.
Each of these departments, agencies, and offices has tended to pursue
its own mandate zealously and exclusively, with little awareness of the
mandates of others. Some agencies have been sympathetic to the steel
companies; a spokesman for the Office of the Special Trade Representative, for example, admitted, "We impose burdens on our industry in
the form of environmental and safety regulations but we do not provide any subsidization or tax relief to offset the costs." At COWPS, in
contrast, an official saw no reason to try to mitigate the effects of free
trade: if "[the U.S. Steel companies' market] share in the U.S. would
. . . drop, from 82% to 75% to 70%; no one has ever explained why
that is a disaster. . . . People do find new jobs and there is no reason to
keep blacksmiths employed forever. . . ."[48]

The Solomon committee of 1977 brought together people from
eight different offices in an attempt to reconcile these different voices.
But, according to one participant (from the State Department), "Solomon tried to keep the task force small, but it kept mushrooming. With
each meeting there were more and more people. As the group got
larger, Solomon began to be more and more independent of it. He began to act on his own, excluding the majority of the committee."[49]
Thus even this effort at interdepartmental coordination succumbed to
divisive pressures inside the government.

The steel crisis and the specter of rising imports in the 1970s have
driven management and labor toward a limited form of cooperation.
In 1973 the two sides signed the Experimental Negotiating Agreement
(ENA), which granted the steelworkers annual wage increases of 3%
plus a cost-of-living adjustment (plus a bonus at the first signing). In
exchange workers pledged not to strike and to lend support to lobbying
efforts against imports. The ENA was clearly an attempt to avoid crisis
bargaining in an already sagging industry, but, as a result, steelworkers' real wages rose well in excess of productivity improvements. Between 1973 and 1979 wages in the mills rose 119%, compared with a
63% rise in the consumer price index. At the same time, the rate
of productivity improvement has slowed alarmingly. Since 1962 it has
grown at only 2% per annum.[50]

These wage gains, even from the union's standpoint, were won at
great cost. Within the USWA there is a sharp division between those
who support the ENA and those who demand an end to "tuxedo unionism," with its close ties to management. In the 1977 union elections,
after a long and acrimonious campaign, the conservatives retained
control of the USWA, although by a very narrow edge made possible
only by wide margins in the nonsteel segments of the union. The second major cost of the ENA has been jobs. Saddled with rising labor

costs and shrinking markets, steel management has closed down marginal operations. Between 1960 and 1979 the labor force fell from 450,000 to 340,000 — a 25% drop.[51] The lists of plant closings in the annual reports of the major firms make dismal reading for the steelworkers. U.S. Steel alone closed sixteen operations in 1980 and 1981.

While trade practices, government intervention, and high labor costs have contributed to the American steel industry's rush into "an involuntary liquidation mode,"[52] organization and industry structure have also played an important part. As we have seen, several factors were gnawing at the industry's health well before 1960: inefficiency and a dearth of innovation.

Before steel imports began to rise, American steel companies felt little pressure to trim excess capacity and contain high costs. These have now become critical problems. Only 80% to 85% of U.S. capacity was utilized during the late 1970s, and there is little prospect for improvement ahead. Most analysts predict that demand will grow at less than 2% per annum during the coming decade.[53] And while the steel supply already exceeds demand, the aluminum and plastics industries have developed their products as inexpensive alternatives to steel. Indeed, two of steel's primary customers, the automobile industry and the food container industry, have increasingly made use of substitutes.[54]

Excess capacity is one sign of inefficiency; inability to cope with rising raw materials costs is another. During most of the steel industry's history, domestic sources of iron ore and coking coal provided American companies with a considerable competitive advantage over foreign producers. In the past two decades, however, rising costs here, the discovery of cheap supplies of raw materials elsewhere, and lower transportation costs have wiped this advantage away. In 1960, for instance, a ton of coking coal sold for $10.56 in the U.S. and $15.63 in Japan; by 1976, the prices stood at $56.04 and $53.60, respectively. This relative change is even more striking in the case of iron ore. In 1960 U.S. producers paid $11.15 a ton for ore while the Japanese spent $12.88; sixteen years later the positions were reversed. Ore cost $27.62 a ton in the U.S. and $15.81 in Japan. Since Japan has virtually no domestic supplies of coal or iron ore and since American steel firms can secure these resources easily (often from wholly-owned subsidiaries), these comparative cost figures are all the more striking. This evidence only underscores the point that U.S. firms have a poor record of efficiency.[55]

Equally damaging is the American steel companies' attitude toward innovation. The best U.S. facilities compare favorably with those found anywhere in the world, although there is too much old technology still in place. Unlike Andrew Carnegie, today's steel managers seem obsessed with sunk costs. In integrated steel manufacture, notes a report sponsored by the National Academy of Sciences,

> Discrete operating units, to realize economies of scale, tend to be massive and capable of high production. Such units also tend to be long-lived. Under these conditions, rapid technological advancement is difficult. New processes are rarely attractive enough economically to justify abandonment of old processes. The rate of adoption of new technologies is more likely to be paced by the rate of wearing out of old equipment and the rate of expansion of steel production capacity than by the availability of superior technology.[56]

As a result of such logic, American steel firms have lagged behind the Europeans and Japanese in discovering and investing in new technologies — BOFs, continuous casting, and computers to coordinate work flows. A chief engineer of one of the major firms recently remarked, "Our management is not innovative. I am not disposed to submit them to innovation. They do not understand it."[57]

The bad habits of past management linger on in other ways. The industry has continued to neglect marketing, particularly outside the United States. Emerging from World War II with a 50% share of the free-world market, the American companies found their share had dropped to about 20% by the late 1970s. Although hindered by international trade politics, U.S. firms gave up foreign markets without much struggle, preferring to sell at home. This strategy typifies a general marketing indolence that has cost the industry dearly in recent years.

U.S. managers also wasted time and money in a pointless struggle against government policies they had little hope of changing. Furthermore, the industry lobby has been equivocal about the proper role of the government. On the one hand, the companies have spent enormous sums on fighting and appealing regulatory decisions and on evading their intent. "The steel industry is a flagrant exception in an otherwise good record of compliance [in American industry]," complains an EPA spokesman. "The steel industry's history is one of obfuscation and litigation regarding compliance."[58] On the other hand, steel companies constantly entreat the government for new tax laws and relief from imports. Thus the industry wants to dictate the terms of its partnership with government and has been unwilling to seek compromise.

Finally, many steel companies remain prisoners of traditional patterns of recruitment and training. There is but one entry level position in most companies — at the bottom. The big companies seldom recruit at the major business schools, nor do they often bring in outside managers at higher levels. They rarely hire senior managers from outside the industry. Top managers normally spend their entire careers in one steel company. Indeed, it is likely that their fathers and grandfathers did so as well.[59] Although most of the major firms have internal management training programs, they appear to be conservative in focus and cursory in practice. Until very recently, quality of work life innovations were unknown in the industry. As *Chilton's Iron Age*, the industry's chief trade journal, finally acknowledged in 1979, "the human side of productivity" is "a long neglected aspect of the problem."[60]

All these factors add up to a major industry crisis. In a recent publication, portentously titled *Steel at the Crossroads*, the AISI portrays the industry's gravest problem as the want of sufficient capital to modernize its plants. The AISI estimates that the industry will require up to $7 billion a year during the 1980s in order to modernize and remain competitive with foreign producers.[61] The human and social cost of the steel industry's plight is equally alarming. About 40,000 workers lost jobs in 1979 and 1980 because *permanent* plant closings. Some cities in the historical center of the industry, in Ohio and Pennsylvania, are withering. Youngstown has lost a third of its population in little more than a decade. Gone with the people and jobs are city services, schools, repair of roads and bridges, even regular airline service. The mayor says: "There is no solution for Youngstown. I shouldn't be saying this. I love this place, but if I were looking for a future, I wouldn't look for it here."[62]

The steel crisis is the result of major changes in the industry's environment that built up over a long period while the major firms failed to adapt. Missing the opportunities of Areas 4 and 5, the steel companies have drifted into the much less favorable conditions of Area 6. Information complexity, represented by increased regulation, new technologies, and increased competition from imports, clearly now concerns the major firms. Resource scarcity, measured by shrinking margins (Figure 3.4) and capital starvation, has risen dramatically since 1960. The result is an industry in serious trouble on both critical fronts — efficiency and innovation.

## ORGANIZATIONAL RESPONSES TO THE STEEL CRISIS

During the past decade, companies have responded to the steel crisis not through organizational innovation, but through diversification away from steel or through merger. It is indeed ironic that the best hope for some of our largest steel firms is to manage their way out of the steel industry. In a recent annual report, U.S. Steel's David Roder-

**Figure 3.4     Steel Companies' Profits After Taxes as a Percentage of Revenues 1954–1978**

SOURCE: Based on tabular material in American Iron and Steel Institute, *Steel at the Crossroads: The American Steel Industry in the 1980s* (Washington, D.C., 1980), Table E-1, p. 89.

ick wrote: "It is essential to direct available funds where they will provide the greatest return" in current circumstances. This means "non-steel businesses" such as oil, chemicals, coal, and fabricated metal products.[63] Other major producers, including Armco and National, are on the same track. Armco's new strategy is perhaps the most dramatic. In 1976 diversified interests accounted for about 27% of Armco's assets; by 1985 the company expects that more than 60% of its assets will fall outside the primary steel business. The biggest change will come in the production of carbon steel, which will drop from 58% to 28% of total assets.[64]

Merger represents a second strategy of crisis avoidance. The 1970s witnessed the industry's first major shakeout in forty years. National Steel (the fourth-largest firm) and Granite City Steel Company (thirteenth-largest) merged in 1971 to form what was briefly the third-largest steel producer in the country, after U.S. Steel and Bethlehem. Jones & Laughlin, for more than a century the oldest privately owned steel company among the majors, was taken over by a conglomerate, LTV, in 1974. LTV added Lykes-Youngstown to its holdings in 1978 (Lykes had earlier swallowed Youngstown Sheet and Tube), and now boasts combined operations that make it the fourth-largest steel company in the nation.

In the core steel business, some firms are responding to the crisis better than others. Armco, for example, has managed its steel operations well. Quick to perceive that innovative compliance with federal regulation could be a competitive advantage, Armco led the way among steel producers in persuading the EPA to authorize a new inexpensive policy to control particulate air pollution. Armco executives attribute their success at least partly to the company's flexible, decentralized organization and a company "spirit" that encourages independent thinking and innovation.[65]

Good management and organization have also helped Inland Steel during the crisis. Inland's reputation as "the best-managed company in the industry" rests on several factors: its geographic concentration, its commitment to reinvestment, and its responsiveness to new technologies. Inland subsidiaries do business in steel warehousing, construction products, containers, metal-forming machines, and manufactured housing, but 66% of sales came from steel in 1981. All of the firm's production facilities are located near Chicago, where its Indiana Harbor plant is the largest integrated steel mill in the country. Inland's primary product is rolled sheet steel, which it sells to the automobile and appliance industries in the Midwest. Close to both its primary materials and its final markets, the company also sits in the center of the Great Lakes transportation network and a well-developed rail system.

Inland's commitment to the latest technology is wholehearted, epitomized by the simple philosophy, "Dollars for the latest equipment is uppermost." The company led the way among U.S. firms in the adoption of computerized rolling. Its eighty-inch hot strip mill set the industry standard when it came on line in the 1960s.[66] The company has steadily converted from open-hearth furnaces to BOFs in the past decade. During the 1970s Inland poured $1.8 billion into capital investments.[67]

Inland has been a pacesetter in other respects, too. It puts greater emphasis on marketing than do most of the major firms, and its facilities and policies render it particularly responsive to changes in consumer preferences. Like Armco, Inland has avoided the pitfalls of fighting the government on regulation—a grateful EPA administrator says it "is a pleasure to do business" with Inland in contrast to other firms in the industry.[68] Finally, Inland has also been anxious to improve productivity through management-training and "participation team programs." For example, the company recently cooperated with a consulting firm to reorganize work in an effort to improve employee relations and productivity in its coal mines.[69]

Inland's financial performance has been generally good, although 1980 and 1981 were bad years. Before 1980, the company had been able to increase its dividend every quarter for forty consecutive years. Earnings averaged 12% higher in the 1970s than in the 1960s, while shipments were up 23% over the previous decade. But Inland has not escaped the steel crisis despite its advantages and progressive policies. Net income fluctuated wildly in the 1970s while returns dwindled; in 1980 profits from steel operations were only $30.9 million — about 13% of the profits two years earlier. In 1974 the company announced a major expansion program, hoping to add 13% to steel-making capacity by investing $2 billion. The company set about raising this sum in an innovative (for the steel industry) fashion. Inland offered the first common stock sale in the industry in twenty-five years, and, with an AA rating, also sought capital in the bond market. However, declining profits and the collapse of the domestic market led Inland to halt the program halfway. The company was even forced to begin layoffs; about two thousand workers were on indefinite layoff at the end of 1981. At present, Inland remains committed to primary steel production and, in spite of its current troubles, appears to be the industry's most competitive large firm.

Outside the ranks of the major integrated producers, two interesting developments are unfolding on the fringes of the industry, in the mini-mills and the service centers. Mini-mills are small, nonintegrated steel manufacturers that typically produce less than 500,000 tons per year for regional markets and specialized customers. The development of the electric furnace and continuous casting made the mini-mills possible, because small operators can now refine steel from scrap. (Previously, the raw materials needed for steel could only be economically obtained on a large scale.) The mini-mills generate a wide range of products, although they cannot produce heavy shapes or rolled sheet steel. In 1981 there were about sixty mini-mills in operation, representing about 15% of total U.S. capacity. It is estimated that the mini-mills may account for as much as 25% of U.S. steel capacity by the late 1980s.[70] Most of the mini-mills are located in the Southeast, Midwest, and West, in areas not heavily served by the major steel companies.

The phenomenal growth of Nucor Corporation, one of the most aggressive mini-mills, makes an object lesson to its much bigger rivals. Averaging a 28% return on equity in recent years, Nucor has increased its capacity from 56,000 tons in 1970 to more than 1.7 million in 1981.[71] The company's unlikely progenitors include the R.E. Olds Company (later Reo Motors), a maker of autos and trucks that twice declared bankruptcy. In 1955 the Reo Holding Company merged with a communications firm to form the Nuclear Corporation of America (eventually Nucor), which manufactured steel joists and nuclear products, and produced rare earth elements.

In the late 1960s new management began to concentrate on steel joists as the company's distinctive competence. Nucor, through its Vulcraft Division, is now the industry leader in that product. It was not until 1969 that Nucor's management, worried about rising costs and cyclical fluctuations in steel supply, began producing its own steel for its joists. The steel business has grown rapidly since then, and Nucor now sells 60% of its annual steel output outside the company. Steel from its four mini-mills (two more are planned) finds its way into farm machinery, oil and gas equipment, transmission towers, highway signs, and even bedframes.[72]

Nucor has been able to achieve this impressive performance in part because it is not saddled with sunk costs and its plants are fully modern. But Nucor's love of competition, its marketing strategy, its commitment to technological innovation, and its human resource practices also set it apart from the major companies. Its technological advantages and its position outside the AISI allow it to undercut prices prevailing in the industry. Moreover, Nucor sells primarily to service centers, thus buffering itself from cyclical slumps in demand and obviating the need for a large marketing staff. As for innovation, the company pours its income back into the business and seeks outside funds as well. As chief executive officer Kenneth Iverson, sounding like a latter-day Carnegie, puts it bluntly, "You must have enough confidence that you're willing to leverage your company to the eyeballs."[73] The company has looked far afield in pursuit of the newest, most efficient technology. When Nucor first decided to make its own steel, for example, company engineers adapted a Finnish design for continuous casting in order to maximize productivity.[74]

Finally, Nucor motivates its nonunion employees with high pay, group incentive plans and weekly productivity goals. The company has successfully transformed unskilled and often uneducated workers into highly efficient and coordinated teams. Bonuses are known to exceed base salaries by more than 100%. Department heads and top managers work under similar plans, which emphasize company performance and overall growth. Thus the good of the whole company takes precedence over the performance of particular departments or divisions.[75] Nucor proclaims "strong feelings of responsibility and loyalty to its employees" and boasts that "for many years we have not furloughed or laid off a single hourly employee for lack of work."[76] Thus Nucor displays all of the organizational features associated with readaptive firms.

Similar readaptive changes are taking place at the edge of the industry where the steel service centers are assuming larger responsibilities for distribution. The earliest steel service centers, or warehouses, stored standardized products for customers in transportation and industry as the big companies turned out steel ahead of orders. Most of these warehouses were independently owned, although some major firms have acquired them in order to locate near customers or to absorb excess capacity. At first the warehouses, or service centers, merely stockpiled standard items such as bars, rounds, and structural shapes. In the past thirty years, however, the service centers have become increasingly active in finishing products and in pursuing customers. Robert Welch, president of the Steel Service Center Institute, estimates that service centers now modify about 80% of the products they handle.[77] Such modification includes cutting, welding, pressing, rolling, and stamping. In short, the service centers have become finishing mills for steel and other metals.

"I think that what has happened over the past ten years," says one service center executive, "is that the metal service centers have gained more expertise, and we have been willing to make heavy capital commitments in terms of equipment." In contrast to most steel companies, the service centers have been quick to detect and respond to customers' needs. "We are extremely aggressive investors in our ability to serve the customer," says another service center manager. "I think we're alive and well and eager to do any damn thing that is necessary to serve the customer's needs."[78]

Such attitudes are borne out by the growth of the service center industry. Service centers now consume about 20% of all domestic steel shipments, up from less than 15% a decade ago; by the end of the 1980s, according to some projections, that figure may reach 30%. Service centers buy metal from foreign as well as domestic producers, and the most efficient of them turn over their inventory forty to fifty times a year. Like the mini-mills, the service centers profit from proximity to customers, but they also have set about their business with a competitive spirit that the major firms would do well to emulate.

## CONCLUSION

Figure 3.5 outlines the progression of the industry from the hordes of small iron-makers in Area 3 in the mid-nineteenth century; through the sudden introduction of the Bessemer process, which created the steel industry in the 1860s (Area 4), Carnegie's rise by vertical integration and horizontal merger (Areas 1 and 2), the founding of the U.S. Steel Corporation in 1901 (Area 5), the growth of its major competitors and long-term market structure by 1930, and the long equilibrium in Area 5 (1930–1960), in which the top firms dominated the domestic and world markets; to the past twenty years, which have seen the rise of imports, the growth of regulation, and the stagnation of U.S. firms.

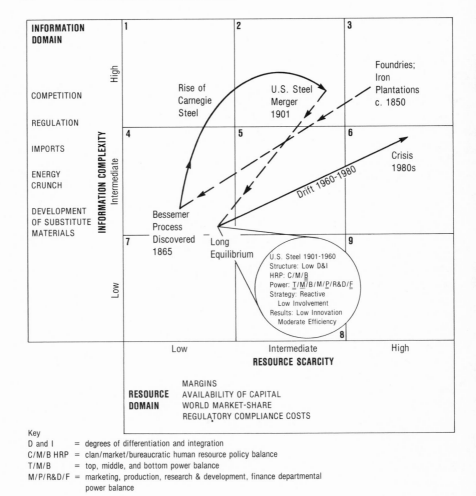

**Figure 3.5    Evolution of the Steel Industry 1850–1980**

The industry currently resides in Area 6, with tighter margins and greater uncertainty, and it faces a long struggle to recover its former greatness.

The present plight of the steel industry makes an even more vivid case than the auto industry of what can happen when firms fail to adapt to their environments. The steel industry environment has changed dramatically since World War II, while the major American firms have remained stubbornly attached to old strategies and stuck in old organizational forms. The industry's experience illustrates that Areas 4 and 5, in spite of their advantages, can lull inhabitants into a false feeling of security and can breed bad habits. Long, comfortable reposes in such environmental conditions can be dangerous. It requires not only good management to capitalize on a favorable environment, but also constant vigilance simply to remain there.

The steel industry crisis, so long in building, will not end quickly. Firms that wish to recover competitiveness in basic steel will not have an easy time of it. They will have to explore new ways to manage in the face of increasing uncertainty and complexity. Traditional defensive strategies and functional structures are unlikely to be successful in the 1980s. Rather, the companies must pursue readaptive strategies that emphasize innovation as well as efficiency. They must also adopt more differentiated structures that give greater voice to personnel in research and development, marketing, and public affairs. Recruitment and training practices must also be made more consistent with the industry's current and future needs. Together with the USWA, steel companies might profit from the experiences of the UAW and the auto companies in simultaneously improving employees' quality of work life and levels of productivity. However, the steelmakers—even when joined by the union—can do only so much to help themselves in current circumstances. At least in the short-term, some coordinated government support will be necessary to encourage research and reward investment in this industry which stood for so long at the center of the American economy as a major regional employer and a large-scale purchaser from and supplier to other basic industries.

So far we have examined two similar industries whose problems are those of older manufacturing firms competing in an oligopoly. In the next three chapters we shall examine very different sorts of industries—hospitals, agriculture, and housing—where the environmental circumstances, industry structures, internal organizational forms, and current problems scarcely resemble those of manufacturing industries. The nine-area model provides a useful common framework for analyzing patterns of industrial growth and organization and will lead us to some interesting conclusions about managerial action and public policy. For instance, the story of how hospitals evolved into Area 1 conditions—low RS but high IC—helps explain some of the reasons for the peculiar organization of American medical care and for its great expense.

# CHAPTER 4

# Hospitals: A Very Special Case

IT IS SOMETIMES hard to recall, in this era of fabulous medical technology and equally fabulous health care costs, that only a century ago hospitals served primarily the indigent rather than the infirm and that doctors once had trouble keeping themselves fed. The transformation of the hospital from a small, precapitalist charitable institution to a large, chaotically administered organization occurred gradually, driven by complex and interdependent forces over a few decades, starting in the late nineteenth century. The changing needs of an increasingly urban society, the discovery of antiseptic surgery, the development of medical research, the rise of the medical profession, the growth of a science of medical administration, and above all, the postwar social commitment to good health at any cost, were all part cause and part effect of this transformation.

After years of rapid expansion and extravagant technological growth through most of the twentieth century, the past decade has represented a second period of organizational change for hospitals. Those institutions now are contracting and searching for new efficiencies, and indeed, some standard medical services are migrating from hospitals to other institutions, such as community health centers, Health Maintenance Organizations (HMOs), and group health practices.

Hospitals have never represented a concentrated industry dominated by a few leading firms, and local circumstances typically create wide variations along several dimensions. A small, rural community hospital differs substantially in resources and organization from a wealthy, urban teaching hospital. Hospital capacity can range from fewer than fifty beds to more than a thousand. There are similar disparities in the range and quality of services and personnel. Nonetheless, for purposes of analysis, this chapter focuses on the "typical" community general hospital, a nonprofit institution with an attending or consulting medical staff. We shall also treat hospitals as an industry, albeit a loosely clustered one, which has evolved along an identifiable path.

## THE EVOLUTION OF THE MODERN HOSPITAL

American hospitals have long intrigued and sometimes bewildered students of organizations. Certainly hospitals are strange institutions. Except in some government and teaching hospitals, doctors are *not* employees of the institutions in which they work. Doctors, not hospitals, admit patients. Doctors, not administrators, decide which technologies are necessary for hospitals to adopt. As Eliot Freidson has written,

> It is as if all professors were self-employed tutors, sending individual pupils to universities where they can themselves administer some special training briefly, but most particularly where they can count on having their pupils trained specially by lesser personnel employed by the university rather than by the professor. The day-to-day service of the organization is supplied by people employed by the organization but supervised by self-employed entrepreneurs committed to their own personal practice and to the individual clients of that practice.[1]

It is often claimed that a turning point in the history of American business occurred with the separation of ownership and control in the late nineteenth and early twentieth centuries. Professional managers gained control of large business organizations from the original family owner-entrepreneurs, raising questions about accountability in these institutions. In American hospitals, the pattern was a little different. Not only were ownership and control separated, but administration also became separate. Since the modern hospital emerged in the same period as the modern industrial corporation, nourished by many of the same forces, many have wondered why hospitals are not more like businesses with professional managers in charge of a centralized bureaucratic administration. The explanation lies in the changing circumstances that supported the growth of hospitals and the rise of the medical profession as against the unchanging goal of American medicine — the provision of the best possible care to every patient.

The modern organization of hospitals evolved gradually over seven or eight decades after the Civil War. In the first phase of this evolution (roughly 1870 to 1910), the increasingly urban character of American life coincided with advances in medical technology to transform the hospital from a traditional philanthropic institution administered by trustees and a very small staff into a large, specialized organization administered in equal part by trustees and doctors. In the second period (roughly 1910 to 1940), competition for resources drove many hospitals out of business, and professional administration and management became critical to institutional success. By the end of the depression, most hospitals, voluntary and proprietary, had similar organizational structures. Trustees or board members looked after long-term financial needs; administrators ran day-to-day affairs, allocated resources in the short term, and managed relations with the supporting community; and doctors oversaw medical research and patient care.

Today's hospitals are descended from traditional institutions with multiple responsibilities, including spiritual care, medical care, and hostelry. Medical care, in fact, was a secondary, and often unattractive, service in the premodern hospital. Patients, or "inmates," often regarded hospitals as places to die, and given the art of medicine in past times, their perception was frequently justified. Medical care was far more commonly provided at home by families or relatives of the afflicted. Institutions designed exclusively to look after the sick (as opposed to the poor, the demented, or the antisocial) and supported by the larger society were relatively rare until the late nineteenth century.

The early development of the hospital is normally broken down into several stages.[2] According to the standard typology, the medieval hospital in Western Europe was essentially an ecclesiastical institution run by clergy, who mingled spiritual guidance with care of the needy and sick. By the late Middle Ages, hospitals' spiritual function began to diminish and, while they still catered to the same population, they were increasingly supported by laymen and communities instead of the Church. Some hospitals in major cities, like London and Florence, were large and wealthy institutions served by large medical staffs, but the typical voluntary hospital was small and chronically short of funds. Two key groups were involved in hospital administration. "Governors," who were prominent citizens or guild members, supplied hospital income through donations. One of their number, a sort of chairman, voluntarily managed hospital finances. The second group, the paid staff including matrons, cooks, stewards, and chaplains, normally looked after patients. Some hospitals employed one or more staff physicians, a surgeon or barber, and an "apothecary" (pharmacist). Many hospitals, however, had no salaried medical staff but relied on independent doctors in the community to visit patients on a voluntary and often rotating basis.[3]

This organizational pattern carried over into the earliest hospitals in the New World. The wealthy Pennsylvania General Hospital, founded in 1751 by Benjamin Franklin among others, retained the medieval structure, although the medical staff included six doctors, and use of the hospital as a training ground for young doctors was encouraged.[4] The Pennsylvania General Hospital was a remarkable institution in many respects, and it served as a model for hospitals founded in the next century in New York and Boston. However, medical care in America, to an even greater extent than in Europe, remained largely a family function until after the Civil War. In 1821 there were only 3 voluntary hospitals in the country. By 1873 there were 120 — a result of population and urban growth and improvements in medical care introduced during the Civil War (Figure 4.1).[5]

If the growth of hospitals in America was remarkable before 1870, the great expansion of health care institutions occurred over the next fifty years. By 1920 there were more than six-thousand hospitals in the United States. Scholars used to attribute this astonishing growth to a single source — the development of modern surgery after Lister's discovery of antisepsis in 1868. It has recently been shown, however, that "Listerism" was slow to take root in America, that antiseptic and aseptic surgery was not widely adopted until the 1880s, and that hospitals catered increasingly to medical patients well before the development of modern surgery.[6]

**Figure 4.1     Growth of Hospitals in America 1820–1980**

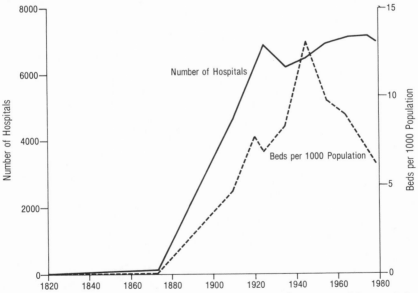

Sources: U.S. Bureau of the Census, *Historical Statistics of the United States, Colonial Times to 1970* (Washington, D.C., 1976), Series B305, 317, 319, 329; U.S. Bureau of the Census, *Statistical Abstract of the United States 1981* (Washington, D.C., 1981), p. 110.

Modern historians of medicine have focused on urbanization and broader social changes as central factors in the rise of the hospital. According to this view, the growth of cities broke up traditional neighborhoods and the extended family, segregated the classes, and obliged working people to live in smaller spaces. Broad social forces therefore created the need for extrafamilial institutions for the care of the poor and the sick. Prominent wealthy citizens occasionally still founded and ran hospitals, but were motivated less by philanthropy than by the desire to maintain social control in rapidly changing circumstances. Other factors also contributed to the growth of hospitals: changing epidemiological patterns and the decline of infectious diseases, the rise of nursing during and after the Civil War, better medical education, and increasing specialization within the medical profession itself all combined to make the hospital a different, healthier place.[7]

The rise of the hospital coincided with the rise of the medical profession. Traditionally doctors had depended on hospital boards for privileges, and the determining criteria were not necessarily medical. Physicians, moreover, typically donated their services to hospitals because the experience acquired in the wards was valuable in attracting paying patients on the outside. Their own income came directly from patients on a fee-for-service basis. As hospitals proliferated and performed more medical than philanthropic services in the late nineteenth century, however, the status of doctors began to grow. After all, it was the doctors who referred patients who could pay mounting hospital expenses. New, costlier technologies made it almost impossible for trustees as individuals or groups to supply the bulk of a hospital's income. Doctors, moreover, increasingly commanded specialized technical expertise hard for laymen (like most trustees) to come by. This economic leverage and technical knowledge put physicians in a better position to dictate the terms of their relationship to hospitals.[8]

In general, doctors preferred the independence afforded by private practice to absorption into the hospital as employees. Where they won greater access to hospitals, then, doctors came in not as employees, but as consultants or members of an attending staff. Patients still paid doctors' bills separately, although hospitals sometimes served as collection agencies. In most early-twentieth-century hospitals, trustees and doctors thus reached a kind of *modus vivendi*. Physicians, prizing their independence, remained outside the hospital while the trustees retained formal control.[9]

The changing nature of the hospital is readily illustrated. For instance, a study of early Boston hospitals reveals that the numbers of patients supported exclusively by philanthropy shrank dramatically between 1870 and 1900. Similarly, by 1922 paying patients supplied two-thirds of total hospital revenues in New York City.[10] At the same time, hospitals became less a place for long stays and convalescences and more a place for short, specific treatments of acute medical problems. At Brooklyn Hospital, for instance, the average patient stayed 31.7 days in 1884 but only 14.6 days thirty years later.[11] As hospitals catered more and more to paying patients, patients were increasingly differentiated on the basis of how much they could pay. One sign of this trend was the growing appearance of semiprivate and private rooms in hospitals in the 1920s. In this respect, American (and British) hospitals came to differ from hospitals in other parts of the world where health care was funded by the state and where the wards remained democratically large.[12]

The changing nature of the hospital also required changes in organizational structure. While traditional institutions could easily be managed by a few people, hospitals became complicated functional bureaucracies by 1910. In addition to a highly differentiated medical staff comprising specialists in medicine and surgery and such new pursuits as radiology and anesthesiology, the modern hospital now housed clinical laboratories and employed a whole new class of personnel, semiskilled medical technicians.[13] Hospitals also elaborated the traditional services of hotels. Thus even medium-sized hospitals typically employed cadres of dieticians, stewards, accountants, registrars, engineers, and various support personnel ranging from cooks to maids to telephone operators (Figures 4.2 and 4.3).

As hospitals grew more complicated, they also became more expensive to operate, straining the abilities of trustee managers and the resources of America's rapidly growing population. In the early twentieth century, hospitals competed for doctors, managers, and community support amid duplication of services. Many hospitals were small — under fifty beds — and catered primarily to religious or ethnic groups or focused exclusively on the treatment of a single disease or infirmity. A single community might have to support several hospitals offering overlapping services. As time wore on, this became a source of concern. "If many hospitals in each city could pool their interests," wrote a dismayed hospital superintendent in 1911, "the result would be greater efficiency and greater economy — and yet nothing is more unlikely than that independent, privately controlled hospitals will pool interests."[14] There was all the more reason for alarm since hospitals' new technical services — chiefly diagnostic — were expensive. Between 1923 and 1927 — a period of mild inflation — hospital costs measured in investment-per-bed rose by half in Pennsylvania and only slightly less rapidly in New York City.[15]

Competition, rising costs, and a darkening financial situation pushed hospitals toward bankruptcy, merger, or increasing reliance on community support in the 1920s and 1930s. The total number of hos-

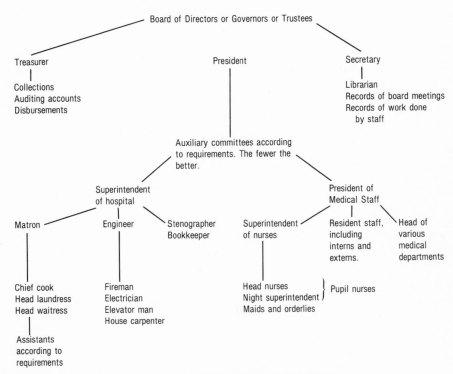

**Figure 4.2    Organization of a Large Hospital (1907)**

SOURCE:Albert J. Ochsner and Meyer J. Sturm, *The Organization, Construction and Management of Hospitals* (Chicago: The Cleveland Press, 1907), p. 43.

pitals in the country peaked in 1924 at 7,370, and declined by 10% over the next five years. The depression devastated some parts of the industry. Between 1929 and 1934 total annual expenditures on hospital construction fell by more than 75%, from more than $200 million to less than $50 million.[16] In the ten years after 1924, the number of hospitals operated for profit dropped by 20%. Over the same period, however, the number of beds per thousand population continued to rise. The trend was thus toward larger, more concentrated hospitals: the proportion of general hospitals rose from 56% in 1923 to 64% in 1929.[17]

Although hospitals were becoming sensitive to market forces, their chaotic administration continued to worry communities and administrators. According to a report sponsored by the fledgling Rockefeller Foundation, "In many American cities there is neither rhyme nor reason in the way hospitals are created, distributed, coordinated, supported, or related to medical research, medical education, or the needs

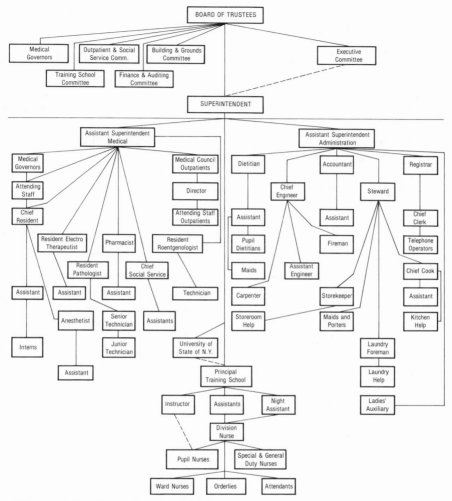

**Figure 4.3    Organization of a Large Hospital (1924)**

SOURCE: Frank E. Chapman, *Hospital Organization and Operation* (New York: Macmillan, 1924), p. 4.

of the community."[18] One expert on hospital organization, C. Rufus Rorem, was appalled that "in contrast to the business world, pressure to achieve the most efficent utilization of fixed assets as been more or less removed from the administration of hospital finances."[19] Although the first textbook on hospital management had appeared in 1911, Rorem was the first to introduce modern techniques of capital accounting to hospitals in 1930.[20]

The expansion of hospital organization and competition for resources therefore placed a premium on good management. As the Rockefeller Foundation report put it, "Thinking men have come to realize that a group of good doctors does not necessarily mean a good hospital and that the welfare of patients depends quite as much on the quality of hospital service as on the skill of surgeons." There was a growing recognition of the critical role of the hospital superintendent, who occupied the key position between the mostly nonprofessional trustees and the medical and support staffs. Superintendents themselves took the lead in agitating for the introduction of "sound business principles" to hospitals and for greater responsibility for managers. "Managing a hospital is largely a business proposition, just as is managing a hotel, department store, or any other business," said a Chicago superintendent, Asa Bacon, speaking at a meeting of the American Hospital Association (AHA). "The fact that most of our hospitals are partly or wholly financed by a kind and generous public, contributing for the purposes of charity, makes the superintendent's position all the more a keen business proposition for the money so contributed is as it were 'trust funds' and every penny should be carefully expended." Men like Bacon earned a symbolic victory in this period when the title of hospital superintendent began to give way to "administrator."[21]

The superintendent, or administrator, confronted daunting responsibilities. Among other things, his job required expertise in community affairs, finance, administration of large organizations, and public health. Yet, according to the Rockefeller Foundation report, this central position was often "held by derelicts who have failed to make good in the kind of work ordinarily expected of them." Although the report emphasized that "the importance of getting high calibered men to raise the level of these positions is urgently felt," no university offered a degree in hospital administration until 1934.[22]

"The hospital situation" became an issue of national concern with increasing public agitation to nationalize the health care system. Indeed, Congress twice considered such legislation in the 1930s.[23] Even inside the industry, rising costs, inefficiency, and poor organization were perceived as serious problems. While few went so far as Frank Gilbreth, a leading apostle of "scientific management," who declaimed "that the *entire structure on which hospital management is built is wrong*," a concerted effort was made to instill efficiency and economy as overriding goals in hospitals. This movement was preempted, however, by a similar movement directly under the control of physicians.[24]

The needs to standardize procedures and to set minimum qualifications for key personnel were also pressing. This movement had gained momentum in 1910 with the publication of the Flexner Report, which found that more than half of the country's medical schools offered inferior and unacceptable training for doctors. This report eventually led to the licensing of medical schools by the American Medical Association (AMA).[25] Acting with similar zeal, the American College of Surgeons initiated a drive in 1918 to set minimum standards for conditions in hospitals, including the definite organization of the medical staff, clear lines of administrative authority, complete and accurate records of patients' care, and adequate diagnostic and therapeutic facilities.[26] The American Hospital Association, founded earlier but effective only after 1918, began regular surveys of hospitals in the 1920s. At the same time, a number of periodicals and journals began reporting on hospital administration, and medical specialty boards were formed to set professional standards. Long-term and perhaps unintended side effects of this increasing specialization included the decline of general practitioners, the further elevation of doctors' professional status, and continuously rising hospital costs.[27]

It would be stretching our definition to regard hospitals as readaptive in this period, especially since most hospital employees worked in unattractive and restrictive conditions for low pay. Nonetheless, hospitals did show signs of coming to terms with a competitive environment. Certainly the status and importance of hospital administrators grew in the 1920s and 1930s. Health care and hospital management stopped short of full-scale corporate organization for several reasons, however, including broader social goals, the nature of hospital technology, the dominance of the medical profession, and the changing nature of hospital finance.

In the first place, despite the impact of the depression and the cry for administrative reform, no one went so far as to say that economic values should predominate in hospitals. The philanthropic character of hospitals, "the samaritan function," remained very much a part of the institution. A national committee that spent five years studying ways to control medical costs pointed out in 1933 that "although a hospital is similar to a business enterprise in its technical processes, it is conducted in a spirit of social or public service prompted by the importance and need of serving individuals and the community."[28] Hospitals continued to provide care to those unable to pay for it and placed the goal of providing the best possible care to patients above the quest for efficiency.

In the second place, hospital service, unlike the "transforming" manufacturing technologies of autos of steel, is a site-bound, "intensive" technology in which "a variety of techniques is drawn upon to achieve a change in some specific object."[29] Put another way, the particular needs of individual patients shape the structure and administration of hospitals. Hospitals are community-based and must respond to community needs. Hence attempts to coordinate medical care beyond local boundaries must usually overcome serious opposition from community, religious, and ethnic groups. And because hospitals are site-bound and wedded to local conditions, medical technology is not employed efficiently. Each hospital in a community tends to duplicate the facilities of every other hospital, no matter how close by.

Moreover, medical technology itself has eluded market forces and administrative planning. As Lewis Thomas has observed, "In medicine, it is characteristic of technology that we do not count the cost, ever, even when the bills are coming in."[30] Thomas has elaborated a distinction between "definitive" and "half-way" technologies in medicine. The former are directed to "the prevention, cure, and control of disease, based upon scientific understanding of the disease process through research," while the latter are "techniques for palliation and repair." Half-way technologies, often heroically employed to save patients' lives, tend to be expensive. According to another expert, Ivan L. Bennett, "The recent history of medicine is replete with evidence that each time a major disease has been controlled, the definitive technology has been much cheaper than the technologies devised before the disease was understood." Bennett offers the history of the treatment of polio as an illustration:

> The [half-way] technologies included costly special facilities, iron lungs, intensive nursing care, hot packs, corrective orthopedic surgery, braces and other prosthetic and orthopedic devices, all technologies ingenious but expensive and by no means definitive. The bill for almost complete control of the disease today is the cost of vaccination.[31]

In the third place, the professional status of doctors was such that they could avoid complete integration into a hospital system. The American Medical Association's resistance to growth of private or public insurance schemes in the 1930s is a notorious example of this independent attitude. Commenting on the recommendations of a national committee that advocated more concentrated community health care funded by private insurance, Morris Fishbein, editor of the AMA's *Journal*, wrote in 1932:

> The alignment is clear—on the one side the forces representing the great foundations, public health officialdom, social theory—even socialism and communism—inciting to revolution; on the other side, the organized medical profession of this country urging an orderly evaluation guided by controlled experimentation which will observe the principles that have been found through the centuries to be necessary to the sound practice of medicine.[32]

Since doctors still supplied patients, defined standards for medical practice and research, and policed their own ranks through the AMA and specialty boards, hospital administrators had little leverage against them. Indeed, in some hospitals, the medical staff bypassed the super intendent and reported directly to the board of trustees. Medicine remained what Eliot Freidson calls a "consulting profession," in which members defined their own goals, as opposed to a "scholarly profession" like scientific research or, presumably, an administrative profession like management, in which goals are set by larger communities or institutions. Doctors are largely independent of hospitals, beyond administrative control. Indeed, it is sometimes remarked that doctors "look like individual entrepreneurs who happen to conduct their business on the hospital's premises."[33]

Finally, the sources of hospital revenues began to change and eroded the rationale for administrative efficiency. A study prepared under the auspices of the American Hospital Association in 1947 points up changing trends in hospital finance. Whereas the proportion of voluntary hospital income supplied by paying patients continued to increase after 1922—from 67% then to 71% in 1935—the remaining share was made up less by private investment and philanthropy and more by government and private insurance programs. At first government investment tended to concentrate on the construction and maintenance of federal hospitals for members of the armed forces and veterans. Soon, however, state workers' compensation programs and several federal programs of the New Deal began to make significant contributions to hospital budgets.[34] Such third-party payments inflated hospital costs almost immediately. For example, when Massachusetts passed a workers' compensation law in 1911, Massachusetts General Hospital and Boston City Hospital raised their daily rates shortly thereafter.[35]

Voluntary prepayment insurance plans began humbly with a few hundred subscribers to an experimental program at Baylor University in 1929. Prepaid insurance programs grew spectacularly thereafter, endorsed by the American Hospital Association as a means to solve the financial crisis of the depression. By 1937 there were some forty programs in operation. The AHA-sponsored Blue Cross program included some 1.5 million subscribers in 1938. Between 1929 and 1940 public funds expended on health care (excluding research and construction) nearly doubled, from $289 million to $570 million.[36] These were the first inklings of a momentous new trend in hospital finance.

## THE GREAT DISCONTINUITY: THE RISE OF THIRD-PARTY PAYMENTS

If the years before World War II promised more efficient hospital management, this promise evaporated after the war with the vast public commitment to good health at any cost. Governments and private insurance companies lavished resources on the health care industry. In the space of a few years, hospitals shifted from the straitened conditions of Areas 5 and 6 to the bounty of Area 1. Hospital organization, however, remained stuck in the awkward balance among trustee, physician, and administrator. Between 1940 and 1948 per capita expenditures on health care jumped from $29.62 to $70.97. Health care rose from a $4 billion business to a $10.6 billion business. Since then, costs and expenditures have skyrocketed. Gross public expenditure and per capita expenditure doubled again by 1958, again by 1967, again by 1974, and again by 1980. Health care expenditures rose from 4.0% of the gross national product in 1940 to 5.3% in 1960 to 9.4% in 1980. Hospital costs have climbed substantially faster than the consumer price index (Table 4.1). Even adjusted for inflation, the average cost per patient day rose more than five times between 1950 and 1976.[37]

The causes of this dramatic inflation are fairly well understood. Rising demand for medical care has been the driving force. Public expectations of the continuing advance of modern medicine have increasingly been high, fueled by some spectacular successes, such as the discovery of "wonder drugs" to control infectious diseases and the mid-century conquests of polio and tuberculosis. Consumer demand for health care has not been subject to normal economic laws, because its costs have been borne by third parties — the government and private insurance companies. Government spending has climbed sharply since World War II with the expansion of the Veterans Administration and the Hill-Burton Act (1947), which supported hospital construction. The government's active role continued through the Medicare and Medicaid programs of the 1960s. Between 1950 and 1975 the percentage of hospital costs paid for directly by consumers fell from nearly 50% to less than 12%. At the same time, the government's share rose from 21.1% to 44.5% while costs borne by private insurance companies climbed from 29.3% to 43.6% (Table 4.2).[38]

The effect of third-party payments has been to subsidize the extravagant growth of hospital technology and services. According to Martin S. Feldstein, hospitals have been encouraged "to produce a more expensive product than consumers actually wish them to produce." Prepaid insurance customers are

> willing to purchase much more expensive care than [they] would if [they] were not insured. . . . This induced demand for expensive care gives a false signal to hospitals about the type of care that the public wants. Unfortunately, the production of high-cost hospital care stimulated patients to prepay hospital bills through relatively comprehensive insurance, while the growth of such insurance makes hospital care more expensive.[39]

Feldstein's interpretation is supported by the numbers. The most powerful force driving up the nation's total health care bill has been soar-

**Table 4.1   Selected Data on U.S. Health Care Expenditures 1929–1979**

| Year | Total Amount (billion $) | % GNP | Per Capita Expenditures | Hospital Care (billion $) | Physicians Services (billion $) | Index of Medical Care Prices (1967 = 100) | CPI (1967 = 100) |
|---|---|---|---|---|---|---|---|
| 1929 | 3.6 | 3.5 | $ 29.49 | .66 | 1.0 | — | 51.3 |
| 1935 | 2.9 | 4.0 | 22.65 | .76 | .77 | 36.1 | 41.1 |
| 1940 | 4.0 | 4.0 | 29.62 | 1.01 | .97 | 36.8 | 42.0 |
| 1948 | 10.6 | 4.1 | 70.97 | 3.20 | 2.61 | 51.1 | 72.1 |
| 1950 | 12.7 | 4.5 | 81.86 | 3.85 | 2.75 | 53.7 | 72.1 |
| 1955 | 17.7 | 4.4 | 105.38 | 5.90 | 3.69 | 64.8 | 80.2 |
| 1960 | 26.9 | 5.3 | 146.30 | 9.09 | 5.68 | 79.1 | 88.7 |
| 1965 | 40.5 | 5.9 | 204.68 | 13.61 | 8.75 | 89.5 | 94.5 |
| 1966 | 45.0 | 6.0 | 224.89 | 15.58 | 9.16 | 93.4 | 97.2 |
| 1967 | 50.7 | 6.4 | 250.77 | 18.15 | 10.29 | 100.0 | 100.0 |
| 1968 | 56.6 | 6.5 | 277.14 | 20.93 | 11.10 | 106.1 | 104.2 |
| 1969 | 64.1 | 6.9 | 311.06 | 24.10 | 12.65 | 113.4 | 109.8 |
| 1970 | 74.9 | 7.6 | 343.44 | 27.8 | 14.3 | 120.6 | 116.3 |
| 1971 | 83.1 | 7.8 | — | — | — | 128.4 | 121.3 |
| 1972 | 93.5 | 8.0 | — | — | — | 132.5 | 125.3 |
| 1973 | 103.0 | 7.9 | — | — | — | 137.7 | 133.1 |
| 1974 | 116.3 | 8.2 | 502.12 | — | — | 150.5 | 147.7 |
| 1975 | 131.2 | 8.6 | 566.61 | 52.1 | 24.9 | 168.6 | 161.2 |
| 1976 | 148.9 | 8.7 | 638.64 | 59.8 | 27.6 | 184.7 | 170.5 |
| 1977 | 169.9 | 8.9 | 729.22 | 67.7 | 31.9 | 202.4 | 181.5 |
| 1978 | 188.6 | 8.9 | 820.68 | 75.8 | 35.8 | 219.4 | 195.4 |
| 1979 | 212.2 | 9.0 | 838.00 | 85.3 | 40.6 | 239.7 | 217.4 |

Sources: U.S. Bureau of the Census, *Historical Statistics . . . to 1970*, series B221, B223, B224, B237, B262, E135; U.S. Bureau of the Census, *Statistical Abstract, 1980*, pp. 104–07, 486.

Table 4.2  Insurance and the Net Cost of Hospital Care

| | 1950 | 1955 | 1960 | 1963 | 1966 | 1969 | 1970 | 1971 | 1972 | 1973 | 1974 | 1975 |
|---|---|---|---|---|---|---|---|---|---|---|---|---|
| Percentage of hospital costs paid by: | | | | | | | | | | | | |
| 1. Private insurance | 29.3 | 44.7 | 52.5 | 56.0 | 51.4 | 44.6 | 45.6 | 45.7 | 45.4 | 45.9 | 45.4 | 43.6 |
| 2. Government | 21.1 | 19.9 | 18.8 | 17.8 | 25.5 | 37.6 | 37.8 | 40.6 | 41.1 | 40.9 | 42.8 | 44.5 |
| 3. Direct consumer spending | 49.6 | 35.2 | 28.7 | 26.2 | 23.1 | 17.8 | 16.6 | 13.7 | 13.5 | 13.2 | 11.8 | 11.9 |
| Percentage of private cost of hospital care paid by: | | | | | | | | | | | | |
| 4. Private insurance | 37.1 | 55.9 | 64.7 | 68.1 | 69.0 | 71.5 | 73.2 | 76.9 | 77.1 | 77.7 | 79.4 | 78.6 |
| 5. Direct consumer spending | 62.9 | 44.1 | 35.3 | 31.9 | 31.0 | 28.5 | 26.8 | 23.1 | 22.9 | 26.3 | 20.6 | 21.4 |
| 6. Average cost per patient day ($) | 15.62 | 23.12 | 32.23 | 38.91 | 48.15 | 70.03 | 81.01 | 92.31 | 105.21 | 114.69 | 128.05 | 151.53 |

SOURCE: Martin S. Feldstein and Amy Taylor, *The Rapid Rise of Hospital Costs*, staff report of the Council on Wage and Price Stability (Washington, D.C., January 1977), p. 31.

All figures exclude hospital costs in federal, long-term, tuberculosis, and psychiatric hospitals.

ing hospital costs (Figure 4.4). At the same time, physicians' fees
have risen dramatically with the advent of third-party payments (Figure 4.5).

All of this is another way of saying that resource scarcity (RS)
ceased to be a problem for most hospitals after World War II. At the
same time, information complexity (IC) continued to rise. The rapid
growth and expansion of health care—the world of Area 1—brought
more services and more expensive services. As a presidental adviser observed in 1972,

> In the case of public health, we are dealing with a loosely organized
> network of private and public agencies, institutions, individuals, and in-
> dustries. There are more than 300,000 individual physicians and 7,000
> independent hospitals providing medical services to some 210 million con-
> sumers. This diversity is at once a strength and a weakness. It provides nu-
> merous opportunities for comparisons of different methods of providing
> health care but at the same time, it vastly complicates the research and
> development process.[40]

Today's hospitals offer newer and better technology than their predecessors, employ more people and pay them better, and perform a
greater number of sophisticated tests on patients.

**Figure 4.4    Selected Trends in U.S. Health Care Expenditures
1929–1979**

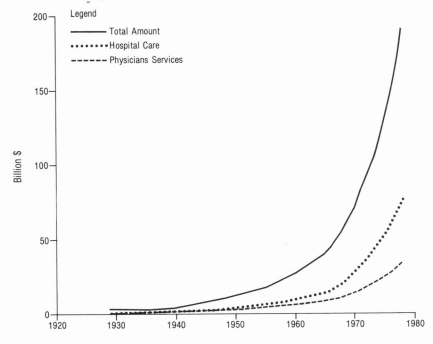

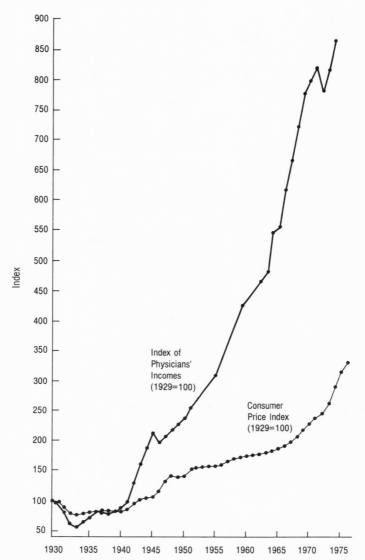

**Figure 4.5    Comparison of Physicians' Incomes with the Consumer Price Index, 1929–1975**

SOURCE: Ronald L. Numbers, "The Third Party: Health Insurance in America," in Morris J. Vogel and Charles E. Rosenberg, eds., *The Therapeutic Revolution: Essays in the Social History of American Medicine* (University of Pennsylvania Press, 1979), p. 192.

The organizational arrangements that have emerged from this turmoil are familiar to the modern reader. Doctors still occupy an anomalous position in hospitals. They have never become employees and are shielded from financial pressures. Nonetheless, they remain arbiters of key policies. Doctors' influence, according to one expert, manifests itself as follows:

> Most elements of hospital and medical care costs are generated or based on professional medical judgement. The judgements include the decision to order various diagnostic or therapeutic procedures for patients, and the larger decision as to the types of facilities and services needed by an institution for proper patient care. For the most part, these professional judgements are rendered outside of any organizational structure that fixes accountability for the economic consequences of these judgements.[41]

In 1978, physicians' income accounted for about twenty cents of the national health care dollar but doctors controlled another sixty cents by specifying hospital services, diagnostic procedures, drugs, and therapies.[42]

Despite these peculiar arrangements, the American health care system generally worked well, since all parties shared the common goal of optimizing patient care. The system also institutionalized some problems in interpersonal relations, however. The hospital administrator held key organizational and financial responsibilities, but his status relative to the trustees and doctors was low. Trustees were normally outstanding wealthy citizens in the community and doctors generally enjoyed higher salaries, more prestigious education, and greater professional status. Quotations from a sociological study of six eastern hospitals illustrate some typical frustrations[43]:

> We have to keep a close watch on expenditures. I suppose I'm an old tightwad, but I like to check on every nickel that's spent. Doctors love gadgets, and always want to buy them right away. I try to quash their purchase of unnecessary equipment.
>
> — A board president

> The trustees don't move fast enough for me. The main trouble is that they don't understand medicine. I don't know when we'll get rid of dead wood, and have some trustees who are really interested enough to keep informed about medical matters.
>
> — A chief of medicine

> You can't fight the doctors. If you try to browbeat them, you will soon become an ex-administrator. What you must do is get their cooperation in making changes you both want. You have to make them think your proposals were their own ideas.
>
> — An administrator

The expansion of hospital personnel and services since 1945 created other organizational problems as well. In the first place, the intensive technology of the hospital requires leaving considerable discretion to the personnel closest to the patient. Thus not only doctors, but nurses and other employees, themselves highly trained, exercise a measure of professional autonomy in their work. Such personnel must be flexible to adapt to the particular circumstances of each patient's case. From some points of view, then, hospitals appear to be decentralized and democratic in procedure. From other perspectives, however, hospitals look like authoritarian bureaucracies. Emergency conditions require rapid and precise mobilization of resources, while such concern for efficiency as there is leads to formal rules and clear lines of authority. Occasionally, these contrary tensions — the democratic and the directive — come into conflict with dramatic results.[44]

In the second place, the number of hospital employees has more than doubled since World War II. These personnel bring new skills but they add to management's already burdensome task of coordination. Indeed, Georgopoulos and Mann have remarked that with the possible exception of governments, "one would have great difficulty . . . finding any other organization whose internal differentiation and structural heterogeneity could match that of a large hospital. . . ."[45] There is thus a great need for internal coordination — better planning, communications, and cooperation — in hospitals. Given the organized anarchy of most hospitals, however, this is exceedingly difficult to arrange.

The inflation of hospital costs and the chaotic organization of medical care have drawn increasing public criticism in the past decade. Once again, as in the 1930s, opinion is polarized between advocates of a national health care system and proponents of a free market in medical care.

## THE CHANGING HEALTH
## CARE DELIVERY SYSTEM

The organizational history of America's health care system is riddled with anomalies. As it developed, the system clearly catered to doctors as much as to patients, while third-party payments froze hospital organization before it became rationalized. Hospitals were highly specialized and differentiated organizations with little hierarchical integration and control. The biggest problem of all, as we have seen, was the "professional dominance" of doctors who remained relatively free of administrative restraint. Such peculiar arrangements evolved because doctors and hospital managers were able to capitalize on two deep-seated American emotions: fear of death and faith in technology. As a result, America's health care system has swelled ominously. Ironically, the nation's heavy investment in health care has not reduced mortality rates. "The most important, and perhaps the most surprising, finding of health economics is this," writes Victor S. Fuchs: "Holding constant the state of medical technology and other health-determining variables, the marginal contribution of medical care to health is very small in modern nations."[46] In short, more money can't buy better health.

A second irony is that just when record amounts of public money began flowing in, public criticism of the industry built toward a crescendo. In 1969, three years after the passage of the Medicaid program in 1966, President Nixon portrayed a "national crisis" in health care, starting a flurry of attacks on the industry. A number of writers have singled out doctors and the American Medical Association for blame. Sociologists like Eliot Freidson warned of the harmful and wasteful consequences of the doctors' dominance.[47] As historian Charles Rosenberg observed,

> If one were to examine the process of decision-making within our most prestigious university and general hospitals in the last half-century it would be found, I think, that such policy determinations were made not only in hopes of maximizing the quality of care provided particular classes of patients but—to put it crudely—to a significant extent to maximize the status and intellectual aspirations of staff members.[48]

Other critics have made different but equally telling points. Costs have gotten out of hand. There has been too little concern for efficiency. Doctors prescribe too many unnecessary tests and encourage unnecessary surgery. Facilities and services are maldistributed across the nation; some areas support too many hospitals while others are neglected. Government and private insurance programs, extensive as they are, nonetheless fail to cover millions of citizens. The latest technologies and techniques—CAT scanners, open-heart surgery, organ transplants, renal dialysis—are exceedingly costly and, for that reason, unavailable to patients on an equitable basis. Some of these new technologies therefore raise thorny questions in medical ethics. Choices about access to care have literally become matters of life and death. Some critics have even gone so far as to blame the system itself for *causing* disease.[49]

In short, in recent years America's health care system has drawn heated debate as well as more measured consideration. The key issue is cost. Lawmakers have focused on economic issues in health care policy, and the resulting legislation and regulation have tried to redirect hospitals toward the needs of the consumer and away from the dominance of physicians. Public policy has pushed in three directions, encourag-

ing local and regional planning and coordination of health care services, the control of hospital costs, and the application of the minimum
technology appropriate to each diagnosis.[50]

Efforts to coordinate planning date from the same period as Medicare and Medicaid. For instance, since 1964, many states have followed New York's lead and have required communities to produce
certificates of need showing that expansion of health care facilities is
warranted. At the federal level, the National Health Planning and Resource Development Act (1974) called for the establishment of more
than two hundred regional health systems agencies (HSAs) across the
nation. Each HSA is required to produce annual long-range and short-
term plans for state and federal review and approval.

As for costs, the Social Security amendments of 1972 set ceilings on
Medicare and Medicaid spending and tightened mechanisms for hospital reimbursement. At the same time, the states were encouraged to
implement local health plans to reduce duplication of services and excess capacity and to consider alternative forms of health care delivery.
Seven states have gone so far as to enact mandatory rate-setting programs to control spending increases.[51]

The third element of public policy, the determination of the minimum technology appropriate to the diagnosis, has developed in two
ways. First, certificate of need legislation has been extended from
construction and capacity expansion to the purchase of new technologies. Since 1974 a certificate of need has been required for purchases
of equipment costing more than $100,000 — a figure well below the cost
of new X-ray equipment, for example.[52] Moreover, since 1972 there
has been a nationwide system of Professional Standards Review Organizations (PSROs) consisting of licensed physicians living in a given
area who are charged with reviewing the quality and cost of health care
funded by federal programs. Using "professionally developed norms of
care, diagnosis, and treatment," PSROs monitor the appropriateness
of admissions, the quality and necessity of services to the patient, and
the patient's length of stay.[53]

There is considerable dispute about the economic effectiveness of
recent government policy toward the health care industry. Economist
Alain C. Enthoven, for instance, has shown that savings from certificate of need programs, cost controls, and PSROs have been negligible.
The reason for this, Enthoven argues, is that regulation has not given
doctors and hospitals sufficient incentives to control costs, and he urges
the introduction of "a system of fair economic competition" as the only
hope of reducing the nation's medical bill.[54] Whatever their economic
effects, however, changing public expectations and a changing institutional environment have already produced a number of organizational
changes in the industry. In particular, under increasing resource con-

straints there has been a renewed emphasis on hospital management, increasing collaboration among hospitals, and a new interest in preventive medicine and the "delivery" of medical services outside the hospital. In our terms, RS is increasing and the hospital industry is moving from Area 1 toward Area 2 conditions.

## HOSPITAL MANAGEMENT REFORM

The hospital industry first responded to increasing RS by attempting to rationalize organization and management. In recent years hospital management textbooks, articles, and organization studies have proliferated. Accounting and control practices have become more sophisticated, while both administrative and medical records have been computerized. Many hospitals have moved away from the balanced management shared among trustees, doctors, and administrators in favor of professional management.

In addition, recent advances in organization theory have been applied to hospitals. For example, contingency theorists have both explained the anomalous organization of hospitals and suggested some remedies for better control. According to Duncan Neuhauser, the peculiar mixture of hierarchy and democracy and the lack of bureaucratic controls in hospitals are results of different levels of specialization required by an uncertain environment. The hospital's chief organizational need, therefore, is to find coordinating mechanisms to bridge its specialized functions. Such mechanisms include management committees of doctors and administrators, revised medical staff organization, unit managers, and patient-care teams. In short, Neuhauser argues that hospitals can benefit from adopting matrix structures. Indeed, some university and teaching hospitals have already done so with good results.[55]

Other recent trends in hospital management reform include the emergence of investor-owned hospitals operated for profit and the rapid growth of hospital management companies. As noted earlier, privately owned hospitals were hit particularly hard by the depression and later suffered because they were ineligible for some federal funding projects like the Hill-Burton Act. Private hospitals accounted for more than half of all hospitals in the country in 1910; they fell to 18% in 1946 and 11% in 1968. Since then, however, the environment for proprietary hospitals has improved and they comprised 13% of the total in 1978.[56] This growth stems partly from the third-party boom which benefited the industry generally, but also from the increasing rationalization of management in investor-owned hospitals.

Investor-owned hospitals differ from traditional proprietary hospitals in several important ways. In the first place, they rely heavily on corporate staffs trained in management skills. Thus the administration has relatively more leverage against doctors. Second, such hospitals operate explicitly for profit and their managers are more likely to be skilled in raising money in the capital markets. Debt financing has grown in importance in recent years, now accounting for about two-thirds of all capital raised by hospitals. This trend is still on the rise, and hospitals with a better understanding of finance are more likely to thrive. (A crucial disadvantage for investor-owned hospitals, however, is that they are subject to taxation.)[57] Finally, those investor-owned hospitals that are part of larger chains can take advantage of administrative economies of scale. Centralizing such functions as purchasing, financial and control systems, and computer services may provide substantial savings. Moreover, large hospital companies employ experts that smaller community institutions cannot afford. Thus in 1977 Hospital Affiliates International, Inc. (HAI) had "staff specialists" in forty distinct fields ranging from accounting to data processing to regulation to expertise in the latest technologies.[58]

Hospital management companies bring together well-paid, highly trained, experienced administrators and physicians into a new style governing group that attempts to balance medical and financial goals. For instance, the largest hospital management company, Hospital Corporation of America (HCA) was organized as follows in 1970:

> Each hospital has a Management Committee, at least two-thirds of whose members are persons connected with the hospital, usually physicians on the staff of the hospital, and the remainder of whom are appointed by the company to supervise the medical, ethical and professional affairs and the daily operations of the hospital. The company supplies management services to each of its hospitals, including the furnishing of accounting forms and controls and of technical personnel to assist in hospital administration and management. Each hospital records its financial and statistical information on a standard chart of accounts which enables the company to aid in the control of expenditures and to compare operations of various hospitals.[59]

Hospital management companies have generally pursued two strategies. Larger companies like HCA have grown by constructing and managing hospitals in Sun Belt cities not fully covered by medical services. In addition, some of these companies arrange contracts to manage hospitals already in existence but usually in financial trouble. HCA, for instance, managed one hundred forty-five hospitals in 1981 in addition to the one hundred sixty-four hospitals it owned in the United States. Contract management is frequently the first step leading to acquisition and it can be a marketing tool for management companies looking to enter new territory. By the mid-1970s, more than thirty management companies operated nearly four hundred hospitals across the nation, adding capacity at nearly ten times the rate of voluntary hospitals. Contract management was big business, too. HCA's annual revenues exceeded $2.4 billion in 1981.[60]

Management firms typically assume total responsibility for the daily operations of an independent hospital in return for a percentage of gross revenues plus incentives. Contracts normally extend from two to five years. It is unusual for management firms to place many of their own employees in hospitals but they do occupy key decision-making positions. The companies also concentrate on training local personnel. The larger firms often assemble task forces from the hospitals they own to serve as consultants to the hospitals under contract. "For example, . . . the management company would borrow an administrator from one of its owned hospitals, a director of nursing from another, a financial executive from a third, and an expert in the management of ancillary services from a fourth."[61] Management companies are, of course, dominated by professional managers, but they also employ some physicians. At HAI, (before its recent acquisition) the governing board consisted of doctors and managers in roughly equal numbers.[62]

In sum, the central thrust of hospital management reform in the past two decades has been toward increasing the power of administrators in order to control costs and provide new sources of income. In general, hospitals and hospital management firms have sought to improve organizational integration in hospitals as the best way to cope with a less bountiful environment.

## COLLABORATION AMONG HOSPITALS AND MULTIHOSPITAL SYSTEMS

Hospitals have responded to increasing RS in a second way by consolidating services in communities or chains. Such collaboration varies from loose agreements to formal mergers.[63] Figure 4.6 portrays the range of possibilities, from "formal affiliations" — agreements to transfer patients and share information and some resources — to "complete ownership," in which the identities and staffs of the component institutions are merged in a single hierarchy. Some of these cooperative forms are not new — religious and ethnic hospital chains have shared centralized services for years while the hospital management companies discussed earlier represent another multi-institutional form.

One of the best known and most widely adopted forms of collaboration is the multihospital system (MHS). This term "refers to a system in which a number of separate institutions are under a single corporate management that has overall authority for operating decisions and for policy formulation."[64] By 1977 there were approximately 350 MHSs in the U.S., representing about two-fifths of the country's bed capacity.[65]

In practice, MHSs themselves embrace a wide range of cooperative agreements. For instance, a recent survey has shown that more than

**Figure 4.6   Classification of Multihospital Arrangements**

| Types or Categories / Characteristics | 1 Formal Affiliation | 2 Shared or Cooperative Services | 3 Consortia for Planning or Education | 4 Contract Management | 5 Lease | 6 Corporate Ownership but Separate Management | 7 Complete Ownership |
|---|---|---|---|---|---|---|---|
| | Less commitment, more institutional autonomy ———— CONTINUUM ———— More commitment, more system control | | | | | | |
| Descriptions, Definitions, Terms | Patient transfer agreements, house officer affiliations, referral agreements | Financial, political commitment over time for selected products or service | Voluntary health planning council for a specific geography; Area Health Education Centers (AHECs) | Corporate-management; full management without ownership | Policy as well as management provided by a single board | Owners do not interfere in the mangement of hospitals even though they have legal authority; absentee ownership | 1. Mergers, consolidations  2. Satellites branch operations  3. Authorities, chains  4. Holding companies |
| Corporate Ownerships | No | No | No | No | No | Yes | Yes |
| Corporate Management | No | No | No | Yes | Yes | No | Yes |
| System Influence on Major Policy Decisions | No | No | Yes | Minor | Yes | Maybe | Yes (Absolute) |

Source: Scott A. Mason, ed., *Multihospital Arrangements: Public Policy Implications* (Chicago: American Hospital Association, 1979), p. 4.

80% of American hospitals share at least one service with another hospital, a trend that has increased markedly since 1975.[66] It is usual to divide MHSs into three types: shared services or consortia, chain organizations, and regional multiunit health care systems. The most common shared services are purchasing, education and training, data processing, and laundry. Chain organizations vary in structure, but typically centralize at least corporate planning and staff functions. In regional health centers, physicians are not attached to specific hospitals but admit patients into that hospital within the MHS with the best facilities for treating the particular case.[67]

A brief description of one regional center illustrates how these systems operate. The Greenville (South Carolina) Medical Center, one of the most famous MHSs, consists of nine hospitals with more than a thousand beds. The system is divided into three parts, each managed by an administrator who reports to the chief executive officer at corporate headquarters. The General Division includes the downtown general hospital and a center for family medicine; the Suburban Division operates four facilities outside the city; and the Center Division has responsibility for new development and management of outpatient care and psychiatric facilities. Headquarters are in the Center Division, "where personnel, fiscal programs, patient accounting, billing and data processing are centralized, [along with] a supply and distribution center." While no hard data are available, it is generally believed that the Greenville MHS is economically efficient. In 1975 Chief Executive Officer Robert E. Toomey listed several advantages of the arrangement, including vertical integration from intensive care to ambulatory care and outpatient psychiatry, shared services, coordinated planning, and the ability to pool depreciation and resources.[68]

A study sponsored by the U.S. Department of Health, Education and Welfare in the early 1970s provides the most complete data on MHSs. From a sample of eight systems matched with a control group of independent hospitals, the authors found the MHSs featured:

- lower levels of average case cost
- slower growth in case cost
- lower price levels
- lower growth in prices
- higher outputs
- comparable services with other hospitals
- lower average lengths-of-stay
- higher wage rates offset by slower growth of the labor force (subject to local variations)
- significant economies of scale in hotel-type services, such as food preparation, laundry, cleaning, etc.[69]

The authors also found in the MHS they examined most intensively, the Samaritan Health Service of Phoenix, Arizona, that one of the most notable changes was the growing status and presence of the corporate staff within the member hospitals. During the six years covered by the study (1968 to 1973), it was discovered that about 40% of the entire system's personnel growth was in corporate staff. At the same time, while the medical staff grew and reflected increasing specialization, the number of physicians added to the system failed to keep pace with the number of physicians who established private practices in the metropolitan area.[70]

To review, the emergence of MHSs and other forms of collaboration among hospitals has been one of the most conspicuous developments in health care organization in the past two decades. There seems to be general agreement that the forces driving such collaboration include public pressure to control costs and the needs to reduce duplicated services and excess bed capacity.[71] In large measure, MHSs appear to be satisfying these needs. Like reforms inside hospitals, the development of MHSs has increased the organizational power of administrators at the expense of trustees and doctors, and improved the degree of organizational integration.

## HEALTH CARE DELIVERY OUTSIDE THE HOSPITAL

The health care industry has responded to increasing RS in a third way, by devising new methods of providing care where it is least expensive—outside the hospital. The past two decades have seen a resurgence of older forms of health care delivery: the growth of physicians' group practices, expansion of ambulatory care and outpatient facilities in hospitals, and the emergence of health maintenance organizations (HMOs).

As we have seen earlier, medical services were commonly provided outside hospitals until the late nineteenth century. It is perhaps the ultimate irony of the American health care system that the hospital is currently losing patients to the very institutions it replaced or eclipsed early in this century. In the quest to hold down expenses, patients are returning to outpatient clinics of various sorts, institutional forms that either antedate or coincide with the rise of the hospital. The model for today's private group practice, for instance, is the Mayo Clinic, founded in the 1880s. Group practices grew rapidly during the 1920s and 1930s but were eclipsed by the expansion of hospital services after the war. These groups worked as follows:

> The physicians who banded together hoped to reduce overhead costs by using common facilities. They pooled income and considered a patient, though he was frequently under the charge of one physician, as the re-

sponsibility of the whole group. Some of these groups conducted general diagnostic surveys and instituted comprehensive therapies; others who were organized only for diagnosis, believed that if therapy were left to the referring physician, he would be encouraged to consult the group without fear of losing his association with the case, and could actively share in restoring the patient to health. At the one extreme, some groups worked under a single roof, its members legally related and incorporated. At the other extreme were groups of specialists who regularly sent patients to each other but had no spatial or legal relationship, except that of one consultant to another. Intermediate forms included independent physicians who leased offices in a "medical building," jointly shared a laboratory, and referred patients among themselves.[72]

Group practices—"formally structured and legally incorporated private group practice, defined as having at least three full-time physicians"—have grown rapidly in recent years. In 1959 there were 546 groups comprising 5% of all physicians in the United States; in 1975 7,773 such groups included 18% of the nation's physicians.[73] The group practice is a competitor to hospitals in two senses. First, it competes for the time and loyalty of physicians. Some hospitals, in fact, have been forced to construct or furnish buildings for group practices in order to attract and retain the services of highly regarded physicians. Second, private group practices compete for patients. By offering comprehensive diagnostic services and, in most cases, facilities for minor surgery, the group clinic can provide all but acute care or long-term rehabilitation services offered by hospitals. At least in theory, then, costs and prices of care in group practices should be lower than costs and prices of similar hospital care. In practice, however, this may not be the case, because third parties typically reimburse private clinics and have removed some incentives to achieve efficiency.*

Another new form of health care delivery with old antecedents is the HMO.[74] Because HMOs can take many organizational forms, they are usually described by listing their behavioral characteristics. These include:

1. A defined population of enrolled members.
2. Payments determined in advance for a specific period of time and made periodically.
3. Services provided to the patients by HMO physicians for essentially all medical needs, with referrals to outside specialists being controlled by the HMO.
4. Voluntary enlistment by each individual or family.[75]

---

*It must also be pointed out that physicians are owners of private group practices, a fact with obvious financial implications. Since doctor-owners are typically compensated by salary plus a profit-sharing arrangement, reducing costs is not a primary consideration. Nor is efficiency, except in the sense that each doctor is encouraged to see as many patients as possible.

Another distinguishing feature is that HMO physicians receive salaries rather than fees for service. There are thus real incentives for doctors and administrators to control costs in HMOs.

HMOs come in many varieties. Some are simply prepaid group practices concentrated in a community. Others are loose individual practice associations, which may be geographically dispersed. HMOs can be operated for profit or not; some insist on full-time employees, others do not. Some HMOs own hospitals, most do not.[76]

One of the earliest models for HMOs was the Ross-Loos group, a prepaid group practice founded in Los Angeles in the 1920s. A model more frequently cited, the Kaiser-Permanente Medical Program, which operates in some western states, began in the 1930s. The rapid development of HMOs, however, dates from the early 1970s, when the Nixon administration searched for ways to coordinate health care delivery and its funding. The Federal Health Maintenance Organization Act of 1973 eased legal problems with the formation of HMOs and empowered the federal government to make grants and loans to help them get started. By 1980 there were about 240 HMOs in the country with some nine million people enrolled.[77]

In economic terms, HMOs have performed modestly well. Harold S. Luft, who has studied HMOs most extensively, concludes that "In all instances, the total cost of medical care . . . for HMO enrollees is lower than for apparently comparable people with conventional insurance coverage." The costs of subscribers to the Kaiser-Permanente plan, for instance, were 10% to 40% less than the costs for people with conventional insurance coverage. The cause of this difference seems to be that HMO subscribers use hospitals less often. "Excluding maternity cases, the hospitalization rate per 1,000 members per year may be as low as half that of people in Blue Cross-Blue Shield plans and those with commercial insurance."[78] This goal has apparently been achieved with no loss of quality of care. Luft's conclusion is even-handed: "The available evidence supports the view that the average HMO offers care comparable or somewhat superior to the 'average' fee-for-service practitioner, but there is no evidence it is superior to that of the 'better' conventional settings."[79]

The central organizational effect of the growing trend toward delivering medical services outside the hospital has been to increase the importance of management at the expense of physicians as health care funding is rationalized. The growth of group practices and HMOs is a clear illustration that the object of the medical care establishment is once again becoming the patient rather than the physician. At this writing the Reagan administration is exploring ways to speed up this trend by introducing more competition to health care. Its general approach is to provide more choice both for insurers and for health care consumers and to provide them with incentives to choose less expensive care. The government is considering retaining the present tax incentive to provide more comprehensive and expensive insurance coverage (tax-free) in lieu of higher wages and salaries. It is also testing the idea of requiring employers to share with employees the savings from choosing less expensive medical coverage. All of these methods can be seen as attempts to accelerate the shift to HMOs and prepaid systems, in order to stem the rising tide of health care costs.

## CONCLUSION

Hospitals have evolved in a peculiar manner. Figure 4.7 recapitulates this evolution and highlights some of the associated organizational patterns. What was once a small, charitable institution situated outside the market economy, the premodern hospital (Area 9), became a highly differentiated organization in the early twentieth century. This transformation was catalyzed by changing social structure, technology, and professional specialization. Just when pressures to consolidate and rationalize services began to take effect in the 1920s and 1930s (Areas 5 and 6), however, the enormous commitment Americans made to health care under the third-party payment system freed hospitals and the medical profession from market constraints. As a result, for more than twenty-five years after World War II, growth of hospital facilities, services, and costs was extravagant (Area 1).

The experience of hospitals in the postwar period provides a rare opportunity to see what happens to organizations that persist for a long period under Area 1 conditions. The result has been a completely lopsided form of competition. Hospitals faced virtually no competitive pressure to economize on new equipment and services. This form of competition created high levels of IC, although RS remained low. Hospitals actually increased their costs in order to attract doctors and patients and thereby survive. Such practices led to high internal differentiation but very low integration, as predicted by our model. Established doctors became the critical resource for hospitals and doctors, in turn, dominated the power structure. Physicians preempted trustees and administrators and hospital employees of all kinds. At the same time, the human resource practices typical of hospitals emphasized clan mechanisms for the doctors and bureaucratic mechanisms for everyone else, reinforcing an unbalanced picture. Hospitals adopted "prospector" strategies as they searched for the latest in technology and services. The level of employee involvement was at best uneven. While the task of caring for people's health is essentially an en-

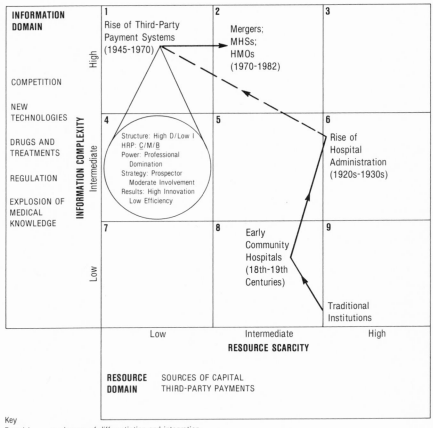

**Figure 4.7    Evolution and Organization of the Hospital 1850–1980**

gaging one, many nurses, technicians, and orderlies complained of long hours, low pay, and exploitation.

The readaptive results are well documented. During the postwar period, hospitals were innovative but highly inefficient. Government action, in the form of Medicare, Medicaid, and tax subsidies of private health insurance, has been the prime creator of Area 1 conditions. Government, therefore, also has the power to push hospitals out of Area 1 conditions. But finding ways to reform the American hospital system has not been easy. Health care has unusual features that make it extremely difficult to reconcile innovation and quality with efficiency.

In the past decade or so, public policy has pressed to increase RS and force the reorganization of health care delivery. The hospital industry is beginning to move from Area 1 to Area 2 with encouraging results. There is more pressure on hospitals to cut costs. The focus of health care policy and delivery is once more on the patient. Organizational anomalies inside the hospital are disappearing. There is less professional domination by doctors, more collaboration between doctors, support staff, and administrators. Hierarchical organization at the top has been strengthened but it has been juxtaposed with horizontal coordination at the level of the patient. These trends in American hospitals seem to have improved employee involvement. Although physicians (as an organized professional group) dislike the changes that have cost them organizational power and, in some cases, income, other hospital personnel — not to mention the patient — are better off.[80] This is partly the result of hospital unionization and the collective bargaining victories of the past decade. But employee involvement has also been promoted by the changing nature of work inside the hospital, where discretion remains with employees closest to the patient but cooperative work is becoming the norm.

In terms of our readaptive outcomes — efficiency and innovation — Area 2 conditions ought to bring better results than those of Area 1. Certainly, all of the evidence cited so far supports the view that efficiency has become a greater concern in hospital management and that improvements have already been achieved. Innovation is a more complicated issue, whose ethical and social implications still tend to overwhelm economic considerations. Changing public policy and changing medical care organization have helped put the brakes on such spending and have increased the time and red tape between the advertisement of new equipment and its purchase and installation. So far, good sense has been balanced by compassion. In one MHS where new decision-making procedures have been implemented, the rate of innovations adopted has not slowed significantly, although some doctors have grumbled at being left out of a process they once controlled.[81] So some of the remedial approaches, such as MHSs and HMOs, that introduce an element of competition at the institutional level, show promise of controlling costs without loss of innovation and quality.

The history of autos and steel revealed the hazards of too little IC and RS. The adaptational record of the community general hospital, as we have seen, has highlighted the very special case of high IC and low RS. For at least three decades the hospital was shielded from market pressures, blocking the evolution of organizational integration, a balanced power structure and high involvement. Next we shall look at the organizational history of another fragmented industry, agriculture, where the hazards of both high IC and high RS are exposed. Aided by direct government action, however, American agriculture has been readaptive since the 1930s, achieving a remarkable record of efficiency and innovation. Let us look, then, at the organizational and environmental circumstances that sustained this impressive performance.

# CHAPTER 5

# Agriculture:
# The American Miracle

ASKED TO NAME America's largest and most successful industry, people on the street might say energy, computers, or even (until recently) automobiles. For some time, however, our largest and most successful industry in terms of employment, assets, sales, and export value has been agriculture. Yet America was not always "the breadbasket of the world." Fifty years ago farming was a big business, but a highly fragmented and uncertain one that kept most of its practitioners at or near a subsistence income and made only a handful of them rich. How the United States became the most reliable and productive supplier of food is not widely understood. Still less well known is the organizational history of this "American miracle": The vast increases of production were achieved not by large-scale or corporate farms, but by the family farm, an operation with only one or two full-time employees.

If we were to trace the full history of this industry we might begin with the environmental conditions of Area 9, since farming, like traditional hospitality, took place outside the market economy for centuries. In more recent times agriculture has been a highly competitive, boom-or-bust business influenced by the weather in the short run and by demographic trends in the longer term. For our purposes we shall pick up the story in the 1920s, when the industry's chronic instability was particularly acute because of excessive competition and uncertainties about the market. These were years of widespread suffering among farmers, with unstable and declining commodity prices. By guaranteeing credit for farmers and by providing incentives to decrease the amount of land in production, New Deal farm policies helped to end the farm crisis. Government policies, in combination with the recovery of other sectors of the economy after the depression, technological innovations in farming, and renewed growth of domestic and foreign markets, set U.S. agriculture on a path toward increasing growth, productivity, and innovation for the next four decades.

## CRISIS IN U.S. AGRICULTURE 1920 TO 1933

In one of the most famous essays in American historiography, Frederick Jackson Turner, writing in 1892, lamented the closing of the American frontier. The Turner thesis, suggesting the psychological, social, and political consequences of the passing of a way of life on our "national character," remains controversial today. There is little dispute, however, that the continental United States was fairly well settled by the time Turner wrote.[1] Most of the good arable land was occupied by small farmers whose settlement had been encouraged by the great land ordinances of the eighteenth century and later legislation like the Homestead Act (1862). Animating these early public policies—and much current federal farm policy—of course, was the Jeffersonian ideal of a republic made up of small, independent, and prosperous farmers.

However appealing, this vision clashed with reality in a number of ways. In the first place, many farmers never owned the land they worked in the 19th century. Farm tenancy increased rapidly after the Civil War, largely because higher real estate values encouraged speculators and made it difficult for younger farm children to buy their own property. Between 1880 and 1930 tenancy increased from 25% of all American farms to 42.4%. This trend was especially marked in the South, where more than half of all farms in 1930 were worked by tenants and sharecroppers, many of whom lived in desperate poverty.[2] Moreover, farming was not always prosperous. In the three decades after the Civil War, for instance, farmers faced failing prices for their goods and their discontent fueled populist politics before prices turned upward at the very end of the century.

These two problems—unstable prices and growing numbers of impoverished tenants—loomed large during two agricultural crises that occurred at the beginning and end of the 1920s. These crises hit with particular force because they followed what is sometimes called "the golden age" of American agriculture. Between 1900 and 1919 farmers' incomes had swelled as production climbed to feed a growing nation and to supply a burgeoning export market. High commodity prices, increasing real estate values, and the growing replacement of animal power by the tractor induced farmers to expand acreage and output — usually relying on increased mortgages. Indeed, farm mortgage debt more than tripled between 1910 and 1920.[3]

After World War I, however, the agricultural boom ended with a sudden crash. Farm prices fell 43% between 1919 and 1921, made a slow recovery over several years, but fell another 56% between 1929 and 1932 (Figure 5.1).[4] The devastation of European national economies and increasing competition from Canada, Australia, and Argentina, combined with the U.S. tariff policy to all but close foreign markets to American exports. While farm income fell spectacularly, fixed costs declined less steeply and, in some cases, such as taxes, actually increased. During the 1920s farmers' realized net income averaged 30% less than during the previous decade.[5] Profit margins were narrow at best and dwindled sharply after 1929 (Figure 5.2).

Moreover, the burden of mortgage debt, contracted when times were good, grew alarming as the 1920s wore on. The rate of "distress transfers" (land transfers forced by bankruptcy, foreclosure, or assignment to avoid foreclosure) quadrupled between 1920 and 1926 and doubled again by 1932 (Figure 5.3). It was said that a quarter of all land in Misssissippi went up for sale on a single day in 1931.[6]

In such circumstances American farmers responded frantically. They were caught up in a vicious cycle, forced to increase production to meet costs, but driving prices downward by that very action. Stories of deprivation, hardship, and starvation were legion in the early 1930s. The plight of poor farmers and tenants was immortalized in the prose of John Steinbeck and James Agee, and in the photographs of Walker Evans and Dorothea Lange. As late as 1937 a presidential commission on farm tenancy asserted that between a fourth and a fifth of the nation's farm population lived in extreme poverty, was chronically undernourished and abnormally subject to nutritional and other diseases, often lacked medical care, and was usually poorly clad.[7]

Less well remembered are the strikes, protest marches, rural vigilantism and violence that occurred even in the most prosperous agricultural regions.[8] At LaMars, Iowa in January 1933, for instance, a mob of about a thousand farmers stormed the courthouse and mauled the sheriff and a representative of a New York mortgage company. All around the state, recalled one protester, crowds of angry farmers

> stopped wagons, dumped milk. They stopped farmers hauling their hay to market. They undertook to stop the whole agricultural process. . . . Some of 'em had pitchforks. You can fix the auto tire good with a pitchfork. The country was getting up in arms about taking a man's property

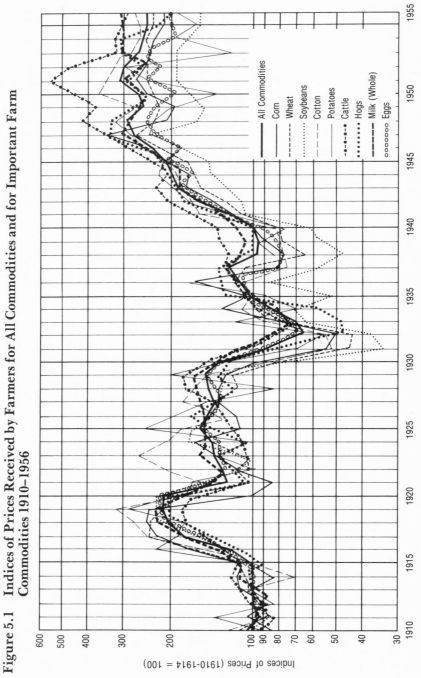

Figure 5.1    Indices of Prices Received by Farmers for All Commodities and for Important Farm Commodities 1910–1956

Indices of Prices (1910-1914 = 100)

Legend: All Commodities, Corn, Wheat, Soybeans, Cotton, Potatoes, Cattle, Hogs, Milk (Whole), Eggs

SOURCE: Willard W. Cochrane, *Farm Prices: Myth and Reality* (Minneapolis: University of Minnesota Press, 1958), p. 14.

122

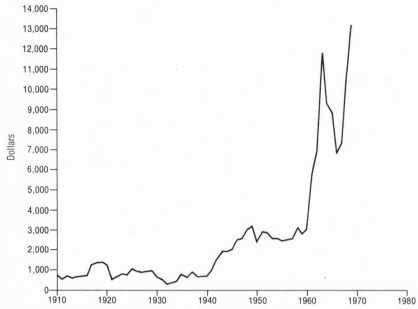

**Figure 5.2 Net Income per Farm 1910–1980**

SOURCE:U.S. Bureau of the Census, *Historical Statistics of the United States from Colonial Times to 1970* (Washington D.C., 1976), series K 259; *Statistical Abstract of the United States*, various years. Note: USDA statistical definitions and procedures are not uniform throughout this period.

away from him. It was his livelihood. When you took a man's horses and his plow away, you denied him food, you convicted his family to starvation. It was just that real.[9]

U.S. agriculture in the 1920s and early 1930s clearly faced extreme RS in shrinking margins and increasing foreclosures. Farmers were also obliged to cope with high levels of IC. Too many farmers created too much competition. Decisions about how much of which crops to plant under what conditions using what seed varieties, fertilizers, and technological aids were paralyzing. Confronted by an abundance of choices and severe financial problems, many farmers simplified matters arbitrarily even when they might have known better. The recollections of Bud Trueblood, an Idaho alfalfa farmer, make a case in point:

> I had to go all the way to college to find out how to farm. My father sure never taught me. He farmed on the principle of let's hurry up and make as much as we can right now and never mind what happens to the soil. It never occurred to him to give nature half a chance. But the things I learned weren't new. A year or two ago, I picked up a copy of the Department of Agriculture's *Yearbook* for 1902 — and it's all in there. Crop rota-

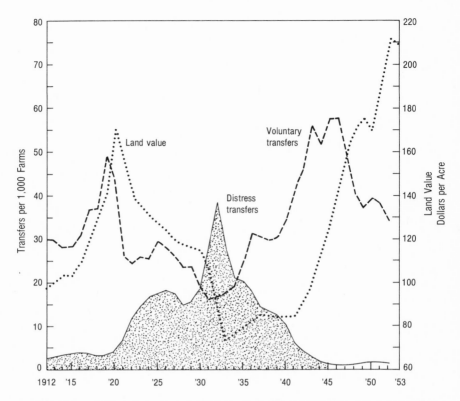

Adapted from a chart supplied by the Bureau of Agricultural Economics. Land value indexes (1912-1914 = 100) refer to value of land and buildings as of March 1; transfer data refer to transactions from March 16 through March 15 of the following year. Distress transfers include assignments to avoid foreclosure, as well as foreclosures.

**Figure 5.3    Distress Transfers, Voluntary Transfers, and Value of Farm Real Estate per Acre, 1912–53**

SOURCE: Lawrence A. Jones and David Durand, *Mortgage Lending Experience in Agriculture* (Princeton: Princeton University Press, 1954), p. 6.

tion. Soil conservation. Cultivation. The Extension Service tried to teach it to my dad, but he couldn't be bothered. He couldn't even be bothered to irrigate right. It was easier to overwater, so he leached his soil away.[10]

## GOVERNMENT POLICY AND THE FARM CRISIS

Area 3 conditions in the 1920s and 1930s brought severe hardship to the nation's farms and proved politically intolerable. Farmers united in demanding government action for relief, but there was no consensus about which possibilities offered most hope. Politicians of both major parties believed that the farm troubles sprang from a common source: overproduction. In addition, some Democrats believed that rural over-population was an equally serious problem and they lobbied for agricultural programs that would either help tenants to purchase their land or, more likely, aid them in resettling elsewhere. In general, however, national debate on the farm crisis centered on the best means to stabilize prices for commercial farmers. Three proposals for federal relief action circulated in the period: expansion of private cooperative agreements, direct price supports, and limitations on planted acreage. In the 1930s the Roosevelt administration chose a mixture of the latter two proposals as the best means to mitigate excessive competition, thereby unleashing massive changes in American agriculture.

The Republican presidents of the 1920s had generally espoused a program of price stabilization through private cooperatives. In California during the early 1920s cooperatives founded by Aaron Sapiro achieved some success in controlling prices through collaborative marketing efforts. As one historian has described it, "The general idea was that farmers could combine in large, national or industry-wide cooperatives and control the flow of their products to the market, operate on the basis of administered prices and, if necessary, dump surpluses abroad or into diversionary, domestic markets."[11] President Hoover's Agricultural Marketing Act of 1929 empowered the Federal Farm Board to loan up to $500 million to cooperatives. The movement no sooner got off the ground than the stock market crashed that October, bringing on a severe financial crisis. In any case, the cooperative movement required a cumbersome bureaucracy particularly unsuited to meeting an emergency situation. Moreover, the program demanded managerial talent of a quantity and quality not then readily available in U.S. agriculture. At best the cooperative movement might have offered a long-term solution to unstable farm income and production, but it never got the chance.

Democrats and farm-state congressmen generally supported a second plan to subsidize agricultural exports. Twice in the 1920s Congress passed bills (the McNary-Haugen Acts) authorizing the creation of a federal export corporation to purchase crops from farmers at a "ratio price" equivalent to the real value of the commodities before World War I. This government corporation "would purchase specified farm commodities at a price well above the world price, and export any of the crop the domestic market could not absorb at that price. The losses on exports would be borne by the producers of the commodity through an 'equalization fee' levied on the marketing of the crop, and imports would be prevented by levying a tariff on the affected commodity at a level high enough to keep out competing products."[12] Although this legislation attracted wide support from farmers' organizations, President Coolidge vetoed both bills, believing they violated the free-market system by fixing prices and that the "equalization fee" was an unconstitutional tax falling unequally on food processing and marketing firms.

M. L. Wilson, an agricultural economist from Montana, popularized yet another policy during the 1920s. According to the "domestic allotment" plan, farmers would be assigned "rights" to produce certain amounts of their crops to sell at subsidized prices. Any crops grown in excess of the allotted amount would not be subsidized and would have to sell at depressed market prices. Wilson and his disciples hoped, therefore, to offer farmers substantial incentives to restrict production.[13] The domestic allotment plan had little appeal for farmers, however, because few of them could believe that producing less might mean earning more. But the plan did interest some members of the "brain trust" gathering around presidential candidate Franklin D. Roosevelt.

FDR's election in 1932 marked the beginning of direct government intervention in the agricultural market system. The agricultural planners of the New Deal approached the farm problem with the general intention of building up farm income through higher prices. From the old McNary-Haugen acts they seized first on the notion of the "ratio price," or "parity" as it was now called, as a device for restoring farm purchasing power to the 1909–14 level. At the same time, the statute borrowed from the domestic allotment plan by offering incentives to farmers to decrease land in production. Title I of the Agricultural Adjustment Act (AAA, 1933) empowered the new secretary of agriculture, Henry A. Wallace, to subsidize voluntary acreage control programs, to regulate marketing by licensing processors and producers, and to determine the rates of processing taxes to pay administrative costs of the program. In addition, price supports were specified for wheat, cotton, field corn, hogs, rice, tobacco, and dairy products.* The AAA and other new legislation of the period also provided for mortgage relief, new federal credit agencies, bank insurance, and other relief and recovery acts for the stabilization of the economy.

While the Supreme Court overturned the AAA in 1936, ruling that the processing taxes were unconstitutional, the New Deal agricultural planners found other means to preserve the principles of price supports and retirement of farmland. These were embodied in the Soil Conservation and Domestic Allotment Act (1936) and the second AAA (1938). The latter program substituted marketing for production controls, authorized the secretary to make "nonrecourse loans" to producers of specified commodities and to make parity payments to supplement other funds, encouraged conservation through land retire-

---

*Other commodities including rye, flax, barley, grain sorghums, cattle, peanuts, sugar beets, sugar cane, and potatoes were added to the list in later years.

ment, and provided for the systematic storage of supplies and surpluses in an "ever-normal granary" for use in emergencies.[14]

In 1935 the Roosevelt administration also addressed itself directly to the problems of tenancy and rural poverty by creating the Resettlement Administration, with Rexford G. Tugwell at its head. Tugwell was concerned that the price-support programs discriminated in favor of large commercial farmers and actually worsened rural poverty in the South. The typical problem was that landlords refused to share parity payments with their tenants and sharecroppers, or worse, simply evicted them, because rental income was no longer necessary.[15] The Resettlement Administration and its successor, the Farm Security Administration (1937), were the chief federal programs aimed at relieving rural poverty. Legislation empowered these agencies to ease credit terms, sponsor educational and land-use programs, and offer long-term loans to tenants for land purchase, special aid to migrant workers and families forced off the land, and community planning.[16]

The government backed up its good intentions and new policies with vigorous administration. Secretary Wallace often spoke of his charge as "the new department" and the official historians of the Agriculture Department (USDA) bear him out: "The agricultural adjustment program transformed the Department from a research and educational institution into an action agency that directly assisted and regulated American farming."[17] In its role as an "action agency" the USDA grew rapidly, creating agencies and bureaus and absorbing heavy appropriations from Congress. Eight major agencies, designed to provide farm relief—the AAA, Farm Security Administration, Soil Conservation Service, Federal Surplus Commodities Corporation, Federal Crop Insurance Corporation, Rural Electrification Administration, Farm Credit Administration, and Commodity Credit Corporation—fell within the department's jurisdiction. USDA's annual budget jumped from $279 million in 1932 to $1.3 billion by 1939.[18] The department reorganized at the top, too. Tugwell was the USDA's first undersecretary and several economists and managers were drawn from universities and business to advise and administer the new policies.

One of the most important functions of the new department became the regular reporting of information. A beefed-up version of *Agricultural Statistics* was separated from the USDA's *Yearbook* and became a useful tool for policymakers and farmers alike. Indeed, more information has since been published about agriculture than about any other sector of the economy. A second significant feature of the new department was that the agencies created by the New Deal legislation required local administration. Thus the USDA actively involved itself in the agricultural industry, providing advice, information, research opportunities, and funds more immediately to farmers, without waiting to be asked.

The full impact of public policy on the recovery of American agriculture in the 1930s is difficult to measure because other factors contributed as well. Several authorities, for instance, claim that the droughts of 1934 and 1936, which wiped out surpluses, affected the recovery of prices as much or more than government action.[19] In addition, the research efforts of the land-grant universities, technological innovation, the recovery of other sectors of the economy, and the stimulus of World War II blended with the New Deal legislation to stimulate innovation and efficiency on the farms, and to bring about a better quality of life to farmers.

The land-grant colleges and universities helped out by working hand in hand with the USDA to expand research facilities and educational opportunities across the country. Research stations and extension services stopped trying simply to increase yields and began to address problems of marketing and the quality of rural life. Budgets and personnel in these institutions swelled enormously. The number of workers in the extension services tripled between 1920 and 1940.[20] Between 1930 and 1940, the number of students enrolled in agricultural programs in the land-grant institutions doubled (Table 5.1) Perhaps the most spectacular growth occurred in high school vocational programs. In 1917 164,200 students enrolled; twenty years later there were 1.5 million.[21]

The expanded services of the USDA and the land-grant institutions in the 1930s were visible everywhere in the countryside. Formerly isolated representatives of remote institutions, county agents became administrators of large staffs actively providing services and information to farmers.

New farm technologies also played a critical role in improving the farm situation. One of the ironies of New Deal policy is that farmers

**Table 5.1    Students Enrolled in Agricultural or Veterinary Science in Land-Grant Colleges and Universities 1915/6–1950/1**

| | |
|---|---|
| 1915/6 | 19,768 |
| 1920/1 | 16,831 |
| 1925/6 | 15,062 |
| 1930/1 | 14,827 |
| 1935/6 | 18,768* |
| 1940/1 | 28,607 |
| 1945/6 | 19,481 |
| 1950/1 | 40,815 |

Sources: U.S. Office of Education, *Bulletin*, (1927, no. 37), (1932, no. 210), (1947, no. 14), (1952, no. 2), *Circular*, no. 168 (1935–36), no. 206 (1940–41).

*No information available on graduate students enrolled this year. None are included in the total.

who were paid to restrain production and retire land invested that money in new techniques that actually increased production. Indeed, while farm population and acreage shrank, agricultural production grew 12% in the 1930s. Investment in labor-saving methods was largely responsible for this increase. The replacement of animal power by tractors, the application of chemical fertilizers and pesticides, and the improvement of seed varieties made possible a 28% rise in the productivity of each agricultural worker in the period.[22] Reductions in transport costs that followed the introduction of diesel-electric locomotives, widespread use of automobiles and trucks, and construction of new and better roads also stimulated production.[23]

Other types of engineering worked wonders as well. The U.S. Conservation Service, founded in 1935, sponsored the building of small dams to control streams and gullies, the planting of gully banks, and even the "Shelter Belt" scheme to plant trees as erosion-preventing windbreakers across the entire Midwest. Other conservation measures included contour plowing, crop rotation, and manuring, while the USDA made its expertise in irrigation available too.

With the growth of production in the 1930s came generally rising prices rather than the catastrophes of the previous decade. The reasons for this turnaround include the depopulation of the countryside, which contributed to a rise of per capita farm income, and the recovery of domestic and foreign markets. Certainly it is true that the restoration of the national economy in the 1930s and the market opportunities created by World War II greatly helped in improving the lot of the American farmer. Prices turned steadily upward in the early 1940s (Figure 5.1).[24]

## THE AMERICAN MIRACLE: THE AGRICULTURAL REVOLUTION

Together, these changes in public policy, the growth of public institutions, adoption of new technology, fortuitous climatic conditions, the recovery of the national economy, and the stimulus of World War II produced a revolution in U.S. agriculture, which we still feel and are only beginning to understand. By the late 1940s farmers no longer toiled amid the uncertain and perilous conditions of Area 3, but reaped the benefits of Area 2 and 5 conditions to increase levels of efficiency and innovation.

The New Deal planners had hoped to raise the standard of living on U.S. farms. Most of them believed that the agricultural sector could be restored to a more favorable balance with the industrial sector by restricting production and supporting prices. Few of them had any clear vision of the magnitude of social change they helped bring about. The farm population plummeted, farms grew larger and fewer in number, farm income soared, and the entire industry became continuously innovative and productive for decades.

### FARM POPULATION, NUMBER, AND SIZE

Every U.S. census since 1820 has recorded a decline in the ratio of rural to urban population. This movement accelerated quickly after the depression. In 1920, 30.1% of the American population lived on farms. By 1940 the figure was 23.2%; by 1960, 8.7%; and by 1979, only 2.8%. "Between 1929 and 1965," writes historian John L. Shover, "more than 30 million people moved away from American farmlands." More people left the farms in this period alone than had immigrated to America between 1820 and 1960 (Figure 5.4).[25]

In most instances the migration from the farms was voluntary, although many tenants and sharecroppers were forced off the land by federal policies that tended to favor large-scale commercial farming,

**Figure 5.4    Farm Population 1910–1980**

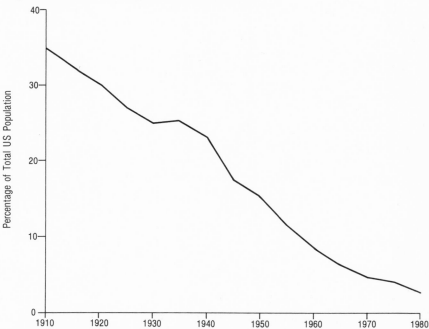

SOURCE: U.S. Bureau of the Census, *Historical Statistics to 1970*, series K1; *Statistical Abstract*, 1980, p. 685.

or by technological innovations that enabled farmer-owners to work larger plots of land. In general, farm workers left the land because material rewards seemed greater in the cities and because they were no longer needed to maintain levels of production sufficient to feed the population.[26] Farm tenancy dwindled to 26.8% of all farms by 1950 and by 1978 tenants comprised only 11% of the total farm population.[27]

The decline in rural population was accompanied by shrinkage in the number of farms and a corresponding increasing in average acreage per farm (Figure 5.5 and Table 5.2). In 1929 there were approximately 6.5 million farms, averaging 150 acres in size; twenty years later there were nearly a million fewer, each averaging over 200 acres. These trends — declining farm population and number of farm units, and increasing acreage per farm — have continued since the depression, although the curves turn sharply around 1945.

Contrary to the current popular notions, most U.S. farms have continued to be owned and operated by families even though capital investments and real estate values have grown very high. A recent study

**Figure 5.5   Number of U.S. Farms 1910–1980**

SOURCE: U.S. Bureau of the Census, *Historical Statistics to 1970* (Washington, D.C., 1976), series K4; *Statistical Abstract, 1980,* p. 686.

### Table 5.2     Number and Size of U.S. Farms 1920–1980

| YEAR | NUMBER OF UNITS (millions) | AVERAGE SIZE (acres) |
|------|---------------------------|----------------------|
| 1920 | 6.454 | 149 |
| 1925 | 6.372 | 145 |
| 1930 | 6.295 | 157 |
| 1935 | 6.812 | 155 |
| 1940 | 6.102 | 175 |
| 1945 | 5.859 | 195 |
| 1950 | 5.388 | 216 |
| 1955 | 4.654 | 258 |
| 1960 | 3.962 | 297 |
| 1965 | 3.356 | 340 |
| 1970 | 2.954 | 373 |
| 1975 | 2.767 | 391/427* |
| 1980 | 2.309 | 453* |

SOURCES: U.S. Bureau of Census, *Historical Statistics to 1970*, series K4 and K7; U.S. Bureau of Census, *Statistical Abstract, 1980*, p. 686.

*1975 and 1980 totals reflect changing USDA definitions of what constitutes a farm.

has concluded that "today farms are usually best managed by two men," although the optimum size and labor force vary from region to region and from crop to crop.[28]

### FARM INCOME

Farm income has lagged behind income in other sectors of the economy every year in the twentieth century except 1973–74. Nonetheless, in the decades following the depression farmers' income rose steadily. In part this increase reflects the growth of income from non-farm sources. With newer technologies, farmers can work their land in less time, and are free to work elsewhere as well. Since the late 1960s nonfarm income has actually exceeded farm income for the average farm worker. The rewards of farming itself have also improved over the years, however (Figure 5.2). For instance, between 1935 and 1940, per capita personal income of the farm population was less than $250 per annum from all sources. From 1970 to 1975 farm income averaged more than $4,000 per person. Such figures must be adjusted downward because of inflation, and the aggregate statistics obviously hide pockets of extreme affluence or poverty. Nonetheless, the general trend in farm income is clear: Farmers continue to make a better living.

Moreover, rural life offers many rewards beyond income. Farming is "not just a business," asserts an Iowa farmwife. "It is still a way of life."[29] Farmers often point to the satisfactions of working close to nature, of making things grow, of providing essential foods, as well as to pride of ownership and the opportunity to preserve traditional family values as reasons why they remain on the land. As for the quality of rural life, opinions flourish. Some extend and embellish farmers' own views and portray life on the farms as sort of a rural paradise; others see only endless backbreaking work and cultural isolation. When all is said and done, however, the comments of rural sociologist Lowry Nelson seem most sensible:

> The truth is that farm family life is neither all black nor all white. There are, of course, families who live sordid, pinched and miserable lives on the land, and on the other hand, many who come as close as the earth affords to meeting the ideal of the romantic's dream of rustic beauty. But, by and large, rural family life is comparable to life everywhere, mixing the bad and good, the joy and sorrow, the littleness and greatness that characterized human kind.[30]

### THE INNOVATIVE CYCLE

From the New Deal through World War II, expanding farm income and credit touched off a cycle of innovation. Farmers adopted new technology, reaped greater harvests, plowed profits back into more technology, and reaped still greater yields. New farm machinery made the most visible impact on farms, but new fertilizers, pesticides and herbicides, and new seed varieties also contributed to the great transformation of American agriculture.[31]

The machine with the most dramatic impact on farming, of course, was the tractor. Before World War I tractors were scarce, although greater numbers appeared gradually over the next decade. In 1930 nearly a million tractors plowed U.S. fields. In the decade after the depression (1935 to 1945) the number of tractors increased by more than 100,000 per year, and by nearly 200,000 per year after that. The number of trucks climbed at roughly the same rate; automobiles appeared on the farms even more quickly. Specialized machines such as cotton strippers and pickers, grain harvesters, hay balers, field ensilage harvesters, and milking machines came into common use in the 1940s.[32] The spectacular achievements of new machines obscured improvements made to older ones. Tractors became lighter while pneumatic tires made them more functional and energy-efficient. Redesign of farm implements led to faster speeds for plowing. Horses and early tractors plowed at about 1–2 mph; by 1940 tractors "did most of their work between 3 and 5 mph."[33] Moreover, new and better roads, changes in modes of transportation, freight handling, and food processing stimulated farm productivity as well.

Chemical and biological engineering also contributed to the agricultural revolution in America, especially after 1945. Scientists from the USDA and land-grant institutions synthesized new fertilizers, pesticides, and herbicides, while geneticists developed new seed varieties and boasted of such greater things to come as "the chicken of tomorrow." Farmers already understood the benefits of fertilizers and lime, consuming 11.5 million short tons in 1930. Consumption more than doubled by 1940 and more than doubled again by 1950. Hybrid seed-corn, first produced commercially by Henry A. Wallace in the 1920s, was widely adopted in subsequent years. New varieties of winter wheat appeared in Kansas in the 1930s and 1940s. The first hydrocarbon insecticide, DDT, was used in the United States in 1943; the chemical herbicide 2,4-D was first marketed in 1945. Indeed, many of these chemical and biological achievements were outgrowths of wartime and warfare experiments.

The contributions of technology to the farms after the mid-1930s seem endless. Mechanical power and biochemical research wrought a revolution in food production, enabling much less labor to yield much more bounty than ever before.

FARM PRODUCTIVITY

The benefits of farm technology combined with other factors to improve farm productivity either expressed as yield per acre or required man-hours. By the end of the 1930s, for instance, wheat yields averaged between 12 and 16 bushels per acre. After the war yields climbed steadily, reaching 27.5 bushels in 1958. Yields of corn, oats, barley, hay, potatoes, tobacco, and cotton followed similar production curves.[34] (See Figure 5.6 for the long view of productivity growth in U.S. agriculture.) In the period 1925–29 it required 10.5 man-hours to plant and harvest an acre of wheat, yielding an average of 14.1 bushels. By 1945–49 only 5.7 man-hours yielded 16.9 bushels. The pace of change has increased since then. Recent figures (1975–76) reveal that only 2.9 man-hours produce a yield of 30.4 bushels per acre. Once again the productivity of wheat farmers mirrors that of other producers. In 1900 one agricultural worker was required to feed seven people; by 1950 one worker produced enough for more than fourteen people. In 1976 one worker supplied enough food for more than fifty-six people.[35]

This revolution in farm productivity has had several important consequences. First, the gains were achieved not only with less labor but also with less land. Marginal land could thus be retired while total volume held constant or even increased. The second major consequence has been the growing importance of the export market to U.S. agriculture. Exports, which had declined during the 1920s and the depression, spurted up again during World War II, and continued to accelerate afterward. Throughout the 1960s and 1970s farm exports con-

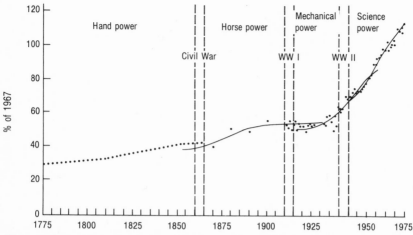

**Figure 5.6    U.S. Agricultural Productivity Growth During the Past 200 Years**
SOURCE: Yao-Chi Lu, *Prospects for Productivity Growth in U.S. Agriculture* (Washington, D.C.: USDA, Economics, Statistics, and Cooperatives Service, 1979), p. 10.

tributed substantially to the U.S. balance of trade, comprising about one-fifth of total America exports (Table 5.3). Agriculture is one of the limited number of industries in which we are clearly outperforming our trade partners. In 1981 the U.S. supplied Japan with 95% of its soybean imports, 82% of its corn imports, and 59% of its wheat imports.[36]

The retirement of farmland and the volume of farm exports generally held farm prices up and eased the government's task of maintaining high levels of farm income. In fact, starting with the Kennedy administration, farm policy became more a "food policy" with emphasis not only on protecting farmers in times of glut, but also the consumer in times of shortage, while letting the marketplace work as much as possible between the two extremes. As we shall see, the social consequences of the agricultural revolution are just as far-reaching.

## IMPLICATIONS OF THE AMERICAN MIRACLE

The great transformation in agriculture that the New Deal planners helped trigger accelerated trends in rural life already under way. Farm population and the number of farm units dropped suddenly and swiftly. The farms that remained grew larger and operated with much heavier capital investments and, somewhat ominously, a higher level of mortgage debt. Throughout the past four decades American farmers

**Table 5.3    Value of U.S. Farm Exports 1920–1979**

| YEAR | TOTAL VALUE (billions of $) | % OF ALL EXPORTS |
|---|---|---|
| 1920 | 3.9 | 48 |
| 1925 | 2.3 | 48 |
| 1930 | 1.5 | 32 |
| 1935 | 0.7 | 32 |
| 1940 | 0.7 | 20 |
| 1945 | 2.2 | 17 |
| 1950 | 3.0 | 30 |
| 1955 | 3.1 | 21 |
| 1960 | 4.5 | 24 |
| 1965 | 6.1 | 23 |
| 1970 | 6.7 | 16 |
| 1975 | 21.9 | 21 |
| 1980 | 41.2 | 19 |

SOURCES: U.S. Bureau of Census, *Historical Statistics to 1970*, series K251-2; *Economic Report of the President Transmitted to the Congress February 1982*, pp. 343, 348.

have led the world in agricultural productivity and innovation. Substantial changes are still unfolding.

The structure and organization of American agriculture have been shaped by government farm policy and by general economic conditions since World War II. Among the consequences of these factors and the trends discussed above have been the growing specialization of farms and the integration of the food and fiber industry. Farmers have tended to concentrate on the production of a single crop rather than mixing livestock and poultry with various commodities. As a result, farmers have left themselves vulnerable to commodity cycles and increased their liability in case of a bad harvest or other disaster. On the other hand, specialization has facilitated the adoption of modern business practices and the rise of "agribusiness," the linkage of producers, processors, and retailers, usually by contractual agreement.

Agribusiness—the systemic coordination of food and fiber production and distribution—is sometimes confused with corporate farming. It is important to distinguish the two concepts.

Corporate farms are owned and sometimes managed by corporations; agribusiness contract farms are normally owned by their operators and are legally distinct from the processing or marketing firms with which they do business. Corporate farming is less common than most people believe, while contract farming may be more common. In 1974, the latest year for which complete data is available, corporations and partnerships accounted for only a tenth of all farms, a quarter of all farmland, and a third of all farm sales (Figure 5.7).

These figures have alarmed some observers because corporate farms control disproportionate wealth for their number. Two points should be remembered, however. First, the vast majority of corporate

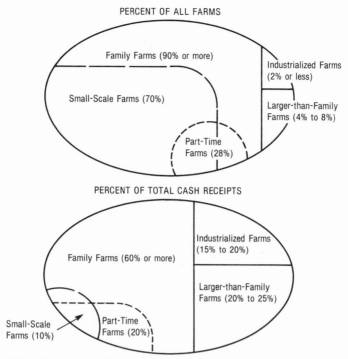

**PERCENT OF ALL FARMS**

Family Farms (90% or more)

Industrialized Farms (2% or less)

Small-Scale Farms (70%)

Larger-than-Family Farms (4% to 8%)

Part-Time Farms (28%)

**PERCENT OF TOTAL CASH RECEIPTS**

Family Farms (60% or more)

Industrialized Farms (15% to 20%)

Larger-than-Family Farms (20% to 25%)

Small-Scale Farms (10%)

Part-Time Farms (20%)

**Figure 5.7    Estimated Current Share of Number of All Farms and of Total Cash Receipts, by Major Farm Types 1978.***

SOURCE: U.S. Congressional Budget Office, *Public Policy and the Changing Situation of American Agriculture* (Washington, D.C., 1978), p. 22.

*These estimates are extrapolated from several sources and limitations exist with respect to both the data and the definitions. Revisions can therefore be expected as new data become available and special tabulations are completed. All farms can be classified, though somewhat arbitrarily, as either family, industrialized, or larger-than-family farms. **Family farms** are farms that use less than 1.5 man-years of hired labor and are not operated by a hired manager; **industrialized farms** use assembly-line production techniques and their capital ownership, management, and labor are highly differentiated; **larger-than-family farms** are nonindustrialized farms that use more than 1.5 man-years of hired labor. Farms can also be classified and defined according to their annual amount of sales or the annual number of days their operator is employed off the farm. In particular, **small-scale farms** are farms with annual gross sales of less than $20,000; **part-time farms** are farms whose operator is employed off-farm 200 or more days per year. The precise overlap between these two types of farms and the other types is not known.

farms in the mid-1970s were privately or closely held by families.[37] Tax benefits have been the chief motive to incorporate.[38] Second, large-scale "business-associated" corporate farming appears to be profitable only under relatively limited conditions. The largest corporate farms are located in Sun Belt states where the climate is relatively predictable. Moreover, they have been successful only with certain agricultural products, such as melons, tomatoes, tree nuts, pineapples, and citrus fruits, which grow in these reliable conditions, or with poultry and egg farming, which can now be done exclusively indoors. Large-scale corporate ventures have had little success in grain production or other types of farming. Indeed, after a brief period in the late 1960s, when conglomerates and large corporations invested heavily in agriculture — typified by Tenneco's 1970 pronouncement that its "goal in agriculture" was "integration from the seedling to the supermarket" — most have withdrawn to seek higher and safer returns elsewhere.[39] A USDA economist now estimates that only seven publicly-owned corporations whose primary business is not agriculture are investors in farmland.[40]

Economists apparently agree that there are no substantial economies of scale in most agricultural production: "In all but a few types of farming, well-managed one- or two-man farms can obtain most of the gains to be had from increased size, as measured by cost of unit of output."[41] The economic logic runs like this. New technologies, such as a more efficient tractor, make larger farms possible. For a particular tractor, then, there will be a particular farm size that optimizes efficiency. Beyond a certain size, the farmer can only increase output by adding another tractor and a hired hand to drive it. "And once a farmer gets much beyond two or three blocs of this nature," Mark Kramer points out, "he is so busy with organizational chores of managing personnel, allocating work and capital, marketing, hiring, and firing that he is no longer driving one of the machines. It is at this point that field efficiences begin to decrease." Or, as Ray Peterson, corporate farmer and economist, puts it:

> As you move from one man with a small operation doing the work himself, and doing the accounting himself, you incur the cost of professional managers. Also, a big farm can be too big for everyone to know everything. This sometimes causes operations to go wrong for a while. There was a case recently [at a very large corporate tomato farm] . . . in which the wrong pesticide was applied to eighty or a hundred and sixty acres, and no one stopped the operator. Economies of scale do stop when you get to the largest production bloc. After that, you proceed in multiples of these units. At a certain point, the cost of administering the multiples decreases the advantage of further expansion.[42]

If corporations are not likely to take the place of the family farm, contract farming may become more prominent. Agribusiness, as originally defined, is simply the application of systems analysis to the total food and fiber sector of the economy and it treats the farm as one element in a chain of organizations that produce, process, and distribute food[43] (Figure 5.8). In recent years, the coordination of the various elements in the agribusiness system has been tightened through the use

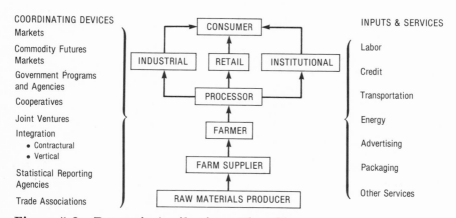

COORDINATING DEVICES
Markets
Commodity Futures Markets
Government Programs and Agencies
Cooperatives
Joint Ventures
Integration
• Contractual
• Vertical
Statistical Reporting Agencies
Trade Associations

CONSUMER
INDUSTRIAL   RETAIL   INSTITUTIONAL
PROCESSOR
FARMER
FARM SUPPLIER
RAW MATERIALS PRODUCER

INPUTS & SERVICES
Labor
Credit
Transportation
Energy
Advertising
Packaging
Other Services

**Figure 5.8   Domestic Agribusiness Flow Chart**

Source: Based on Ray A. Goldberg, *Agribusiness Sector* (HBS Case Services, 4-581-012), pp. 8-9.

of production and marketing contracts between farmers and their buyers. In part, this has been a necessary adaptation to increasing domestic and international commitments, although it is also a response to technological innovations that have supported food and fiber processing and marketing on a larger scale. Contract farming is still not very extensive, although it may be on the rise. It accounted for about 17% of total agricultural output in 1970 and 21% in 1974. Only 9% of farms with annual sales exceeding $2,500 participated in contract farming in the latter year. Like large-scale corporate farming, contracting networks are typically associated with particular crops, such as dairy farming, sugar beets, and poultry.[44]

Agribusiness contracts are sometimes criticized as symbols of the surrender of farmer autonomy to "nonfarm decision-makers." In fact, farmers have plenty of reasons to enter into contracts willingly, because by doing so they reduce their own risk and uncertainty and guarantee themselves an income and definite access to markets. Moreover, contracting is frequently managed through voluntary cooperatives. One-third of all contracts reported in 1974 were negotiated by farmer cooperatives and bargaining associations. In short, there is little evidence that farmers are exploited by agribusiness contracting.[45]

While corporate farming and agribusiness have become more pronounced since World War II, the more interesting organizational phenomenon is the survival of the family farm. As of 1974, more than 90% of U.S. farms were still classified as "family farms," that is, they were not operated by a hired manager and used less than 1.5 man-years of hired labor per year.[46] The typical family farm is growing larger and more heavily capitalized, spurred on by the innovative cycle and public policies that, like price supports, favor larger units. A recent USDA report (after much hemming and hawing about the methodological problems) presents this picture of a typical farm: The most viable farm has annual sales in the range of $40,000 to $99,000, assets of nearly $500,000 (70% of which are in land), 80% equity ownership by the farmer, and net cash farm income of $18,500 with $6,000 in nonfarm earnings and $34,600 unrealized capital gains on real estate. In addition, the USDA report notes that

> Today, many farming operations are combinations of rented units. It is not uncommon in the Midwest, for example, to find farmland owned by retired farmers and widows and heirs of farmers, but consolidated through rental into larger farming operations.[47]

This sort of consolidation is made possible by new technologies that permit farmers to work larger plots of land.

Today's family farm, of course, is far removed from the traditional family farm of decades past. As farms have grown larger and require more intensive cultivation, they demand new skills and sources of capital. Farmers and their families must be well versed in agricultural science and technology and in business management. Nonetheless, a small amount of labor suffices to run even a large, technologically advanced farm. The family farm, then, remains a prosperous organization with a continuing capacity for further growth. Its structure combines high integration with modest differentiation: Farmers coordinate a variety of specialized tasks and they mitigate their uncertainty by linking themselves into larger processing and distributing networks.

Like any great transformation, the revolution in agriculture has had negative as well as positive effects. The social consequences of rural depopulation have obviously been far-reaching. A leading rural sociologist, for instance, has shown that the great migration away from the farms between 1950 and 1970 produced a decline in services in the smallest communities.[48] Another study reveals poignantly the social changes in one rural town. In 1920, Ostrander, Ohio, a rural center near Columbus, contained a livery stable, two grocery stores, two restaurants, two barbershops, a bank, a drugstore, an opera house, a poolroom, a bakery, a small hotel, a machine shop, the railroad station, a new grain elevator, and one doctor. In 1970 Ostrander's population was nearly the same as fifty years before, although its citizens' average age was much higher. The town included only a branch bank, a filling station, post office, one restaurant, one barbershop, one grocery store, and one "general equipment chain store." For supermarkets, hardware, medical service, and the movies, residents must now go elsewhere. A town that once offered about fifteen economic services now supplies six or seven.[49]

It may also turn out that the technology that produced the agricultural revolution is a tool with a double edge. Farm machinery has become much more expensive and the pressure to adopt falls heavily on smaller farmers who can least afford it. As rural wisdom has it: "There's two kinds of farmers. There's the one that's got weeds and the one that's got money."[50] Between 1950 and 1975 the cost of farm machinery tripled; such indispensable items such as tractors may now cost more than $50,000. Energy costs, once an insignificant part of a farmer's budget, are an increasing concern as well. Such expenditures, along with high real estate values and current tax policy, have obviously raised barriers to entry in farming, as illustrated by the steady increase in gross farm debt. In 1960, for example, total farm debt stood at $24.8 billion; in 1980, the figure was $157.3 billion. This trend has been partially offset by inflation and rising real estate values, but the ratio of debt to assets has risen from 11.8% to 17.1%.[51] Entry barriers are also reflected by the increasing age of the farm population. Average age of farm operators rose from 48.7 to 51.7 years between World War II and 1974. Fewer young people enter farming because the capital requirements are so high.[52]

Moreover, as a host of environmentalist critics and consumer advocates point out, the costs of technology may be more than financial. Scientists have discovered that many pesticides and herbicides—DDT is only the most spectacular example—have deleterious effects that may outweigh their benefits. In 1974 the Environmental Protection Agency claimed that "virtually every American adult carries pesticide residues in his or her body fat. . . . The entire population of the U.S. has some storage of these chemicals."[53] U.S. farmers have become heavily dependent on chemical fertilizers, which, like farm machinery, cost more and more. Some of these fertilizers stimulate plant growth at the same time as they kill nitrogen-fixing bacteria found naturally in the soil. Other scientists worry about our gradual loss of top soil and the lowering of underground water tables. Well-known social critics like Barry Commoner, Ralph Nader, and George Wald, and organizations like the Sierra Club have lined up to attack features of modern farming. The early 1970s saw the birth of the "Agribusiness Accountability Project," formed to criticize what it calls the "inbred and even incestuous" relations between USDA officials, leaders of the land-grant institutions, and managers of giant food corporations.[54] Consumer groups have kept a sharp eye on government policy since the Russian grain deal of 1972, which immediately boosted bread prices to the public.[55]

Some people argue that we are now facing a farm crisis that looks dangerously like the one that plagued the country fifty years ago. It may well be that American agriculture is moving away from Area 5 toward Area 6 conditions under the pressure of increasing RS. Production costs are rising along with energy costs. Real farm profits were down to $13.4 billion in 1980, from $31.5 billion in 1973, and the near-term outlook is disturbing. Credit is becoming tight, break-even points are high, and gross farm debt is climbing with high interest rates. The Reagan administration is severely cutting back price-support programs. The dependence of U.S. farmers on foreign markets parallels that of the World War I years. American farmers are part of the world market, placed there by their own astonishing productivity, the volume of exports, government food policies like the Marshall Plan, Food for Peace, and the 1973 Agriculture and Consumer Protection Act. All these programs emphasize production rather than its limitation. Moreover, recent foreign policy has led the United States to commit itself to long-term grain deals abroad. As a result, American farmers are once again selling one-third of their produce overseas, and most of it at the world price rather than at the level maintained by price supports.

Furthermore, new technological developments may be unable to stimulate growth rates like those that followed 1945. There is a limit to what machines and chemicals can do, and there are indications that future rates of productivity growth may be slower than in the past. It is hard to see how payoffs from current USDA and land-grant research can match earlier results. Bioengineering, itself a highly controversial subject, may be the best hope and its impact is still some years away.[56]

Finally, there are increasing tensions between the still-Jeffersonian intentions of federal farm policy to preserve the family farm and the way that policy works out in practice. Current benefits are apportioned according to volume. Large-scale farms receive more aid than smaller farms. Continuation of current policies will therefore produce a continuation of current trends in rural population and farm size.[57] Big farms will dominate gross sales even more than in the past. Small farmers will face more pressure to meet capital costs and will be tempted to sell out to their larger competitors or to real estate speculators. At some point, the agrarian myth, increasingly at odds with agricultural reality, may die of attrition.*

## CONCLUSION

Farming has always been arduous work focused on production but it has changed dramatically in a number of ways in this century. Today's farmers need a familiarity with agricultural science and technology more than ever before. They must also acquire new skills in financial

*Congress clearly worries about this. In the mid-1970s, Senator Gaylord Nelson (Wisconsin) conducted hearings on the rise of agribusiness and warned of the dangers of increasing concentration in farming. Since 1978 the USDA has been required to submit annual reports to Congress on the status of the family farm.

management. With the spread of contracting networks, leasing arrangements, and cooperatives, farmers have had to develop more sophistication in business. It may even be that farmers will surrender their independent entrepreneurial roles altogether—although this is clearly an event of the far future.[58] Some even speculate that coming generations of farmers will be highly trained, specialized agricultural technicians rather than the home-grown inheritors of an agrarian tradition. But this bleak prophecy is not likely to come true, for, as a number of corporate investors have learned at great cost, one aspect of farming has remained constant over the years. Success still demands intense involvement and an almost spiritual dedication to the land itself. As a county agent in Idaho sums it up:

> The day of the hick is long gone. Farming is a real profession now. It demands a lot of man. I've never seen a good farmer who wasn't above average in intelligence. He has to know how to handle men, he has to be able to plan, and he has to be able to manage land—he has to understand the land. I've known potato growers to get a yield of three hundred and fifty hundred-weight to the acre and still go belly up. They were thinking yield when they should have been thinking quality. Quality is work. You don't get quality by sitting around the cafe drinking coffee at ten o'clock in the morning. You have to live with the crop. That's one thing that hasn't changed. The best fertilizer is still the grower's shadow.[59]

The risks of farming have been reduced but it still remains an uncertain business and the organizational structure most likely to survive is one that is designed to cope with the local vagaries of growing crops—the family farm unit, coupled with agribusiness networks to ease market uncertainties. It may be that America faces a coming agricultural crisis. One cause for optimism, however, is the historical performance of the family farm when freed from the extreme environmental conditions of Area 3. Past public policies helped shield farmers from oppressive RS and eventually helped moderate the high level of IC. This historical record is portrayed in our summary chart (Figure 5.9). With government help in the 1930s, farmers proceeded to assist themselves, reinvesting and purchasing new equipment, adopting new techniques of farming, and arranging contracting networks to reduce market uncertainty. Farmers have, by and large, moved from defensive to readaptive strategies.

The experience of agriculture in the past fifty years is truly the story of an American miracle. Today the chief hazard to farming may be a serious lack of awareness and understanding of this success story and its implications on the part of the general public and its representatives in Washington. Somehow the idea seems to be abroad that farmers are coasting on government handouts, that they are receiving unwarranted subsidies at the taxpayers' expense. In particular cases, of course, such

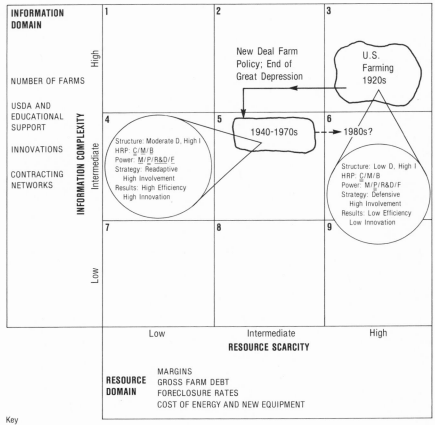

**Figure 5.9    Evolution and Organization of U.S. Agriculture 1920s–1980s**

charges are certainly true. But particular exceptions cannot be allowed to obscure the industry's overall record of high efficiency and innovation. We must recognize that agriculture is one of our healthiest industries. Every city dweller depends on farmers not only to put food on the table but to pay for a big chunk of U.S. imports. Another farm crisis seems to be looming on the horizon and failure to perceive what is at stake and the special needs of agriculture is alarming. The family farm remains the basic productive unit but it needs to be understood and supported. If fundamental change threatens this industry, then our farm policymakers in Washington might profitably take a lesson from their predecessors, the New Deal planners, who spurred this century's first agricultural revolution.

The story of U.S. agriculture bears many similarities to the subject of the next chapter, the residential construction industry. Both industries are highly fragmented, populated by large numbers of competitors. Both are characterized by traditional organizational forms—the family farm and the general contracting firm. Both have been buffeted by excessive competition (Area 3). The housing industry, however, has not enjoyed the sort of sustained liberation from extreme environmental conditions that the New Deal created for farming. Public policy, in the form of shifting interest rates, has subjected housing firms to periodic fluctuations in RS. Yet the industry has performed well in terms of our readaptive outcomes over the years. Let us look, then, at the organizational form that does so well in an unstable environment.

# CHAPTER 6

# Residential Construction: A Hidden Resource

THE BUILDING OF SHELTER, like agriculture, is one of humanity's oldest occupations. It is also one of the largest industries, at least in the United States. The most recent Census of Construction Industries (1977) reported that more than 100,000 firms transacted some $40 billion of housing business. Despite the industry's scale and revenues, however, the organization of most homebuilding firms has changed little over the centuries. A general contractor normally oversees the construction of houses—perhaps after designing them—while a small number of special trade subcontractors perform much of the labor. Housing, again like agriculture, did not follow the trends toward bigness, vertical integration, and oligopoly structure that affected other industries. Individual firms remain small and simple in terms of administrative coordination and the division of labor.

Because the organization of homebuilding has changed so little, the housing industry is often berated as outmoded and inefficient, resistant to new technology and innovation. When there are housing shortages it is common to hear cries for a "General Motors of housing" to mass-produce inexpensive homes. In fact, however, the housing industry has been continuously innovative and efficient over the years; it has achieved readaptive results. Furthermore, the growth of manufactured or industrialized housing has transformed some aspects of production in the industry during the past several decades. More building takes place off-site and labor has become increasingly productive. All

146

this has been achieved through an organizational form that probably evolved first in classical times and has been common in Europe since the Middle Ages.

Today's housing industry is largely shaped by its basic task and technology—it normally builds customized products—and by financial conditions linked to federal monetary policy. Homebuilding firms are able to adapt to these special circumstances over time because they are organized to ensure maximum flexibility. Small, simple establishments are often linked by subcontracting or less formal arrangements into a larger organizational unit that Robert Eccles calls "the quasi-firm."[1] The quasi-firm permits general contractors to employ a variety of specialized craftsmen as needed while maintaining centralized coordination and control. Thus, on a small scale, the typical housing firm replicates the differentiated and integrated structures of much larger, more complex organizations. The quasi-firm also balances power between general contractors and their employees and makes use of a variety of human resource practices to sustain the involvement of its members. Indeed, the residential construction industry, as a whole, has a remarkably strong record of sustaining all aspects of the readaptive process.

## TECHNOLOGY AND ENVIRONMENT IN RESIDENTIAL CONSTRUCTION

The organization of construction projects larger than one person can manage has probably changed little since the building of temples, coliseums, and aqueducts in classical times. Certainly since at least the thirteenth century in Europe, large-scale projects have been built by a designer/master-builder and a team of laborers contracted by trade specifically for the job. Masons and common laborers were employed under separate arrangements in the building of cathedrals and they were compensated at different rates. Similar organization, on a smaller scale, seems to have typified homebuilding in the past.

There have been few changes in these basic arrangements over the centuries. In the 1600s the function of the architect grew distinct from that of the builder, and with the gradual evolution of market economies in Europe, cash contracts became more common in construction. The term *general contractor* gained currency in the nineteenth century as the industry became more professionalized and its practitioners often acquired formal training in civil engineering. Then and now, however, most of the actual work of building has been carried out by subcontracted labor. Indeed, the trend toward increased subcontracting appears to be accelerating in the twentieth century.[2]

It is clear that the organization of homebuilding firms has evolved to match the peculiar characteristics of the product, the technology, and the marketplace.[3] Houses are in many respects so unlike most manufactured products that it may be misleading to refer to housing as "an industry" in the same sense that we speak of the automobile or steel industries.

First, houses are specialized and, except for mobile homes and certain types of manufactured housing, unique. Buyers prize features that distinguish one house in a development from another. Indeed, buyers usually specify what features they want in the houses they buy and also initiate the construction process. This sort of specialization in the product entails a diversity of technical requirements and expertise for the builder.

Second, the core technology of home building, like that of hospitals and farms, is site-bound. As James Thompson says, "In the construction industry, the nature of the crafts required and the order in which they can be applied depend upon the nature of the object to be constructed and its setting; including, for example, terrain, climate, weather."[4] Except for mobile homes, houses are stationary products, tied to local topographical, real estate, and market conditions.

Third, an irreducible amount of labor must be performed on-site. In recent years an increasing proportion of construction has occurred in factories, but the sheer size of most houses and high transportation costs make off-site assemblage impracticable. Houses with foundations must be built where those foundations are poured.

Fourth, houses are durable and costly. They normally represent the largest capital investment their owners ever make. They are expected to last for generations under a fairly stable line of ownership.

Fifth, demand for new housing is highly seasonal. This stems in part from the pattern of mobility in the United States — people tend to move during the summer. It also results from the extra costs of construction that winter imposes in some areas of the country.[5]

Sixth, housing is unusually susceptible to outside financial conditions. Unless it is an outright cash purchase, a person's decision to buy a house depends upon the availability of an acceptable mortgage. Because of this intimate relationship with federal monetary policy, therefore, construction activity follows fluctuations in the condition of the economy very closely.

Finally, housing firms depend upon outside research and development. Materials suppliers, tool and equipment manufacturers, engineering firms, architects, and universities produce most of the industry's innovations.

Residential construction is a volatile business characterized by cyclical fluctuations of demand and growing numbers of firms of all sizes. The number of contractors and large scale "operative" (speculative) builders in the industry has increased rapidly in the past decade. The Bureau of the Census, which has kept statistics on construction since 1967, records that a total of 72,573 firms produced single-family dwellings in that year. A decade later, the number had risen to 124,470—a 70% increase (Table 6.1). This increase in the number of firms occurred independently of growth in demand, because the average number of annual housing starts in the 1970s was only slightly higher than that of the previous decade. The typical firm is becoming smaller while competition among general contractors is increasing.

A glance at the number of housing starts in America since 1945 reveals the marked instability of the industry's environment (Figure 6.1). Housing is subject to short-term cycles of three to five years—there have been eight since 1950—in the volume of starts. The two most recent cycles have been the most pronounced. In 1972 the industry reached a record level of starts, nearly 2.4 million. Three years later the industry hit its lowest number since 1946, less than 1.2 million starts. Sharply climbing interest rates have made the 1980–82 slide deeper still with less than one million starts in 1981 (Figure 6.2). There seems to be little doubt that the cause of this extreme volatility lies in the interrelationship of the housing industry, interest rates, and the housing finance system.[6] Whatever the causes, the consequences are clear. In the short run, downturns may "lead to idle plant and construction equipment, to underutilized material manufacturing capacity, to homebuilder bankruptcies, and to unemployment of construction workers."[7]

Resource scarcity (RS), as measured by the housing cycle or fluctuations in the home mortgage interest rate, is thus very real.[8] Information complexity (IC), represented by the growing competition among housing firms, is intermediate to high. Innovations appear more fre-

**Table 6.1  Construction Firms and Receipts 1967–1977**

| | GENERAL CONTRACTOR PRODUCING SINGLE-FAMILY UNITS | | GENERAL CONTRACTOR PRODUCING OTHER THAN SINGLE-FAMILY UNITS | | OPERATIVE BUILDER | |
|---|---|---|---|---|---|---|
| | *Number* | *Receipts (billion $)* | *Number* | *Receipts* | *Number* | *Receipts* |
| 1967 | 59,336 | 12.0* | 4470 | n.a. | 13,237 | n.a. |
| 1972 | 90,207* | 23.2* | 7651 | 6.4 | n.a. | n.a. |
| 1977 | 100,993 | 21.3 | 4775 | 4.4 | 23,477 | 19.8 |

SOURCE: U.S. Department of Commerce, Bureau of the Census, *Census of Construction*, 1967, 1972, 1977.

*Totals include general contractor *plus* operative builders.

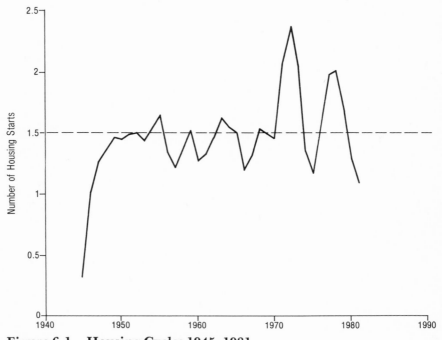

**Figure 6.1    Housing Cycles 1945–1981**

SOURCES: U.S. Department of Commerce, Bureau of the Census, *Housing Construction Statistics, 1889-1964*, Table A-1; Bureau of the Census, *Housing Starts*, Feb,
1982, p.3.

quently while greater competition creates new uncertainties about
products, technologies, and markets. Thus on our model, the housing
industry cycles between Areas 5 and 6, close to Areas 2 and 3. Area 5
depicts moments of expansion and innovation while Area 6 represents
contraction and the struggle for survival through increased efficiencies.

## THE ORGANIZATION OF
## HOMEBUILDING FIRMS

The size and organization of homebuilding firms are well suited to the
industry's exacting environmental conditions. An abundance of small,
locally based general contractors and special tradesmen is able to produce most housing efficiently. These widely dispersed firms are sensitive to local demand and financial conditions as well as to local building codes and zoning laws. Such factors, which vary across
geographical and governmental units as small as neighborhoods in

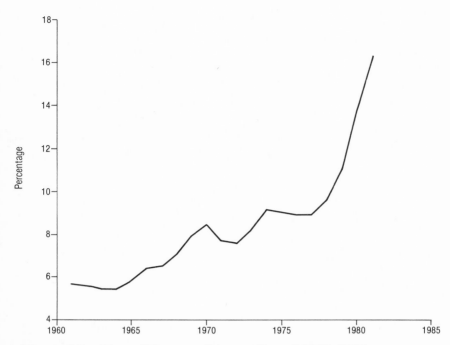

**Figure 6.2     Home Mortgage Interest Rates\* 1961–1981**

SOURCE: *Federal Reserve Bulletin*, various issues.

\*Conventional new home mortgage interest rates. Housing and Urban Development series.

some municipalities, make it difficult for housing firms to operate on a national scale. Thus more than 90% of the firms surveyed in the 1977 census of construction industries employed fewer than ten persons full time; far less than 1% employed as many as a hundred.[9]

Subcontracting is an organizational device that helps these small contractors cope with the industry's demanding environment. It allows them to survive periods of low demand and to employ labor efficiently when the economy improves. General contractors with small permanent payrolls can ride out seasonal slumps or recessions. On the other hand, they can respond quickly to new opportunities simply by hiring subcontractors. Subcontracting also helps contractors estimate and fix construction costs, thereby reducing an additional uncertainty.

Subcontracting is also an efficient adaptation to the uniqueness of houses. It frees general contractors from the burden of finding productive employment for all their tradesmen all the time. For instance, a contractor need not maintain masons on salary while building houses made entirely of wood. He is also relieved of training and sustaining new specialists when new techniques are discovered. Thus, in a peculiar way, the system facilitates the adoption of new technology. When a project requires a new technique, the general contractor merely seeks out a subcontractor who is properly equipped. Finally, increased subcontracting appears to be a response to the growing percentage of construction work done off-site. Many components of modern homes are factory-built and require only brief employment of specialized subcontractors during installation.[10]

Labor too generally prefers subcontracting to more rigid forms of organization.[11] Construction, unlike most manufacturing, requires skilled labor for a significant portion of the work. Carpenters, bricklayers, plumbers, and other skilled craftsmen have maintained a strong tradition of independence in their work for centuries. Prizing this autonomy, craft unions have generally resisted the employment of their members in most large-scale organizations.[12] Moreover, general contractors are typically themselves representatives of one of the specialized trades, often rising from the ranks of the subcontractors. Thus subcontracting reflects a historical accommodation between employers and skilled labor that has no parallel in the later development of manufacturing. Although the importance of unions in residential construction has eroded in recent decades, the tradition of independence lingers on. Tradesmen generally regard subcontracting as beneficial because they enjoy being their own bosses and the contractual relationship encourages them to achieve high levels of productivity.

Eccles has shown that subcontracting in construction is better suited to efficient production than is vertical integration.[13] The economic logic that confers greater transactional advantages to hierarchies than to markets simply does not apply in the housing industry.[14] The nature of homebuilding technology and the peculiarities of the housing market militate against hierarchical organization. Subcontracting helps general contractors cope with the cognitive limits that constrain all organizations as well as the special problems of homebuilding itself. Most attempts at vertical integration in homebuilding have failed for these reasons. We might also add that the historical conditions that fostered vertical integration in manufacturing and the beginnings of "big business" in the nineteenth century—the revolutions in transportation, communications, mass marketing, and mass production—obviously could not stimulate the growth of large-scale housing firms because of the characteristics of the product: houses are too large and complex.[15]

In practice, however, subcontracting occurs not as a pure market form but rather as a more stable informal arrangement. In a study now several decades old, Sherman Maisel observed that "practically no shifting of trade contractors occurs as the builder moves from one job to the next. He tends to work very closely with a picked group of subs and does not seek independent bids for each job."[16] Eccles lent empirical support to this view from a survey of approximately thirty small homebuilders in Massachusetts.[17] His research demonstrates that general contractors normally negotiate contracts with previous associates and actually resort to free market bids only about a fifth of the time. Even then such bids are often merely a test of "the going rate" for particular kinds of work. As proof of the prevalence of this organizational arrangement, the quasi-firm, Eccles found that general contractors tend to rely on a few subcontractors in each trade, to form long-term associations with those in the skilled trades especially, and to employ a high percentage of "labor-only subcontractors" (workers whose tools and equipment are supplied by the general contractor). In turn, these subcontractors seldom work for a single employer but rather a small set of general contractors with whom they establish long-term flexible relationships.

The quasi-firm, a hybrid between the pure market form and a hierarchical organization, serves particularly well to counter the uncertainties and complexities of the housing industry. General contractors are able to reap the advantages of subcontracting while also enjoying the security that comes with ongoing relationships. For similar reasons the arrangement appeals to subcontractors, who can count on regular sources of employment while maintaining their own independence.

## LARGE-SCALE HOMEBUILDING AND THE QUASI-FIRM

We have argued that three factors shaped the structure of residential construction firms: the characteristics of the product, the site-bound technology it requires, and the cyclical fluctuations of the housing market. The same factors militate against the predominance of large-scale housing firms and an oligopoly structure in the industry. The quasi-firm (with the exceptions noted below) appears to be the standard structure of construction firms regardless of type or size.

The Bureau of the Census classifies residential construction firms in three categories: general contractors of single-family units; contractors who specialize in multifamily units or apartments; and "operative builders," who are real estate developers or speculative builders. Most of these firms rely heavily on subcontracting. The advent of industrialized or manufactured housing since World War II has affected the organization of the industry only in certain markets. Mobile home manufacturers, which can produce shelters on a massive scale, have all but captured the market for low-income housing outside urban centers.

Similarly, in certain parts of the Southwest, manufactured-housing firms produce inexpensive conventional houses employing unskilled labor at factory wages while performing much of the construction off-site. Such strategies have so far been successful only in restricted areas, however, and, as we shall see, it is unlikely that there will be many imitators in other parts of the country. Moreover, techniques of industrialized housing are less useful in building large structures and manufactured-housing firms have been less successful competing in the growing market for multifamily units.[18]

Despite some economies of scale, large-scale manufacturers have not dominated the industry. The largest firm, U.S. Home, commands barely 1% of annual housing starts (excluding mobile-home manufacturers). Moreover, recent surveys suggest that large firms, while growing rapidly, are actually earning a shrinking share of the total housing dollar. *Professional Builder's* survey of firms with sales over $15 million shows a decline in share of housing starts from 27.5% in 1974 to 23% in 1980.[19]

In the most substantial study of the subject, Leo Grebler has shown that the effects of scale are not uniformly advantageous.[20] Larger size may permit the tract developer bulk purchase of materials at a discount, more effective and lower-cost marketing, greater continuity through housing cycles, opportunities for expansion into related industries, and lower costs of financing and land development. These advantages, however, are sometimes outweighed by the disadvantages of size, including different forms of administrative troubles. Overhead costs grow rapidly with size, as do strains on managerial coordination. Furthermore, large firms that operate across great distances face tricky problems in financial planning and dealing with local political, legal, ecological, and labor conditions. Some giant firms — U.S. Home, Centex Corp., and others — certainly prospered in the 1970s, but there were spectacular casualties, too. The fates of the Great Southwest Corp., Boise Cascade, and Levitt & Sons illustrate the perils of building homes on a vast scale.

It is significant that most discussions of economies of scale in housing have little to say about the construction process itself. Indeed, at the production level, the giants behave simply as large general contractors. "There is a good deal of careless talk about the bureaucratization of construction and the introduction of mass production by operative building of tract homes," Arthur Stinchcombe has observed. "The central innovation of operative building is in the field of marketing and finance rather than in the administration of production."[21] Some firms openly admit as much. U.S. Home, for instance, "generally acts as its own general contractor, entering into contracts with various subcontractors for the construction of its projects."[22] This firm considers itself "essentially a management organization."[23]

Very large homebuilders generally practice decentralized or coalition management, at least partly because of the historical pattern of growth in the industry. Most of the giants have grown by acquiring or merging with other large builders. This explains the apparent paradox that some such firms grew rapidly while the group as a whole was losing market share. Put simply, the giants who prospered did so at the expense of those who failed, and the most successful ones leave their subsidiaries largely autonomous.[24] U.S. Home, for instance, has been the largest on-site builder of single-family houses in the country for most of the past decade. Its 1980 sales exceeded $1 billion, while the company built more than 15,000 homes in 303 communities in 121 cities in 18 states (most of its business is concentrated in the Sun Belt). U.S. Home's product mix in 1980 consisted of 72% detached single-family units, with most of the rest made up of attached single-family units and some garden apartments and other construction. In contrast to most of its competitors, U.S. Home has not diversified substantially outside the housing industry; in 1978 89% of its total operating revenues came from sale of single-family units. The company's product, in the opinion of a recent commentator, is "functional, if aesthetically uninspired, and reasonably well put together."[25] In 1980 the average price of U.S. Home's houses was $66,800, substantially beneath the national average calculated by the Bureau of the Census.[26]

U.S. Home has grown primarily by acquiring smaller contractors and operative builders, which become divisions or profit centers in the parent corporation. The company allows considerable discretion to these local divisions. Before a new acquisition is made, U.S. Home and the prospective subsidiary sign a provisional agreement to work together for three years. At the end of that time the smaller company is free to go its own way, although apparently none has done so yet. The local company supervises construction while U.S. Home itself helps with accounting, tax and financial planning, cash management, internal auditing, insurance advice, marketing and sales training, land development, and construction management advice.[27] In addition, U.S. Home has understood that management recruitment and training are critical to its development. Indeed, the company attributes its success to the attention it pays to management.[28] It seems fair to add that U.S. Home's success also derives from its loosely connected organization, which replicates the quasi-firms typical of the industry in general.

At the project level most very large housing firms rely heavily on subcontracted labor. In fact, they function as giant general contractors, at the center of giant quasi-firms. Two recent surveys indicate that the use of subcontracting actually increases with the size of the firm. A survey by the National Association of Homebuilders found that 55.6% of freshly formed housing firms that produce more than five hundred units per year subcontracted 100% of their labor in 1976.

This figure contrasts with a 29.2% incidence of subcontracting in small firms that build fewer than ten houses per year.[29] *Professional Builder* (1979) revealed that its "large" and "giant" firms subcontract nearly 80% of their construction labor, while "small" and "medium" firms subcontract 57% and 72%, respectively.[30] The largest firms remain wedded to traditional construction techniques. As U.S. Home's 1974 annual report puts it, "Today we find conventional on-site building still produces the best quality home. We utilize factory construction methods only where they cut costs and improve quality."[31]

Subcontracting in these large firms differs in one important respect from that prevailing among small general contractors. Subcontractors employed by the giants often work exclusively for them. Since the relationship tends to be labor-only—that is, the firm provides tools and equipment and purchases building materials—the line between subcontracting and an employee relationship can be very fine indeed, as Eccles has commented.[32] The fact that subcontracting is preferred to a hierarchical arrangement nonetheless suggests that the quasi-firm generates greater efficiency, or at least greater profitability, as well as being a more adaptive organizational form.

If U.S. Home's growth can be traced to its management and operation as a quasi-firm, the converse is true of firms that have experienced trouble. The well-known story of Boise Cascade provides "the classic case of unsuccessful diversification into housing production and land development."[33] Originally a timber and wood products business, Boise Cascade grew rapidly in the late 1960s to become the biggest housing firm in the country. The company built products for all markets, from recreational vehicles to mobile homes to conventional houses to entire communities. It also invested heavily in real estate, some Latin American businesses, and timber reserves. Boise Cascade's strategy, evidently, was to become an enormous building firm integrated vertically from the forests to several consumer products.

In 1972, however, the firm suddenly collapsed, writing off $150 million in losses. Grebler has identified three causes of this catastrophe. First, Boise Cascade attempted to integrate a full range of businesses without a clear strategy for balanced growth among them. Second, the firm grew too quickly and was unable to find experienced managers for all of its activities. This problem was compounded in at least one case by Boise Cascade's inability to retain experienced personnel in an acquired company. Third, the proportion of realty liabilities in the firm's total liabilities was alarmingly high—between 40% and 42% in 1970. According to Grebler, the credit crunch of the late 1960s finally had its impact in 1971–72, when the company experienced critical shortages of cash. Boise Cascade was forced to divest some of its profitable operations merely to survive.[34]

It is clear, however, that the firm's disaster also resulted from poor management and poor organization. Given the product, technology, and market conditions, full-scale vertical integration of housing is difficult to manage. Looking back on the crisis, Boise Cascade's executive vice-president remarked, "You're competing with the independent builder who is willing to work for wages. We can't do that. A large corporation must also get a return on investment, and the economics (of on-site building) aren't sufficient to give a good return on investment."[35] The only way for big corporations to compete with quasifirms in this industry, it seems, is to adopt that form of organization.*

Successful examples of complete vertically integrated production of housing are exceedingly rare. The production system of Fox and Jacobs, Inc. illustrates both the advantages and the limitations of such a process. This Texas subsidiary of Centex Corp. experienced rapid and steady growth throughout the 1970s, specializing in single-family detached units in the $30,000 to $50,000 price range in Dallas, Fort Worth, and Houston. The firm employs unskilled, nonunion labor in factories to prepare frames, trusses, panels, floors, and ceilings. When all components are ready, Fox and Jacobs uses other unskilled workers paid at factory wages (roughly $6 per hour in 1978) to assemble the houses on-site. According to founder Dave Jacobs:

> We design our house and our process so you don't need real high skills. We don't need a man who's learned how to cut roofs and joists, how to build a window and order wood and do all the things a journeyman carpenter needs to know. Same thing for paint — we don't need a painter who knows how to mix paint and stain. They don't need — because of the way the work is laid out — to ask a whole lot of questions.[36]

The company is capable of turning out a house in three weeks, from frame to finished product, and builds more than five thousand homes per year. Such is the success of this system that Fox and Jacobs almost alone of large-scale builders was able to maintain growth during the slump of 1975–76.[37] The company has few imitators, however. Even Centex's other housing subsidiary, Centex Homes, constructs its product in the conventional manner. The reasons for Fox and Jacobs's unique performance are clear. In the first place, the company benefits from labor and real estate conditions peculiar to the area. Houston and Fort Worth are among the fastest-growing cities in the country, and builders there are relatively shielded from the effects of the housing cycle. Second, heavy transportation costs and the quirks of local laws limit factory production to small areas. Fox and Jacobs

---

*Thanks to the value of its other assets, Boise Cascade survived the crisis and, in addition to its extensive forest products operations, has since become a leading producer of manufactured housing.

has had to build factories in each of the three cities where it operates and so far, because of complex legal, environmental, and employment regulations, has been unable to promote its system outside of Texas. (Other firms, such as the Del E. Webb Corp., use similar methods in restricted markets elsewhere, however.) Third, factory-built houses have a strictly limited appeal, since a standardized product is unattractive to all but the lowest income buyers. The Fox and Jacobs system is unlikely to accommodate the demands of more well-to-do buyers or the variable conditions of other parts of the country. In effect, Fox and Jacobs pursues a "niche strategy" with a carefully defined market.

In sum, the organizational form typical of most large home building firms remains the quasi-firm. The quasi-firm has proved adaptable in markets regardless of scale of operations. The most successful of the giants employ what is essentially a franchise system of production, supplying national management and marketing services while allowing considerable discretion to its local divisions at the project level. This seems to be a characteristic of site-bound technology industries that have found an equilibrium in the conditions of Areas 2 and 3.

## READAPTIVE RESULTS IN
## RESIDENTIAL CONSTRUCTION

Critics have often ridiculed the housing industry's time-honored mode of production. "Housing is the one industry God forgot and the industrial revolution overlooked," asserts one advocate of mass-produced shelters. "No major part of our economy has been as backward as housing."[38] When demographic pressures build up, or when young people find it hard to purchase homes, as in the years following World War II, the late 1960s, and the 1980s, the housing industry is particularly scorned. In 1969 Department of Housing and Urban Development (HUD) Secretary George Romney planned a military-sounding "Operation Breakthrough" to produce more houses more quickly at lower cost. A recent HUD task force found that "the high cost of shelter" for many Americans "is not merely serious, it is too often an insurmountable crisis."[39]

The housing industry makes an easy target for its critics, although, as we shall see, it achieves better readaptive outcomes than commonly believed. Casual observation of the product and conventional indexes of productivity suggest that the industry is backward, inefficient, and resistant to new technology. Except for mobile homes, there is little mass production, and the house of today looks pretty much like the house of thirty years ago. Moreover, as shown in Table 6.2 prices of new houses have risen dramatically in recent years — more than 100%

**Table 6.2     Average Sales Prices of New Houses 1967–1980**

| Year | Price | |
|------|-------|---|
| 1967 | $24,600 | |
| 1968 | 26,600 | |
| 1969 | 27,900 | average change 3% per annum |
| 1970 | 26,600 | |
| 1971 | 28,300 | |
| 1972 | 30,500 | |
| 1973 | 38,900 | |
| 1974 | 42,600 | average change 9% per annum |
| 1975 | 48,000 | |
| 1976 | 48,800 | |
| 1977 | 54,200 | |
| 1978 | 62,500 | average change 12.1% per annum |
| 1979 | 71,800 | |
| 1980 | 76,300 | |

Sources: *Construction Review*, various issues; and U.S. Department of Housing and Urban Development, *Construction Reports, New One-Family Houses Sold and For Sale*, May 1981, p. 7.

in the last decade — and rising labor costs and production inefficiencies are frequently held to blame.

As if this were not bad enough, productivity growth in housing construction is generally reported to be low. Productivity can be measured in many ways, but none reveal more than minimal annual increases ranging from 0.5% to 3% per year in the period 1945 to 1970.[40] Comparable figures for other industries are hard to come by, but it appears that since 1955 productivity in construction has grown far more slowly than in manufacturing and agriculture.[41]

Economists and scholars who specialize in the construction industry consider such statistics misleading, however. The central problem in constructing productivity indexes, according to their view, is that units of output are not strictly comparable.[42] A house produced in 1980 has qualitatively different features from a house built even a year earlier. Even the best indicator available, the "Price Index of New One-Family Homes Sold" prepared by the Bureau of the Census, which attempts to hold certain factors constant, does not take into account improvements in size, equipment, and amenities.[43] Thus it seems that present indicators of productivity in construction are subject to considerable dispute.

A recent detailed examination of the productivity problem by economists Rosefielde and Mills, argues that the usual measures of productivity are biased downward and make the industry seem stagnant when in fact it is dynamic.[44] A more accurate statistical measure (a "quality-adjusted Lespeyres index") would raise the annual rate of improvement in postwar labor productivity from 2% to 5.2%, a figure roughly equal to the rate in other industries. "Thus instead of characterizing construction as a backward sector," the authors conclude, "we should view it as a quality-intensive industry in which the heterogeneity of the final product obscures and biases conventional quantitative estimates of factor productivity."[45]

This revisionist view is confirmed by other sources. After an analysis of the components of housing costs, the chief economist at the National Association of Homebuilders found that both materials and labor have declined as a percentage of total cost in the past several decades.[46] In 1949 materials and on-site labor accounted for 69% of the cost of a new house; by 1977 these two factors made up only 46.7% of the total. (Table 6.3.) In other words, most of the increase in housing costs is not attributable to the housing industry itself, but reflects the rise in land values and development costs. In addition, growing costs of financing, settlement, and closing now represent a larger part of the housing dollar.[47]

These findings indicate that, contrary to popular belief, the housing industry has become more efficient over time and is receptive to new technologies. Off-site manufacture of components such as walls, trusses, and electrical and plumbing cores have reduced costs throughout the industry. Houses are now constructed more quickly and more efficiently than ever before. Procedures have become standardized, more work is done off-site, and many parts of the actual process of construction have been mechanized. There have been important technological improvements in assembly methods (prefabrication of structural components, doors, windows, and cabinets), production aids (automatic gun-nailers, panel cranes, truss assembly forms, framing tables, sheathing machines, adhesives, and adhesive guns), and materials (prestressed and precast concrete, plastic and fiberglass assemblies, aluminum and steel frames). Computers and new management techniques have aided the design and scheduling of construction projects as well.[48] The sources of these innovations are to be found largely outside the construction firm, in materials and equipment suppliers and engineering firms, although large-scale manufactured housing enterprises have contributed some new technologies.

The product is constantly improving too. A study by the Bureau of the Census points out that contemporary houses, compared to houses built a decade earlier, are more likely to have central heating and air conditioning, more bedrooms, more floor space, more bathrooms, a full basement, a fireplace, and a two-car garage.[49] Furthermore, new homes tend to be more energy-efficient. New types of insulation, redesigned windows, increased attention to siding, and (in some cases) installation of solar panels for heating and electricity make the house of the early 1980s very different from the house of the past.

The residential construction industry is therefore both productive and innovative. That it sometimes appears to be stagnant and anti-

**Table 6.3    Distribution of Single-Family Home Costs by Major Category**

| | PERCENT DISTRIBUTION | | | | PERCENT CHANGE IN SHARE OF |
|---|---|---|---|---|---|
| CATEGORY | 1949 | 1969 | 1974 | 1977 | TOTAL COST |
| Land acquisition and site preparation | 11.0 | 21.4 | 24.6 | 25.0 | 127.2 |
| Structure | 69.0 | 54.6 | 48.4 | 46.7 | − 32.3 |
| Building materials | 45.0 | | | 30.0 | − 33.3 |
| On-site labor | 24.0 | | | 16.7 | − 30.4 |
| Financing | 5.0 | 7.0 | 10.0 | 10.8 | 116.0 |
| Overhead and Profit | 15.0 | 17.0 | 17.0 | 17.5 | 16.6 |
| Total cost | 100.0 | 100.0 | 100.0 | 100.0 | |

SOURCE: National Association of Homebuilders (1977) reported by Arthur P. Solomon, "The Cost of Housing: An Analysis of Trends, Incidence, and Causes," in Federal Home Loan Bank of San Francisco, *Proceedings of the Third Annual Conference: The Cost of Housing* (San Francisco, 1977), p. 17. Reprinted by permission.

quated is due more to the inappropriateness of conventional statistical measures and the cyclical instability of the market than to the techniques of housing production. This is not to say that the industry cannot be made more efficient and innovative. To ease the housing crisis, however, public policy and research might better focus on financial arrangements and rewriting building codes and zoning laws. There is little in the organization of homebuilding firms or the structure of the industry that retards the adoption of new technology or the use of efficient methods.

## ORGANIZATIONAL FEATURES OF THE QUASI-FIRM

It is very revealing to compare the typical organizational form found in the housing industry with readaptive manufacturing organizations. At a superficial level they have little in common. How can a handful of small independent contractors of various sorts, each operating out of a garage, a pickup truck, and a backroom office be compared to sophisticated organizations in a complex business environment? Yet a closer look at the residential construction industry reveals every feature of the readaptive process in place. We have looked at the environmental conditions that place these quasi-firms in the cycle between the upper edges of Areas 5 and 6. What about the internal factors?

Many clues about the internal conditions have already been discussed but they need a sharper focus. The key is that general contractors establish ongoing relationships with selected subcontractors. Predictability and mutual support grow out of these relationships that go beyond the strictly legal contact that governs any one job. But these mutual obligations stay fluid. Normally, the general contractor is not dependent upon a single plumber nor is the plumber dependent upon just a single contractor.

The quasi-firm achieves several useful organizational goals at once. First, as we have noted, it provides for a relatively high D and I structure. The general contractor integrates an extensive set of differentiated subcontractors, any portion of whom can be employed on a given project. Second, this form provides a built-in power balance between the top of the quasi-firm (the contractor) and the bottom (the subcontractors). Each side needs the other but is not totally dependent on the other. Each brings some chips to the bargaining table. Similarly, the horizontal power distribution among the various subcontractors on a given job is not rigidly determined by any vested interests. Subcontractors are normally treated as peers and if any one of them becomes more powerful on a given project, it probably reflects the importance of his skill to the task at hand.

The quasi-firm also incorporates an automatic mix of clan, market, and bureaucratic human resource practices. Consider that, while the legal form of the relationship is a *market* contract, the recurring nature of the relationship reflects clan bonds of obligation and friendship that go beyond legal requirements. This is the essence of the quasi-firm. The bureaucratic features arise naturally through the obvious need to keep track of time, materials, equipment, and schedules. All parties have to maintain some bureaucratic practices to regularize their work and maintain competitive levels of efficiency.

The final and probably most essential ingredient of the readaptive process is involvement. Both statistical and qualitative evidence show the quasi-firm, combined with the very nature of construction work, generates high levels of member involvement at all levels. It is common knowledge that construction work pays well and that members of the skilled trades command hourly wages that place them in the vanguard of American labor. As with agriculture, however, less tangible rewards are substantial motivators as well. *Professional Builder's* recent survey (1980) reports that home builders not only enjoy high incomes but like their work because it is creative.[50] "The tradesman considers himself in an artistic field," says Gil Wolf of the National Plastering Institute. "He takes a bunch of nothing and builds something from it." Other contractors quoted in Martin Mayer's book, *The Builders*, speak with the same voice: "Our business is a business and a hobby, too," claims one. "What's hard to grasp," concludes Mayer, ". . . is that this has been mostly a *pleasurable* occupation. Homebuilders get addicted to it."[51] Moreover, like farmers, builders enjoy being their own bosses and they relish their independence. This combination of motivating factors produces high involvement in residential construction, and this seems to be the factor connecting its structural form to its readaptive results.

## CONCLUSION

The story of the housing industry demonstrates that readaptation is possible in site-bound industries even when they are unusually vulnerable to economic cycles. When many simple firms and trades are joined into a fairly stable contracting network, the quasi-firm, readaptation can occur. The individual components of the network reflect the range and degree of differentiation required by the specific construction task, while the general contractor effectively integrates this set of firms based on prior working relations. The quasi-firm is, in effect, a high D and I form that is able to reconcile generally high efficiency with continuing innovation through the high involvement of its members. Figure 6.3 summarizes both the movement of typical firms as they swing with the business cycle and the organization form, strategy, and results that vary only modestly with the economic cycle.

The homebuilding industry has been unfairly maligned by critics who have been unable to appreciate its performance in an environment alternately bountiful and barren. The quasi-firm is an adaptive organizational form that, in combination with high involvement, can cope with the roller-coaster swings of the housing cycle. After all, Americans have reason to boast that they are the world's best-housed people, with two-thirds of all heads of households owning their own homes. Yet the severity of the most recent cycles is disturbing. Can even this resilient industry sustain itself in the face of such pressures? Can it continue to be readaptive? As with agriculture, the threat to the homebuilders is largely a lack of public and governmental understanding of how the industry has, in fact, performed so well. High interest rates may be a necessary part of the cure for inflation, but government policymakers need to be aware that the home construction firms are absorbing a disproportionate amount of the resulting punishment. Government policy inevitably plays a major role in the readaptive process. Residential construction has been a healthy and productive industry to date, but severe environmental conditions in Area 3 may be too much even for the flexibile quasi-firm to overcome.

We have now completed the last of three studies of site-bound, fragmented industries that populate the higher part of our nine-area model. A common theme has been the importance of contracting networks to mitigate high IC and help promote readaptive outcomes.

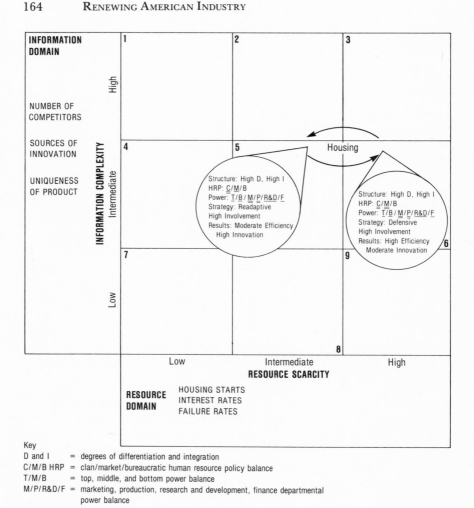

Key
D and I        = degrees of differentiation and integration
C/M/B HRP   = clan/market/bureaucratic human resource policy balance
T/M/B         = top, middle, and bottom power balance
M/P/R&D/F  = marketing, production, research and development, finance departmental
                    power balance

Underline indicates weight

**Figure 6.3    Movement and Organization of a Typical Quasi-Firm in the Residential Construction Industry**

Multihospital systems represent a rudimentary form of this approach; agribusiness contracting is somewhat older, while the housing quasi-firm is the fullest and most mature example of the high D and I structure on a small scale. These studies also suggest that Area 1 organizations have a poor record of efficiency, while Area 3 conditions tend to thwart innovation. Involvement tends to be high in these industries, although the hospital industry is a partial exception because of the professional domination of doctors. Finally, public policy has had a considerable impact on the pattern of organization as well as on the outcomes in all three of these industries.

Our next study shifts attention from the industries facing high levels of information complexity to one that faced very different environmental conditions for most of its history. Coal producers, beset by declining demand and formidable obstacles to the use of coal, were mired in Area 9 conditions—low IC and high RS—from the turn of the century to the past decade. Since the first energy crisis, however, the fortunes of most coal companies have changed for the better. A once unattractive product in declining use has become an increasingly valuable industrial fuel. A once-stagnant industry has found new markets and attracted new investment. How well the coal industry is coping with its changed circumstances, its new opportunities, and its managerial choices is the subject of the next chapter.

# CHAPTER 7

# Coal: The Born-Again Industry

THE UNITED STATES is often described as the "Saudi Arabia of coal," sitting atop one of the largest proven energy reserves in the world. For most of this century, however, coal has been in declining use. After about 1900, when coal supplied 90% of our national energy needs, coal's importance as an energy resource slowly faded. In 1974, for instance, coal accounted for less than 20% of total U.S. energy consumption. In recent years enormous increases in the price of imported oil have reversed this trend and the fortunes of coal have begun to look up. Indeed, President Carter's National Energy Plan (1977) called for coal production to increase by more than 80% by 1985, from 660 million tons to 1.2 billion tons annually.

There is now an abundant literature showing why such goals will be difficult to achieve. This literature focuses principally on how industry growth is inhibited by problems related to the consumption of coal—a dirty, messy fuel, awkward to transport, handle, and burn. Far less attention has been paid so far to problems in coal production, which include mining technologies that have reached their limits and a labor force that has been divided and restive over the years. One of the most critical problems of coal production has hardly been noticed: Is there enough managerial talent in the industry capable of directing the resurgence of coal? Does the industry as presently structured possess the organizational capacity to meet public expectations or objectives? The

166

coal industry has spent most of the twentieth century facing conditions of high resource scarcity (RS) and low information complexity (IC). An organization that has adapted and survived in these unusual circumstances may not be suitable for the different environment that the 1970s and 1980s have brought. Indeed, the history of the coal industry poses in vivid relief our central concern with the adaptability of organizations in a dynamic economy.

## HISTORY AND STRUCTURE OF THE U.S. COAL INDUSTRY

The amount of coal underlying the United States is normally expressed in numbers so staggering — trillions of tons or quadrillions of BTUs — that they are difficult to comprehend. It is perhaps easier to grasp the size of U.S. coal reserves in other ways. Roughly 13% of the country sits above a coalfield. There is enough coal presently identified in the ground to sustain our current rate of production (roughly 700 million tons annually) for at least two hundred and possibly five hundred years.[1]

There are four major coal-producing regions in the country, the Appalachian Mountains, the plains of the Midwest, the Rocky Mountains, and the northern plains of Wyoming, Montana, and the Dakotas (Figure 7.1). About 60% of U.S. reserves lie in regions west of the Mississippi River. American coal occurs in several types and grades. The cleanest-burning and most energy-intensive form, anthracite, is unfortunately rarest in nature. Most of our coal is of the softer bituminous type. There are many grades of bituminous coal distinguished by sulfur, BTU content, and combustion properties. The least satisfactory type of coal is lignite, a substance low in energy content but plentiful in Texas and the Dakotas, where it is marginally economical to mine.

Coal has traditionally been used in two principal ways: "steam coal" is burned directly for heat or conversion of energy; "metallurgical" or "coking coal" (bituminous grades) is treated to produce coke, an important ingredient in the manufacture of steel. In addition, a number of valuable by-products are produced from coal, including synthetic fibers and plastics, even aspirin. In recent decades another new application has been found for coal: synthetic liquid fuel and synthetic gas (synfuels) from coal have potentially a wide range of commercial uses.

The United States has hardly begun to tap its vast coal resources. There has been nothing exotic or promising about the traditional use of coal in this country. It simply has been ripped from the earth, transported, and burned. Coal became the major source of the nation's en-

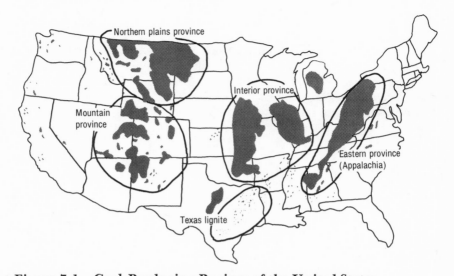

**Figure 7.1     Coal-Producing Regions of the United States**

SOURCE: Martin B. Zimmerman, *The U.S. Coal Industry: The Economics of Policy Choice* (Cambridge, Mass.: MIT Press, 1981), p. 4.

ergy during the second half of the nineteenth century, when the industry grew with the spreading use of the steam engine. Coal fueled the industrial revolution and the expansion of America's railroad network. Its importance as an industrial, transportation, and residential fuel peaked around 1900, when coal supplied nearly 90% of the country's total energy demand (Figure 7.2). After the turn of the century, however, the relative advantages of oil and natural gas created trouble for the coal industry. While total production continued to expand with the growing U.S. economy until 1918, coal's share of total energy consumption fell steadily to a low point in 1974. Since then its fortunes have improved slowly and, according to some projections, coal will furnish about one-third of our energy needs by the year 2000.[2]

Declining demand is the salient fact about the U.S. coal industry through most of its history. Its once-great customers, the railroads and industry, have either faded themselves or turned elsewhere for energy supplies. Despite the great expansion of the U.S. economy in this century, only 8% more coal was mined in 1974 than in 1920. Electric utilities have been the industry's one steady customer over the years, though even this relationship has been precarious at times. In the early 1960s, for instance, the prospect of a coming age of nuclear power spread gloom throughout the coal industry which has only recently been dispelled. Until 1973, the coal industry's profitability was generally poor. A study prepared for the U.S. Bureau of Mines reported that

**Figure 7.2  Consumption of Coal as a Percentage of Total U.S. Energy Consumption 1850–1980**

SOURCE: U.S. Bureau of the Census, *Historical Statistics of the United States, Colonial Times to 1970* (Washington, D.C., 1976), series M83–85; *Statistical Abstract of the United States, 1980* (Washington, D.C., 1980), p. 602.

the coal companies earned very low rates of return between 1951 and 1972, an average of 1.2 or 1.3%. These figures are well below those found in other mining industries.[3]

Coal's dubious investment potential is one of several reasons why the industry did not become concentrated in an oligopoly of large producers. The vast dispersion of coalfields across the nation also works against industry concentration. Not only is it nearly impossible for a small group of companies to control all this territory, but the very abundance of coal has made it easy for small producers to enter the business. Thus, almost from the beginning, hordes of companies have competed in the coal industry. In the nineteenth century there was a brief period of concentration in the industry when the railroads were both the largest consumer and the only means of transportation out of the coalfields.[4] The subsequent decline of the railroads permitted independent coal producers to regain lost territory and opened up a fierce competitive struggle for remaining customers. In West Virginia alone, the number of mines shot up from 325 in 1900 to 2,102 in 1920.[5]

The coal industry has remained fragmented ever since. At last count nearly 4,000 companies operated some 6,200 mines in the United States. As Table 7.1 shows, no firm or group of firms has been able to dominate the industry. The great majority of these coal companies are small operations producing less than 100,000 tons per year. Moreover, the market shares of the top companies have been declining in recent years. From 1950 to 1970 it appeared that an oligopolistic structure might form, but since 1970 industry concentration has decreased. The U.S. Department of Justice, required by law to investigate the state of competition in the industry annually, has repeatedly concluded that there is no danger of monopolistic concentration or restrictive practices. Even when the country is divided into regional markets (a reasonable framework of analysis in light of coal's transportation problems) no single firm or group of firms is dominant.[6]

There is yet a third reason for the coal industry's fragmentation: the nature of mining technology and the low capital requirement necessary for a coal company to get started. Traditionally, all that a prospective producer needed to enter the business was some land, a pick, and a shovel. Miners worked alone or with a single partner and attacked the coal seam in whatever manner and for however long they pleased. By these primitive means, miners in the nineteenth century could dig out one to three tons per day, depending on the accessibility and consistency of a coal seam.[7]

New technologies changed the nature of mining only slowly. Big investors, therefore, enjoyed few advantages over their smaller rivals.

**Table 7.1    National Coal Production Concentration Ratios 1950–1980**

| YEAR | PERCENTAGE OF TOTAL COAL PRODUCTION ACCOUNTED FOR BY THE LARGEST | | |
|---|---|---|---|
| | Four Firms | Eight Firms | Twenty Firms |
| 1950 | 13.6 | 19.4 | 30.4 |
| 1955 | 17.8 | 25.5 | 39.6 |
| 1960 | 21.4 | 30.5 | 44.5 |
| 1965 | 26.6 | 36.3 | 50.1 |
| 1970 | 30.2 | 40.7 | 56.5 |
| 1975 | 26.4 | 36.2 | 50.6 |
| 1976 | 25.1 | 34.2 | 49.7 |
| 1977 | 22.9 | 30.6 | — |
| 1978 | 20.9 | 28.0 | — |
| 1979 | 22.4 | 30.7 | — |
| 1980 | 21.2 | 29.7 | — |

SOURCES: U.S. General Accounting Office, *The State of Competition in the Coal Industry* (Washington, D.C., December 30, 1977), p. II-6; *1981 Keystone Coal Industry Manual* (New York: McGraw-Hill, 1981), p. 714.

Mechanized cutting machines, introduced in the 1880s, became universal only in the 1950s. Mechanical loaders first appeared in the 1920s and likewise spread slowly through the industry, reaching a high level of use only in the 1950s (Table 7.2). The growth of strip mining depended upon the development of the steam power shovel, a technology too expensive for most coal operators to afford. Invented in the 1870s, the steam shovel found less immediate use in the coal industry than in the mining of copper and metallic ores. As late as 1940 strip mining accounted for less than 10% of bituminous coal output and it only surpassed underground mining in production in the 1970s.[8] Gradual mechanization also meant slow improvement in productivity in the coal industry—between 2% and 3% per year until the 1950s, with somewhat more rapid increases in the next decade as strip mining became more prominent (Figure 7.3).

The historical conditions of declining demand, a fragmented but competitive industry, and the slow diffusion of technology have greatly affected patterns of organization and employment in the industry. Most companies managed well with a small hierarchical structure because of the simple nature of the coal business and its undifferentiated product. Since production scheduling was tied to market prices, central offices had little work to perform and little need of sophisticated management.[9] Of course, new technologies altered the actual work of coal production. Before mechanization, miners had been fully responsible for choosing where, how, and how long to work under a piece-rate system. All this changed with the introduction of mechanical cutters and loaders. Miners began to work under management supervision in groups around cutting and loading machines. Moreover, coordinating activity across several coal faces in a single mine led to specialization of work. Individual miners no longer performed a variety of functions but instead tended to concentrate on a single task, like fixing timbers, working with explosives, running the machines, or loading coal.[10] As mining became a less-skilled job, minors lost proprietary interest in their work.[11] Now more tightly controlled by supervisors and managers, the work also became less well paid and less secure because of the economics of the industry. Mining was a filthy and dangerous job as well. Between 1906 and 1935 nearly 1,600 miners died on the job annually.[12] These conditions, added to the marginal finances of the small operators, contributed to the exploitation of the miners.

The same factors that shaped the miner's job—lack of growth, industry fragmentation, unskilled tasks—impeded unionization of the coal industry. While a number of local and regional unions formed in the nineteenth century and the national United Mine Workers (UMW) was founded in 1890, labor did not gain a secure foothold until the 1920s and 1930s under the leadership of John L. Lewis. Brutal and

**Table 7.2  Production of Bituminous Coal by Mining Methods 1900–1980**

| Year | Total Production (thousand short-tons) | Surface Mines Production % of total | Underground Production Mechanically Cut (%) | Underground Production Mechanically Loaded (%) |
|---|---|---|---|---|
| 1900 | 212,316 | — | 24.9 | — |
| 1905 | 315,063 | — | 32.9 | — |
| 1910 | 417,111 | — | 41.7 | — |
| 1915 | 442,624 | 0.6 | 55.3 | — |
| 1920 | 568,667 | 1.6 | 60.7 | 1.2 |
| 1925 | 520,053 | 3.2 | 72.9 | 1.2 |
| 1930 | 467,526 | 4.2 | 81.0 | 10.5 |
| 1935 | 372,373 | 6.3 | 84.2 | 13.5 |
| 1940 | 460,772 | 9.4 | 88.4 | 35.4 |
| 1945 | 577,617 | 19.0 | 90.8 | 56.1 |
| 1950 | 516,311 | 23.9 | 91.8 | 69.4 |
| 1955 | 464,633 | 24.8 | 88.1** | 84.6 |
| 1960 | 415,512 | 29.5 | 67.8 | 86.3 |
| 1965 | 512,088 | 32.3 | 53.9 | 89.2 |
| 1970 | 602,932 | 40.5 | 46.1 | 97.2 |
| 1975 | 648,438 | 54.8 | 32.0 | 99.8 |
| 1978 | 665,127 | 63.6 | 25.0 | 99.9 |
| 1979 | 776,299 | 58.7 | — | — |
| 1980* | 830,000 | 69.7 | — | — |

SOURCES: U.S. Bureau of Mines, *Minerals Yearbook*, various years, and U.S. Department of Energy, Energy Information Administration, *Bituminous Coal and Lignite Production and Mine Operations—1978* (Washington, D.C., June 16, 1980), pp. 45–46. *1981 Keystone Coal Industry Manual* (New York: McGraw-Hill, 1981), p. 713.

*1980 totals preliminary
**Declining totals indicate replacement of mechanical cutting machines by continuous mining machines, which combine cutting and loading.

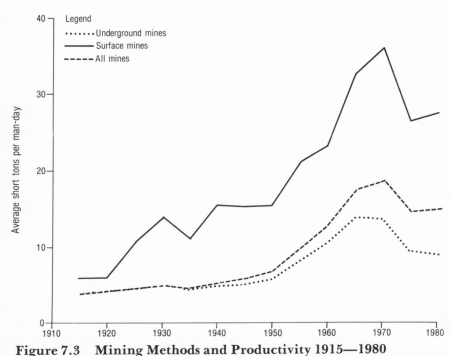

**Figure 7.3   Mining Methods and Productivity 1915—1980**

Source: Congressional Research Service, *The Energy Fact Book: Data on Energy Resources, Reserves, Production, Consumption, Prices, Processing, and Industry Structure* (Washington, D.C., November 1980), p. 552; *1981 Keystone Coal Industry Manual* (New York: McGraw-Hill, 1981), p. 713.

bloody confrontations punctuated the union's early struggle for recognition and established a pattern of violence that has endured ever since. In the 1913 "massacre" in Ludlow, Colorado, three miners, two of their wives, and eleven children were killed by National Guardsmen. Sporadic guerrilla wars between strikers and operators in southern Illinois; in Harlan County, Kentucky; and in several counties along the Tug River in West Virginia were common in the 1920s and 1930s.[13] The UMW managed to organize some major coalfields in the East in the 1920s, but its real success came with the New Deal and the establishment of the National Labor Relations Board. By the mid-1930s Lewis's UMW represented about 90% of the nation's 430,000 miners, a considerable achievement in such a widely dispersed and marginally profitable industry. The legacy of bitterness between management and labor lives on, however, and strikes and frequent violence have attended virtually every national contract settlement in this century.

John L. Lewis was an unusual labor leader, to say the least.[14] His vision extended beyond the immediate needs of the miners, to the health of the industry itself. Lewis recognized that the coal business needed technological advances, consolidation into larger units, and lower levels of employment. Only after these changes were made, Lewis believed, would the lot of the individual miner improve. "Shut down 4,000 coal mines, force 200,000 miners into other industries, and the coal problem will settle itself," declared Lewis in 1923.[15]

Lewis was not in a position to pursue this program until after World War II, however. In the late 1940s, after a series of long, bitter strikes and shutdowns, the UMW won the right to establish a welfare and retirement fund from royalties on each ton of coal produced or each hour of labor performed. This fund, designed to pay for the miners' medical care, insurance, unemployment compensation, and pensions, had two important effects besides immediately benefitting members of the UMW. It further eroded the margins of smaller producers and forced some bankruptcies and consolidations. In addition, Lewis used the proceeds of the fund, kept in a Washington bank owned by the UMW, to make loans to larger coal companies for the speedier adoption of new technologies and for the outright purchase of smaller coal companies.[16]

The effects of these actions were dramatic. Between 1950 and 1970 (when the practice was stopped) the four-firm, eight-firm, and twenty-firm concentration ratios in the industry nearly doubled (Table 7.1). At the same time, continuous miners quickly replaced older cutting machines (Table 7.2), strip mining became more common, productivity tripled (Table 7.3), and membership in the UMW plummeted. In 1950 some 416,000 miners carried union cards; when Lewis retired in 1959 there were only about 180,000 members left on the rolls.[17] Just before his retirement, when a reporter asked Lewis if the UMW cooperated with the industry, Lewis snorted:

> The United Mine Workers not only cooperates with the operators on that—we invented the policy. We've encouraged the leading companies in the industry to resort to modernization in order to increase the living standards of the miner and improve his working conditions. . . . It's true there aren't as many miners. But those young men who have been absorbed in other industries are better off than working in a coal mine far underground.[18]

Whatever one makes of the legality or propriety of John L. Lewis's management of the UMW welfare and retirement fund—at the very least, it represented a conflict of interest and set a dangerous precedent for his less scrupulous successors—it was in one sense an act of great industrial statesmanship. At a time when the coal companies and the government were neither able nor inclined to help a stagnant industry, Lewis used UMW money and power to improve the lot of miners and operators alike.

During most of the twentieth century the coal industry has faced a very hostile environment, stiff competition for diminishing markets, low profitability, and low rates of efficiency and innovation. These conditions—high RS and low IC—are characteristic of Area 9. Simple bureaucracies, poor working conditions, and labor exploitation typified most firms struggling to survive in the industry. Lewis's controversial actions of the 1950s improved the coal industry's fortunes, although they could not alter them fundamentally. That depended upon other developments. Changing patterns of ownership, the advent of government intervention, and the energy shocks of the 1970s propelled the industry from Area 9 to Area 5, where new opportunities and challenges lay waiting.

## COAL'S CURRENT CHALLENGE

Hopes for the coal industry have risen dramatically in the past decade. Since the mid-1960s the big oil companies have been investing in coal by buying up independent companies and reserves. While horizontal integration of the "energy" industry is a controversial development, new ownership opens up the potential of new skills, new technologies, and new markets to the coal business, thereby increasing IC. Both IC and RS have been increased by federal regulation of land use, air and water quality, and safety as well. The biggest jolt of all, of course, came with the oil shock of 1973. Between 1973 and 1977 the price of coal increased nearly 140%. Suddenly coal was once more a competitive source of energy, freed at a single stroke from the oppressive RS of Area 9.

The industry now faces the potentially rewarding conditions of Area 5 under intermediate IC and RS. Coal producers at last have some room to pursue readaptive strategies. It is not at all clear that they will do so, however, for the increased use of coal still faces serious obstacles. Problems with the increased production and consumption of coal have been discussed at length elsewhere and we shall do no more than summarize them here.[19]

In the first place, coal operators' incentives to increase production are uncertain. Since the early 1960s large independent coal companies have lost ground to owners from other primary industries. Indeed, of the top fifteen coal producers in 1980 only three were independent; five were owned or partly owned by energy companies, and three by conglomerates (Table 7.3). These developments raise an intriguing set of issues. The energy giants possess the capital and management skills to upgrade coal production and increase both innovation and efficiency considerably. The costs of gasification and liquefaction pro-

**Table 7.3  Top 15 Coal Producers and Parent Companies 1980**

| Company | Tonnage | Status* | Ownership |
|---|---|---|---|
| 1. Peabody Group | 59,083,123 | d | Newmont Mining Co., Williams Co., Bechtel Corp., Fluor Corp., Equitable Life Insurance Society, and Boeing |
| 2. Consolidation Group | 48,955,000 | e | Continental Oil, Du Pont |
| 3. AMAX Group | 40,547,065 | d | AMAX, Inc., Socal |
| 4. Texas Utilities | 27,590,768 | u | Texas Utilities |
| 5. Island Creek Group | 20,017,040 | e | Occidental Petroleum |
| 6. Pittston Group | 17,775,693 | i | Pittston Corp. |
| **7. NERCO Group | 16,900,000 | u | Pacific Power & Light Co. |
| 8. Arch Mineral | 15,818,000 | e | Ashland Oil, Hunt Oil |
| **9. U.S. Steel | 14,223,502 | s | U.S. Steel Corp. |
| **10. Amer. Elec. Power | 14,052,665 | u | American Electric Power |
| 11. Peter Kiewit Group | 13,450,000 | d | Peter Kiewit Group |
| 12. North Amer. Group | 12,669,521 | i | North American Coal Corp. |
| 13. Westmoreland Group | 12,656,515 | i | Westmoreland Group |
| **14. Bethlehem Mines | 11,706,772 | s | Bethlehem Steel |
| 15. Exxon Coal Group | 11,400,000 | e | Exxon Corp. |

Source: Based on tabular material in *1981 Keystone Coal Industry Manual* (New York: McGraw-Hill, 1981), pp. 714, 717.

*d = diversified corporation;  e = energy company;  i = independent;  s = steel company;  u = public utility.

**captive producer

176

cesses are so huge as to exclude smaller investors. However, critics charge that the oil companies may raise prices or hold back production of coal in order to keep oil prices up. Critics also assert that the oil companies and conglomerates skim the profits of their coal subsidiaries to meet cash needs elsewhere. For example, a witness at a Senate hearing in 1977 claimed that SOHIO used profits from its coal properties to build the Trans-Alaska pipeline and to develop Prudhoe Bay, and that Occidental Petroleum milked 60% of its Island Creek subsidiary's income in 1975.[20] Once again, hard evidence is hard to come by and the results of a host of congressional and executive-branch studies have been inconclusive to date. All that can be said with confidence is that while the giant investors are clearly in the best position to improve the fortunes of U.S. coal they will not do so automatically or inevitably.[21]

Greater production and consumption of coal will also depend on meeting objections to its undesirable environmental qualities. Coal industry managers must deal with complex regulations and policies, which can delay increases in production for years (Figures 7.4 and 7.5). Government controls on coal production revolve around three issues: land use, water use, and worker safety. In 1977 Congress enacted the Surface Mining Control and Reclamation Act, which requires mining companies to restore lands disfigured by strip mining to their original contours. In addition, reclamation must include isolating and disposing of toxic wastes and the replacement of topsoil. The Clean Water Act (1972) established "effluent limitations" on discharges from coal mining and preparation plants. The federal government has not yet acted on the related question of water rights, leaving determination to state regulatory agencies. At present, no clear policy has emerged. Nonetheless, the production of synfuels and the slurry process would require enormous amounts of water whose quality must be controlled once its availability is established.

A third area of federal regulation of the industry involves mine safety. In 1969 Congress passed the Federal Coal Mine Health and Safety Act, in the wake of an explosion in a West Virginia mine that killed 78 miners. This accident climaxed more than a decade of mounting casualties from mining and served to dramatize other occupational hazards of the industry as well by focusing public attention on conditions in the mines. During the 1960s more than 250 miners died on the job each year and another 10,000 suffered disabling injuries, often stemming from "coal workers' pneumoconiosis" or "black lung disease." Federal legislation now mandates strict standards for the amount of dust, harmful fumes, and gases allowed to circulate in the mines and for the amount of noise permitted. It also calls for the periodic unscheduled inspection of the mines by federal officials and stiff penalties for noncompliance.[22]

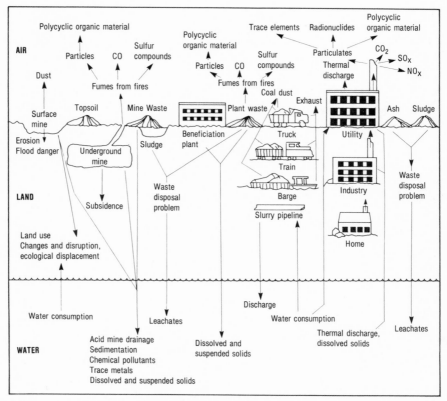

**Figure 7.4    Environmental Disturbances from Coal-Related Activities**

SOURCE: U.S. Congress, Office of Technology Assessment, *The Direct Use of Coal: Prospects and Problems of Production and Combustion* (Washington, D.C., 1979), p. 184.

After decades of environmental abuse and negligence toward worker safety, there can be little doubt that federal regulation of the industry is necessary. The consequences of regulation, however, have been mixed. Long lead times—as much as eight to sixteen years—are now required before new mines can satisfy federal requirements and begin to operate.[23] The capital expenses and management expertise necessary to cope with regulation, moreover, place smaller companies at a disadvantage.

Federal air quality regulations seriously impede increased consumption of coal as well. Simple burning of coal leaves corrosive residues in boilers and chimneys, spews cinder and ash over the surrounding countryside, and pollutes the atmosphere chemically, thermally, and olfactorily. The Clean Air Act of 1970 and amendments in 1977

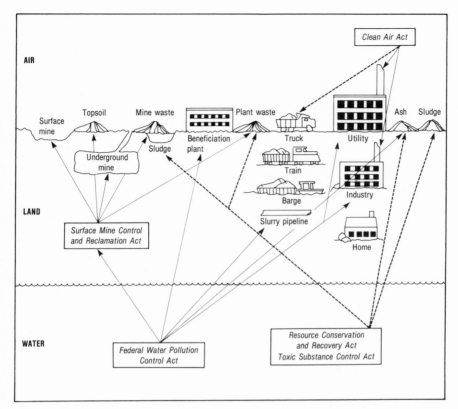

**Figure 7.5   Jurisdiction of Federal Control Legislation**

Source: U.S. Congress, Office of Technology Assessment, *The Direct Use of Coal: Prospects and Problems of Production and Combustion* (Washington, D.C., 1979), p. 185.

mandate that sulfur dioxide, nitrogen dioxide, and "particulate matter" must be removed from emissions into the atmosphere. Since the sulfur content of much U.S. coal (and nearly all eastern coal) exceeds federal limits, coal-burning utilities and industries have been required to invest in "scrubbing" technologies to clean up emissions. Scrubbing is expensive and poses the additional problem of a noxious sludge by-product that accumulates rapidly and is difficult to dispose of.

Shorter-term constraints on the supply of coal center on ownership of lands in the mineral-rich western states. It is estimated that the federal government owns more than 70% of the reserves west of the Mississippi River. In 1971 the government placed a moratorium on the leasing of coal rights because of opposition from local ranchers and the need to determine water rights and provide for land reclamation after stripping. The Reagan administration ordered that leasing be renewed in 1981, although there will be a lead time of four or five years for development of the lands. Thus no coal may be produced from these lands until 1985 or later.

Finally, the government is now examining public policy issues which, while not directly affecting the industry, threaten its rapid growth. These are the social and political consequences of a sudden increase in coal production. A vast expansion of coal mining will create "boomtowns" with their attendant problems: changing real estate values, and uncertain quality of public services, such as schools, health care, and maintenance of highways and transportation networks. Neither the federal nor the state governments will deliberately prevent coal's rapid growth, although hearings on such public policy matters will surely slow the process.

The big changes in the value of coal have serious implications as well. Since 1974 coal's price has reflected its value in comparison with other energy sources as well as its cost of production. The rapid price increases have strained traditional methods of marketing coal. Ordinarily, coal of all ranks and grades is sold either by contract or on the spot market. Most larger companies sell according to long-term contracts with principal users, such as the utilities or steel companies. These contracts generally contain price-escalation provisions to offset inflation, overhead, labor, or tax increases as well as a *force majeur* clause freeing the seller from obligations in case of a major setback. Some contracts permit an annual revaluation of the price along with developments in the spot market. Most smaller companies sell either through their larger competitors or at the spot, or open-market price, which varies with the supply/demand relationship, the quality of the coal, and the competitive price of other fuels. The price rises of the 1970s, which far outstripped inflation, have had the effects of boosting smaller companies and discouraging long-term contracts, and have left ripple effects in coal-consuming industries.[24]

Next, there are problems with creating new demand for coal.[25] Obviously, if none of coal's buyers prosper, then the industry cannot grow. Figure 7.6 displays postwar trends in the consumption of coal by different types of users. While total consumption has climbed, the coal industry's heavy reliance on a few critical industries is likely to constrain future growth. As we have seen (Chapter 3), the growth potential of the steel industry is negligible. Moreover, after a thirty-year period of 7% annual increases, the growth of the electric utilities industry has slowed since the early 1970s. Demographic trends and conservation of electricity militate against achieving such rapid growth again, although demand will remain high in some areas, such as the Southwest. On the other hand, the recent troubles of the nuclear power industry and the prospect of further oil price increases make coal a more attractive fuel in the long run for generating electricity. The use of coal as a boiler fuel in general industry has dwindled since World War II, and now accounts for less than 10% of all coal consumed (down from nearly 50%). Once more, formidable barriers threaten to block reversal of this trend. According to a recent study by the Congressional Research Service, "more than 90% of existing industrial boilers cannot physically burn coal."[26] Thus coal's prospects are tied to the rate at which industry will install new boilers, a dim prospect in view of the longevity of existing equipment.

Some analysts predict that exports of coal will assume an increasingly larger role in the industry. In 1980 about 90 million tons of coal were exported — more than twice the amount shipped overseas in 1978. By 1990 exports may reach 150 million tons — about 10% of total production — although port and dock facilities will have to be built to accommodate this traffic.[27]

Synfuels represent a final market for coal. However, gasification and liquefaction of coal on a large commercial scale are a long way off, according to best estimates. Because of environmental uncertainties and long lead times for development and construction of technologies, even if there were a full-scale national commitment, synfuels could make no significant contribution to U.S. energy consumption before

**Figure 7.6 Coal Consumption by End-Use Sector**

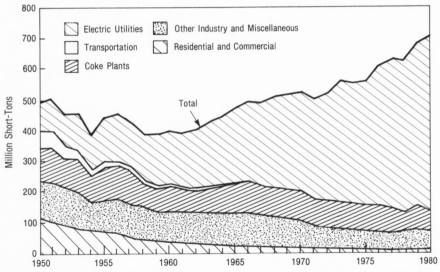

SOURCE: U.S. Department of Energy, Energy Information Administration, *1980 Annual Report to Congress* (Washington, D.C., 1980), vol. 2, p. 128.

1990 and possibly much later. Even with present inflated oil prices, synfuels are not nearly economical to produce. It may well be, as Mel Horwitch has concluded, that "the need for a synthetic fuels capability is more a matter of national security than of comparative fuel economics. . . ."[28]

Transportation problems will also restrict increases in coal production. Coal is an awkward fuel to use even after it is dug from the ground and prepared for shipment. Because most U.S. reserves (60%) are in the West and most markets for coal are in the East, transportation is a critical problem, made worse by western coal's lower average BTU content — a higher volume must be burned to produce as much energy as Eastern coal. Coal is too heavy to be transported efficiently and safely by truck and the inland waterways of America form an insufficient network for barge transportation. Most coal is thus carried by rail, and so is subject to the capital and managerial limitations of the railroad industry. The development of adequate rail networks in the West would require enormous investments, and it is difficult to see where such money can be raised. Moreover, the prospect of high-volume train traffic — one expert has calculated that trains will depart major mines every eighteen minutes, twenty-four hours a day — has stirred up a hornet's nest among citizens who fear the impact of such traffic in their communities.[29] The transportation bottleneck may be relieved in the late 1980s by the increased use of slurry pipelines carrying pulverized coal mixed with water from mine mouth to junction or destination. The railroads oppose slurry pipelines vehemently, however, and several public policy and environmental issues (granting rights of eminent domain to the pipeline companies, and resolution of western water rights) remain to be resolved before slurry pipelines can make a significant contribution to coal transportation.

It is unlikely that advances in coal mining technology will have a significant impact on the economics of the industry in the foreseeable future. The Congressional Research Service predicts that "no large degree of innovative substitution is expected in the next twenty-five years."[30] Longwall mining has been the most promising innovation in coal since the continuous miner. However, its deployment is subject to limitations on the quality of the seam and heavy turnaround costs to reposition the machine on the next face. Other innovations now concentrate on improving existing equipment and processes — matters such as roof control, ventilation, haulage, and machine designs in underground mines and better conveyors and shovels in surface mines. Some companies are experimenting with underground gasification of deep or otherwise hard-to-reach seams. Through the application of enormous heat and pressure, coal can be converted to gas *in situ*. If such processes are successful, much coal that is otherwise inaccessible or uneconomical to mine may indeed become available. At present, however, the technological and environmental problems surrounding the process are forbidding.[31]

Other constraints on the expansion of the coal industry stem from declining productivity in recent years. Indeed, the national statistics are sufficiently alarming to make Tennessee Ernie Ford's song "Sixteen Tons" a fond memory. Between 1969 and 1979, the average figure for all mines has declined from 19.9 tons per man per day to 13.5 tons. Productivity has fallen in both underground and surface mining (Table 7.3). Experts claim that the easy coal seams have all been identified and are being mined out. Newer mines are located in less hospitable environments. Moreover, changes in the work force have hurt productivity. Miners are now younger and less experienced and, some say, more often absent. It also has been argued that no significant advances in mining technology have been made for more than a decade. The continuous miner, this century's chief innovation, was all but universally adopted by 1969. Finally, growing federal regulation has forced companies to hire many personnel for jobs that do not contribute to production and interrupt work with frequent inspections.[32]

Declining productivity also reflects the history of troubled relations between management and labor in the industry.[33] Since the late 1960s the miners have been sporadically hostile toward both management and their own UMW leaders. The miners' attitude stems partly from the producers' historical disregard for safety measures and benefits. A more serious problem since Lewis's time is that the union leadership has had trouble controlling its membership. Lewis was followed first by weak then by shamelessly corrupt successors, Thomas Kennedy and W.A. "Tony" Boyle.[34] Although Boyle was turned out of office in 1972 (and later convicted of ordering the murder of his chief opponent), and replaced by more democratic leaders and organization, miners continue to balk at official union policies. In particular, the mid-1970s saw a wave of wildcat strikes called over the opposition of the UMW. In 1976 the industry lost more than two million man-days to wildcat strikes. There is little consensus on the causes of these strikes, although various explanations have been advanced. Dissatisfaction with the union leadership and policies, declining UMW membership (it now represents only about half of all miners and only about 20% of surface miners in the West), the demographic split between young miners and older union leaders, the antiquated and authoritarian hierarchies of most coal companies, poor industry response to federal safety standards, and generally unattractive working conditions—all these have contributed to the industry's decline in productivity.[35]

Clearly, the growth of the coal industry faces a plethora of problems. One of the most serious may be the want of managerial expertise to deal with the other difficulties. Regulation has multiplied the need for capable managers. It has been claimed that 15% to 20% of the employees of a large underground mine are concerned with complying with federal safety regulations alone.[36] A private study commissioned by Exxon's coal subsidiary predicted that the ranks of managers will need to grow by 5% annually through 1985 in order to meet industry needs. This represents a far faster growth rate than will be necessary among miners themselves.[37] In the pedestrian prose of the National Coal Association, there is "a gap in the management talent bank for the industry."[38] It is difficult to see where these managers will come from, given the industry's historical conservatism and stodgy image. The need to train and recruit managers to preside over the resurgence of coal represents yet one more serious constraint on production.

## PERFORMANCE AND STRATEGIES OF SELECTED COAL COMPANIES

The complicated maze of regulations, restrictions, and constraints on the coal industry poses a difficult challenge to coal operators. Navigating a consistent course through this maze will require more than ordinary skill. Such skill is not necessarily concentrated in the larger, new entrants to the industry, as is sometimes argued. The larger companies do enjoy economies of scale and access to capital markets denied to their smaller competitors, and they can support more ambitious and intensive R&D as well. But, as we shall see, there is an alternative way for small companies to increase innovation and efficiency and balance short-term and long-term interests by the imaginative management of their human resources.

These points are illustrated by the performance, organization, and strategies of seven coal producers. Four of the cases discussed here are based on Balaji Chakravarthy's recent study of adaptation in the coal industry.[39] For purposes of contrast, we have also assembled profiles of several other companies differing in size or primary market.* According to our criteria of innovation and efficiency, we see three firms — Exxon Coal, Northern Energy Resources Company (NERCO), and Kentucky Coal Mining Corporation — as being readaptive. Two other companies — Armco, Inc., and Consolidation Coal Co. — show promise but display fewer indications of readaptation. Finally, two compa-

---

*We have used a set of business school teaching cases on a small producer in Kentucky and recent management literature on a quality of work experiment at a mine in Rushton, Pennsylvania, in order to show options available to companies without enormous financial resources. In addition, we have relied on company reports and trade literature to examine the performance of two "captive producers," a steel company and an electric utility company.

nies—Island Creek Coal Company and North American Coal Company—seem not to be making the best use of the opportunities presented by Area 5 conditions.

## Exxon Coal, U.S.A.

Exxon Coal, U.S.A., a wholly owned subsidiary of the Exxon Corporation, is a recent entrant into the coal business.[40] In the early 1960s Exxon began thinking about sources of oil to develop once domestic production peaked. Accordingly, in 1965 it established a subsidiary, the Carter Oil Company, to buy up coal reserves and to concentrate on the synfuels business. In its first eighteen months, Carter Oil accumulated more than seven billion tons of reserves in Ilinois and the West, and it has since become the fifth-largest holder in the country. By 1969 Carter Oil realized that commercial production of synfuels was further off than first believed, so it established its own subsidiary, Monterey Coal, to mine and market steam coal for utilities in Illinois. A year later, when the Clean Air Act made its western low-sulfur coal more valuable, Carter Oil established a second subsidiary, the Carter Mining Company, to begin production in Wyoming. These various properties were gathered under the umbrella of Exxon Coal, U.S.A. in 1980.

Exxon Coal's history is a classic illustration of how outside capital and management skills can create a major coal company from scratch. Virtually everything the company has done so far reflects Exxon Corporation's abundant resources, long experience, and impressive capacity to implement new strategies. The parent company has provided not only the cash to buy coal reserves, but the geologists and engineers to find and develop them. Exxon Corporation supplies central services in marketing, control, planning, public affairs, and human resources management. The corporation drew from its own managerial ranks to staff Exxon Coal's hierarchy. Exxon encouraged its subsidiaries to be responsive to their new communities as well. In Gillette, Wyoming, for example, the Carter Mining Company built a multimillion-dollar office building as a declaration of its intention to stay and invest there. The company further strengthened its ties to the communities where it operates by collaborating with local universities on environmental programs.

Exxon Coal has also taken advantage of its standing as a newcomer in the coal business. Better lighting, ventilation, and other coal-dust control measures have created excellent underground working conditions. These practices, combined with upgraded supervision, have contributed to better safety records, more harmonious relations between labor and management, and higher tonnage per man-day than comparable competitors. Exxon Coal's production from mines in Illinois and Wyoming climbed rapidly during the 1970s, reaching a total of 11.4 million tons in 1980, when the company ranked as the fifteenth largest producer in the country. New mines in the West and West Virginia are expected to add to a total production of 21 million tons by 1982. All of this amount is already committed to utilities under long-term contracts.

Exxon Corporation has long been studying synfuels technology and it has placed its expertise at the disposal of its coal subsidiary. Recognizing that population growth in the Sun Belt will soon outstrip the capacity of natural gas producers to supply energy, Exxon Coal recently established a small gasification pilot plant near its lignite reserves in Texas. The corporation plans to build an experimental coal liquefaction plant on the same site. This project, managed by Exxon, is funded by a consortium including the Department of Energy and several other petroleum companies with interests in coal.

Exxon Coal has clearly established a record of both innovation and efficiency. It expects to remain readaptive and to stay in Area 5. With the advice and help of its parent corporation, Exxon Coal has maneuvered to the leading edge of developments in the industry. A company forecast predicts production of 24 million tons of coal in 1985. If any company can achieve such a goal, it is Exxon Coal.

### Northern Energy Resources Co. (NERCO)

Based in Portland, Oregon, Northern Energy Resources Co. (NERCO) is a wholly owned subsidiary of Pacific Power & Light (PP&L), a public utility that generates electricity and steam heat and operates waterworks, telecommunications systems, and coal mines in eight Northwest states. PP&L also is engaged in coal mining in three Midwest and Southern states and oil and gas exploration in the West and Southwest.[41] Originally a producer of hydroelectric power, the utility company has since invested heavily in coal and nuclear energy as well as several other businesses. NERCO manages PP&L's coal properties in Montana, Wyoming, Indiana, Tennessee and Alabama, which yielded 20.4 million tons of steam coal in 1981. PP&L's coal-fired stations burn NERCO coal exclusively, although NERCO also sells steam coal to utilities in the Midwest, East, and Southwest. According to company data, 28% of the total produced in 1981 was sold to the parent utility and the rest was sold outside to other customers.

Between 1970 and 1981 NERCO jumped from the forty-fourth ranked position to become the fifth-largest producer of coal in the United States, largely because of the output of its Montana operations. NERCO is half-owner of the Decker Coal Company, which operates a gigantic surface mine in the Southeastern part of the state near Sheridan, Wyoming. The mine was opened in 1972, with a long-term contract to sell steam coal to Commonwealth Edison in Chicago. It has since acquired other customers and, by 1975, the Decker mine was the largest in the country, although it has since slipped to third place.* At present the Decker mine has a capacity of 19 million tons per year, but current annual production is in the range of 10–12 million tons. NERCO has also opened another mine, Spring Creek, nearby and has arranged long-term contracts with utilities in Michigan and Texas.

NERCO is not strictly a "captive" owner of coal. The company has continued to purchase coal reserves and owns some 1.3 billion tons, about half of which are not presently committed for development. The utility treats its coal subsidiary as a profit center and pays out a portion of its income in dividends. In the Decker mine's first year of operation, for instance, coal contributed seven cents per share; within four years it added thirty-seven cents; and by 1981 NERCO contributed sixty-eight cents per share even though there has been a large increase in common shares outstanding during this period. There are several reasons for this impressive performance. First, although it sponsors little R&D directly, PP&L has been a pioneer in land reclamation techniques, new emission control technologies, and water conservation policies. Moreover, in 1980 the company's western mines averaged between 65 and 80 tons per man per shift (productivity was substantially lower in the Alabama mines: an average of 11.8 tons per man-shift in 1979). These figures, well above the national average, are largely attributable to new equipment and a relatively thin "overburden" above the coal seams. But NERCO also pays good wages and expects its supervisors and employees to attend periodic training sessions. Company managers, outside consultants, and faculty of the Colorado School of Mines teach not only technical material and subjects required by law—safety, equal opportunity—but also such topics as interpersonal communication, management of stress, and NERCO policies.

It is clear that NERCO is taking advantage of the coal industry's improved fortunes in Area 5. The company has the resources and the managerial skills to expand coal production. By pouring fresh capital into the business, by mining its well-chosen seams intensively, and by cultivating its work force, NERCO is managing readaptively.

### Kentucky Coal Mining Corporation (KENCO)

KENCO, a small independent producer in western Kentucky, was founded in the 1960s by a former coal salesman and three partners,

---

*In 1980 Decker began operating a second mine near the original one, now called West Decker.

with a start-up capital of only $400,000.* This sum enabled the partners to purchase 10,000 acres of land holding about 40 million tons of high BTU (but high sulfur) coal, which they planned to market to utilities. KENCO management took advantage of its position as a new entrant to the business. The company began with a well-chosen, well-prepared site and with the latest equipment. KENCO's management chose not to hire trained UMW miners, in part because nearby companies who employed union labor had experienced high absenteeism and frequent wildcat strikes. Rather, the company employed unskilled employees and offered them a benefits package superior to that won by the UMW in its most recent contract. In particular, the schedule of wages, hours, and vacations matched the union's, but KENCO employees received incentive bonuses based on production, provision for profit-sharing, full salary while disabled because of a work-related injury, and full medical coverage.

The KENCO management also tried to inculcate a company spirit among the miners by showing its interest in the men in other ways. The company took special care to improve safety in the mine and endeavored to improve working conditions. KENCO formed its employees into work teams and gradually trained each team member to perform a variety of tasks so that they could fill in for each other as needed. The mine supervisor decided against holding periodic formal meetings with the miners, remarking, "Other mines have these 'bull sessions.' But KENCO is a family. You don't have weekly meetings in a family."

KENCO's concern for its workers paid handsome dividends. Although its first mine was not highly mechanized, the productivity rate was astonishing. Even after the industrywide decline began in 1969, KENCO maintained its rate at 25 tons per man per shift and beyond — more than twice the rate of its competitors. Within three years the company increased production from 700,000 tons to more than one million tons annually. Furthermore, KENCO avoided the disturbing problems of absenteeism and wildcat strikes that plagued nearby mines. And all this was accomplished *before* the energy crunch made coal a more attractive fuel. A large energy company subsequently bought out KENCO, but the parent has continued and improved the innovative labor management policies, extended them to other mines, and still maintains a productivity rate (41 tons per man-day in 1980) substantially higher than the industry in general.

The experiences of another small producer, the Rushton Mining Company in Pennsylvania, provide a second illustration of the options open to small producers. From 1973 to 1976 Rushton management co-

---

*KENCO is a disguised name. Its story is summarized from the case series, *Kentucky Coal Mining Corporation* (HBS Case Services 9-678-101 to -103).

operated with the local UMW chapter to rearrange the normal duties and responsibilities of some miners. The men assigned to one face of the mine were organized into a semiautonomous work group. In most union mines, management, in the person of the foreman, determines where the crew will work, how they will attack the face, and how much coal they will mine from it. At Rushton, however, each miner was trained to perform more varied tasks; loaders became drillers, and vice versa. Finally, the work crew joined with management to review all grievances arising in the experimental section.[42]

The Rushton experiment achieved modest gains in productivity (about 3%) but striking reductions of absenteeism and grievances, and a substantially improved safety record. The miners who volunteered to participate in the experiment endorsed it almost universally. "Suddenly, we felt we mattered to somebody," said one.

> Somebody trusted us. . . . The funny thing is, [in the new system] the crew, we don't really get tired anymore. We probably work twice as hard as before, but we don't get tired. . . . It's like you feel you're somebody, like you're a professional, like you got a profession you're proud of. . . .

"We see that work gets done," said another, "that the safety law is kept up. We learn how to run all the equipment. You want to come to work now. We all work together, like a team."[43]

Unfortunately, the Rushton experiment ended on a sour note. In a heated meeting at the end of 1976, the UMW local voted to discontinue the program. The reasons for this vote are not entirely clear, although it is speculated that the Rushton workers who did not participate in the experiment resented the workers who did, and that the majority of the union viewed the program as a management ruse to divide its labor force. However, the Rushton experiment promised, as the KENCO case shows, that small coal producers can take advantage of Area 5 conditions by innovative management of human resources. Large size and substantial capital are obviously helpful, but other roads can also lead to readaptation.

### CONSOLIDATION COAL COMPANY (CONSOL)

Consol, a subsidiary of Continental Oil and Du Pont, has been the second largest producer of coal in the nation for more than a decade.[44] Consol operates both underground and surface mines in northeastern Appalachian states, North Dakota, Colorado, and Utah. Its principal product is steam coal, although about 14% of its output is metallurgical coal mined in joint ventures with steel companies. Consol's efficiency and production volume did not escape the industrywide declines of the 1970s. In 1970 Consol mined 57.4 million tons; in 1980, 50.0

million. Consol's chairman, Ralph Bailey, reported decreases of 40%
and 25% in underground and surface productivity, respectively, between 1969 and 1976.[45] Like Exxon Coal, Consol has been able to turn
for help to a rich parent. Conoco has given Consol central engineering,
resource management, and R&D services as well as a time-tested, efficient central control system.

Consol's top executives seem genuinely concerned with declining
productivity. The company reorganized in 1975, seeking to rationalize
its functions and establish a more consistent image across its far-flung
operations. It has further attacked the productivity problem by increasing capital expenditures, adopting new technology (chiefly
longwall mining) and engineering systems, and building closer ties
with its work force. Consol has established a management development
institute for training senior administrators and has implemented intensive training programs for lower-level supervisors, who are required to
learn company safety, engineering, and machine-operating procedures
and review them annually.

Conoco has invested heavily in new technologies to provide new
markets for its coal subsidiary. An R&D subsidiary, the Conoco Coal
Development Company (CDCC) has built pilot gasification plants in
Ohio and South Dakota with outside financing. In addition, CDCC has
investigated new scrubbing techniques that might make coal more attractive to conventional consumers. This long-term strategy is deliberate and well planned. As Eric Reichl, head of CDCC, puts it: "If the
nation eventually decides that it needs a synthetics industry, our company will have the coal and the expertise to lead in the development."[46]

Consol recently announced its plans for expansion in the 1980s. Total production will increase to 90 million tons by 1985. Most of this coal
will be steam coal destined for utilities and industry, but 6 million tons
will be reserved annually for gasification. Consol has adopted an intel-
ligent, diversified strategy that is likely to serve it well. The company
seems poised to enjoy the benefits of continuous growth and innovation
in Area 5 for some time to come.

ARMCO INC.

Armco is a large, diversified steel company that is also a captive
producer of metallurgical coal.[47] In 1980 the company had $3 billion
in assets, of which about 50% were in specialty and carbon steel, with
the remainder spread through five other business areas including coal.
By 1985 Armco's diversified interests (nonsteel) are projected to account for more than 60% of the company's business. Coal production
will assume increasing importance as Armco moves away from its roots
in the steel industry.

In 1980 Armco operated sixteen mines in West Virginia and Oklahoma and owned 929 million tons in coal reserves. All but three of the mines are underground. While most of its 1980 production (4.6 million tons) was targeted for the company's own coke plants, Armco also sold steam coal on the profitable spot market. Recently, the company has also negotiated long-term contracts with utilities, opened new steam coal mines, and sold coal for export. One of Armco's four coal preparation plants has been modified to handle steam coal exclusively. The company expects sales of steam coal "to grow swiftly," reflecting a new attitude about coal. As Armco's chief executive officer, Harry Holiday, Jr., puts it:

> I think if you go back into Armco's history, you'll find we got into the coal business to meet our needs as a steel producer. However, in today's world we see the opportunity to have our coal reserves provide profit to our company right away, rather than think of them for use in our steel plants a hundred years from now. We are expanding our facilities for coal mining expressly for the purpose of selling coal to whoever wants to buy it.

Armco's West Virginia mines were very efficient in the 1970s, achieving a productivity rate (13 tons per man per shift) that is 60% higher than the statewide average. This performance can be traced partly to Armco's newer mines with high seams and balanced mining methods, but the company believes that its innovative management practices are also responsible.

Armco has focused on the intensive training of production foremen in a twenty-week development program that includes eight hundred hours of class time. The curriculum concentrates on safety and medical training, engineering, new mining techniques and technology, union contract administration, environmental law, and management of working groups. Holiday believes the program is a success:

> We've worked many, many long hours trying to improve labor relations and the personal relationships between the miners and management. And, we have been successful . . . getting the miners to realize that we are a responsible citizen in their area, that we are a reasonable company to work for, and that, when things are worked out on balance, we can get along together. I think the men have been responsive to our interests and to their interests, and they're doing a crackerjack job of running the equipment.

Armco's new approach seems to be paying off. The company produced nearly five million tons in 1980 and hopes that production will reach ten million tons by 1985. Its productivity rates continue to be high. Armco is finding new markets for its coal and is investing in new technology. In late 1979, for example, the company opened a new coal, coke, and energy laboratory to improve its R&D. More and more

Armco coal will be sold to utilities as the company diversifies from the slow-growth steel industry. Armco appears to be managing its coal properties well, and should benefit from Area 5 conditions for the foreseeable future.

### ISLAND CREEK COAL COMPANY

Island Creek, a subsidiary of Occidental Petroleum (Oxy), ranked as one of the top ten producers of coal throughout the 1970s,[48] reflecting balanced production of steam and metallurgical coal and judicious acquisition of western reserves after the passage of the Clean Air Act. Like many other companies, Island Creek has suffered declining production and productivity since 1969. Efforts have been made to offset these trends through new labor-management programs and reliance on the resources of the parent company. Mine managers and division presidents work under incentive plans, earning bonuses for improvements in output, productivity, safety record, capacity utilization, and cost. Lower-ranking supervisors can earn bonuses for improvements in those factors or control of overtime. The company provides community services for its miners and has tried to improve labor relations through training programs, enhanced employee benefits, and public relations.

Island Creek has been associated with Oxy since 1968. Oxy furnishes capital and central services—finance, planning, engineering, public affairs—the coal company would be hard pressed to provide by itself. Oxy's investment enabled Island Creek to purchase reserves of high-quality steam coal in Wyoming in 1975. A new subsidiary there, Sheridan Mining, is projected to produce three million tons annually in the 1980s. Although Occidental is an oil producer, it has not yet involved Island Creek in the production of synfuels. In 1980, however, Island Creek opened a "portable plant" to produce coal-oil mixtures, an experimental boiler fuel. Oxy has also invested in several joint ventures with the government and private industry to evaluate the feasibility of underground gasification of coal. If this process proves commercially viable, Island Creek will probably benefit from new markets.

In light of its advantages, Island Creek's recent production figures are disappointing. Although it is well positioned to prosper in several markets, and possesses obvious management skills, coal output fell from nearly 32 million tons in 1970 to about 20 million tons in 1980. At the same time, Island Creek dropped from third to fifth place among major producers. Explanations for this performance, beyond the industry's general laments about government and labor, are not easily found. One suspects that there may be some truth to the claim that Oxy removes profits from coal without returning comparable investments.

In theory Island Creek, like Exxon Coal and Consol, ought to remain in Area 5. In practice, however, it seems to be drifting into the conditions of Area 6.

## North American Coal Company (NACCO)

Based in Cleveland, with mines chiefly in Northern Appalachia, North Dakota, and Texas, NACCO is one of only three independents to be ranked in the top fifteen coal producers.[49] NACCO grew into prominence in the 1950s and 1960s as a producer of steam coal for the utilities market. Since the company lacked capital, it developed mines as joint ventures with utility partners. NACCO provided coal reserves, engineers, and miners while its partners arranged financing. In 1970 NACCO launched a long-term program to acquire reserves in the West, although by then the prime available reserves had been bought up by other investors. By 1976 NACCO managed to build up its reserves by more than 400%, from 1.2 billion tons to 5.1 billion tons. Most of these holdings consist of lignite, the lowest grade of coal, which is not economical to burn commercially, although it does have possibilities as a feedstock for gasification. NACCO has arranged joint ventures with Getty Oil and American Natural Gas to develop synfuels form its coal.

NACCO's output increased about 30% between 1970 and 1980 despite a 50% reduction in productivity rates. The explanation for this apparent paradox is that NACCO's surface mines in North Dakota and Texas greatly increased their production while its underground mines in Ohio and Pennsylvania struggled to maintain constant volume. The company blames federal regulation and labor unrest for the problems of its older mines. In particular, the Clean Air Act has hurt the market for NACCO's high-sulfur eastern coal. The company has tried to combat its labor troubles with training programs for supervisory personnel. Begun in 1975, these programs run one full day each month and include sessions on technical, managerial, and safety problems. The results so far have been modestly encouraging. After severe troubles in the late 1970s—the company was hit particularly hard by a national coal strike in 1977–78—production has improved.

In 1977 NACCO announced plans to more than double its annual output to nearly 25 million tons. The company anticipated that most of this total would come from western strip-mining operations and subsidiary companies financed by long-term utility contracts.[50] These goals are no longer realistic and NACCO may have to struggle to achieve much less ambitious growth. NACCO's troubles stem partly from regulatory compliance costs and labor unrest, but also from inflated expectations for its western coal, lack of capital, and lack of organizational capacity. As of 1977, NACCO remained a centralized, functional bureaucracy with restricted ability to promote long-range planning, marketing, or new products. The company maintained tight financial controls over its geographical divisions and subsidiaries with "a predominately efficiency-oriented administrative focus."[51] With its present strategy and organization, it will be difficult for NACCO to hold its position in Area 5.

## CONCLUSION

Figure 7.7 summarizes the adaptational record of the U.S. coal industry over the last century. For most of the period, the industry declined slowly from its onetime monopoly position as consumers preferred rival fuels to coal. From about 1920 to the 1970s the coal industry was stagnant, mired in Area 9 conditions of high RS (lack of capital, declining demand, competitive pressure for resources, and labor unrest) and low IC (few competitive, technical, customer, or product variations). Despite modest improvement in the 1950s, the industry's fortunes changed substantially only with the advent of new ownership, federal intervention, and the sudden energy shocks of recent years. As the preceding case studies illustrate, coal companies are now responding to the more hospitable environment in Area 5 conditions in various ways. Some firms have stuck with traditional ways of doing business, while others are pursuing readaptive strategies to meet current challenges and opportunities. New capital investment, more flexible organizational structures, and innovative management of human resources are the approaches which seem most promising.

Our analysis of the coal industry suggests two general conclusions. First, the companies in the best position to thrive are those that are organized to bring new ideas and methods to traditional markets while they are preparing themselves for new uses of the product in the future. The best-performing firms — Exxon Coal, NERCO, Consol — are bringing new management skills and new technologies to the industry. They are managing through organizations with greater capacity for readaptation. Summing up his case studies, Chakravarthy observes that the better-performing firms are characterized by (among other things) more differentiated and more integrated structures than lower-performing firms. Taking Exxon Coal and NACCO as the extremes, Chakravarthy points out that the former has nearly twice as many functional departments at the corporate level providing such services as long-range planning, industrial relations, public affairs, and synfuels management. Exxon Coal also uses a greater variety of coordinating devices — formal interdepartmental meetings and project teams — to

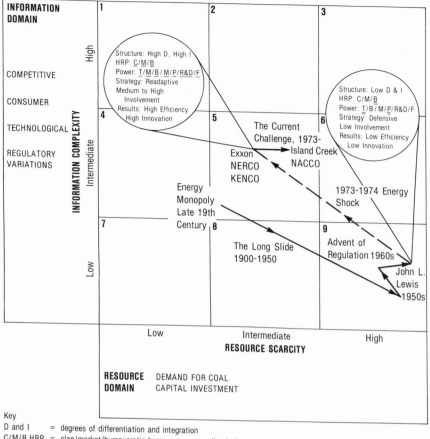

**Figure 7.7   Evolution of the U.S. Coal Industry 1880–1980**

bridge its specialized subunits. In short, Exxon Coal (like Consol and NERCO) is especially well organized to balance sustained innovation and efficiency amid the new challenges and uncertainties of the coal industry.[52]

Our second general conclusion is that mechanistic, authoritarian human resource practices are inappropriate if coal companies are to take full advantage of Area 5 conditions and become truly readaptive. Indeed, the evidence clearly shows that companies with higher levels of innovation and efficiency have made greater efforts to increase member involvement in the mines. This is especially good news for smaller coal operators. Small firms can achieve readaptive results and the possibility of a sustained cycle of growth through human resource programs designed to increase miners' involvement in their work. In our terms, KENCO added both clan and market mechanisms to the industry's traditionally bureaucratic procedures. The company supplemented its emphasis on bonuses and a "family" feeling at work with enlarged jobs and shared power and decision making. KENCO is a company that pulled itself up by the bootstraps from Area 9 toward Area 5. Among the larger companies, Exxon Coal and Armco are using similar human resource and power-sharing practices. All these cases highlight the importance of improving relations between management and labor, and, by extension, suggest that the traditional hierarchical and frequently autocratic organization of work in the mines can be counterproductive. Decentralized management are careful cultivation of labor — the high D and I structure, power sharing, and balanced human resource practices — are important sources of competitive advantage in today's coal industry.

From the coal industry we now move to the last of our case studies to consider the telecommunications industry. Although at first glance the industries seem very different — fragmented versus concentrated, low-tech versus high-tech, stagnant versus dynamic, poor versus rich — there are some interesting parallels. Chief among these are the magnitude and direction of recent environmental changes. In the case of AT&T, by far the dominant firm in its industry, new technologies and public policies have pushed the organization from its historic position as a regulated monopoly in Area 8 conditions toward the more uncertain and competitive world of Area 5. Let us look now at the Bell System's organizational responses to its new circumstances and its opportunities to sustain the readaptive process.

# CHAPTER 8

# Telecommunications: New Rules for the Bell System

IF A CITIZEN of the nineteenth century had somehow been frozen in a time capsule to wake up in the 1980s he would scarcely recognize the world around him.* Most of the differences that would strike him can be attributed to the development of information handling and the advances in electronics that followed from it. Improvements in communications underlay the industrial revolution and the growth of modern enterprise in America. They have affected the nature of the home and the family no less than the workplace and the employee. It would be difficult to overestimate the social and economic impact of "the communications revolution" and the dawn of "the information age."[1]

Among its other effects, the coming of electric and electronic communications transformed the structure of business in America. The growth of large-scale enterprise could not have happened without rapid communication between corporate headquarters and various far-flung administrative and operating departments. The communications industry was itself a pioneer in this evolution of business from

---

*Note: This chapter was written simultaneously with a set of teaching cases, *AT&T: Adaptation in Progress* (HBS Case Services 9-481-074 to -077 and -120), now expanded in book form as *Recasting Bell: From Monopoly to Competition at AT&T* by Leonard A. Schlesinger, Davis Dyer, and Thomas N. Clough (forthcoming, 1983). Portions of this chapter draw heavily on information collected for and included in these cases.

small firms owned and run by families to large bureaucratic organizations in which ownership has been separated from management.[2] For most of Western history communications were managed, if at all, by government. National monopolies controlled postal service and, in case of war, signaling services. This pattern first broke in nineteenth-century America, when private enterprise developed telegraph service. Western Union, the survivor of an intense struggle for supremacy, became the first giant business in the country, bigger even than the railroads in the 1860s, and an early prototype of an administrative hierarchy organized around functional responsibilities. The story of Western Union's rise bears marked similarities and contrasts in the later development of a still larger communications giant, the Bell Telephone System, which has dominated the industry since the 1880s.

In the past two decades the changing business environment that has affected so many U.S. industries has challenged telecommunications as well. New technologies, the explosive growth of electronics firms, the blurring of the distinction between data processing and data transmission, the new willingness of regulatory agencies to foster competition, the emergence of new participants from hitherto separate businesses, and foreign competition have subjected the industry and its leading firms to intense pressures. As a result, AT&T has redefined its strategy, moving from "the service business" to "the knowledge business" and reorganized from a formal, functional bureaucracy to a less structured, more adaptive form. Early in 1982, the forces of change came to a dramatic climax, when AT&T and the Department of Justice negotiated a consent decree to break up the Bell System into separate competitive and regulated businesses.

## TELECOMMUNICATIONS IN AMERICA: AN ORGANIZATIONAL HISTORY

To understand the strategic and organizational issues facing today's industry it is helpful to look at the development of communications in America and the formation of its dominant firms. Western Union and the Bell System rose to monopolize their markets because of far-seeing strategies, clever management, good fortune, and (later) public policy. They were also buttressed, however, by functional structures that served their needs and supported their growth. In the case of AT&T, the functional organization proved remarkably enduring.

There was nothing foreordained about the rise of America's communications giants. In preindustrial societies communications were generally controlled by governments. National post offices are almost as ancient a part of central bureaucracies as treasuries and war departments. Postal service in America has been a centralized function since colonial times. In addition, governments sometimes employed rapid signaling services during wartime that were occasionally adapted to commercial uses in quieter periods. Napoleonic France, for instance, boasted a preelectric "telegraph" system of 224 stations that transmitted simple messages — the outcome of battles, arrival of ships — through line-of-sight semaphores.[3]

Central control over the diffusion of information remains typical in many Western nations where postal, telegraphic, and telephonic services are a government monopoly.* In the United States, however, electric transmission of messages developed in private hands after the government turned down the opportunity. Samuel F.B. Morse and his partner, Alfred Vail, received a government grant to build a line between Baltimore and Washington in 1844. The grateful Morse then hoped that the government would take over the expansion of the service. In fact, the U.S. Post Office Department did administer the Washington-Baltimore line for several years but could not persuade Congress, then distracted by the Mexican War, that the telegraph was potentially a profitable instrument.[4]

Once the government abandoned the telegraph, the business grew, in the words of one historian, "with weed-like rapidity and often with no more than weed-like stability."[5] The original Morse patentees feuded and competed among themselves, while inventors and promoters of similar equipment — Bain, House, Hughes — also scrambled to wire the nation. A host of firms sprang up in the 1840s: Morse's own Magnetic Telegraph Co.; Henry O'Rielly's Atlantic, Lake, and Mississippi Co.; the New York, Albany, and Buffalo; the Erie and Michigan; the Western; the New York and Boston; the Boston and Portland; and the Washington and New Orleans, to name only a few of the major companies formed by the end of 1846. Soon scores of smaller companies mushroomed between the major trunk lines. This rapid growth was supported by the voracious demand of three major customers: newspaper editors, who found the telegraph a wonderful conveyancer of news; an emerging network of "small competitive enterprises and independent merchants, wholesalers, and speculators;" and the railroads, who used the telegraph to schedule and coordinate the movement of trains and freight.[6] The railroads, in fact, granted rights-of-way and in the 1850s commonly formed alliances with telegraph companies to open new territory.

The first shakeout in American industry followed quickly in the 1850s. The ruinous effects of competition — price wars, needless dupli-

---

*Deregulation of telecommunications is now underway in several countries, including the United Kingdom and Australia.

Figure 8.1  Formation of the Western Union Telegraph Company 1844–1900

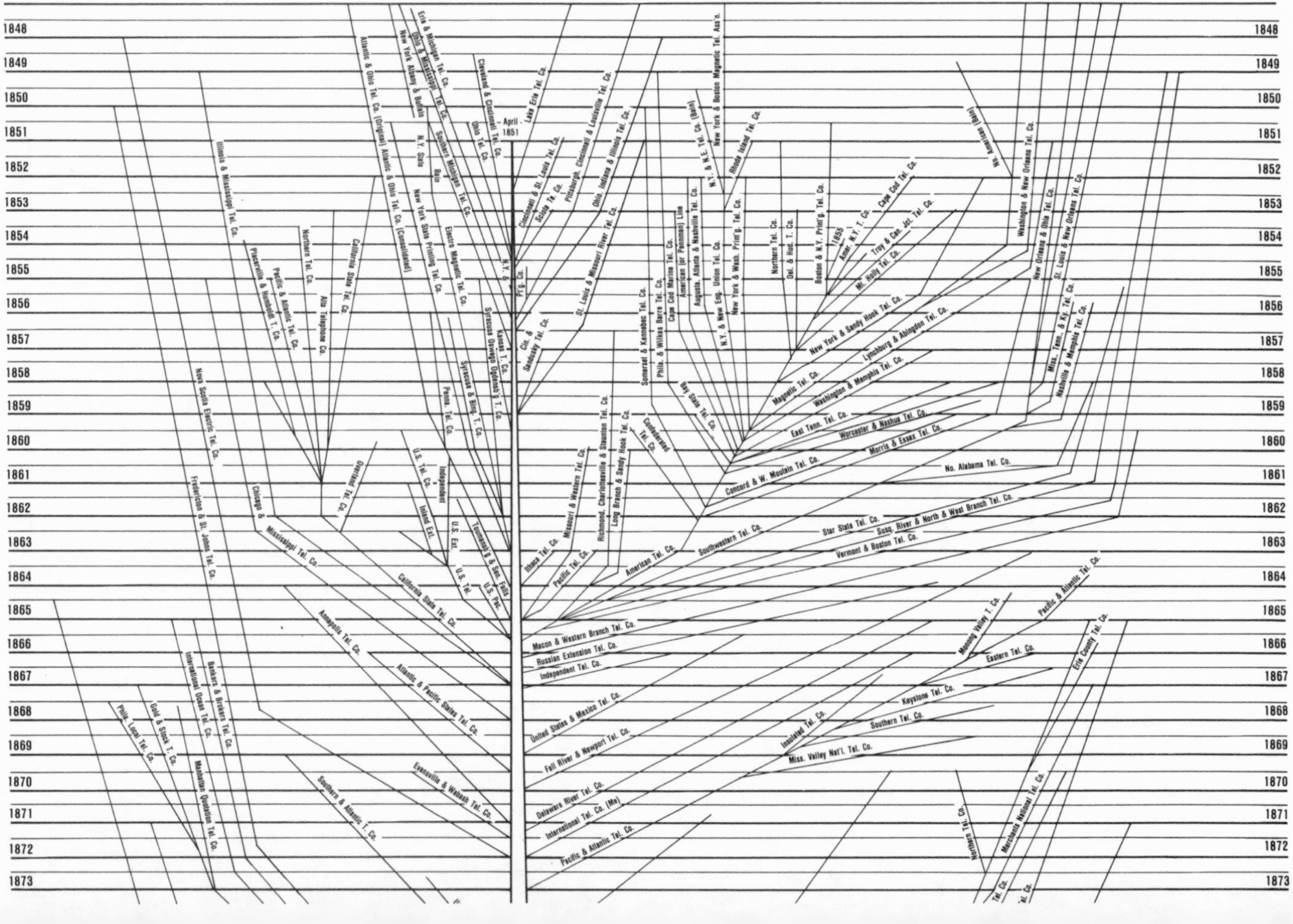

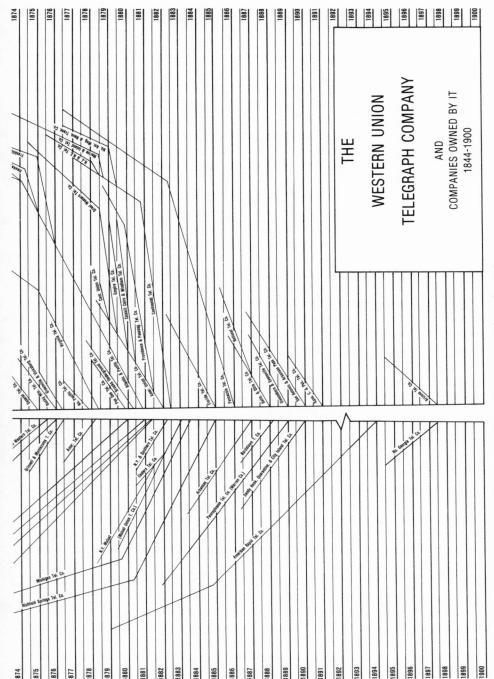

THE

WESTERN UNION

TELEGRAPH COMPANY

AND

COMPANIES OWNED BY IT

1844-1900

SOURCE: Robert Luther Thompson, *Wiring a Continent: The History of the Telegraph Industry in the United States, 1832–1866* (Princeton: Princeton University Press, 1947), facing p. 422.

201

▼

cation of service, incompatibility of equipment between firms, the shoddiness of hasty construction, and the draining of capital—led to pools and combinations. Bankruptcies and predatory competition exacted their toll, although there were surely sound business reasons to form alliances. The winners in these competitive struggles emerged first as regional powers or as monopolists on particularly valuable trunk lines. One such firm was the New York and Mississippi Valley Printing Telegraph Company, a dominant force in the Midwest before it outgrew its borders and changed its name to the Western Union Telegraph Company in 1856.

The ongoing consolidation was epitomized in 1857 by a contract— "the Treaty of the Six Nations"—in which six leading firms carved up the eastern United States into exclusive territories. Although this "treaty" was supposed to endure for thirty years, the destruction of networks in the South and border states during the Civil War left all in the hands of three companies, one of which, the United States Telegraph Company, had not even existed in 1857. The final step was taken in 1866 when the big three—Western Union, the U.S. Telegraph Co., and the American Telegraph Co.—merged under Western Union's leadership (Figure 8.1).[7]

Thus twenty years of fierce competition ended with a virtual national monopoly. Scores of small companies still remained in 1866, but Western Union dwarfed them all in assets, stations, and mileage, and it was the only one offering national service. According to the company's annual report of 1869, Western Union controlled nearly 90% of the telegraphic business in the United States.[8]

Figure 8.2 recapitulates the early history of the telegraph in terms of our model of adaptation. Initially, barriers to entry were low and a spate of telegraph companies sprang up in Area 4 conditions during the 1840s. The first wave of competition in the 1840s and early 1850s increased information complexity (IC) and resource scarcity (RS) and propelled the industry into Areas 1 and 2. Margins began to shrink and capital dried up. The Magnetic Telegraph Company (a Morse company), for example, could manage annual dividends of only 2% in 1850 and 1851 despite a fast start in the 1840s. Even Western Union paid no dividends in its first seven years.[9] The early casualties, the first attempts to cooperate, and the regional consolidations pulled the industry down through Area 5 conditions in the late 1850s. Western Union's dominance during the next decade continued the downward trend, leaving the industry in 1866 poised in Area 7 conditions, where the nation's telegraph service was provided by a monopoly.

A closer look at Western Union's history fills out this general pattern of growth. In 1851, when its predecessor company was founded, the firm possessed only 535 miles of wire at a capitalization of

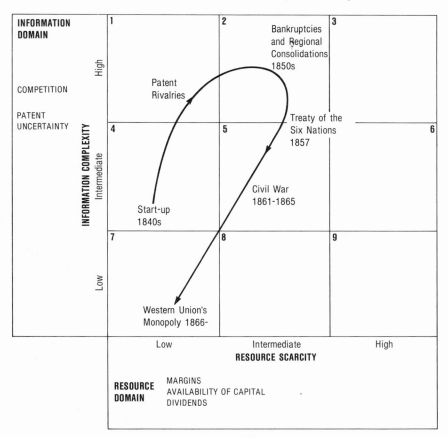

**Figure 8.2    Consolidation of the Telegraph Industry 1845–1866**

$170,000. Fifteen years later Western Union claimed more than $40 million in capital and controlled more than 75,000 miles of wire and 2,250 stations.[10] Luck played a significant role in this success — for example, the Civil War did relatively little damage to the lines — but Western Union's management had been unusually shrewd. The key figure was Hiram Sibley, whose strategy was far-reaching for the time and the business. Sibley was a system builder who believed that telegraphy could never pay in a highly competitive environment. Perhaps impressed by the growth and structure of several railroad companies, he extended Western Union's organization far beyond the capacity of any other single firm.

Western Union first grew by concentrating on a particular geographic market, the Midwest. Sibley diminished competitive uncertainties by buying up the rights to the House printing telegraph and by maintaining close control of it. By offering to lease or buy struggling companies in the targeted region, Sibley kept himself well informed of the financial condition of each company and, at opportune moments, he and his associates bought up stock at nominal prices. With his lieutenant, Anson Stager, he negotiated a series of favorable contracts with railroads beginning in 1854. In one case, the railroads agreed to build lines from Cleveland to Chicago in return for priority use of the telegraph for their own needs. Thus Sibley gained a major trunk line at no cost. Western Union consolidated its dealings with the railroads by securing agreements that excluded contracts with other telegraph companies.

As the company grew larger and more profitable (Table 8.1), Sibley located and exploited cracks in competing telegraph systems. He secretly bought out two of three partners in one rival operation and he broke up another competing system by purchasing its weakest but still essential links. After this conquest of the Midwest, Sibley became a prime mover in bigger causes, such as the Treaty of the Six Nations and the construction of telegraph lines to California and Europe.[11]

The organizational innovations of Sibley and his successor, William Orton, proved as significant as the company's strategy. The rapid consolidations that created the telegraphic empire brought with them the need to integrate Western Union's sprawling operations into a single harmonious system. In the late 1860s Western Union adopted a centralized structure with well-defined rules and regulations to achieve this goal. The company borrowed some of its organization, including the distinction between line and staff officers, from the railroads. The

**Table 8.1    Western Union Dividends 1857–1863**

| MONTH/YEAR | CAPITAL | % DIVIDEND | |
|---|---|---|---|
| Dec. 1, 1857 | $    369,700 | 8 1/2% | (cash) |
| April 1, 1858 | 369,700 | 5 | (cash) |
| July 6 | 369,700 | 8 | (cash) |
| July 24 | 379,700 | 20 | (cash) |
| Aug. 19 | 379,700 | 33 | (stock) |
| Sept. 22 | 385,700 | 414.40 | (stock) |
| 1859 | 2,263,300 | 2 | (cash) |
| 1860 | 2,329,500 | 5 | (cash) |
| 1861 | 2,355,000 | 5 | (cash) |
| July 16, 1862 | 2,355,000 | 27.26 | (stock) |
| | 2,994,800 | 9 | (cash) |
| March 16, 1863 | 2,979,300 | 100 | (stock) |
| | 5,993,400 | 9 | (cash) |
| Dec. 23 | 5,962,600 | 33 1/3 | (stock) |

SOURCE: James D. Reid, *The Telegraph in America* (New York: John Pohlemus, 1886), p. 484.

influence probably ran both ways, however, since the telegraph company reached its national boundaries more than a decade before the first of the large railroad systems was created.[12]

At Western Union's New York headquarters, "believed to be the most extensive and well-appointed telegraph office in the world," an "executive committee" consisting of the president, several vice-presidents, and a treasurer maintained "a general supervision over every department of the service." Headquarters also included an auditor and an "electrician" or chief engineer. After the Civil War the central office for supply and purchasing was moved to New York. The executive committee's purview extended to two "manufactories" of electrical equipment as well. In 1872 the company and one of its officers acquired controlling stock in a fledgling electrical supplier in the Midwest, Gray and Barton, later known as the Western Electric Company.[13]

Western Union's operations spanned four regions — East, South, Central, and Pacific — headed by general superintendents. Beneath them were some thirty-three district superintendents and approximately three thousand offices (Figure 8.3). Each month office managers forwarded to the district superintendents reports containing the number of messages transmitted, gross receipts, and accounts, "all expenditures in detail." The district managers collated these reports and sent them on to the central auditor. In addition, the district superintendents prepared "detailed statements" of disbursements for construction and maintenance for the general superintendents every month.[14]

By the late 1860s and early 1870s, then, Western Union was "the first multiunit modern business enterprise in the United States," a highly organized, vertically integrated company with a national monopoly on long-distance telegraph operations between major cities.[15] Over the years, however, Western Union was unable to sustain its success and adapt to new competitive threats. As competition waned, the company faced growing public criticism and internal organizational troubles. One of the earliest targets for populist opponents of big business, Western Union spent the rest of the nineteenth century fending off legislation in Congress to nationalize telegraphy.[16] Popular resentment sprang chiefly from the company's monopolistic control of the market. However, Western Union also suffered from its reputation as a stern employer. Telegraph workers complained about long hours, low pay, cramped conditions, strict rules, and close supervision. Employee discretion in low-ranking positions was limited, while turnover ran high.[17]

We have dwelled at such length on Western Union's past because it was in many respects the prototype of later communications firms,

206

## Figure 8.3 Organizational Structure of Western Union 1869

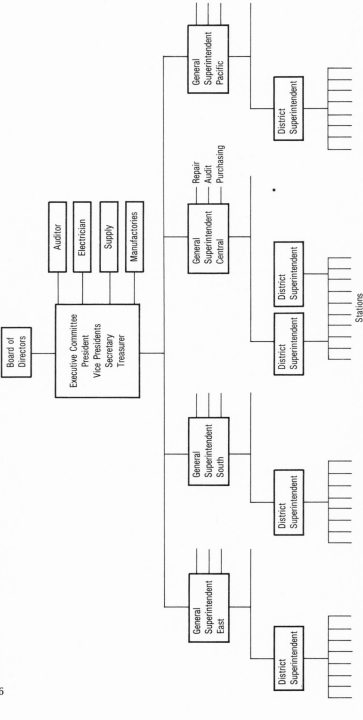

SOURCES: The Western Union Telegraph Co., annual reports of 1869 and 1873; Alfred D. Chandler, Jr., *The Visible Hand: The Managerial Revolution in American Business* (Cambridge, Mass.: Harvard University Press, 1977), pp. 177–178; James. D. Reid, *The Telegraph in America* (New York: John Polhemus, 1886) pp. 485–486.

most prominently AT&T. Many of Western Union's business methods—its control over technology, entrepreneurial strategy, and management of consolidation—emerged in the Bell System. In at least
one important respect, however—organization—AT&T came to differ
from Western Union.

## THE RISE OF AT&T

The rise of AT&T is both the most spectacular and the most enduring
in the annals of American business. AT&T's history can be divided
into four periods. In the first (1875 to 1894) the Bell Association and
companies flourished as a patent monopoly. The company's fortunes
improved steadily but not dramatically in these years, while its distinctive organization as a holding company and as a system was laid out. In
the second period (1894 to 1913) the Bell System struggled in competition with other telephone companies. The holding company organization and the structural relations between the parent and the associated
companies were formalized in these years. During the third period
(1913 to the early 1970s) AT&T resided fairly comfortably in an organizational and strategic equilibrium with its environment under state
and federal regulation. With the opening of a new era of competition
in the past decade, AT&T has entered a fourth period of its development.

### PATENT MONOPOLY (1875 TO 1894)

When Alexander Graham Bell invented the telephone in Boston in
1875 he had already sold shares in the patent rights to two local investors, Gardiner G. Hubbard (Bell's future father-in-law) and Thomas
Sanders. These two gentlemen, Bell, and his assistant, Thomas Watson, formed the Bell Patent Association, the first organization to develop the telephone for commercial purposes. Some of the company's
most famous practices were sketched out in these earliest years. For instance, Hubbard, impressed by the example of a former client in the
shoe machinery business, made the fateful decision to rent rather than
to sell telephone equipment to customers. The Bell Associates believed
that three sorts of benefits would accrue from rentals: more money,
better control over the telephone patents, and an image as a service
company rather than a manufacturing business.[18] Certainly the example of Western Union's experience led the Bell Associates to maximize
the benefits of patent control and they challenged encroachments vigorously.

The early growth of telephony was constrained, however, by limited technology and lack of capital. Since telephone instruments were

developed before it was discovered how to interconnect them, there was little likelihood of a booming growth like that of the early telegraph. Indeed, the telephone was initially perceived and advertised either as "a speaking tube" between two users only, or as a device for home entertainment, like the radio, in which a central station would broadcast to many end users.[19] The first local exchanges to interconnect multiple customers opened in 1878, although it took several years to establish the best technology.

Lack of capital posed more immediate organizational problems for the Bell patentees. To expand the business beyond Boston, they had to arrange for agents to run the business elsewhere, under temporary licensing agreements. This was the germ of the future relationship between AT&T and its operating companies. Agents provided service and were charged "to collect the rentals and royalties from the users, and transmit the collections, less a specified discount to cover their services, to the parent Bell company."[20] The need to attract capital also forced the associates to surrender control of the business early on to outside investors and managers.

One of the first outside managers to enter the Bell organization was Theodore N. Vail, a cousin of Morse's first partner. Theodore Vail had begun his career in the telegraph business and had recently climaxed a three-year tenure in the U.S. Post Office Department by rising to become general superintendent of the Railway Mail Service. Hubbard noticed this "thousand horsepower steam engine" in Washington and offered Vail a job as general manager of National Bell in 1878.[21] Thus when Vail came to the telephone company he was already schooled in the ways of managing the nation's two largest industries, telegraphy and railroading. At National Bell, Vail became responsible for the company's growth strategy and long-term organization. Hubbard had acted on the belief that most income would flow from telephone rentals. In contrast, Vail, like Hiram Sibley (and several railroad managers) before him, believed in the commercial value of systems. As he himself put it, "It is more the system established in connection with the telephone, than the telephone itself, that makes the value of the telephone."[22] Accordingly, he changed Bell's policies toward licensing, patents, R&D, and the development of long-distance exchanges.

Early on Vail expressed his general strategy: "to protect to the fullest extent, the present and future interests of our Company without hampering . . . by . . . unnecessary conditions, the fullest possible use of the Telephones."[23] Scrapping Hubbard's loose coalition of agencies, Vail eventually granted permanent licenses "to build and operate telephone exchanges in return for an equity interest in the licensee" — usually 35% to 40%.[24] Vail thereby found more willing takers for the Bell franchise at the same time as he countered the uncertainties of his own business. One of the chief virtues of the new licensing policy (from the parent's point of view) was that it transferred to the licensees the burdens of raising capital and coping with local business environments. Vail also made it company policy to buy up majority stock whenever possible.[25]

Furthermore, Vail recognized that National Bell's distinctive competence included the exchange business as well as the telephone itself. While the old management defended the telephone instrument patents ferociously, it was Vail who saw the need to invest in R&D, particularly on the exchange. In 1880 the company established an "electrical and patent department," to monitor patents and test equipment.[26] "Just as quick as we started into the district exchange system," Vail later testified, "we found out that it would develop a thousand and one little patents and inventions with which to do the business which was necessary, and that was what we wanted to get control and possession of."[27]

Vail's emphasis on the exchange and control was matched by a determination to develop a long-distance network. His tenacious adherence to this goal was partly responsible for a crucial event in early Bell System history. In 1876 Western Union's president, William Orton, had turned down an offer to purchase Bell's patents for $100,000. Within a year, the telegraph company regretted this decision and determined to enter the telephone business. The Bell interests countered with a suit against infringement of their patents. The case was eventually settled in 1879 when Western Union agreed to drop out of the telephone business in return for a 20% share in Bell's royalties during the life of the patents, Bell's purchase of its telephone properties, and a pledge from Bell to stay away from telegraphy.[28]

Historians have often been puzzled by Western Union's capitulation, because the telegraph company seemed outwardly prepared to dominate the telephone business. In 1879, however, the statement looked less like a surrender than a convincing victory. By relinquishing the telephone, Western Union avoided the uncertainty of managing a questionable business while hedging against Bell's future growth through the claim on royalties. Western Union also escaped a final judgment in a case it might well have lost. Moreover, the telegraph company's attention had not been fully focused on the case, because throughout 1879 its directors were absorbed in fighting off a takeover bid by financier, Jay Gould.[29]

Western Union may have acted on technological grounds as well. The technology of the telephone proved to be less similar to the telegraph than it first appeared. The crucial difference was the local exchange and switching network, which in 1879 was still a messy and uncertain business. The telegraph had never penetrated the residential market and did not require interconnectability in anything approaching the same degree. Indeed the two devices initially seemed more complementary than competitive. The telephone, without long-distance exchanges, seemed suited only for local markets; the telegraph, in contrast, was largely excluded from local markets because it required skilled operators to send and receive messages.[30]

Finally, organizational differences underlay Western Union's decision to relinquish the telephone. The telegraph company was, as we have seen, a national enterprise under centralized management. Company rules clearly circumscribed the activities of office managers, the agents in the field. The telephone business, however, required leaving discretion to the men at the lowest level. Bell agents in the field had to get out, sell, and interact with customers. The company's licensing policy gave them every incentive to do so. Indeed, Vail considered the differences in organization between the telegraph and telephone companies to be an advantage. As he wrote to one anxious agent, "You have too great an idea of the Western Union. If it was all massed in your one city you might well fear it; but it is represented by one man only, and he has probably as much as he can attend to outside of the telephone."[31] Western Union simply did not have the right kind of organization in place to compete with Bell, despite its vast advantages of capital and its preexisting national network. Its functional bureaucracy could not adapt to the challenges of selling a new product and managing a new service.

After the settlement of 1879, one of the great turning points in the history of the telecommunications industry, Vail pushed forward in his drive to turn the telephone business into a system. From the start, equipment manufacture, like service operations, had been performed under a license contract. All telephones were built initially at a small electrical shop in Boston. However, the growing volume of business quickly strained the shop's capacity. Fortunately, as part of the settlement of 1879, Western Union had agreed to part with its telephone manufacturing interests in Western Electric. By 1882 Vail negotiated the purchase of Western Electric for American Bell, thereby establishing the telephone company as a formidable vertically integrated industrial enterprise.[32] That same year American Bell reached another milestone. The first long-distance line opened between Boston and Providence. As the long-distance business grew, American Bell formed another subsidiary, the American Telephone and Telegraph Company (AT&T), to manage the new service in 1885.

By the time Vail left the business in 1887, the general structure of the Bell System was in place: a central holding company with equity interest in operating exchanges, central R&D and manufacturing, and a central long lines business. The fortunes of the telephone company during the patent monopoly are laid out in Table 8.2. At first, growth was slow. In April 1879, stock was selling at $50 a share. As Bell's competitive position improved, however, its value shot up. When the settlement with Western Union was announced, Bell shares sold for $1,000 each.[33] From then on, the Bell companies enjoyed steady and sure growth.

After Vail's departure, Bell's management became less innovative. Vail's successors pursued a defensive strategy of slow expansion with earnings dependent on high rental charges. Indeed, geographical growth was probably constrained by these monopoly rents. In New York in 1893, for instance, business customers paid $240 per year while residential users paid $180. By way of contrast, in London, where the government managed the telephone, subscribers of both types paid approximately $100 per year. All in all, telephone rents accounted for 70% of Bell revenues.[34]

**Table 8.2   Financial Performance of the Bell System 1881–1899**

| YEAR ENDED | NET INCOME/ REVENUES (%) | DIVIDENDS/ NET INCOME (%) | REINVESTED EARNINGS/ NET INCOME (%) |
|---|---|---|---|
| February 28 | | | |
| 1881* | 53.0% | 80% | 20% |
| 1882 | 67.5 | 74.1 | 25.9 |
| 1883 | 72.4 | 61.2 | 38.8 |
| 1884 | 75.7 | 65.0 | 35.0 |
| December 31 | | | |
| 1884* | 78.7 | 80.4 | — |
| 1885 | 74.5 | 91.3 | 8.7 |
| 1886 | 73.6 | 84.8 | 15.2 |
| 1887 | 70.0 | 77.8 | 22.2 |
| 1888 | 70.3 | 75.1 | 24.9 |
| 1889 | 72.8 | 70.0 | 30.0 |
| 1890 | 73.2 | 75.0 | 25.0 |
| 1891 | 71.0 | 84.3 | 15.7 |
| 1892 | 73.1 | 81.2 | 18.8 |
| 1893 | 67.2 | 91.6 | 8.4 |
| 1894 | 61.8 | 98.7 | 1.3 |
| 1895 | 63.6 | 95.7 | 4.3 |
| 1896 | 62.9 | 96.1 | 3.9 |
| 1897 | 65.8 | 87.4 | 12.6 |
| 1898 | 60.9 | 90.1 | 9.9 |
| 1899 | 55.6 | 90.9 | 9.1 |

SOURCE: U.S. Federal Communications Commission, *Investigation of the Telephone Industry in the United States* (Washington, D.C., 1939), Exhibit 1360C, p. 81.

*Ten-month periods

## COMPETITIVE INTERLUDE (1894 TO 1913)

The second period of Bell System history opened with the expiration of the basic telephone patents. After 1894 independent exchange companies and manufacturers mushroomed in a growth reminiscent of the early years of the telegraph. Some eighty-seven telephone companies invaded the business in 1894; by 1902 a federal census showed independents controlling 1.5 million miles of wire and 1.05 million phones.[35] The independents fed on populist resentment of the telephone monopoly. A great many of them had names like "the People's," "the Citizens'," or "the Home" Telephone Company. Most of the new companies appeared in small cities and towns and in rural areas not served by the Bell System. These operations ranged from mom-and-pop telephone companies and farmers' mutual lines to large, well-funded enterprises. Independent companies occasionally challenged the Bell System directly, as in Washington, Chicago, and Cleveland, where the newcomers offered service at substantially lower rates.[36]

American Bell's initial reaction to the new competition was a mixture of fear and aggression. Some of the early Boston and New York investors sold their stock in the 1890s. Indeed, this period marked the permanent separation of ownership and control in the organization.[37] While the original investors quailed, the management of the company responded vigorously to competition. The price of service to Bell customers plunged by more than two-thirds (from $5.74 per instrument rented to $1.87) between 1893 and 1896. The operating companies joined battle with the independents through fair means — refusal to sell equipment or to interconnect, legitimate takeovers, expansion, propaganda, and continued litigation in patent suits — and foul — pricing below cost and secret buy-outs.[38]

American Bell intimidated the independents but could not stop them from growing. Bell's trump card, however, proved to be the management of long-distance exchanges. Only American Bell had the technology, capital, and managerial experience to offer long-distance service. It was easy enough for the independent companies to get started, but quite another matter for them to grow beyond their local borders. If they wanted to connect to the wider world they had to rely on the Bell System — which was rarely cooperative. "The Long-Distance Company," as AT&T was called in those years, was obviously a well-managed organization. Long-distance traffic accounted for an increasing portion of Bell System income in the 1890s. In 1894 the subsidiary brought in less than $400,000 in net income; within five years AT&T's net income reached nearly $3 million.[39]

After 1907 Bell's attitude toward the independents changed for two reasons. First, a group of New York bankers led by J.P. Morgan —

whose jaundiced view of competition was well known (see Chapter 3) —
acquired control of the management of AT&T. With the support of
the Morgan interests, the presidency went to Theodore Vail, who, at
the age of sixty-two, still had a dozen years of progressive management
remaining to him. Vail had no love for competition, which he thought
wasteful and ultimately harmful to the consumer, and immediately
moderated AT&T's hostile behavior toward smaller telephone companies. He wanted AT&T to grow by acquisition rather than by squan-
dering resources to duplicate service, and he began preaching the virtues of the Bell System's "universality." In 1908 Vail ordered Western
Electric to modify its long-standing policy of selling exclusively within
the system in order "to secure uniformity of equipment among non-
Bell companies, so as to facilitate their connection with the Bell System."[40]

The second factor in AT&T's changing outlook was public pressure. The first regulatory agencies to monitor telephone rates were
formed in Wisconsin and New York in 1907. Federal antitrust enforc-
ers regarded AT&T suspicously, too, especially after Vail arranged a
merger with Western Union in 1909. The Interstate Commerce Commission undertook federal auditing of telephone accounts in 1910 and
the Wilson administration launched an official antitrust investigation
of AT&T early in 1913. These public pressures eventually forced
AT&T to make an historic concession, the Kingsbury Commitment, in
1913. AT&T agreed to divest Western Union, to forswear future acquisitions of the independents without prior approval of the ICC, and
to interconnect with all responsible independents.[41]

In organizational terms, the era of competition brought some important changes to the Bell System. At the end of 1899 the subsidiary
AT&T became the parent of American Bell in a two-for-one stock
swap. This change was partly motivated by a desire to move headquarters to New York, where corporation laws were more liberal, but it also
made the system's organization more consistent with its actual workings. AT&T had held the stock of the operating companies and acted
as their most important central contact. American Bell, in contrast,
had held AT&T's stock, some patents, some of the licenses, and Western Electric. Gradually, after 1899, all was transferred to the central
holding company, the new AT&T, completing the general form of the
Bell System that would endure for more than eighty years.

Vail added characteristic twists to the organization after his return.
One of his innovations was to separate the long lines department from
the general operating department at headquarters. Henceforth the
holding company and the operating company aspects of AT&T became distinctly separate. Vail also centralized research and development. The research group at headquarters (such as it was) had been a

branch of the engineering department; each operating company and Western Electric had also maintained separate research staffs and dabbled in new products. As a result, the system lacked uniform engineering standards and procedures. Moreover, AT&T's attitude toward research had been defensive. It often preferred to buy up patents or to test existing equipment rather than conduct research and invent new products itself. One of Vail's first priorities upon his return was to stimulate a new interest in research. Accordingly, he moved the technical staff from Boston to New York and appointed a new chief engineer, John J. Carty, who worked out definite procedures and standards for the engineering department. Carty and Vail also clarified its relation to the operating companies and to Western Electric. The new central research group ("the 1907 Lab") began conducting fundamental as well as practical research. Vail was determined that AT&T stay abreast of all developments in communications, including radio, that might affect the future of the telephone business.[42]

### REGULATED MONOPOLY (1913 TO 1970s)

For more than six decades after 1913 the Bell System reposed in an adaptive equilibrium with the external world. The Kingsbury Commitment stabilized AT&T's environment while the second coming of Vail stabilized its management. The company embarked on a distinguished period of its history as the country's largest and the world's richest corporation, dynamic and well managed. This is not to say that the period was uneventful. On the contrary, AT&T weathered two massive antitrust suits, the intense scrutiny of the Federal Communications Commission (FCC), and frequent attacks by muckraking journalists and authors. Moreover, the period was one of significant technical accomplishment, as indicated by Bell Labs' pantheon of Nobel laureates and new products, from radio and motion picture soundtracks to radar, transistors, and lasers. But the passage of time brought no serious challenge to AT&T's fundamental strategy or structure. Its status as a regulated monopoly permitted its organization to stabilize as a functional bureaucracy, while critics charged that the innovation and efficiency in the system suffered as a result.

The telephone business was now considered a public utility and a natural monopoly and AT&T was granted a virtual national monopoly to deliver phone service. By the 1930s rates were regulated at the national, state, and sometimes municipal levels, with rates of return generally allowed at 5% to 7% — substantial profits in a preinflationary economy. Public outcry at AT&T's sheer bulk led to a number of government investigations, and the company has been inundated by an unending stream of litigation for most of this century. The most serious problems stemmed from federal antitrust suits filed in 1913 and 1949 and an exceedingly thorough investigation by the FCC shortly after its founding in 1934.

AT&T emerged from each of these ruffled but intact. For a brief period (1918 to 1919) the government nationalized telephone and telegraph service but eventually conceded that private management was more efficient. The FCC investigation reinforced the public image of a giant company sprawling out of control, but otherwise led to no substantive public policy changes. The second antitrust case (1949 to 1956), which aimed at breaking up AT&T's vertical integration by forcing the divestiture of Western Electric, achieved the opposite result. According to the consent decree that terminated the suit, AT&T was permitted to retain Western Electric but henceforth Western sold only within the system, to the government — Western was then a prime defense contractor — or occasionally to foreign customers. Western Electric was also forbidden to enter data processing markets. This settlement proved costly as the computer business took off, but it legitimated AT&T's basic organization as a holding company. Indeed, all of the major telephone companies in the U.S. are holding companies at least partly modeled on the Bell System.[43]

## AT&T'S TRADITIONAL STRATEGY AND STRUCTURE

The growth of the Bell System was shaped by strategy as well as technology and environment. Once again, Vail charted the company's course. In his early years at National Bell Vail preached the value of creating a unified telephone system. After 1907 he coined the company's early slogan: "One system, one policy, universal service." Elaborating on this notion some years later, he wrote that the Bell System's mission would be

> to develop the possibilities of service and to give the best possible service; to anticipate all the reasonable demands of the public as to service, either as to quality, quantity, or extent; to distribute the charges for such service in such a manner as will make it possible for everyone to be connected who will add to the value of the service to others. . . .[44]

Vail's emphasis on service was condensed into an even more famous slogan in 1927 by President Walter S. Gifford, who pronounced that the Bell System's aim was "to furnish the best possible service at the lowest possible cost consistent with financial safety."[45] This motto formed part of AT&T's public image for nearly fifty years. In the words of one recent company publication: "The Bell System's basic aim has been and continues to be the widest availability of high-quality communications services at the lowest overall cost to the entire public. It is this aim that governs the design of our services and the way they are marketed and priced."[46]

The manner in which the company approached its goal of universal service varied over time. Under regulation, strategic planning was essentially network planning, designing products and allocating funds to develop and expand the network. The Bell System initially controlled costs through its manufacturing policies. Bell Labs and Western collaborated on the design of new products and Western eventually produced them in rigidly standardized, cost-efficient forms. Later, as public policies changed in the 1940s, the company began to subsidize local service with long-distance revenues. These tactics meshed perfectly with AT&T's plans and with the demands of the American public. By the 1960s the Bell System had achieved its goal of a wired America. The cost of basic local service was within reach of nearly everyone. In 1970, 92% of domestic households included at least one telephone.

Over the years AT&T felt little pressure to reshape the structure developed in the early part of this century. Many features of the company date to its founding but its internal organization was virtually fixed by Vail's death in 1920. AT&T, according to Vail, was

> primarily a holding company, holding stocks of the associated operating and manufacturing companies. As an operating company it owns and operates the long-distance lines, the lines that connect all the systems of the associated operating companies with each other.
> In addition . . . it assumes what might be termed the centralized general administrative functions of all the associated companies.[47]

The general organization and equity relationships of the Bell System are shown in Figure 8.4. AT&T as a holding company owned stock in hundreds of smaller companies, but the principal subordinates were Western Electric, the Bell Telephone Laboratories (Bell Labs), and a cluster of operating telephone companies (OTCs) spread over the nation. Bell Labs, established in 1925 out of the Western Electric engineering department, was owned 50% by AT&T and 50% by Western Electric.

The traditional structure of AT&T's headquarters is laid out in Figure 8.5. At the very top (not shown) was the board of directors, to whom the president reported. In the first decade after the bankers acquired control in 1907, the board exerted considerable influence on the president, especially in financial affairs. After 1920, however, the board's authority diminished before such dynamic senior managers as president Gifford (1925 to 1948). Reporting to the president were the heads of R&D, general operations, accounting and finance, legal affairs, public relations, information, long lines, and the secretary. For

**Figure 8.4  Functional Organization of the Bell System**

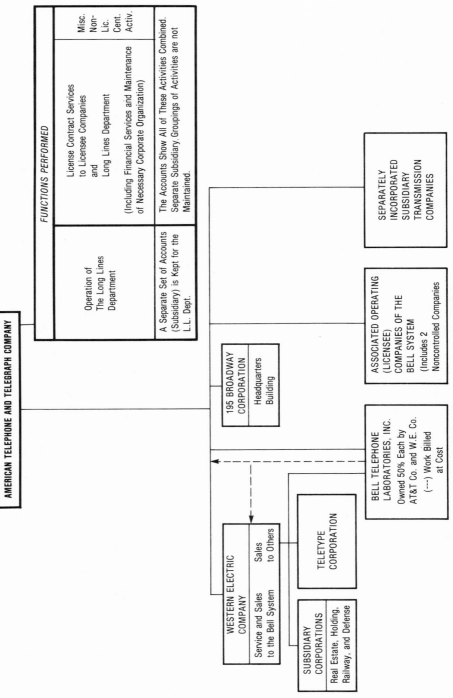

SOURCE: *AT&T: Adaptation in Progress (A) 1875–1974* (HBS Case Services, 9–481–074), p. 31.

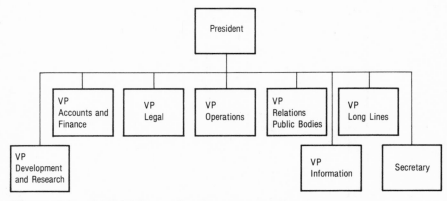

**Figure 8.5     AT&T Organization—Traditional Structure**

SOURCE: U.S. Federal Communications Commission, *Investigation of the Telephone Industry in the United States* (Washington, D.C., 1939), p. 108.

most of the twentieth century, the majority of work at headquarters was concentrated in two of these departments, the "general departments" (operations) and long lines. The general departments provided services to the operating companies, including R&D, advice and assistance to functional departments, and legal and financial help, including assistance in marketing securities and raising money. The long lines department managed interstate and international long-distance traffic.

The twenty-three operating telephone companies were the legatees of the earliest licensed agents and represent the end product of consolidations of hundreds of smaller local companies. By the 1930s AT&T had acquired controlling ownership in all but two of the companies. Each OTC paid AT&T a proportion (about 2%) of its gross revenues in return for access to the long-distance network, central administrative help, and central R&D.

The organization of the early OTCs was described in a company document as "a purely geographical arrangement," or "territorial organization."[48] General managers at the local level oversaw many functions, including planning, sales, service, and the management of the local plant. After 1907 Vail and vice-president Edward J. Hall led a drive to standardize the organizations of the OTCs and to tighten their relations with headquarters. OTC structure became modeled partly on the organization of the AT&T central office and partly on the general structure of public utilities. Departments were established on the basis of functional skills (Figure 8.6).

The work of the commercial department included rate negotiations with state utility commissions, revenue collection, advertising, publica-

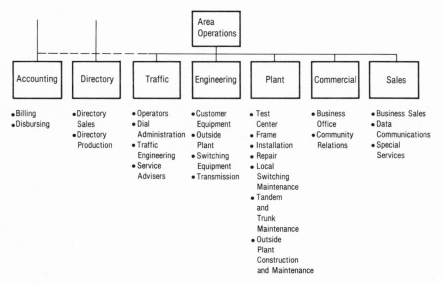

**Figure 8.6    Traditional OTC Organization**

SOURCE: *AT&T Adaptation in Progress (A) 1875–1974* (HBS Case Services, 9–481–074), p. 38.

tion of directories, and routine customer relations. The plant department built and maintained central offices and performed routine wiring and installation. The engineering department enforced Bell System engineering standards and handled technical problems requiring special skills. Finally, the traffic department included operator services and personnel responsible for smoothing the flow of telephone traffic. In addition, each OTC had a separate accounting function. Over the years, the lines between departments grew rigid. Individual careers tended to develop exclusively within departments and there was no general coordination across them below the vice-presidential level. Nonetheless, the functional organization of the OTCs proved very successful in the Bell System's regulated environment, when task responsibilities were well defined and growth was achieved by expanding basic services.[49]

AT&T's relationship with the operating companies was generally one-sided. As an exhaustive FCC study of the 1930s put it:

> In exercising its control over these regional subsidiaries, [AT&T] licenses their operation under its patents, controls their financing; elects their directors; appoints their officers; directs their rate-making, advertising and public relations policies; standardizes their equipment; requires them to render periodic reports; and checks the latter by means of traveling auditors.[50]

Compared with the operating companies, the other parts of the Bell System — Western Electric and Bell Labs — were less closely watched from on high.

The Western Electric Company has been AT&T's major supplier since the 1880s. By the middle of the present century, Western had grown to become the largest single component of the Bell System and one of the country's biggest manufacturers. In 1972 Western Electric employed about 200,000 people and achieved more than $7 billion in sales. Its general role, according to the FCC, is twofold:

> First, it is the manufacturing branch of the Bell System; and second, it is the purchasing and supply department of the Bell System. In connection with its latter function, Western Electric is also a developer, storekeeper, installer, repairer, salvager, and junker of the Bell System.[51]

Since the 1956 consent decree Western Electric has not normally sold telephone equipment outside the system. Because of its peculiar legal status, and because it has such a large captive market (the OTCs) Western's manufacturing policies were not affected by competition. It has tended to count on extended production runs and capitalize on enormous economies of scale to hold down costs.

Bell Labs, one of the world's largest R&D institutions, has long enjoyed its reputation as one of the world's best. AT&T managers speak of the Labs as a "unique national resource." Over the years it has remained committed to Vail's research strategy and it represents a formidable competitive advantage for the company.[52] The list of significant innovations invented or developed at the Labs — radio equipment, radar, wave-guide transmission, transistors, semiconductors, fiber optics, lasers, and electronic switching equipment — is an impressive one. By tradition, employees at the Labs have received relatively little direction from AT&T and sometimes engage in basic research only tenuously related to the company's operational needs. By the early 1970s the Labs operated in seventeen locations, employed some 17,000 people (including 2,000 with Ph.Ds), and had an annual budget of about $500 million.

During AT&T's long, quiet period of strategic and organizational stability under regulation, the company developed a conservative management that placed relatively little emphasis on sales or marketing. In part, this was a matter of style. From the outset, most of AT&T's top managers had hailed from blueblood backgrounds, Boston Brahmins and Ivy Leaguers. Most senior AT&T executives were trained as engineers and many also prided themselves as humanists. A formal training program of the 1950s even sent managers back to school at the University of Pennsylvania, Swarthmore, and Dartmouth for liberal arts courses.[53] Many senior managers spent their entire careers in the Bell

System and almost all of the very highest circulated through one or more of the OTCs, Western Electric, or Bell Labs in order to acquire familiarity with its various parts. The organizational style of AT&T has been captured by John Brooks:

> There is a certain sameness about AT&T people. Their dress and manner is conservative, but not to the point of stuffiness. . . . They seem far more vivid, dashing, and enterprising than a building full of government bureaucrats, but far less so than, say, the brainy and hungry young hotshots of some rising new high-technology company. . . . Top AT&T people's tastes and interests tend to be similar, and for those who are going places, their primary interest is the Bell System. . . . Life at 195 [Broadway — company headquarters in New York], on the surface at least, is bland and civil; only very occasionally does one catch a sniff of the corporate jungle. . . .[54]

AT&T's record of employee relations has been generally favorable. Because of the nature of the business, the company was an enormous employer almost from the beginning. By 1885, the end of its first decade, American Bell employed nearly 6,000 people. By the eve of the depression some 325,000 people were on the rolls, and by the mid-1970s the company employed nearly a million workers.[55] The company's record as an employer is not without blemish. Although Vail introduced an employee pension plan in 1913, eligibility was tightly restricted — workers had to serve a minimum of twenty years with the system to qualify — and the plan was administered solely by management. N.R. Danielian, an FCC investigator in the 1930s, estimated that 80% to 90% of employees would never benefit from the plan.[56]

Despite generally thriving business, AT&T was slow to share its good fortune with low-ranking workers. These employees enjoyed little job flexibility or security and, in some cases, shockingly low incomes.[57] Workers followed standardized routines and were subjected to rigid supervisory controls.[58] Operators and service representatives, for instance, had to observe strict protocols in dealing with callers or customers while supervisors hovered nearby or randomly listened in. For many years employees were appraised according to inflexible standards which permitted very little employee discretion. Not surprisingly, employee turnover in many low-ranking positions was high.

If AT&T was a strict employer, it was seldom a capricious one. Nonetheless, employees were sometimes sacrificed to new technologies and to commitments to shareholders. During the depression, for instance, about 185,000 workers lost their jobs, although the business continued to thrive. The value of Bell stock remained high and the company continued its "habitual" (since 1922) dividend of $9 per share. Danielian has calculated that a reduction to an $8 dividend would have saved 18,000 jobs.[59] In AT&T's defense, however, it should be pointed out that the company refused to lower the wages of the employes it retained.[60] Moreover, during these years AT&T was in the midst of a conversion to dial telephones, which reduced the need for operators and other personnel in switching units.

Like many other leading American corporations, AT&T resisted unionization. Some Bell companies recognized the International Brotherhood of Electrical Workers before World War I, but, writes John Brooks, "The record is quite clear . . . that Bell System companies . . . opposed the incursion of a national union, and did so very effectively."[61] The means were never violent. AT&T paid relatively good wages and maintained a kind of paternalistic care for most of its workers. It is significant that one of the landmark studies of organizational behavior—the Hawthorne Experiment—took place in the Bell System with company support.[62] Nonetheless, the National Federation of Telephone Workers formed in 1939, finally reached a national agreement with the Bell System in 1946, after a series of local strikes and walkouts. The next year the union, now renamed the Communications Workers of America (CWA), called a national strike over wages and the desire to set up a national bargaining contract. The company and the CWA narrowly averted several other major strikes in the 1950s and 1960s.[63] In general—and especially in comparison with other companies in older industries—AT&T's relations with labor have been harmonious, the result of good pay, paternalistic policies, and justifiable employee pride in the high quality of Bell service.

## THE READAPTIVE RECORD

AT&T's financial performance has been spectacular over the years (Table 8.3). By the mid-1970s it boasted $75 billion in assets, almost a million employees, and nearly three million stockholders. Even its component parts were enormous. Western Electric, if a free-standing company, would have ranked among America's top twenty industrials in size. AT&T dominated the domestic telecommunications industry by a wide margin. Although more than 1,700 telephone companies operated in the U.S. in 1975, AT&T controlled more than 80% of the business (Table 8.4). The next largest telephone company, GTE, claimed a market share of less than 10%, while no other single company held more than a few percentage points.[64]

In view of its market dominance, the Bell System's sustained record of innovation and efficiency has been impressive. AT&T has been responsible for most of the significant inventions and new technologies in the communications industry during this century, from loading coils to

**Table 8.3   Bell System Operating Revenues and Net Income, 1935–1980**

| YEAR | TOTAL OPERATING REVENUES | NET INCOME |
|------|--------------------------|------------|
| 1935 | $        94,249,444 | $      125,806,505 |
| 1940 | 121,143,740 | 188,344,032 |
| 1945 | 233,896,054 | 171,640,228 |
| 1950 | 3,261,528,032 | 358,866,924 |
| 1955 | 5,297,043,174 | 546,045,367 |
| 1960 | 7,920,454,000 | 1,212,966,000 |
| 1965 | 11,061,783,000 | 1,850,185,000 |
| 1970 | 16,954,881,000 | 2,189,400,000 |
| 1975 | 28,957,241,000 | 3,147,722,000 |
| 1980 | 50,791,200,000 | 6,079,700,000 |

SOURCE: AT&T annual reports

transistors and from coaxial cables to fiber optics. Bell Labs has been a prolific innovator, producing on average more than one patent every working day since its founding.[65] On the other hand, many of these inventions were adopted slowly, if at all, by the system. By tradition, Bell Labs initiated its own projects subject to AT&T's approval. Instead of focusing on the system's operational needs, the Labs tended to conduct basic research that affected system architecture very slowly. Because the characteristic procedure was first to generate new ideas and then to look for applications, products actually discovered at the Labs, like the transistor, often took years to turn up in Bell products. Nonetheless, by conducting basic research and generating new products, AT&T was an atypical monopoly, one producing an abnormal amount of innovation and uncertainty.

Given AT&T's size and complexity it is difficult to measure efficiency in any meaningful sense. On one hand, most impartial observers would say, and even critics admit, that the United States has the best telephone service in the world. One study shows that the annual rate of

**Table 8.4   Five Largest Telephone Holding Companies, 1980**

| | NUMBER OF COMPANIES* | NUMBER OF TELEPHONES | PERCENT OF TOTAL U.S. TELEPHONES |
|------|------|------|------|
| Bell System (AT&T) | 23 | 145,515,000 | 80.1 |
| GTE | 10 | 15,756,400 | 8.7 |
| United Telecommunications | 6 | 4,697,500 | 2.6 |
| Continental Telephone Corp. | 8 | 3,125,800 | 1.7 |
| Central Telephone and Utilities Corp. | — | 1,806,600 | 1.0 |

SOURCE: U.S. Independent Telephone Association, *Independent Telephone Statistics for the Year 1980* (July, 1981), pp. 2, 8.

*1978 data source: U.S. Federal Communications Commission, *Statistics of Communications Common Carriers*, year ended December 31, 1978, pp. 213–214.

improvement in "total factor productivity" (TFP) of the communications industry averaged 4.2% between 1948 and 1976—the highest measured in any American industry and nearly twice the TFP rate of the economy generally. On the other hand, the sheer size of the Bell System guaranteed much bureaucratic waste and inefficiency. A team of researchers at the University of Wisconsin found a lower rate of TFP (about 3%) in the Bell System itself, but a figure still exceeding prevailing rates in American business. [66]

When the efficiency of component parts of the system is considered, however, the debate is much hotter. AT&T has argued on microeconomic grounds that its vertical integration creates efficiencies.[67] The Justice Department suit of 1949 and a host of critics, on the other hand, have charged that the costs of the Bell System as a whole, and Western Electric in particular, have been artificially high in the absence of competition. Consequently, in this view, rates ultimately paid by consumers also have been too high. Moreover, the government suit claimed that AT&T was slow to adopt several products developed outside the Bell System, including automated switching, unattended dial central-office equipment, and the modern telephone hand set.[68] The consent decree of 1956 quieted this debate until recently, because there was no external standard for evaluating Western's costs.

## THE BRAVE NEW WORLD OF TELECOMMUNICATIONS[69]

For most of AT&T's history, there was a tight fit among Bell System strategy, its structure, and its environment. Since the 1960s, however, a combination of pressures has disturbed this equilibrium: new technologies of transmission and increasingly sophisticated terminal equipment, a dramatic growth in the volume of business, the availability of competitive products and services outside the Bell System, and the willingness of regulatory agencies to promote competition. As a result, AT&T's natural monopoly in the telecommunications industry came under siege.

In the market for terminal equipment (attachments to the basic network, such as telephones or computer terminals), the distinctions between the previously separate functions of data transmission and data processing—in layman's terms, between telephones and computers—have become blurred. Since Alexander Graham Bell's time, voice has been transmitted by analog signal. That is, the actual voice pattern with all its inflections is directly converted into electrical impulses of varying strength and duration by the transmitter and reconverted by the receiver. In recent years, however, digital transmission has come into vogue. Voice inputs are converted into binary code and packed together for transmission. Thus, what is essentially a digital computer sits at either end of a telephone call, packing and unpacking information. Among the many advantages of digital transmission is that the same equipment can be used to transmit both voice and data with minimal interface.

New technology has also affected Bell's local exchange business in a number of ways. In some respects, CB radio and pocket page services already bypass the telephone central office, while one of AT&T's own products in development, the Advanced Mobile Communication Service, portends a future telephone without wires. Domestic satellites with housetop or neighborhood receiving stations present an alternative to the entrenched network. Cable TV presents yet another, because in some scenarios of the home of the future, the "smart TV" will be the primary device for communication as well as entertainment and education.

Some of the same technologies are challenging AT&T's monopoly of the long-distance exchange business. "With a satellite investment of one or two hundred million dollars," claimed one expert in 1979, "a company could duplicate the long lines capacity of the terrestrial network."[70] This threat stands somewhere off in the future and the national security implications are forbidding. Already, however, AT&T has been seriously challenged by competitors who offer long-distance service to both business and residential customers via microwave radio. The Bell System itself has a heavy investment in microwave, which now accounts for nearly half of the trunk mileage in the country. Finally, it is conceivable that future competitors will emerge from fiber optics suppliers who expand into operations either through contracts or subsidiaries.

A tremendous growth in demand for communications products and services has accompanied these new technologies. The sheer volume of telephone business has grown at an accelerating rate. Between 1950 and 1972 the numbers of telephones and conversations increased 200% while the number of local central offices accommodating this traffic increased 85%. In 1950 there were 30 million routing combinations linking central offices; the 85% growth of these offices by 1972 multiplied the routing combinations nearly four times. The market for telephones is not nearly saturated and it is not even limited by demographic trends: "Telephone use, it turns out, increases markedly faster than the square of population growth, with no leveling off in sight."[71] Data communications, which includes not only the linking of computer systems and data bases, but also electronic funds transfer, credit card verification, and biomedical and law enforcement applications, is growing still faster.

Changing technologies and growth of demand have paved the way for competition to open up in the telecommunications industry. Some of America's largest corporations — IBM, Xerox, Exxon, RCA, and others — which traditionally served different markets, have begun to invade AT&T's territory. At the same time, other communications companies like ITT, Western Union, and GTE are mounting fresh competitive assaults. Figure 8.7 describes some of the new competition by technological function and suggests the range of present and future competition. The stakes are enormous. By the late 1970s revenues in the industry approached $50 billion in the domestic market and some forecasts predict annual revenues of $250 billion by 1985. "Plain old telephone service" accounts for more than 90% of present income, but the remaining business (data and facsimile transmission) is growing twice as fast as voice transmission. In 1972 revenues for data communications added up to less than $1 billion. By 1985, these revenues may reach $20 billion or more. The market for hardware is growing rapidly as well. In 1978 the total expenditure for electronic equipment in the industry exceeded $16 billion, after an annual growth rate of 9% in the preceding decade.

AT&T is by far the dominant firm in most markets, although each year brings new challenges. The company has lost some residential sales to retail outlets, but the competition is fiercest in the markets for business products and services. The business market comprises two segments: the "interconnect" market (essentially terminal equipment), and the long-distance exchange. The 1970s witnessed rapid growth in the interconnect market, with revenues approaching $1 billion at the end of the decade. Between 1975 and 1977 the market for private branch exchanges (PBXs) alone grew 54% per annum.[72] Specialized common carriers (SCCs) have achieved similar figures. "Landline SCCs" (microwave companies) earned $134 million in 1977, up from $30 million in 1972. Satellite carriers earned $250 million in 1977 and, according to some estimates, may achieve revenues of $2 billion by the mid-1980s.[73]

These technological and competitive pressures combined to change the FCC's historical belief that communications is a natural monopoly. Indeed, the development of today's competitive industry stems from two FCC decisions of the 1950s. The Hush-a-Phone decision (1956) established for the first time that independent suppliers could sell equipment to be attached to the network without AT&T's permission; and the Above 890 decision (1959) allowed private firms to use the radio spectrum above 890 megacycles (microwave frequencies) for transmission needs not met by common carriers.

Two parallel decisions of the 1960s opened the door still wider. The Hush-a-Phone was not an electrical device, but the FCC's Carterfone

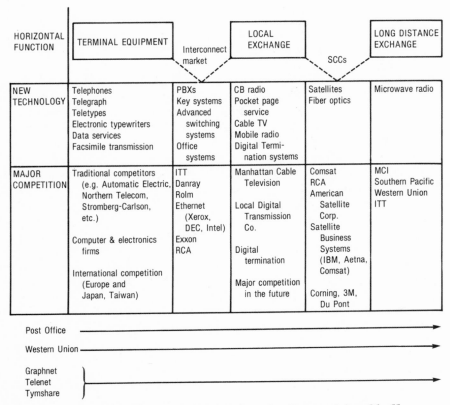

| HORIZONTAL FUNCTION | TERMINAL EQUIPMENT | Interconnect market | LOCAL EXCHANGE | SCCs | LONG DISTANCE EXCHANGE |
|---|---|---|---|---|---|
| NEW TECHNOLOGY | Telephones<br>Telegraph<br>Teletypes<br>Electronic typewriters<br>Data services<br>Facsimile transmission | PBXs<br>Key systems<br>Advanced switching systems<br>Office systems | CB radio<br>Pocket page service<br>Cable TV<br>Mobile radio<br>Digital Termination systems | Satellites<br>Fiber optics | Microwave radio |
| MAJOR COMPETITION | Traditional competitors (e.g. Automatic Electric, Northern Telecom, Stromberg-Carlson, etc.)<br><br>Computer & electronics firms<br><br>International competition (Europe and Japan, Taiwan) | ITT<br>Danray<br>Rolm<br>Ethernet (Xerox, DEC, Intel)<br>Exxon<br>RCA | Manhattan Cable Television<br><br>Local Digital Transmission Co.<br><br>Digital termination<br><br>Major competition in the future | Comsat<br>RCA<br>American Satellite Corp.<br>Satellite Business Systems (IBM, Aetna, Comsat)<br><br>Corning, 3M, Du Pont | MCI<br>Southern Pacific<br>Western Union<br>ITT |

Post Office ⟶

Western Union ⟶

Graphnet
Telenet        ⟶
Tymshare

**Figure 8.7    Changing Technology and the Competitive Challenge to AT&T 1970–1980**

SOURCE: Based on *AT&T: Adaptation in Progress (A) 1875–1974* (HBS Case Services, 9–481–074), p. 37.

decision (1968) extended the principle of permitting "foreign attachments" to electrical equipment, thereby legalizing the interconnect business. The next year the commission prepared the way for the SCCs by approving MCI's application to offer intercity communications for businesses via microwave (in essence combining the Above 890 and the Carterfone decisions).[74]

AT&T protested the liberalization of competition before the commission and the courts, all to no avail. The company's case boiled down to four points. First, AT&T charged that the FCC orders were unfair. In certain markets, AT&T was not permitted to compete against its rivals. For instance, some firms sold both data processing and transmission services as a package while Bell was not legally free to follow. (This constraint did not stop AT&T from threatening to compete, however. In the mid-1970s the company announced that it would shortly unveil its Advanced Communications Service (ACS), a data processing service to link computer terminals of different manufacture into a single network. ACS, however, only became available in 1982).

AT&T also charged that regulatory decisions allowed competitors to "skim the cream" of its business, taking away the lucrative intercity business traffic and leaving the Bell System to deliver the much costlier residential service. Historically AT&T had achieved universal service by, in effect, subsidizing residential service at the expense of business. The company claimed that if cream-skimming continued unabated, then residential rates would rise across the board and dramatically in rural areas. Third, AT&T claimed that since its publicly mandated accounting practices allocated costs among the local exchanges and the long distance network, competing long-distance companies ought to pay a "network access charge" to the Bell System to recover the costs shared by the local exchange. Otherwise, said AT&T, the price of local service would rise. Finally, AT&T argued that if competition in the industry brought savings to the public in the forms of efficiency and innovation, it would be at the cost of public service. In a fully competitive environment AT&T would be far less willing and able to redistribute its work force during emergencies or to build costly back-up systems into the network.

Rate of return regulation was also a growing hindrance to the Bell System as competition increased. AT&T's rates were traditionally set to provide the company a fair rate of return on investment in place. This kind of regulation encouraged short-term planning. AT&T could not go to public agencies for rate hikes to cover the long-term investment necessary to position itself for competition down the road. The company's accounting for depreciation according to schedules fixed by public agencies was also increasingly unsuitable in a competitive marketplace. AT&T traditionally depreciated its assets on a straight-line basis over very long periods. Conduits to protect cable in some local areas, for instance, were written off over eighty years and central office equipment over forty years. Such timetables tended to discourage innovation, since early replacement of plant would cause huge write-offs and probably lead to higher rates or lower profits. In the 1970s and 1980s, when the economic life of electronic equipment was measured in months, the traditional depreciation policies imposed on AT&T were a definite disadvantage.

At stake in the public debate on competition and regulation in telecommunications was nothing less than the structure of the Bell System itself. In the early 1980s the federal government reached two momentous decisions. The FCC and proposed legislation in Congress aimed to restructure the Bell System *horizontally*, by isolating the competitive parts of the company's business in a subsidiary at "arm's-length" from its regulated business. In perhaps its most dramatic ruling on telecommunications since 1934, the *Final Decision* in the Computer II Inquiry (CI-II), the FCC recognized a distinction between "basic services" (switching and the core network), which should remain a natural monopoly, and "enhanced services" and "customer premise equipment" (data processing and terminal equipment), which should be open to all comers, including AT&T.[75] Thus the commission ruled that AT&T would be free to compete in data processing markets from which it had been excluded by the 1956 consent decree. In order to comply with CI-II, AT&T would be required to divide itself into two separate vertically integrated parts, a regulated network monopoly and a competitive telecommunications manufacturing and marketing organization.

At the same time, however, the Department of Justice sought to break up the system's *vertical* integration. In an antitrust suit filed in 1974, the government aimed to force AT&T to divest Western Electric, the OTCs, and those parts of Bell Labs directly concerned with manufacturing and local service. If the original suit had succeeded, AT&T would have become a long distance transmission company with general capabilities in telecommunications research. However, in January 1982, AT&T and the Justice Department agreed to settle the suit out of court. Under the new consent decree, AT&T retained Western Electric, Bell Labs, and its long-distance transmission business, but agreed to divest the twenty-three OTCs, which will become independent local exchange companies. This agreement is the most important policy decision affecting the communications industry since the Kingsbury Commitment of 1913, because it dismantles the unified management of the nationwide telephone network.

## ORGANIZATIONAL ADAPTATION AT AT&T[76]

By the late 1960s AT&T found itself in much the same situation that Western Union had faced a century before. It was a functionally organized, complacent monopoly, increasingly unable to respond to new conditions, new technology, and competition. Unlike Western Union, however, AT&T recognized the inadequacy of its organization by functional specialties and strived to reshape itself for a new competitive world. The decade since has witnessed tumultuous change inside the Bell System.

The competitive business environment strained the traditional organization at many levels and in many ways. The earliest symptoms were a series of urban service crises in 1969 and 1970 and worrisome losses of terminal equipment and long-distance sales to other firms. The most dramatic service crisis occurred in New York City in 1969, when a fire destroyed one central office and disabled thousands of telephones for months before service was fully restored. The sheer volume of business in the city also affected New York Telephone's ability to provide prompt service. In the early 1970s customers frequently complained of long waits for dial tones, installation, or repairs.

The increasing complexity of the business made it extremely difficult for top managers to trace accountability in the functional structure. One OTC vice-president reported the following scenario:

> I would meet with my subordinates, trying to identify responsibility for breakdowns in metropolitan service. The operations people claimed there was too little new plant to meet growth, the engineers pointed to traffic estimates, and the traffic engineers pointed to commercial forecasts. Although oversimplified, this scene repeated over and over reflects the shortcomings of the traditional system. . . .[which] fragments responsibility for customer service and does not lend itself to quick responses to unusual demands.

At the same time, competitors began to eat into AT&T's once-secure markets. The company lost some income to retailers selling telephones, but the fiercest competition came from suppliers of business products and services. Within three years of the Carterfone decision, rival interconnect companies sold 1,800 PBXs with features not available in Bell products. An internal AT&T study in 1973 painted a disturbing picture:

> Competitive PBX and key system losses are multiplying—a trend that shows every sign of continuing. . . . Each year the forecast of losses has been alarmingly high and has evoked many expressions of disbelief. The fact is that all forecasts to date have proven to be too low. The forecast for 1973 anticipates the loss of 9,600 PBX and key systems. If the first eight months of 1973 are a good indicator, that total loss figure will be closer to 12,000.

Competition in long-distance transmission from the SCCs grew rapidly over the same period.

By the early 1970s senior managers at AT&T were seriously alarmed by what they perceived as an organizational crisis in the Bell System. Not only was basic service a problem, but the traditional functional organization of the OTCs was not responsive to change. As new technologies increased the sophistication of the network and terminal equipment, the system required new levels of technical expertise and managerial ability. Moreover, advanced technology reduced the need for operator services and thus created an imbalance of power among the functional departments and threatened to block some career paths. At the same time, as customer products like PBXs became more complex, so did service orders, which required more interdepartmental co-ordination than the traditional structure could deliver.

AT&T confronted its organizational troubles in two ways. First, the company commissioned a major consulting firm to analyze the changing nature of the telephone business and the appropriateness of the Bell System organization. At the same time, AT&T began to look at the relationships among various parts of the system in a new and critical light.

At the beginning of John deButts's tenure as chairman in 1972, AT&T established a new marketing thrust. The company had had a small separate marketing department since 1959, but it was closely aligned with the traditional functional departments. Chairman deButts began to delegate authority affecting different departments at lower levels in the system hierarchy and he took the unprecedented step of recruiting key managers from other companies. About half the managers in the new marketing department came from outside, including many from such market-oriented firms as IBM, Procter & Gamble, and Xerox. Under the direction of Kenneth Whalen, a former president of Michigan Bell, and Archie J. McGill, a former vice-president of IBM, AT&T designed an elaborate system for segmenting the market in the mid-1970s. This system and the associated sales organization had features quite novel for AT&T — new incentive schemes, performance appraisal standards, team marketing efforts, and skip-level and matrix reporting patterns. McGill in particular worked at transforming AT&T from a technology- and product-driven company to one that responds primarily to customer and market needs.

The second major thrust of the early 1970s was the reexamination of the relationship between AT&T and the operating companies. When Vail and his officers standardized the functional organization in 1908 and 1909, they intended to tighten coordination between headquarters and the operating companies. Over the years this tight coordination relaxed with changing executive styles and operating company environments. By 1973 only seven of the twenty-three operating companies retained the traditional functional structure in its original form. Many had added beefed-up marketing departments (ahead of AT&T), or expanded commercial services, or had combined plant and engineering functions into new network services departments. These changes, coupled with minor realignments at AT&T over the years, had led to confused and tangled reporting channels. In 1970 the operating company presidents listed organizational problems as the number-one issue for the coming years. An internal AT&T study warned that

a great deal of diversity still exists among these companies. Allowing independent reorganization to continue risks increasing diversity throughout the Bell System and a consequent erosion of the unity derived from the historical similarity of structures.

The 1970s became a period of massive organizational turmoil in the Bell System. In 1972 a committee of AT&T's highest officers asked the corporate planning officers to recommend a new organizational structure. The planners considered three alternatives: retaining the traditional form, moving directly to a competitive structure built around market segments, or some combination of these extremes. In the end, the company settled on a hybrid form organized around work flows and processes — still a functional structure. Thus one department, customer services, was based on the service order flow; another, network services, centered on switching and trunk line maintenance and planning; the third, operator services, resembled the old traffic department (Figure 8.8). As competitive and regulatory pressures continued, the company was forced to recognize the inadequacy of this hybrid form and accept the argument of marketing managers like McGill that a complete market-segment organization was necessary. In 1978 AT&T reorganized again, this time on a much more massive scale. Explaining this second reorganization in five years, Chairman Charles L. Brown, who succeeded deButts in 1979, wrote that

> the 1973 transition to a customer services orientation was one step down the reorganization road. But the need to go farther became increasingly clear to Bell senior management. Trends pointed to a 1980s decade in which customer needs would be still more diverse, technology more flexible, and competition still more vigorous. . . . Marketing no longer must be assigned to a single department but reinforced as an overall corporate effort.

Thus general operations were organized into three segments: business, residence, and network. Marketing managers held key positions in the first two segments, while the network segment combined most of the old management functions (Figure 8.8).

In the operating companies, organization by segments has called for a new kind of management, involving project teams and matrix structures. "The reason to use matrix management," said the president of one OTC,

> is that it gives us an opportunity to change from a militaristic style of management which demands methods, procedures, practices, and structure to a system that pushes decision responsibility down to where the information and action is, that encourages contention over priorities at lower levels of the organization. An orientation to service as the customer sees it precludes top-down, authoritarian style, and requires more interaction among the departments. Under the traditional structure, the departments established their budgets independently of each other, without

Traditional Functional Structure (1907-1973)

1973 Reorganization—System Structure

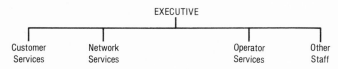

1978 Reorganization—Market Segment Structure

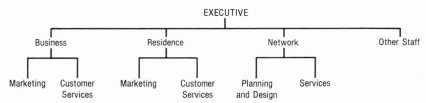

**Figure 8.8**    **Evolution of Organization Structure at AT&T 1907–1978**

Source: *AT&T: Adaptation in Progress (B)* (HBS Case Services, 9-479-041), p. 5.

taking into account the effects on other departments. The budgets and priorities they reflected rose all the way to the top before there was any challenge. The matrix idea helps people understand that contention at lower levels is all right, that it's necessary.

Employees found themselves working for more than one boss and working with other employees whom they had never seen under the old order. Employee performance is no longer appraised on the basis of internal measures like the Green Book, but on external measures like customer surveys.

The vice-president of personnel at the same OTC reports that the transition to the new form has not been easy:

> There was an immense amount of frustration in the beginning, mainly because most people did not have the skills required. We were used to a structure where . . . the lines of authority were clear and people followed correct procedure. People didn't have any understanding of how to work across organizational lines, or with people at different levels. You were

supposed to stay within your own unit, and when you had to go outside, the protocol was to talk to someone at your own level. . . . Traditionally, power came from direct control of resources. Plant had the capital funds and the construction program; Traffic had all the operators. Now in this new environment it's what you do with what you don't control that matters. You have to learn not to use your staff as a hammer, to ask questions of your opposite number yourself. All of this was new to us.

At this writing (1982), the FCC's CI-II decision and the new consent decree have forced yet another reorganization on AT&T. The company must design a new structure to manage its new competitive products and services along with the regulated long-distance business. The company will establish a new regional organization, drawing some employees from the OTCs, while the OTCs must prepare themselves for separation and independence from AT&T. The trauma of this major change has been partially absorbed by AT&T's earlier strategic reorientation and reorganizations. Yet the coming transformation of the Bell System will be fundamental. It marks the passing of an era, the end of Theodore Vail's definition of the telephone business as a universal system.

## CONCLUSION

The translation of AT&T from its historical position in Area 8 into the less comfortable (although potentially more rewarding) world of Area 5 is an excellent illustration of mutual adaptation between organization and environment (Figure 8.9). As environmental uncertainty (especially IC) increased in telecommunications, AT&T responded by altering its strategy and form to gain greater control over its changing circumstances. The company began pursuing new markets and targeting innovation to customer needs. Its new organization was both better differentiated and better integrated than the structure bequeathed by Theodore Vail: better differentiated at all levels, because the marketing impetus added to the system new professionals who sought to drive the traditional departments; better integrated at the top, because headquarters rationalized the bureaucracy, tightened relations with the companies it owned, and took a more active role in operations; and better integrated lower down, because the new matrix structures and project teams required more teamwork across the specialties.

In addition to adopting the high D and I form, AT&T altered its traditional internal balance of power. As the old engineering standards and manufacturing policies gave way in the competitive marketplace, so the dominance of engineers and production managers was countered by marketing managers. In terms of human resource policies, AT&T clearly moved away from strict bureaucratic controls. Tradi-

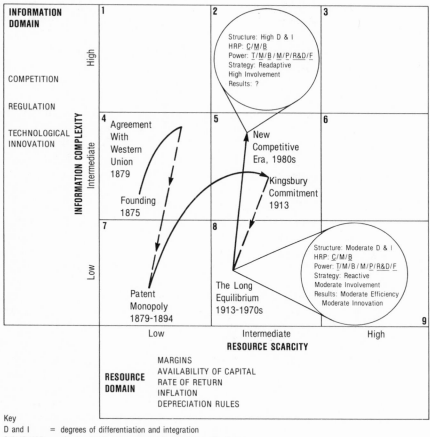

Key

D and I = degrees of differentiation and integration
C/M/B HRP = clan/market/bureaucratic human resource policy balance
T/M/B = top, middle, and bottom power balance
M/P/R&D/F = marketing, production, research and development, finance departmental power balance

Underline indicates weight

**Figure 8.9     Evolution of AT&T 1875–1980**

tional performance measures, once the bane of hourly workers and first-level supervisors, were replaced. At the same time, the company increased market incentives for its sales force and instituted quality of work life programs for employees at all levels. Thus AT&T's mix of clan, market, and bureaucratic mechanisms became more evenly distributed.

The organizational upheavals of the past decade obviously affected AT&T's readaptive outcomes, although it is still too early to measure exactly how and how much. The advent of a new era of competition has created a standard of comparison, albeit a crude one. For instance, one expert argues that "the market entry of firms offering products competitive with Western Electric has prompted Western to embark on a cost reduction of products exposed to an outside benchmark." Such products include private branch exchanges, dial services, and new keying and transmission systems. Competition similarly spurred Bell Labs to new telecommunications innovations and has foreshortened timetables for product development.[77] While proof is difficult, Bell executives themselves believe that efficiency and innovation have improved as a result of the reorganization. A vice-president at one of the OTCs claims that "inefficiency is disappearing. Competition in the long run will squeeze out inefficiency. We look at costs much more seriously now and are determined to drive them down."

Greater innovation is also claimed, and the company has speeded the flow of new products and services to the marketplace. "Our near-term product line is incredible," boasts a business marketing manager. "You wouldn't believe the products we'll have ready in the next two years. Payoffs to the customer will be ten to one. The teleconferencing possibilities are staggering and so are improved network and PBX services!"

Member involvement at AT&T is indeed changing, although whether it has improved is a subjective judgment. The transition from a service company to "the knowledge business" forced managers to rethink their traditional values. The satisfaction of customer needs has replaced the provision of high-quality technical service as the company's driving motive. To some Bell managers, particularly the marketing staff, it has been exciting and challenging to manage attitudinal change, to be at the leading edge of events as they are unfolding. But the change is not without cost. In 1973 Chairman deButts warned that

> the service motivation has been bred in the bones of telephone people through the course of a hundred years. To supplant that motivation with a market motivation might make us a no less profitable business and a no less effective one, though by different standards. But we would be a different business and I, for one, cannot help but feel that we would be the poorer for it and so would the public we serve.

Many employees joined AT&T precisely because it was a monopoly and not a competitive, pressure-filled, risky business. Many of these old-timers are unhappy. With one voice, AT&T senior managers agreed that the most pressing problems facing the company in the late 1970s were the difficulties in changing corporate values and in accommodating those who resist such changes. New and unclear responsibilities, complicated reporting patterns, altered power relationships, and the need to take risks have created a great deal of discomfort in the Bell System.

From all outward appearances, then, AT&T's recent performance seems readaptive. It remains to be seen whether the reorganized Bell System will continue on its new path. How successful the company will be in the new telecommunications industry is also unclear. It is unreasonable to expect a continuation of the dominance the company enjoyed in its first hundred years, but AT&T's recent behavior augurs well for its future.

# CHAPTER 9

# The Readaptive Process:
# Fitting It Together

WE HAVE REVIEWED the development of seven basic American businesses with an eye to the readaptive process—that is, the environmental and organizational conditions that favored (or hindered) continuously reconciling innovation and efficiency. The nine-area "map" of adaptation helped us keep our bearings in moving from industry to industry and from era to era, but must now be put to a sterner test. Does it lead to some useful generalizations about organizational and industrial adaptation? How might these ideas be applied in practice?

Deferring the question of a practical application until Chapter 10, we can move toward some general propositions by taking up four more specific questions.

1. What are the broader forces that influence our key variables of information complexity (IC) and resource scarcity (RS) which seem so critical to adaptation? Can we identify factors that help us account for the amount of IC and RS across our seven industries? In particular, we will look at the effects of core technology, public policy, interindustry and foreign competition and organizational choice.

2. What are the various types of organizational adaptation? How do organizations survive without being readaptive? We shall look at the kinds of organization forms and strategies that tend

to appear in Area 1, in Area 3, in the combined Areas 6 and 9, and in Areas 7 and 8. It is in these general areas of our model that we found industries and organizations persisting for significant lengths of time. Are there any patterns that can help us account for the phenomenon of the mature, nonreadaptive organization?

3. Does the evidence support our basic contention that intermediate IC and RS (the conditions of Area 5), along with readaptive strategy and form, are essential to the readaptive process? Is it as difficult to reconcile innovation and efficiency and stay in Area 5 as we expected and, if so, why? What part does the involvement of organizational members play in the readaptive process?

4. How do the various patterns of adaptation we have seen in the United States compare with the experience of the leading Japanese firms? We shall explore why the United States seems to be such a favorable locale for industrial start-up and early development while mature industries are more likely to be readaptive in Japan.

Before turning to these major questions we need recall our adaptation model in more general terms. Figure 9.1 recapitulates our model of the readaptive process introduced in Chapter 1; Figure 9.2 displays the recent history of the seven industries we studied. These figures emphasize the two-way flow of influence, the mutual adaptation between

**Figure 9.1   Relationship Among the Factors in the Readaptive Process**

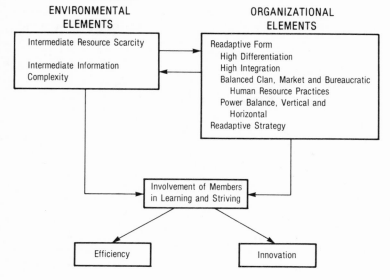

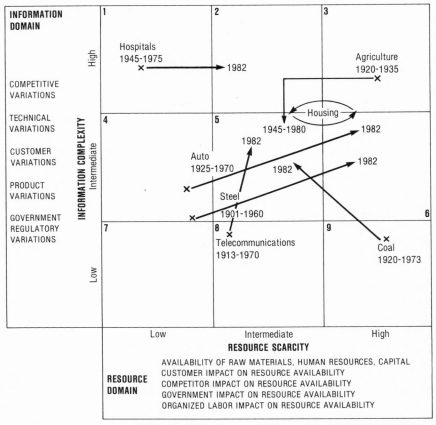

**Figure 9.2    Selected Historical Locus of Seven Essential Industries**

the organization and its environment. With the framework in mind, we can now consider what factors influenced RS and IC in each industry.

## FORCES AFFECTING INFORMATION COMPLEXITY AND RESOURCE SCARCITY

RS and IC are ways of characterizing the environmental factors that, along with internal factors, help explain the results firms achieve. At any point in time IC is determined by environmental variety and RS by resource availability. Beyond this, however, we can now review the overall record to identify the longer-term forces that lie behind RS and

IC. The first of these is *core technology*, whose primary impact is on information complexity.

### CORE TECHNOLOGY

Think of the difference between agriculture and telecommunications. Agriculture (like housing) involves a technology that is heavily site-constrained. The inescapable fact that farmers must farm on arable soil forces geographic dispersion, which in turn has always favored small firms (the family farm) over any larger corporate effort. It is no accident that the kinds of farming that are exceptions to this rule employ more site-concentrated technologies, such as irrigation and hothouses. Farming's intensive technology is also an important reason why, in spite of massive and prolonged efforts in the Soviet Union, large collective farming has had difficulty matching the family farm's ability to readapt.

Thus the technology of farming creates the industry structure, with thousands of independent farm production units and hundreds of potential ways to do farming (varying the choices of crop mix, method, and market segment). The resulting high IC far exceeds the cognitive capacity of any single farm family to collect and process all the information relevant to making rational strategic choices. Farmers are not stupid, but circumstances force them to make somewhat arbitrary, often questionable decisions unless aided by outside groups such as the Department of Agriculture. Our analysis underscores the wisdom of the apocryphal story of the farmer who declined to buy a book on advanced farming techniques with the explanation that he already knew a lot more about better farming than he could use.

At the other technological extreme, the need for a completely interconnected network among all of the geographically dispersed telephone customers led to a natural monopoly in telecommunications. This natural monopoly supported a very large AT&T with an enormous collective cognitive capacity. With few competitors or other external sources to generate strategic questions, however, AT&T faced little information stimulation beyond what it created internally. Because of the nature of its technology, AT&T existed under conditions of low IC.

Between these technologically driven extremes, we find more conventional manufacturing industries, such as steel and autos. These industries are not constrained by their technologies either to use widely dispersed production sites or to be tightly interconnected. This makes it easier to achieve the economies possible with larger manufacturing units. These industries are likely to shake down to a few relatively large firms. In such cases oligopoly is by no means as ominous as the word itself would suggest to many people.

These generalizations about the impact of technology on the size and number of firms are not newsworthy to economists or to other students of industry structures. More interesting is the way that certain industries have to some extent maneuvered around these technological constraints to achieve the economies of larger units on one hand (housing and agribusiness) or the advantage of multifirm information stimulation on the other (telecommunications). In the case of housing we saw that the semipermanent contracting network centered on the general contractor represents a very useful organizational form that allows for not only survival but even readaptation in the face of fluctuating RS and fairly high IC.

This organization network, the quasi-firm, has appeared in a somewhat different form in agribusiness and has cropped up as franchise systems and chains in such fields as restaurants, food stores, soft drinks, motels, hotels, and clothing and appliance stores. All of these enterprises are forced by their technology to locate near where their customers live. This reality has in the past favored the survival of thousands of independent local firms. The invention of the loosely connected quasi-firm has made it possible to reduce uncertainties and achieve economies that improve resource conditions, thereby edging those industries from Area 1 into Area 5.

Technological influences, then, are not immutable forces but rather constitute a predisposition that can be significantly modified by the organizational choice of an appropriate strategy and form. The quasi-firm provides a way to develop a more sophisticated organization with more differentiated units without losing integration. This form, therefore, has a better chance of innovating while maintaining efficiency than would its legal parts as stand-alone units.

The example of telecommunications is also instructive. The accommodation worked out between AT&T and the government in 1913, the Kingsbury Commitment, essentially made the company a regulated monopoly for several decades. Ironically, it was AT&T's own choice to make large investments in advancing its technology that led to the new technical developments that are now bringing competition back to all phases of the business. Without the transistor and its technical offspring, computerized switching gear, without microwave point-to-point transmitters, and without laser-driven optical fiber transmission systems (all Bell Laboratory developments), AT&T's natural monopoly would still be intact. Within the Bell System, Bell Laboratories created the equivalent of an environment of intermediate level IC. Technology can break as well as make natural monopolies—and at times this force for change is home-grown.

We have seen how technology by impacting the size of firms has influenced the level of environmental IC in the industries studied, but we must not miss the influence of size on the internal process of involving firm members in learning and striving. We need only recall that achieving involvement was not a problem in the relatively small firms in agriculture and housing while it was an enormous problem in the big steel and auto firms. It is not a mysterious point but it is often overlooked that large firms have a much harder time involving their large numbers of middle and lower level employees in the productive challenges posed by their environments. The fact that AT&T, with the largest employee group of all, for years was able to achieve a reasonable level of involvement in learning and striving throughout its ranks is a testimonial to its managerial ability to overcome adverse conditions. The organizational arrangements that can induce involvement, such as the use of clan as well as market and bureaucratic human resource practices and a reasonable balance of power from top to bottom, are especially important in large organizations where the external realities can so easily be lost in the multiple layers.

### PUBLIC POLICIES

Our industry survey demonstrates that public policies are a second major force significantly affecting IC and RS. The government — and behind the government the values, aspirations, and beliefs of the public — defines the ground rules for playing out the accommodations and exchanges between any organization and its immediate environment. Public policy has probably been the major force influencing adaptation in the hospital and coal industries, for example, and has significantly supplemented the primary force of core technology in agriculture and telecommunications.

Public policy has had a primary influence on the hospital and health industry since the early twentieth century but the clearest examples are from the post-World War II period. It was then that the combination of the Hill-Burton Act, Medicare and Medicaid legislation, and the tacit support of private third-party insurance systems, moved hospitals from a condition of intermediate RS to one of distinctly low RS. This shift, in combination with massive public support of medical R&D, created the rather special circumstance of a significant industry with a large number of organizational units remaining for an extended period in Area 1. Behind the government's policy was, of course, the public's great interest in health care. The country was affluent and generally willing to spend a significant amount of its resources on health. This mood was fostered by the dramatic examples of the wartime wonder drugs and other technological advances. It was public policy that lowered hospitals' RS and kept it low. Only now is public policy gradually changing in this regard.

In coal public policy had a more indirect, although potent, impact on industry adaptation during the 1930s through the early 1950s. During the Depression, the economic problems of the coal operators (Area 9) reinforced their traditional exploitation of the scattered, largely unorganized work force. This picture began to change with the New Deal legislation. The National Recovery Act, and then the Wagner (NLRB) Act gave official support to collective bargaining. It had always been difficult to organize the coal mines but John L. Lewis had the disciplined cadre and drive to do it, given government support. Membership rose, the war later strengthened the market for coal, and postwar technology brought the continuous mining machines. These factors supported Lewis's efforts to push up wages and, at the same time, to support the technical changes that increased productivity and reduced the size of the work force. As a result of this combination of actions, coal temporarily moved toward Area 5, but it could not stick. Once Lewis retired, tendencies toward union and industry fragmentation again took hold. But the temporary decrease in RS and improvement in efficiency, involvement, and innovation was due in significant measure to a shift in public policy toward the support of unionization.

In the case of agriculture, New Deal planners had a fairly direct impact on price stability and support, moving the industry toward a more intermediate level of RS. It was largely this public policy intervention that permitted improvements in innovation and efficiency and accelerated the reduction in the number of farming units, completing the shift from Area 3 into the upper edge of Area 5. This was perhaps the clearest and most dramatic example of government intervention supporting the readaptive process. It should be noted that this was accomplished by reducing competition in the industry, contrary to the implications of classical economic theory.

Finally, public policy has had a major impact on the telecommunication industry. The recent federal move toward deregulation is only the latest of a sequence of public policy impacts that began with the government's decision to get out of the telegraph business in the 1840s.

We cite these among many possible examples of government intervention to make it very clear that public policy affects both RS and IC directly and indirectly. The policy impact may move a given industry away from Area 5 (hospitals) as well as toward Area 5 (agriculture). Wise government choices are absolutely critical to the readaptive process.

### INTERINDUSTRY AND FOREIGN COMPETITION

The third general influence on IC and RS is the competitive effect coming from outside the customary domain. In the industries we examined, such impacts come from interindustry effects and foreign competition.

Changed circumstances in related industries can have major influences on any industry and its key firms. The interplay of the oil and coal industries provides the most salient example in our sample. The oil industry's initial rapid growth paralleled the development of the internal combustion engine and the automobile. The convenience and relative cleanliness of oil, however, soon allowed it to invade other markets where coal had dominated, such as home heating, electric generation, and railroads, dramatically increasing RS for all the coal companies. Much later, in the 1970s, oil again had a major impact in the reverse direction. It was, of course, oil shortages and the OPEC cartel that drove up oil and, in turn, coal prices. To a lesser extent we have seen similar interindustry effects in steel (from substitute materials such as aluminum and plastics) and telecommunications (from the computer industry).

Steel and autos will be at once recognized as industries whose RS and IC have been much influenced by increased foreign competition. In the last twenty years foreign competition in those industries surged from an insignificant to a dominant source of competitive variation and resource pressure, laying bare the partially hidden weaknesses in the key U.S. firms. Their adaptive state simply did not stand up to the pressures of foreign competitors.

## ORGANIZATIONAL CHOICE

The final force affecting RS and IC is any choice made by organizational leaders that makes a significant difference in the adaptive pattern. The arrow in Figure 9.1 that points to the left, from the organization to the immediate industry environment represents the force of such choices. Within the limits of particular circumstances organizational leaders can choose their strategy and form, and, in time, these choices can shift an organization from one environmental area to another.

The steel industry (Chapter 3) offers a useful example. The circumstances surrounding the formation of U.S. Steel in 1901 had a major influence on the future development of the industry. This historical event was not heavily constrained by technical or public policy considerations, but hinged significantly on Andrew Carnegie's age and succession plans, the availability of a man with Judge Gary's traits, and especially J.P. Morgan's unique position of power and his antipathy to competitive turmoil. This combination of leadership circumstances started U.S. Steel's corporate life with a deeply entrenched defensive strategy and a fragmented internal organization. In many ways the company has ever since been managed as a "cash cow," drifting slowly to its present, mired-down position in Area 6.

That this critical event in steel hinged largely on a choice of leadership is shown by the nearly simultaneous reorganization of AT&T by the same Morgan banking group. The man available to lead the refinanced AT&T was Theodore Vail, whose characteristics and aspirations were very different from Gary's. AT&T started off on a different track. Its strong commitment under Vail to continuing technical innovation was not environmentally forced, and it has had consequences that are still being felt.

We could cite other examples but the point is made. Historical analysis does uncover key turning points, often in the very early years of an industry, when a central figure makes a critical choice that, in turn, casts a long shadow on subsequent events.

## VARIETIES OF ORGANIZATIONAL ADAPTATION

Our study of seven industries has shown various points in time when the major or typical firms were not achieving readaptive results in terms of strong records of efficiency and innovation. As the next step in testing our model's ability to explain all types of organizational adaptation, we shall examine the organizational forms and strategies that evolved in the nonreadaptive organizations. The forms observed seem to vary in regular patterns depending upon the area of the model.* Let us begin by analyzing Area 1 and Area 2 with a review of hospital development.

Most hospitals have existed in Area 1 (low RS and high IC) since shortly after World War II. During this period, despite their resource affluence, urban hospitals had surprisingly little choice about the implicit strategy they had to follow. To survive, they had to attract enough patients to achieve a reasonable bed occupancy level. A half-occupied hospital could not keep going even under low RS conditions. Hospital leaders recognized that to induce enough doctors to refer enough patients, a hospital needed a full range of expensive technologies and services. These factors made the difference in occupancy levels, regardless of cost, since all rate increases could be painlessly passed through to the third-party insurers. So the tacit strategy was to spend and spend on equipment and services in order to survive.

---

*In the Appendix we have also reviewed the form of adaptation that tends to exist area by area, with attention to the descriptions found in the organizational literature instead of in our histories of seven industries.

These special historical circumstances have provided a unique opportunity to see what happens when an industry remains in Area 1 a long time. The organizational form that emerged was high in differentiation but very weakly integrated. Specialists of all types were abundant but managers charged with coordination were not. Hospitals' human resource practices had many clanlike features, especially among the professional personnel, and made a more limited use of hierarchical and market methods than the other industries studied. As we saw, the power distribution became unbalanced, with the doctors gaining dominance relative to their trustee and administrative partners in the top triumvirate, and relative to the less skilled hospital employees further down in the hierarchy. This pattern of organization might have been deduced from our general framework, as could the readaptational consequences, relatively strong innovation and poor efficiency.

Other somewhat similar but less extreme organizational forms can be found in some high-tech industries, including minicomputers and microprocessors. Some firms in these industries exist for a time in Area 1 but probably more frequently in Area 2. Firms in such settings have been characterized by Henry Mintzberg as *adhocracies*.[1] These organizations are probably as highly differentiated as hospitals but are somewhat more integrated, through such mechanisms as cross-functional task forces, liaison roles, matrix structures, and so on. Even so, the looseness persists. It is not surprising that such organizations are noted for their remarkably high innovation but not for conspicuous efficiency. The powerful people in these organizations are usually gifted professionals, researchers and engineers. They dominate the organization rather than the other way around. Their complaints may be loud at times, but they have more the ring of the prima donna than the downtrodden employee.

From a broader social perspective it may be desirable that some organizations remain in Area 1, if the value of rapid innovation strongly outweighs the value of efficiency. The point, however, is that organizations that survive and remain in Area 1 are likely to take on the characteristics of an organized anarchy or adhocracy. We should assume that this form is a reasonable response to these special environmental conditions, and that low efficiency must be expected.

Area 3 is defined by the twin conditions of high information complexity and high resource scarcity. It is in this area that hundreds of thousands of small businesses live, and frequently die. As we saw in Chapters 5 and 6, farmers and general contractors can be found struggling with these conditions and searching for ways to ease the tension and uncertainty. Many of these organizations deal with high IC by ignoring it, and might even deny that it exists. For example, does an independent clothing store in a busy urban area face high IC? We argue that it does, even though the owner-manager may claim that he has never considered doing anything else but run, say, a youth-oriented shop featuring a limited selection of jeans and T-shirts. We suggest that such a person is handling the enormous number of potential products he could stock for a wide variety of market segments by an arbitrary simplification of his strategic choices. His response is easy to understand and even predictable, given the resource implications of preparing a more sophisticated analysis of options. So the resulting strategic choice will be relatively unexamined. If it proves wrong, the firm will be hard pressed to find resources to correct the error. That is, the fact of high RS will tend to dominate the response of the small firms that frequent Area 3. High IC exists but is largely unrecognized by the managers involved. Adaptation occurs more by natural selection in the Darwinian sense than by a learning process.

With RS the dominant influence, and IC largely unrecognized, Area 3 is characterized by a *simple* organizational form, to use Mintzberg's term. Simple organizations are run in a centralized way by a manager who is often a partial owner. Simple structure will usually follow a functional pattern, with the work of subordinate managers directly coordinated by the top manager. These relatively small organizations seldom have more than two levels of management and very limited staff support resources. The firm, therefore, makes relatively little use of specialists and needs relatively few integrating mechanisms to supplement the work of the general manager. Such firms can make quick responses to environmental shifts but can draw on only a very limited repertoire of potential responses. If the environmental shift is great enough to fall outside the firm's range of responses, it will fail. Largely dependent on the learning capacity of a single person, the simple structure does not have the highly differentiated organizational form needed to increase its range of possible responses. Its ability to adapt is severely limited.

Ways can be found to soften the impact of Area 3 conditions, as our examination of construction quasi-firms made clear; the loosely coupled franchise system and the chain store approach represent analogous organizational devices designed to cope with adverse environmental pressures. By achieving a scale that permits more specialized units and more integrative devices, such firms can increase their repertoire of adaptive responses. Such organizations can acquire some buffer resources that give them time to learn new approaches and put them into place as needed. Of course, as we have seen over and over again, having such resources and using them effectively to be readaptive are two different things. For firms in site-dispersed industries, which tend to show up in Area 3, even the helpful organizational inventions that we have seen provide only an opportunity for readaptation; its realization remains problematic.

Since Area 3 most closely approaches the conditions of perfect competition, it has been idealized by many economists ever since the time of Adam Smith. They argue that the competitive market forces at work on large numbers of firms will generate the greatest public good, in the sense of making the desired products available to the consumer at the lowest possible prices. We cannot treat this argument in detail here, but it should be noted that today it is probably less in favor with economists than with the general public. The simplistic "efficient market" economic model tends to assume unchanging technology and consumer preferences. In the end, the consumer is usually not well served except under limited conditions and over short periods of time. Despite temporarily depressed prices, the agricultural industry of the 1920s did not serve the public nearly so well as the present industry does. The small, simple firms are severely limited in their long-term readaptive capacity. The trial and error form of decision making that predominates in Area 3 firms is costly. As conditions change over time, many firms will fail, causing economic waste and often personal tragedy.

Areas 6 and 9 will be treated together because their firms tend to be adaptive in a similar manner. These areas are characterized by high RS and low or intermediate IC—conditions experienced by many commodity industries where undifferentiated bulk and mass-produced products are sold almost entirely on the basis of price.* The Area 6 and Area 9 industries we studied were steel, autos, and coal in recent years, and hospitals in earlier years.

The dominant organizational form in Areas 6 and 9 can best be labeled *machine bureaucracy*,[2] the kind of large-scale organization that best fits the popular stereotype of a monolithic pyramid with a few bosses creating detailed instructions for the many. The machine bureaucracy governs its internal relations with a heavy reliance on the chain of command and the rule book. It expects its employees to be diligent and reliable in executing detailed instructions in return for fair treatment and standard wages. The highest level of involvement it usually achieves from employees is their time, physical effort, and obedience in exchange for money. If resource conditions become more severe, it is likely to exploit labor unless restrained by countervailing forces such as strong unions backed by government policies. Power usually concentrates in the hands of top-level operations management.

The management strategy associated with this environment can be summed up as defensive. Top management is preoccupied with limiting competitive pressures by such means as blocking new entrants to the industry and seeking protective tariffs and other barriers to foreign

---

*Area 9 is also the locus of small preindustrial handicraft and cottage firms that operate on a local subsistence basis. We have not studied such firms. '

competition. It is defensive about the product improvements of others and tries to block the use of substitute products. It avoids risk.

Firms that operate with a machine bureaucratic form and a defensive strategy are unlikely to be innovators. What little innovation occurs is apt to be directed toward reducing costs rather than improving the product. Such firms can be expected to be moderately efficient and occasionally highly efficient. They can be very disciplined about making efficient use of established production methods but their efficiency is often limited by their reluctance to develop new products and to adopt new production and marketing techniques. In essence their form and strategy permit them to be highly integrated firms but their insistence on conformity inhibits the differentiation that nourishes innovation.

Of all the industries we have studied, steel is the clearest example of the organizational form expected in Area 6. Although exceptions exist, most steel firms are machine bureaucracies with defensive strategies. These organizational patterns create a set of vested power relations that, once established, become self-reinforcing. Organizational inertia takes over. And some of the major steel firms have had a very long time to establish these patterns.

Our examination of the auto industry showed a similar slow drift into such patterns but also, recently, a more vigorous effort to break away. Their internal transformation is under way, although positive financial results from this readaptive process have yet to emerge.

Coal represents a rather unusual case. For many years its characteristic firms, the smaller independent operators, hovered on the line between Areas 6 and 9. It was a truly depressed industry that continually lost market share to oil companies offering cheaper and cleaner energy. Management methods in coal were antiquated and its work force was exploited. Even Lewis's efforts to help management modernize the industry had a limited and temporary impact. The major shift in oil prices starting in 1973 has, however, opened up new possibilities in coal. The industry's RS has markedly decreased even as its IC has increased. It is now in Area 5, with a chance to enter a readaptive period. The key variable will be the commitment and the quality of management in the larger firms that are now the pacesetters for the industry. Will they commit to a readaptive strategy, make significant investments in new technology, and work toward collaborative relationships with labor and government? The early indications are that some, but not all, of the major firms are launched on such a course.

Areas 7 and 8, where IC is low and RS low to moderate, are where monopolies or near-monopolies will appear. Our primary example is the regulated telecommunications industry. We might also expect to find here other utilities whose technology is deemed to justify a natural monopoly, including electric power and gas utilities and also, to a lesser extent, the railroads, and airlines. All of these enterprises share network technologies.

This area also includes some government agencies that provide services the public has no other way of obtaining. The Post Office Department occupied such a position for many decades but now alternative services are beginning to appear. The list of services supplied exclusively or predominantly by the government includes primarily local services, such as fire and crime protection, waste disposal, water, parks, schools, and roads; and state and national services, such as unemployment insurance, old-age insurance, defense, highways, harbors, flood control, and so on. Even such highly diverse activities are clustered together in our adaptational field, and can be compared in terms of their organizational form, strategy, and adaptive outcomes.

With neither enough RS to generate striving nor enough IC to stimulate learning, the organizations of Areas 7 and 8 are notoriously nonreadaptive. The impatient public's strong desire to increase the RS for all these organizations is clearly reflected in the voters' support of tax ceilings from California to Massachusetts. The best way to increase efficiency is not at all clear, however. We shall come back to this question in the next chapter. For now it is important to take a closer look at the kinds of organizational form and strategy that characterize this area.

The term that seems best to describe the organizational form typical of Areas 7 and 8 is *professional bureaucracy*.[3] Like machine bureaucracies, these organizations employ a fairly conventional hierarchical command structure and make extensive use of rules and standard operating procedures. Professional bureaucracies, however, differ in the sense that they rely to some extent on indoctrinating their employees with a code of professional service. We clearly saw this approach taken in AT&T. Thus these organizations use some clan methods to buttress their primary reliance on bureaucratic methods of achieving social control. They are much less likely to employ such internal market methods as profit centers, incentive bonus plans or piece-rate systems. Because of the structure of their industries, these organizations are often large ones. For their size, they tend to have relatively low levels of both differentiation and integration.

Because these organizations are under only slight environmental pressure, power is distributed by internal criteria—it is there to be taken by those who are most skillful in seeking it, not necessarily by those with the greatest capacity to cope with outside pressures. Members of these organizations tend to become preoccupied with organizational "politics" in its customary usage. ("It is not what you know but who you know.") Sometimes a clique defined by ethnic origins or social class will become the dominant power group. For instance, New England Telephone and Telegraph for many years was dominated at the top by old-line establishment Yankees and in middle management and below by Irish-Americans.

Our adaptational framework suggests that organizations in these areas are likely to have relatively poor outcomes in both innovation and efficiency. By our assessment, AT&T has, over the years, generally achieved better results than our model would predict. Government rate regulation created an intermediate level of RS as expected. The unexpected event was the extra amount of IC that Bell Laboratories internally generated for the rest of the organization.

Area 4 was described in Chapter 1 as the place where new successful industries are born. Our historical studies, however, revealed variations in the pattern of development of different industries. Steel, automobiles, and to some extent telecommunications followed the developmental trajectory anticipated in Chapter 1; housing, hospitals, coal, and agriculture did not show such a clear pattern. The first set of industries all began with a major technical breakthrough that led to a rapid growth period. Starting in Area 4, these industries moved rapidly into 1, then into 2 and 3 before reaching a temporary equilibrium point near the line between 4 and 5 (steel and auto) or 8 (telephone). These movements were marked by some dramatic turning points and jumps into different areas. Examples were the founding of U.S. Steel, the switch of General Motors' leadership from Durant to Du Pont and Sloan, the expiration of Bell's telephone patent, and the Kingsbury Commitment at AT&T. We expect that the developmental sequence of these industries, including the sudden jumps, will prove to be fairly typical of new science- and technology-based industries. The other four industries are all site-bound and started at a local trade level, which helps explain their very different developmental pattern.

Our study generated limited new evidence on the organizational conditions characteristic of Area 4. Typically, a small entrepreneurial group forms to manage the new business. Because of their relatively small size and clanlike features, member involvement is not apt to be a problem. A "prospector" strategy is characteristic, to borrow a term recently used in a study by Raymond Miles and Charles Snow of the various organizational forms observed in the book publishing, food processing, hospital, and electronics industries. To quote from their study:

> Prospectors are organizations which almost continuously search for market opportunities and they regularly experiment with potential responses to emerging environmental trends. Thus, these organizations often are

creators of change and uncertainty to which their competitors must respond. However, because of its strong concern for product and market innovation, these organizations are usually not completely efficient.[4]

Our evidence would tend to support these conclusions.

## THE PROCESS OF READAPTATION: AREA 5

Area 5 is of special interest because of our key idea that intermediate RS and IC favor the readaptive process. Area 5 was the locus of firms in agriculture, housing, autos, and steel at various times, and, very recently, coal and telecommunications.

Agriculture is the industry that most clearly reflects our basic framework. Here we saw that external events, in the form of the New Deal action, a drought, and a strengthening export market, were necessary to improve the resources available to farmers and to begin lifting them out of the crisis conditions of the 1920s and 1930s. This combination of events permitted farmers to anticipate reasonable returns from their crops, and induced them to invest more in labor-saving and yield-improvement methods. Farm families became able to manage additional acreage. Those inclined to migrate to cities could usually realize higher prices for the land they left behind. The number of farmers rapidly declined and the size of the average farm increased. Innovation in farm methods brought continuing productivity improvements.

Various challenges to the dominance of the farm family as the basic production unit have periodically been noted with alarm but have not in fact made significant inroads. And the farm family, not surprisingly, has had few problems in securing high involvement from the family members who stayed on the farm. We estimate that farming is now operating in the upper right-hand corner of Area 5. It is currently challenged by the inflated prices of its basic inputs, especially energy; by high interest rates; by uncertainties about the use of pesticides, herbicides, and growth hormones; and by pressures for other uses of the land. The truly remarkable performance of agriculture continues, however. In 1981 $43.3 billion of farm products were exported, making it possible to offset more than half of the $78 billion of petroleum products we imported. Agriculture continues to be readaptive under Area 5 conditions.

The story of steel offers a sharp contrast, demonstrating that intermediate IC and intermediate to low RS do not *assure* readaptation. Most steel firms have existed for most of this century near the line between Areas 4 and 5, but their behavior has been more like what we might expect of firms in Area 6. Our historical analysis indicates that

Carnegie's steel firm was readaptive until it was merged into U.S. Steel. The newly established firm followed a remarkably consistent course during the next 75 years, reflected in the very steady decline of its U.S. market share. Consistently following a defensive strategy, U.S. Steel fostered price stability, not price competition. It was a late follower rather than a leader in technical innovation, and was slow to carry out organizational reforms and modernization. It clung to the twelve-hour day and fought unionization. It led in buying its way out of the labor strife of the 1950s and fought government regulations. U.S. Steel was formed as a defense against Carnegie's aggressive behavior and its record has been consistent with its genesis. It merged its way rather than earned its way into Area 5. The roots of the last two decades' troubles go far back in the industry's history. Eventually Area 6 organizational behavior at U.S. Steel led to Area 6 resource conditions. In pursuing its chosen strategy and organizational form, U.S. Steel was following the conventional wisdom at the time of its founding. The name of the game was only to make money for the financiers and the stockholders. They saw a steel organization as a production system, not as either a learning or social system. Their organizational mold was cast before the coordinated, multidivisional structure was developed.

To conclude, our analysis indicates that the steel industry's environment was too good to the key firms for too long. Environmental press was not great enough to induce the learning and striving needed for readaptation. U.S. Steel even came through the Great Depression with only one year of losses. The evidence indicates that being on the border between Areas 4 and 5 induces complacency rather than readaptation.

The auto industry experience near the line between Areas 4 and 5 shares some similarities with steel but also shows some important differences. Both industries existed under favorable conditions for a long time and have recently drifted into Area 6. Both went through similar early growth periods associated with technological breakthroughs. The auto firms, however, earned rather than bought their way into Area 5. The early Ford organization developed the standardization, the high volumes, and the innovative production methods that secured efficiency in the industry. With DuPont and Sloan, General Motors developed the product, organizational, and market innovations that others eventually had to match. Ford of the 1910s and General Motors of the 1920s achieved readaptive outcomes.

Under its aging founder, Ford clearly lost this capacity during the 1920s, while General Motors gradually became complacent and less innovative thereafter. In time, a more conservative, defensive strategy predominated in each of the Big Three, reflected in their product design, recruitment and management development practices, in their freezing of organizational form, and in the adversarial relationship that evolved with the UAW. The environmental blows of the 1970s came on strongly and quickly. The automakers' response has been painfully slow but a turnaround seems to be coming. They have further differentiated their organizations, changed product design radically, and made significant efforts to develop a partnership with the UAW in improving the quality of work life and member involvement in the hourly ranks.

Both AT&T and key coal firms are such recent entries into Area 5 that is too early to judge the full import of their changed circumstances. Coal now has the resources needed to innovate in basic ways. AT&T now has the competitive stimulation that can induce both more innovation and efforts to be more efficient. There are clear signs that these anticipated effects are being realized in AT&T and in some of the coal companies. In the past six years AT&T has gone through two major reorganizations and has undertaken the spin-off of the local operating companies. The reorganizations were designed to overlay a market-oriented structure on the company's traditional, geographic and functional organization. AT&T has launched intensive training programs, extended the range of its recruiting efforts, and begun a number of promising worker-involvement programs, most recently in conjunction with the Communication Workers of America. All of this bodes well for the company's capacity to become readaptive.

The recent environmental changes experienced by the coal industry resulted not only from the dramatic price jumps of the 1970s but also from the infusion of capital from the big oil companies and increased government regulation. The kinds of internal changes necessary to bring higher levels of innovation and efficiency have been initiated by several firms in the industry. Exxon Coal has demonstrated that a deep mine can be a humane, safe place to work, where cooperative relations with the unions and their members can encourage efficiency and the introduction of new methods. Exxon Coal also has shown that western strip mining need not destroy either the physical ecology or the more fragile social ecology of a rural/small town area. Armco's coal subsidiary and others have demonstrated the big payoff possible from intensive and progressive management education, especially at the foreman level. Kenco showed the potential of the semi-autonomous mining group. But these potentials still have to be realized in persistent and large-scale ways. If the resources and the knowledge are available, why hasn't the change come faster? Perhaps it is moving as rapidly as possible, or perhaps sufficient pressures and incentives are not at work on the industry. This question deserves a more definitive answer than we can give.

We argued in Chapter 1 that the involvement of organization members in learning and striving was the intervening variable that linked environmental and organizational conditions to readaptive outcomes. The evidence from the seven industries in general supports this idea. The evidence from earlier periods regarding Carnegie's steel operations and General Motors is limited, but more recent information is more conclusive. High involvement is present when members are engaged in a rich and complex exchange with their organization. In addition to the limited exchange of time for money; ideas, loyalty, energy, trust, and support enter into the two-way flow. The recent efforts of GM to switch from a restricted level of exchange to an enriched involvement with their hourly workers is a graphic example of the distinction. To put it bluntly, GM has found it very difficult to produce high quality, inexpensive cars with an antagonistic work force. GM's label for the effort, quality of work life, makes the point that involvement can be not only a means to innovation and efficiency but can also be an end in itself. It can reasonably be thought of as a third outcome of the readaptive process.

We have hypothesized that the results of the adaptive process, in terms of efficiency and innovation, flow from a combination of environmental and organizational elements. The combinations of these elements that tend to appear together are shown in Figure 9.3, a more formal and detailed statement of our adaptational findings. It could be argued that the steel and auto industries existed for some years at the margin between Areas 4 and 5 without being readaptive, but these industries were eventually pushed into Area 6, establishing a fit between their internal and environmental conditions. Housing seems, on the other hand, to have achieved both efficiency and innovation by means of its special version of readaptive form and strategy without consistently enjoying the environmental condition of Area 5. The housing, auto, and steel industries are thus only temporary exceptions to the pattern. *Overall, the historical evidence indicates that successful readaptation is consistently associated with the internal form and strategy and usually with the levels of IC and RS we anticipated.* In other words, certain organizational features are essential to readaptation and certain environmental conditions are clearly supportive of it.

In addition to our historical approach, there is another entirely different and perfectly reasonable way to explore the question of readaptation: to choose a sample of firms, regardless of industry or national origin or environmental conditions, that seem to be readaptive and try to find the common denominators of their success. This is the approach used in recent studies focused on understanding the differential success of the leading Japanese firms and their U.S. counterparts.

## JAPAN AND THE READAPTIVE PROCESS

There can be little question but that Japan has a very strong record of keeping mature industries readaptive. Our examination of the U.S.

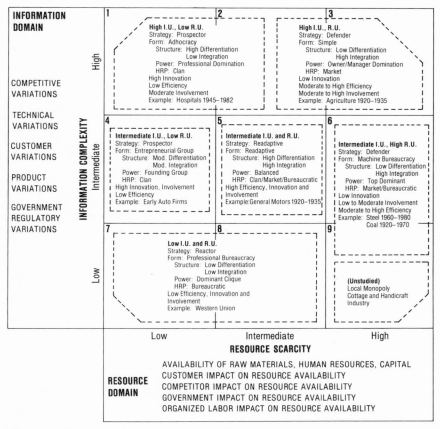

**Figure 9.3    Summary of Findings by Areas**

auto and steel industries gave ample evidence of Japanese firms' record of high efficiency and innovation in these areas, and, to our knowledge, the Japanese have accomplished as much in every industry they have seriously entered. Nearly every observer has remarked upon the high member involvement in Japanese firms. A brief review of this literature may be useful as a further test of our adaptation findings. We will look primarily at two contemporary studies: William Ouchi's *Theory Z* and Richard Pascale and Anthony Athos's *The Art of Japanese Management*. Both address the question of why several U.S. industries lag competitively behind Japan, drawing on numerous other studies of the same phenomenon. While neither book makes extensive use of the concept of adaptation as developed here, both judge performance in much the same way as we have, in terms of efficiency and innovation. Both are essentially empirical studies that try to identify the practices and methods associated with high performance. Their data bases are complementary: Pascale and Athos have more evidence on the internal workings of leading Japanese firms, especially Matsushita Electric, while Ouchi takes a closer look at Japanese-like U.S. firms he calls Type Z. The two studies produced very similar findings, with only one important exception to be noted below. Neither book emphasizes the institutional conditions surrounding the firms studied; to fill in this void we will later turn primarily to Michael Yoshino's *Japan's Managerial System* and to Ezra Vogel's work, *Japan as No 1?*

Ouchi and Pascale and Athos conclude that the higher-performing, readaptive firms they studied in both Japan and the United States are very similar hybrid systems using a mix of Western and Eastern management methods. These firms employ both the multidivisional organization structure and the product-line strategic planning that have become commonplace in modern industry. Both books include many examples showing that these organizations are not only structured into differentiated product divisions employing specialists of many kinds, but also employ a wide variety of integrating mechanisms. Matsushita, for example, maintains very large corporate staffs not only to achieve financial control but also to conduct centralized hiring, promotion reviews, and training. In addition, they make extensive use of task forces, rotational assignments, and other lateral means of linking divisions. These structural characteristics are not as widely practiced in U.S. industry.

In terms of formal accounting and control systems, the two studies disagree. Ouchi reports that the leading Japanese firms rely on informal control systems. Pascale and Athos describe very explicit, stringent, and elaborate formal control systems in use at firms such as Matsushita, in addition to informal methods. These market control mechanisms include profit centers, borrowing capital at interest from the headquarters "bank," and performance bonuses. We find the latter evidence quite persuasive and consistent with what both studies found in the high-performing U.S. firms.

Both studies found the greatest divergence between typical U.S. management practices and those of the hybrid U.S. and Japanese firms in the areas of human resource practices, management skill and style, and corporate philosophy and goals.

Both studies report that the high-performing U.S. firms enter into longer-term employment commitments to their members at all levels than is typical of most U.S. corporations — in this way approaching the well-known Japanese practice of extending lifetime employment to a significant number of employees. They find an emphasis in both hybrid types on in-company education programs, extensive rotation among assignments in the interest of developing managerial generalists, a longer-term orientation in reward systems, slower evaluation and promotion practices and a general interest in the life of the employee that extended to his or her immediate family. Although the career prospects for new employees recruited from high school are distinctly different from those for recruits from college, a unified set of human resource practices applies to both and there is significant career overlap in the lower managerial roles. Class distinctions are minimized. In our study we have borrowed Ouchi's term *clan* to denote this particular set of human resource practices, which we see as an important means, along with more customary bureaucratic and market methods, to achieve high levels of member involvement. Both Ouchi and Pascale and Athos illustrate the influence of human resource practices on readaptation, and tend to confirm our findings in this regard.

Both studies explore the issue of managerial skill and style in the U.S. and Japanese readaptive firms. Ouchi stresses the high levels of trust among the members of Type Z firms and the subtlety and intimacy of their working relationships. Similarly, Pascale and Athos note the ease with which managers in high-performing firms have learned to live with interdependence, ambiguity, and uncertainty. Both studies point out that the broader Japanese culture tends to support these practices much'more than does the U.S. culture. Nevertheless, the U.S. hybrid firms have found it possible to instill similar practices even given American values. Our historical approach has not brought us close enough to the organizations we studied to make such discriminating observations, but the management style reported by Ouchi and by Pascale and Athos is entirely consistent with and supportive of clan human resource practices. And our observations of the power balance in readaptive firms is consistent with these two studies' findings on management style. Trusting work relations do not thrive in the face of extreme power differentials. Both books offer many examples of how firms worked to reduce and offset power differences, striving to create an egalitarian system in spite of inevitable role differences.

Finally, both books emphasize the critical importance of a firm's developing an explicit statement of beliefs about its broad mission in society, its operating principles, and its ethical standards, what we have referred to as strategies. Similarly, we have argued that a firm is more apt to be readaptive if it explicitly emphasizes its strategic commitment to involvement with all its members, to innovation, and to efficiency.

Hewlett Packard, one of the firms cited as a high-performing U.S. hybrid, has a statement of corporate objectives that exemplifies this point.

> FIRST, the most capable people available should be selected for each assignment within the organization. Moreover, these people should have the

opportunity—through continuing programs of training and education—
to upgrade their skills and capabilities. This is especially important in a
technical business where the rate of progress is rapid. Techniques that are
good today will be outdated in the future, and people throughout the organization should continually be looking for new and better ways to do
their work.

SECOND, enthusiasm should exist at all levels. People in important
management positions should not only be enthusiastic themselves, they
should be selected for their ability to engender enthusiasm among their
associates. There can be no place, especially among the people charged
with management responsibility, for half-hearted interest or half-hearted
effort.

THIRD, even though an organization is made up of people fully
meeting the first two requirements, all levels should work in unison
toward common objectives and avoid working at cross purposes if the ultimate in efficiency and achievement is to be obtained.[5]

These three "fundamentals" could hardly be a more focused and
explicit statement of the value of innovation, involvement, and efficiency. Finally, under the heading of "citizenship," Hewlett Packard
summarizes its mission by saying, "Objective: To honor our obligations
to society by being an *economic, intellectual and social* asset to each
nation and each community in which we operate." [italics added]
This, we submit, is a readaptive strategy statement.

To conclude our discussion of Ouchi and Pascale and Athos, we
must point out that their approach, by focusing on prominent large
firms, would make it difficult to recognize the readaptive success of industries with smaller units, such as agriculture or housing. Nor does
their approach help us understand the less adaptive firms. The particular contribution of these two studies is their clear recognition of the
internal similarities between readaptive firms in the U.S. and Japan.
We shall now turn to the question of what contextual and environmental factors have helped so many readaptive firms to emerge in the postwar years in Japan.

Japan's postwar industrial record has been much admired. It is,
however, still hard to comprehend the magnitude of the achievement.
The country came out of the war with very tight resources and a flood
of new ideas brought in by the occupying powers. It is easy to forget
just how turbulent the immediate postwar years were for Japan. Unions
were quickly formed in the leading industries, often with Communist
leadership. There was a wave of prolonged strikes in major firms. Unions pressed for employment security and met with determined resistance from managers. Violent clashes resulted. The government became very active in trying to resolve this conflict. In effect, a bargain
was struck at government's instigation between management and unions that industrial peace would be granted in exchange for employ-

ment security. The so-called lifetime employment contract is of fairly recent origin in Japan and was accepted with great reluctance by Japanese management.

Gradually, over the years Japan has evolved a very complex and rich set of integrating mechanisms that tie business, unions, and government together at multiple levels in mutual problem solving on a large array of topics. As Vogel and Yoshino have emphasized in describing these mechanisms, the basic assumption of all three parties is that at bottom their relationship will be one of collaboration, marked by occasional outbursts of conflict.

Out of these relationships has grown a general understanding of a rough formula that seems to work for the Japanese in creating and maintaining readaptive firms. They expect to have a relatively small number of leading firms emerge in every newly developing industrial area. The more promising firms are encouraged to grow by the extension of capital from the banks and government and by other forms of support. These leading firms are then expected to engage in strenuous competition with each other for their respective shares of the domestic market. It is only after they have proven their mettle at home that they are encouraged seriously to seek overseas markets. Of course, some firms move into exports without official encouragement. The government's control in such matters has apparently waned in recent years. The point should not be missed, however, that these leading firms face very real, but not overwhelming, domestic competition (intermediate IC and RS). They must prove in this competitive arena that they are efficient and innovative. These firms have long since learned that they cannot meet the standards of an increasingly discriminating domestic market without securing the daily concern and involvement of their employees throughout the ranks. We have already seen the care with which this is done.

As an additional contextual factor, we should recognize that leading Japanese firms are mostly financed by long-term bonds owned by an interlocking set of banks and other operating firms. Stock is primarily owned by the same people. Owners do not expect their stock to pay substantial dividends but rather expect it to appreciate at a somewhat better rate than prevailing interest rates. This capital structure tends to give the owners a longer-term outlook than is typical in the United States. If things start going wrong, the owners react with corrective advice and perhaps some additional management talent rather than a "sell" order. Owners are largely locked in. Therefore, they are concerned with management succession, the next generation of technology, the demographics of the work force, and other long-term issues as well as current sales and earnings. They can be counted on to join forces with relevant government agencies in helping the firm stay healthy.

Japanese management does not now need to be convinced, if it ever did, that their organizations are learning and social systems as well as production systems. This insight is implicit in all their actions. And the culture of Japan tends to reinforce this outlook. Our review of the Japanese record sets the stage for pulling together our own historical findings on readaptation.

## READAPTATION IN REVIEW

We started our inquiry with the simple idea that organizations and their members could have too much or too little information stimulation for innovation to thrive, and too many or too few resources for efficiencies to be achieved. We judged neither of these two outcomes could be sustained without the high involvement of the organization's members in learning and striving; on closer examination, the element of involvement became not only a means but a legitimate end in itself, a high quality of work life.

We can now see that this way of looking at the relation between an organization and its environment is also a useful framework for examining what happens inside the organization. Does the sales department face enough or too little IC to induce learning? Does the production unit have too many or too few resources at its disposal to encourage efforts toward efficiency? Do we have the kind of employment understanding with the people in purchasing that gives them a stake in the long-term health of the whole enterprise? Are we using all three means — clan, market, and bureaucratic — to link corporate interests with employee interests so that high involvement follows? We cannot claim to know the optimal information and resource levels for any given unit, in a given firm, in a given industry, at a given point in time. Even with detailed inside information, gauging pressure is a matter of judgment and feel. But if an organization is to be readaptive, management must find a way to translate the intermediate uncertainties of its environment into intermediate uncertainties for its separate units and its individual members, up and down the line.

This same reasoning applies to the working relations between an organization's component parts. Are these units, such as sales and production, sufficiently differentiated to induce learning and innovation? Are they effectively integrated, in spite of their necessary differences, to secure the efficiencies of coordination? Are the power differentials in reasonable balance, so that joint problem solving can proceed up and down as well as laterally? Is the strategy explicit about the outcome components of readaptation?

In talking about organizations as learning systems we do not mean to suggest that they have human properties. Organizations do not think, do not learn in a literal sense. Only people do. It is true, however, that members of an organization can not only learn as individuals but can transmit their learning to others, can codify it and embody it in the standard procedures of the organization. In this limited sense the organization can be said to learn. When certain organizational arrangements are in place, an organization will foster the learning of its members and take the follow-up steps that convert that learning into standard practice. Then it is functioning as a learning system, generating innovations.

Similarly, organizations, as such, do not expend effort to achieve efficiencies. People do. But when involved organization members strive in coordination with the efforts of others, we can fairly say that the organization is efficient as a production system. Treating organizations as production systems is probably the most venerable way of looking at them. Frederick Taylor popularized this outlook in his famous time and motion studies in the steel mills. The same idea, however, underlies the even older definition of economists of the three factors of production as land, capital, and labor. These ideas are still valid but need to be supplemented by other ways of looking at organizations.

The idea of organizations as social systems was seriously introduced into contemporary thought by the work of Elton Mayo and Fritz Roethlisberger and their experiments at the Hawthorne plant of Western Electric. Both abstractly and empirically, they argued that to manage organizations only as production systems and not also as social systems was wasteful in both human and economic terms. The very title of the book that reported this research, *Management and the Worker*, suggests their major finding, that the social systems of the workers and of management were two different worlds. The challenge was to join these worlds — to blend production logic and social logic into a unified system. Their ideas have been pushed forward in more recent years by the advocates of sociotechnical design of work. Leaders in this effort, such as Eric Trist and Kenneth Rice, have developed specific ways to build on the earlier insights so that management can design for both technical and social effectiveness.

Even the idea of organizations as learning systems is by no means new. This was the central theme of James March and Herbert Simon's classic 1958 work[6], which argued that many of the features of organizations were designed to overcome the limitations on any one individual's thinking, thus helping people handle very complex information and decision issues.

Our effort is an attempt to integrate these three ways of looking at organizations — seeing them as socio-techno-learning systems, to make the perspective clear but unpronounceable. This point is embedded in our definition of readaptive results in terms of efficiency, innovation and now, involvement. It is built into our emphasis on the active processes of learning and striving. We can now propose a definition of the readaptive organization's goal: to have every employee at every level define himself or herself as a manager (learning), as a worker (striving), and as a member (belonging). We believe that organizations have lived up to this potential only in limited and sporadic ways. By understanding organizations as trimodal systems we will have a better chance to bring them to fulfillment as truly readaptive systems.

Our examination of the adaptive process has uncovered systematic relationships between the RS/IC balance and both industry and organization structures. The range of industry structure, from monopoly to perfect competition, can be seen as a continuum running across our model from Area 7 to Area 3, as shown in Figure 9.4. Similarly, organization structures range from the mechanistic or bureaucratic form to the organic, clanlike form, varying most sharply along the diagonal

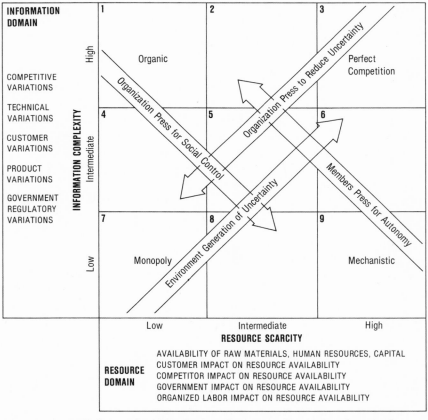

Figure 9.4    Schematic of Relation Between Organization and Economic Theory and Associated Dynamics

from Area 1 to Area 9. The large arrows in Figure 9.4 are an attempt to convey the dynamics of this overall pattern. The organization generally seeks to reduce both information and resource uncertainty and thereby dominate its environment. At the same time, environmental forces normally generate uncertainty for the organization and in other ways press to dominate the organization. In a similar fashion the members of the organization generally tend to push for autonomy while the forces of the organization press for member control. That these existential tensions are best balanced in Area 5 is another reason why the broadly constructive outcomes we call readaptation are most likely to occur here.

In our concluding chapter we shall consider some of these ideas at greater length, as we present our suggestions about the implications of our findings for the management of firms and for public policy.

# CHAPTER 10

# The Readaptive Process: Putting It to Work

THE SHEER COMPLEXITY of the American industrial scene is a formidable stumbling block in efforts to see its specific problems and its overall condition. Simplifications too often distort reality; analyses too often treat living, changing organizations as if they were static entities. Our way of analyzing an organization's behavior with the readaptive framework is different; with it the extremely complex phenomena that inhibit or contribute to an organization's adaptive and readaptive behavior can be simplified and patterned without taking gross liberties with reality. In addition to its being a practical descriptive framework, our model is based on concepts which, in themselves, provide help for diagnosing particular situations, for clarifying goals, and for distinguishing among the options available to an organization for proceeding toward these goals. In brief, the readaptive framework points the way to reconciling innovation and efficiency in the total organizational environment and over the long term. It provides a reasoned way for an organization to chart as well as execute a turn toward renewal.

In spite of its multifaceted flexibility, the readaptive framework is not by any means an across-the-board solution to industrial malaise, for each organization confronts its own mix of obstacles and opportunities. Solutions to individual problems can come only when management—and government—adapt the tools to particular problems and use them to move, in sequence, through the three steps of diagnostic assessment, strategic goal setting, and tactical planning for change.

266

How, specifically, can managers and government officials proceed to put the readaptive process to work? Our answer begins with ten general implications for action; suggestions for specific managerial and governmental action follow.

## GENERAL IMPLICATIONS FOR ACTION

1. *Although organizations can get by for a time being only efficient or only innovative, over the long term there must be a simultaneous achievement of both efficiency and innovation.* The current plight of the automobile industry is an example of the inadequacy of limiting goals to efficiency; the plight of hospitals, an example of overemphasis on innovation. Working toward both efficiency and innovation is particularly important for industries facing worldwide competition.

2. *Achieving and sustaining readaptive results is difficult for an organization, but it is by no means impossible.* The history of the auto and steel industries demonstrates the difficulty organizations experience in sustaining readaptive results once they are achieved, while the history of agriculture and housing show that continued success is not impossible. Organizations can also move from long periods of nonreadaptive operation to readaptive operation. Depending upon the circumstances, the necessary initiative can come from within the organization or from the environment. In telecommunications the initiative was mostly internal; in coal, external.

3. *Member involvement is essential to the simultaneous achievement of both efficiency and innovation.* We found no instance of an organization's having a record of high efficiency and high innovation without evidence of active involvement throughout the organization.

4. *The current circumstances of any given organization determine what particular actions will best foster readaptation.* What might be helpful for hospitals will not necessarily be good for coal. Good planning for agriculture in the 1930s will not necessarily work for the industry in the 1980s. What works for AT&T will not necessarily work for Chrysler. There is no single road, no panacea, to assure the renewed vigor of American industry; the point is not obscure, but it is often ignored to the detriment of all parties concerned.

5. *Overall, both industry and government have a part to play in any drive toward achieving strong readaptive outcomes; the degree and nature of the initiative each takes will depend on the particular environmental pressures and possibilities of a given situation.* Readaptation in industries whose site-dispersed technology (such as agriculture) tends to put them in Area 3 is relatively dependent on government action; firms whose transforming technology tends to put them in Ar-

eas 4, 5, or 6, depend more directly on internal initiatives. Totally "free enterprise" is no more the key to readaptation than is complete state ownership and control. Ezra Vogel's term "guided enterprise" is closer to the mark.[1]

6. *Readaptation can be achieved only if industry as well as government see their goals in terms of concrete sources of wealth rather than in terms of money which is only a symbol for wealth.* This is an important distinction. Money as a symbol for wealth is highly distracting and easily confused with what it stands for. Actually it expresses only a claim on real resources. In household terms, the family bank balance is not a resource but a claim on the purchase of a car or a house. In industrial terms, profits, by the same token, are only the bottom line of a periodic income statement, the abstract summation of many concrete resource transactions between a firm and its environment, and a balance sheet represents the current status of tangible resources employed and reserved by the enterprise. Together the income statement and balance sheet indicate the level of resource scarcity in only an approximate and short-term way. Over the long-term, if the firm is relatively efficient, its outputs will compare favorably with its inputs; if it is innovative, it will remain efficient; and if it is involving its members, these two outcomes can be reconciled. If this readaptive process goes forward, wealth, the real bottom line, is generated and the symbol of it, profit, will take care of itself. If this process, illustrated in Figure 10.1, does not go forward, no amount of financial wheeling and dealing to make the numbers come out right is going to suffice for long. Figure 10.1 highlights the point that information and its internal processing must guide the transformation of raw inputs, step by step, into "information added" outputs that have extra value for customers.

7. *If both government and industry are aware that intermediate levels of resource scarcity and information complexity favor readaptation, the destructive suspicion and animosity usually associated with debate on broad economic issues will be significantly lessened and the focus of discussion turned to questions amenable to constructive solution.* Too often government officials act as if companies is Area 3 striving to move into Area 5 are, in fact, trying to push through to become Area 7 monopolists. Likewise, companies on the edge of Area 7 are afraid that government will enforce anti-trust laws so as to force them into the extreme competition of Areas 3 or 6. With agreement on both sides that there can be too much as well as too little competitive pressure, government and industry might have an easier time finding the happy medium.

8. *In addition to being production systems, organizations have great potential for being learning and social systems as well.* This is as true for public as well as private organizations, for profit as well as

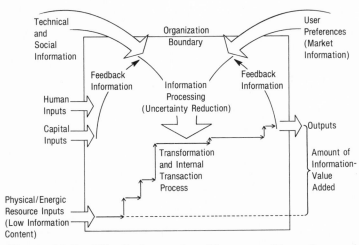

**Figure 10.1    The Information/Resource Transformation Process of an Organization**

non-profit organizations. Our research showed that one of the positive outcomes of the readaptive process is a particular kind of high quality work life. While readaptive firms are by no means free of pressure and stress, they do provide opportunities for their employees to experience a sense of competence.

9. *In their efforts to achieve innovation and efficiency, managers who understand the readaptive process can identify and employ a wide variety of organizational mechanisms that may not have been recognized or fully utilized.* For example, students of organization have only recently identified how the quasi-firm has helped the housing industry be readaptive; these semipermanent contractors' networks have considerable potential for other applications.

10. *Industrial managers and government officials who achieve readaptive results perform a difficult and valuable service that deserves recognition.* The public, and even organization members, often fail to appreciate and encourage the kinds of constructive efforts needed to sustain readaptation.

## IMPLICATIONS FOR MANAGEMENT: DIAGNOSIS

Management that wants to use the readaptive framework to help a firm move toward the overall strategic goal of becoming more efficient and innovative must distinguish clearly between the need to diagnose the firm's condition and the need to decide on tactical changes that would improve that condition.

The first diagnostic step for management to take is determining what area of the adaptation model the firm is currently in. To do this it must look first to the firm's environment to assess its information complexity and resource scarcity. It must also look inside the organization at its current form, strategy and performance record.

Answers to these inquiries are not easy, and they cannot be precise. Still, a pattern should emerge that can than be compared to those found in our research. (See Figure 9.3.) In particular, the pattern ought to be evaluated in relation to the organizational features we found associated with readaptation in Area 5. The differences between the model and the descriptive pattern identify the features of the firm that need to be changed.

In considering specifically how to diagnose an organization's conditions, we can think of the concepts of the readaptive framework as themselves being diagnostic tools.

One way to describe the structure of a given firm is to determine the degree of its *differentiation (D)* and *integration (I)*. A sufficiently high degree of differentiation (our term for the use organizations make of specialized individuals and units to bring differentiated skills and orientations to problems) is essential if a firm is to sustain innovation. The more an organization is faced with information complexity, the more it needs differentiation. Specialists consume resources, however, so that, if an organization is small, as high IC firms commonly are, the practical dilemma of how far to carry differentiation becomes acute. Small organizations are usually forced to take their chances by employing jacks-of-all-trades; larger firms have a greater degree of freedom.

Integration is the reciprocal of differentiation, since an increase in D tends to lower I. As a result, the more D there is, the more integrative activity is needed to pull things together. Integration also tends to build up as resource scarcity increases, since integration clearly fosters efficiency. Hospitals are chronically too poorly integrated to keep up with their galloping differentiation. Auto firms, on the other hand, have stressed integration at the expense of differentiation. For the readaptive process to work, a balanced level of high D and high I is essential.

*A balanced mix of clan, market, and bureaucratic human resource practices* is also essential to achieving readaptive outcomes. How is such a mix expected to help? The basic idea is that because achieving innovation and efficiency depends on involvement, no tool that might help involve members in the work of the organization should be neglected. Each of the three methods provides a different and fundamental way of involving people. Clan mechanisms appeal to people's need to identify with a social entity in which they can join others to achieve common goals and mutual support. Clan mechanisms, of course, were the mainstay of feudal societies — and Japan, incidentally, only in the last century emerged from feudalism. Market mechanisms work on the reinforcement principle of rewarding individuals or groups for desired behavior. Business has invented a wide variety of reinforcement methods, from profit centers to performance bonuses and piece rates. Bureaucratic methods have recourse to two appeals: rules and leaders. Thoughtfully designed rules satisfy people's need for order. Following legitimate leaders who are wise and strong is a time-honored and sensible way to help solve some problems of organization members. All three approaches have some potential for abuse: clans can become inbred; market methods can induce greed; bureaucratic methods can bog down in red tape. The balanced use of all three methods will minimize the potential for abuse of any one. It will also enhance involvement if employed in a unified and consistent way at all levels.

Based upon our familiar adaptation framework, Figure 10.2 shows where each of the three kinds of human resource practices can be expected to dominate. Every organization can be expected to make some use of all three forms but larger firms in the lower part of the framework can be expected, in their concern for order, to emphasize bureaucratic methods. Smaller organizations of the upper tier, when pressed for resources, tend to emphasize market mechanisms such as the piece rate of small garment firms. On the other hand, small high-technology firms in Areas 1 and 2 are apt to develop a clanlike spirit and group commitment. In the significant areas of overlap the emphasis is more a matter of organizational choice. A balance of all three mechanisms is more likely to appear in Area 5.

*A balanced power distribution* is the final element of organizational form necessary for readaptive results. No organization can be expected to strike a perfect balance between the power and influence of the various functions and divisions (horizontal power distribution) or between the top and bottom (vertical power distribution), and it probably should not try to. Certainly there are times, for example, when giving extra power to the top level will help an organization through a crisis situation. The point is rather that extreme and persistent power differentials will block readaptation.

Blocking takes two forms. The lack of a reasonable horizontal power balance makes it significantly more difficult for managers to integrate specialized sub-units in a constructive and creative way. The differences in orientation and approach that contribute to creative problem solving will not be brought to bear if, in the end, one party

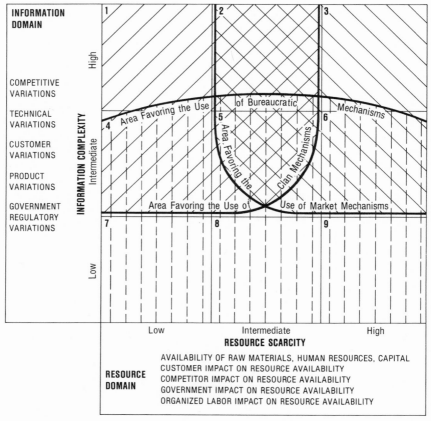

**Figure 10.2    Expected Usage of Market, Bureaucratic, and Clan Human Resource Practices**

can be expected to make an arbitrary decision. This point is particularly relevant to the horizontal power distribution. Figure 10.3 illustrates how major functional units are likely to bring contradictory built-in biases to any general decision. For instance, production managers are apt to stress efficiencies on a short-term unit cost basis to the point of ignoring important longer-term factors. This practice, if persistent, would pull a firm toward Area 6.

The lack of vertical power balance affects readaptation in a less obvious and more controversial manner. It affects the distribution of the wealth generated by the enterprise. The fruit of a readaptive enterprise is the real wealth it generates by taking less valued inputs and transforming them into more valued outputs. The organization must attend to the distribution of this wealth in some way that does not, in itself,

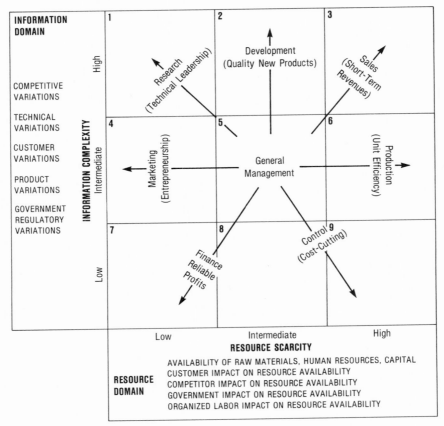

**Figure 10.3    Schematic of Functional Tendencies**

stifle the ongoing readaptive process. Success can breed success in the sense of generating the resources needed for continuing investment in efficient innovations, but it can also lead to dissension among the contributing members over the division of the surplus. The continuing involvement of members of all types and at all levels depends upon their sense that the distribution of the wealth is reasonably equitable. One way to achieve equity is to rely on top management's sense of fairness. While this method can work, the human tendency to see one's own contribution more clearly than that of others, makes the method a less reliable means of achieving equity than having a reasonable balance of power between the parties. The inevitable conflict of interest in the distribution of rewards must be dealt with by some bargaining process, implicit or explicit. Large organizations particularly tend to create large power differences between the people at the top and people at the bottom. Whether management likes it or not, unions and collective bargaining methods reduce this power differential and improve the probability of an equitable distribution of rewards. And again, ongoing high involvement and readaptation require a reasonable sense of equity about rewards. We are not so naive as to think that sharing power and wealth will come easily to many influential and wealthy people. We are simply pointing out that readaptation will eventually be self-limiting unless a sense of reasonable equity is achieved.

We do not want to imply that unions' traditional role in bargaining about the distribution of resources is the only contribution that unions can make to the readaptive process. We saw in Chapter 2 the vital, constructive partnership role that the UAW is playing at GM and at Ford in the involvement of hourly employees. This effort is proceeding at three levels, shop floor groups, plantwide sponsoring committees, and a joint top-level coordinating committee specified in the union contract. Somewhat similar efforts have begun between the Communications Workers and AT&T, and between the Steel Workers and some of the major steel firms. Japanese unions regularly work with management in projects concerned with innovation, efficiency, and product quality. The increasing willingness of American union leaders to join with management in working toward readaptation is encouraging.

Although the need for an explicit *readaptive strategy* is obvious, its importance and complexity are apt to be overlooked. Even firms that are relatively readaptive frequently hobble themselves by narrow strategic thinking and platitudinous public statements. (We should emphasize that we are using the term *strategy* to include not only the standard idea of product line and market planning but also the firm's broadest sense of purpose, its basic operating principles, and its ethical standards.) Too many firms make meaningless statements like "the goal of the enterprise is to make profits." Again, profits are only a symbol. How much more meaningful to say that the purpose of the enterprise is to create specific forms of wealth—for example, to produce high-quality cars efficiently whose value will be known by the premium they command in the marketplace. Such statements engage members' commitment, and keep the focus on the basic values of efficiency and innovation. Firms are also often reluctant to state their operating principles and ethical standards explicitly. If carefully and forthrightly prepared, such statements can act as guidelines for decisions down the line that then need not be referred to the top for time-consuming consideration. When managers live by their own explicit guidelines, such statements have a positive, unifying effect.

# IMPLICATIONS FOR MANAGEMENT: TACTICS FOR CHANGE

After management has diagnosed those aspects of its organization that must be modified if the goals of efficiency and innovation are to be achieved, it must consider its tactical options for change. A consideration of the actions that could be used to move an organization toward Area 5 from four distinctly different points in our framework will illustrate these possibilities for change.

First, what does it take to become readaptive in an organization that is being pushed from the quiet world of Area 8 into the competitive pressures of Area 5? This challenge faces any organization that has been existing rather comfortably in a low IC condition with minimal strategic alternatives or competitive challenges from its environment. Now it finds the world changing with new competition, new product and technical options, new ground rules from government, and perhaps a new internal desire to be readaptive. Such are the circumstances now facing AT&T, as we saw in Chapter 8.

To make this move successfully, organizations must increase the diversity of views inside the organization to keep up with the increasing IC of their environment. Many mechanisms are available. To consider some examples is helpful. Outside directors and senior advisers with diverse views helped GM make its decision to downsize ahead of its domestic competition. AT&T now recruits nontraditional specialists from outside the organization and appoints them to key posts. Job rotation among senior managers can stimulate new thinking. Carefully orchestrated face-to-face meetings between senior executives and panels of influential outsiders are often useful. The same is true for outside executive education programs and internal seminars drawing on diverse outside resources.

For lasting differentiation, some companies need to enrich their formal structure by adding to the traditional geographic and functional categories of their organizations. Depending on the circumstances, this new structural dimension might be based on product, market, or technological categories. Sometimes these new dimensions will displace old ones; and sometimes it may be more appropriate to use the new dimension as a formal matrix overlaid on the old structure.

Human resource practices may well have to include a larger proportion of clan and market features to achieve a better balance. Members will need to be challenged more by situations that engage shared goals and values. Current and candid business information should be shared from the top of the organization to the bottom. Factory and clerical jobs can be enriched by adding some integrative functions (I), such as unit safety, primary equipment maintenance, or inventory control, to the existing specialized role of each member (D). More might need to be done to diminish the customary vertical power differential. The means might include multilevel educational sessions, shared parking lots and cafeterias, open office architecture, grass roots task forces on business problems, and doors that really are open. Relevant new strategies must be explicated and widely communicated. An increased emphasis on innovation and efficiency can be very straightforward.

As these various moves begin to have effect, care must be taken to avoid shattering old belief systems before new ones take hold and disrupting old work habits before new ones are understood. Pace and timing will be continuing problems. It is hard to overestimate the difficulty of executing such an important, multifaceted change in a large Area 8 organization. One might even question whether it can be done at all, if there were not clear evidence that this kind of massive change is well underway at AT&T. Such a transformation will inevitably require both time and leadership with a sensitive appreciation of the old system and a clear vision of the new.

To move from the conditions of high RS in Area 6 toward the conditions of intermediate RS in Area 5 represents the current challenge to major firms in the steel and auto industries. Again, action implications can be stated in only a brief, suggestive way. One good way to start such a change is by ensuring that everyone in the organization feels a sense of resource pressure and urgency. Senior managers often buffer those in the lower ranks from the bad news of high RS. This is a dubious kindness. Members throughout the organization need to understand the economic facts. Some of the strongest shock waves from an adverse environment may be partially absorbed at the top to avoid excessive anxiety, but certainly no one should be left in a fool's paradise. Business facts should no longer be kept to an inner circle but widely disseminated.

One of the trickiest aspects of moving from Area 6 to Area 5 involves increasing the attention given to the long-term issue of innovation while continuing to keep a reasonable focus on the importance of short-term results. In terms of organizational structure, it will probably be necessary to add both more differentiation and, to keep pace, more integrative mechanisms. Greater differentiation is likely to be needed in the research and development function to strengthen the innovative effort, and in the human resource function to foster involvement. It will be essential to add clan mechanisms to any existing market and bureaucratic methods. Such methods as short-term executive bonus schemes will need to be cut back or phased out in order to balance long- and short-time orientations appropriately. The need to strike a better power balance and make strategy explicit will also be important.

A move from the low RS conditions of Area 4 toward the intermediate RS conditions of Area 5 is one that few firms currently face — but this situation could reoccur. In our historical sample it was the unrecognized problem facing some steel firms before 1960 and some auto firms before 1970 when they were in Area 4. In many ways this often unrecognized problem where affluence fostered complacency was a general affliction of American industry in the 1950s and 1960s. The key to solving this problem is to recognize it and then to get one's associates to recognize it. Finding the means for correction is then not overly difficult.

Overcoming complacency requires its own action planning. Digging out and spreading information about any and all competitive challenges at home and abroad is a much needed step. Firsthand examination of competitive products and technologies helps to drive home the information uncertainties. Some firms have even been known to give indirect support to competitors so that they will have worthy future challengers. The fact that U.S. Steel can claim to have done this in the early part of this century is an indication, however, that this is not enough. AT&T's experience shows that the generation of internal competition can partially substitute for external competition. The innovator and the entrepreneur need to be brought on board and rewarded. The risk taker must be supported even while a tougher attitude is taken toward operating costs.

Complacency associated with affluence must also be fought with hard-nosed control methods. Accounting and general management functions may need to grow in order to increase pressures for economy and coordination. Integration can be increased by using cross-functional task forces or permanent teams to devise and implement efficient innovations. Other means of achieving lateral integration, such as the use of liaison roles or even the establishment of a regular department committed to the full-time task of integration, should be considered. Additional long-term market mechanisms may be needed to round out the mix of human resource practices. Horizontal power rebalancing could give additional clout to the forces for both innovation and control.

IBM is an example of a firm that stayed remarkably readaptive for many years even while dominating its world market. In effect, IBM's senior management amplified and exaggerated actual environmental uncertainties to create an internal environment of intermediate IC and RS. In recent years both greater market competition and an antitrust suit, have obviated need for self-generated ways to "run scared."

One unconventional remedy for the Area 4 firm could be the voluntary splitting of the organization into two or more independent firms. In fact, why shouldn't a highly successful competitor whose very success has moved it from Area 5 into Area 4, undertake a voluntary split to promote its own readaptation? This suggestion may seem bizarre, but only in terms of traditional thinking. Stocks can easily be split, and multiple factory and distribution sites can be parceled out without great difficulty. If such action creates two or more worthy competitors who can challenge each other to be readaptive, who is the loser? If professional managers realize that real wealth creation, not monopoly profits, is the purpose of enterprise, such a move may become sensible, particularly if the government may otherwise take the decision out of management's hands and pick the time and form of the split. What would have happened if U.S. Steel had decided to split following World War I and General Motors following World War II? Would we now have stronger firms to face international competition? Although the U.S. at present has few if any mature firms enjoying the affluence of Area 4, such conditions can return, making it important to explore multiple ways to avoid the mistakes of the auto and steel industries.

Moving from Area 2 to Area 5 might be the goal of firms in volatile high-technology fields, such as minicomputers, bioengineering, and semiconductors. The starting point, Area 2, is where IC is high and RS low to intermediate but where there is the potential for a rapid swing to high RS. The problem for firms in these circumstances is probably not innovation or involvement, but one of efficiency. Of the industries we studied, hospitals most clearly face this special challenge.

The key to becoming readaptive from this starting point is to simplify complexity so that the world becomes more manageable for the organization's members. A few strategic priorities should be chosen and faithfully pursued. For example, Digital Equipment Company has consistently stressed the dual concepts of distributed data processing and engineering compatibility throughout a period of great churning in its industry. A necessary corollary is that performance should be measured and rewarded in terms of the chosen priorities. Strive to simplify the organization. Restrain tendencies toward further differentiation. Put the emphasis on more integration, detailed planning, and stringent budget reviews. In the human resource realm, those organizations which already have pervasive clan mechanisms, need a strong dose of bureaucracy: more job descriptions, more standard procedures, more organization charts. Adding these features carefully will make organizational life less chaotic for the average member without eliminating clan and market mechanisms. Power balancing may not be much of a problem, but there could be a need to trim the influence of certain professional specialists in favor of general managers.

This review has offered a range of change tactics available to management for consideration in particular situations. Figure 10.4 summarizes the action implications for management.

## IMPLICATIONS FOR GOVERNMENTAL ACTION

The American public and government have a large stake in whether or not the United States contains a large mix of firms that are both efficient and innovative. When firms are staying on the readaptive track without government's help, there is no need or justification for government to become involved. There are cases, on the other hand, when

**Figure 10.4    General Action Implications for Management**

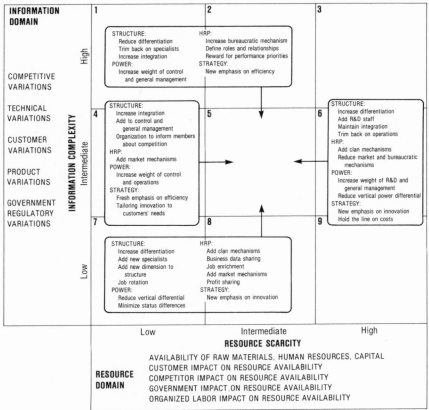

government, by actions either large or small, can significantly improve the likelihood of an organization's becoming and remaining efficient and innovative. Some industries need only a helping hand; others need more extreme measures. In other words, a blanket policy of either hands-on or hands-off makes no sense but fitting policy to need does. At just this point when assessment and planning for action are necessary, the readaptive framework proves its usefulness.

For most people, appreciating ways in which the framework is helpful in shaping policies for industrial management is probably easier than seeing its possible role in shaping policies for government agencies. Prior attitudes and unfamiliarity with the concepts ought not to keep us from fully exploring its potential, however, for by the same token that the conceptual framework of adaptation and readaptation can serve as a tool for simplifying, assessing, and planning for industrial renewal, so it can provide a new and constructive way to consider the pros and cons of government involvement with industry.

At this point it is appropriate to point out — and emphasize — that certain aspects of governmental action are beyond the scope of our discussion. We will suggest some possible lines of governmental action for fostering readaptive results, but we will not pursue the complexities and difficulties of implementing these ideas in the national political context. Likewise, we will not address the important national economic debates on Keynesian economic theory, demand- versus supply-side policies, tight versus loose monetary policy, deficit versus balanced budgets, and tax impacts on low- versus high-income families. Our focus is restricted to finding ways to renew American firms and industries and assure their continuing health.

In business circles one hears many justifiable complaints about the inconsistency of government policy. Some agencies, for instance, encourage foreign trade, others discourage it. Some agencies foster industrial research, others inhibit it. Even a given posted price may be attacked by one group for being "punitive," by another for being "fixed." Figure 10.5 shows the contrary thrusts that government agencies can have on business firms. Clearly, finding the means to minimize counterproductive governmental actions is a pressing challenge.

One value of our model lies in its potential for reducing inconsistencies in governmental policy. It provides a basis on which different agencies could work together toward agreement on whether a given industry needs more or less IC and RS to foster readaptive results. With agreement on these points, the firms in that industry could then be treated consistently by government agencies, even as other industries are treated differently, in a manner appropriate to their condition. Such an approach could provide the foundation for a national industrial policy focused on the basics of innovation and efficiency.

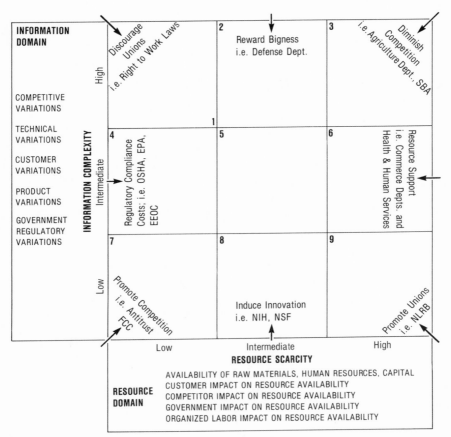

**Figure 10.5    Impact Tendencies of Selected Government Agencies**

By way of example, we will discuss some actions government might take to foster readaptive results. Specifically, we shall look at some of government's options for shifting an industry toward Area 5 from each of five different locations on the readaptive framework.

We begin with the situation in which government may decide to help move an industry cluster from the high RS and IC conditions of Area 3 toward the moderate levels found in Area 5 by lessening competitive pressures. Some government actions of this kind have been proceeding for years, but they have had to be carried out in an ad hoc, uneasy way without theoretical justification or a unified approach. The most conspicuous example encountered in our historical studies was in agriculture. Chapter 5 sketched the ways in which the government reduced the level of competition that raged in the 1920s and early 1930s and thereby contributed to the readaptive process in the entire industry. While one can undoubtedly find examples of government wastage in agricultural support programs, on balance the cost of agricultural programs over the years has been dwarfed by the benefits of a readaptive industry. The history of U.S. farming demonstrates that there is a time and place to lessen competition. While this example stands out as the clearest and probably most successful government action of this kind, it is by no means the only one. Various small business and fair trade programs all share the common denominator of restraining dog-eat-dog competition. Most of these support efforts take the form of some combination of educational programs, government-sponsored research on new products or methods, programs to increase the availability of capital, special tax breaks, and, probably most controversially, price supports. It is beyond our scope to discuss the merits and demerits of these various approaches to putting together a coherent program. What we want to emphasize is the legitimacy of restraining competition in selected industries in the interest of readaptation.

The government will usually have an important role in shifting an industry cluster from the conditions of high IC and low RS in Area 1 toward Area 5. This is true because government policies are usually a primary cause of an industry's being in Area 1 in the first place. The prime example is hospitals. Both the general public and government officials are at last keenly aware of the need for government to play a role in constraining the continuing escalation of hospital costs. The debate continues, however, as to the appropriate means. Our model suggests that the answer lies in finding mechanisms that will enhance competition and increase RS, certainly not in more forms of third-party insurance that pass through the costs. There are various plans coming forward that are designed to increase price competition at the level of the institutional payer. Having a choice of HMOs with a potential rebate to the insured is another promising approach. Such approaches based on incentives are more attractive than efforts to cap costs and license capital projects. It is too soon to say which approach will work best, but the need for change is clear as is the desired general direction of movement.

The government employs a variety of policy tactics to move firms from the conditions of low IC and RS in Areas 7 and 8 toward Area 5 by increasing competition; probably the principal one is the federal antitrust program. Recently there has been renewed interest in examining antitrust policy to see whether it is an effective tool for its purpose. Interest is also strong in employing deregulation as another way of increasing competition. Our study can reinforce these efforts by providing a fresh perspective on when and why competition needs to be enhanced. It can also suggest other means to supplement existing methods.

The implications we see in our model for antitrust policy start with the point that most antitrust action is used to induce readaptation by preventing firms from operating under conditions of relatively low IC and RS. Under these conditions suspicion of "monopoly" profits is often justifiable. However, our model suggests that bigness is not, per se, evidence of such conditions. Furthermore, our model suggests the need for examining internal factors as well as marketplace conditions. For instance, what is an appropriate level of industry concentration depends on the nature of the core technology. Network technologies, such as telecommunications, require more concentration than other technologies. And even though tacit price collusion is easier when an industry includes only a few competitors, our historical evidence indicates that sometimes it happens and sometimes it does not. If a smaller number of competitors results from defensively oriented mergers, collusion is more likely than if the market structure is achieved by internal growth of the stronger firms. By the same token, the question of whether to challenge a proposed merger on antitrust grounds could be translated into the question of whether it is being undertaken for defensive or readaptive reasons. Although facts will still be difficult to ascertain, the target would be much clearer.

Governmental action aimed at increasing competition through deregulation is a policy tool that is being used increasingly. To date, the action has occurred almost entirely in industries with network technologies which are often found in Area 8: airlines, trucking, railroading, banking, and telecommunications. We saw the process of deregulation at work in the changing stance of the Federal Communications Commission toward the Bell System. The enormously improved technological capacity for moving and processing data is one of the principal developments making deregulation feasible. Although careful trial and error efforts are necessary if the deregulation of an industry is to proceed with minimal negative side effects, the tool has great potential for improving both efficiency and innovation.

Government agencies that have a monopoly in providing services to the public are likely to be in Area 7. A limited amount of thought and action is under way aimed at shifting them toward the competitive conditions of Area 5. Such a shift is being tried with the postal service and some municipal sanitation systems; it is being discussed with regard to primary and secondary schools; one can think of trying it with license bureaus, road maintenance, occupational safety enforcement, and many other public services. In some instances the government might

shift from being a monopoly supplier of services to playing a more limited role as the public's purchasing agent. While such a shift is not always possible, some services might well become more efficient and innovative in a more competitive environment.

One of the difficult public policy questions highlighted by our research is what should be done (if anything) with a mature industry in
Area 4 where affluence induces complacency rather than readaptive
behavior? Can the government, in representing the public interest, sit
on the sidelines for several decades while an industry that is vital to the
entire economy slides off the competitive edge? The most conspicuous
example in our study was steel, followed to a lesser extent by autos.
Even though it may be argued that government policies contributed to
the decline, our review indicates that for a significant period the internal practices of key steel and auto firms were clearly not readaptive.
Many groups besides stockholders are now paying the price for this behavior.

What position the government can and should take in such matters
needs to be widely explored and discussed. The answer is by no means
obvious. Some people have gone so far as to suggest state takeover of
the companies in question. Our model indicates this would be no remedy. Such action would move the industry into Area 7 with predictably
unfortunate consequences. In a more practical vein, the government
could require, for example, that under Area 4 conditions a majority of
a firm's board of directors be nonmanagement outsiders, with one director an official of the federal government. Another approach would
be to assemble a highly trained staff, say in the Commerce Department, organized along industry lines, as is done in Japan, to review and
report continually on the readaptive state of the industry. Such reports
would deal with internal conditions as well as market conditions, and
would be made widely available as a constructive pressure on the industry leaders. Such reports might even induce the voluntary split-up
of a mature Area 4 firm. Of course, government always has the final
resort of forcing a split in spite of the high cost and time-consuming
nature of antitrust proceedings.

An additional question is that of defining government's proper role
in fostering the early development of promising new industries that
usually get started in Area 4. This is by no means a new question. Our
patent laws have long acted to encourage new industries. As we saw,
government was intimately involved in the start-up of the telegraph industry in the beginning of the last century. America has a uniquely
strong record over many decades in providing new industries a favorable setting for a fast, strong start. We believe that the most important
reasons for this, however, have little to do with government actions.

Our critical strengths are simply our great national diversity, our entrepreneurial tradition, our large internal markets, and the availability of physical resources and venture capital. Several of the industries we studied thrived in their early years because of these general conditions. The government has provided supplementary support by sponsoring research or giving tax breaks for small firms. Such support has seldom, if ever, been crucial. Our findings about developing new industries suggest that government, by and large, should keep hands off. Rapid growth and innovation still seem to be occurring without direct government involvement and, except in special circumstances, involvement might impede such development. Such a posture by government should be subject to change, however, if, for instance, the kind of support the Japanese government provides their new industries gives them a significant advantage.

Government action is often needed to move firms in the resource-constricted conditions of Area 6 to Area 5. What can be done for firms like some of the steel and auto companies that are without sufficient resources to invest in their own future? Although the primary initiative must come from management in the firms involved, government needs to face up to the fact that in these instances a reasonable amount of resources will be necessary to get the readaptive process started and to keep it going. A solid case can be made for supporting Area 6 firms if they meet strict conditions at the outset. We suggest two possibilities. The first one might be that resource support—whether loan guarantees, import relief, or whatever—be given for an explicitly limited time, so that no long-term dependency can take root. The second might be that support be strictly conditional on a commitment to a detailed, realistic plan of what the firm intends to do to become readaptive. Some level of support would seem sensible in the interest of achieving readaptation, even in those industries, such as steel, where there will probably be a lasting reduction in the U.S. share of the world market.

Perhaps the best hope lies in devising means by which governmental action can help prevent an industry from being in Area 6 in the first place. An instance where this kind of action might be useful involves firms still in Area 5 that are moving toward industrial maturity after an early period of rapid and prosperous growth. This is a critical stage in their development. Can they stay readaptive given their larger size and changing environmental pressures? Senior managers in such firms frequently feel pressured by capital markets to focus entirely on short-term financial results. The enhanced capacity to generate, transmit, and process data rapidly has given the financial community instant access to current operating information about companies with publicly traded stock. Analysts use this instant information to influence not only individual investors but, more importantly, the portfolio managers of the huge investment pools in pension funds, mutual funds, insurance companies, and so on. The rewards and punishments associated with these portfolio managers' jobs tend to make them particularly responsive to short-term stock price fluctuations. After all, their immediate superiors can easily track the value of their portfolios on a daily basis. The net effect of this causal chain is that senior people in many firms in Area 5 feel pressured to get positive and consistent figures every quarter, even at the expense of the longer-term success of the firm. Top managers feel vulnerable to negative reports on their firms which can suddenly depress stock prices, limit their ability to attract capital, and encourage takeovers. These pressures can eventually move such firms into Area 6 and away from readaptation. This is a fairly recent development and still a difficult one to assess, but the hazard seems great. Government action of some kind may be the only effective remedy. Carefully constructed tax policy designed to discourage the rapid turnover of stock is an example of the kind of preventive measure government might consider. There also are lessons that could be learned from a careful study of the Japanese capital market system.

For firms in or near Area 6, other, more everyday forms of government action are also needed. It is unfortunate that the wolf must be at the door before representatives of firms in an industry sit down with each other and government representatives to explore joint solutions to common problems. All firms in an industry face common problems in complying with the myriad regulations government has applied to serve the public interest. It is to everyone's advantage that compliance be achieved at the least possible cost. Firms and government could hold continuing discussions at several levels, to explore the definition of reasonable standards and the most efficient compliance and monitoring methods. The meetings could serve several functions, including the application of joint pressure on noncompliers to ensure that delaying action does not yield a competitive advantage, the joint support of experimental approaches, and the joint drafting of workable compliance details. Union leaders could at times join such discussions with the agenda moving on to issues like employment levels and workforce mobility. Such discussions have been inhibited by the antitrust rules, and, even more, by suspicion and antagonism on all sides. These inhibitions can and should be overcome.

In this regard we can learn from the Japanese practice of joint consultations. We can also develop social skills for handling cooperative as well as adversarial relationships between the same people. Although a crisis may sometimes be the spur to acquiring these skills and appreciating their rewards, we ought to be aware that they are also effective for the ongoing improvement of non-crisis conditions.

Government policy in relation to business is often inconsistent — a series of knee-jerk reactions to threatening crisis. Present policy tools range, therefore, from indirect, arms-length techniques, such as tax rules on depreciation affecting marginal investments, to more drastic measures like increased antitrust activity, emergency credit, and radical new legislation. Middle-range tools and techniques, such as federal charters, industry studies, and tripartite industrial panels, are seriously lacking in the repertoire of government policy, however. The development of these middle-range tools is seriously inhibited, when government officials, primarily using the concepts of economics, see organizations as super-rational, profit-optimizing machines. Were there a more sensitive appreciation of the variations that exist within organizations and of the impact these variations have on innovation and efficiency, the constructive influence government could have on business in the United States would be greatly enhanced.

The health of our major economic organizations is a matter of legitimate public interest. Government officials find it next to impossible to let key firms die. Such crises might be avoided if government officials were to study the problems industry by industry in order to decide, in terms of individual industry need, on appropriate, coordinated policy. Such informed action could prove a significant help to those many managers who want their firms to be readaptive.

Figure 10.6, in giving a summary of possible government actions of the sorts we have been discussing, points up that although there is no one best way for government to influence industry, there are clearly many possibilities for its making a significant — and positive — difference on the American industrial scene.

## CONCLUSION

One of the questions that sparked this inquiry into the pattern of behavior in American organizational life was why the United States, with its tremendous ability to start new industries, has had such an uneven record in keeping them healthy. The reasons are many and complex, of course, but as we surveyed our research findings, the frequency with which maturing firms have drifted into seemingly immutable adversarial relationships with both their work forces and the government was striking. Moreover, the cost in terms of lost productivity has been high. The antagonism between management and labor has had a long history. With the industrial revolution making inevitable the development of large firms, distance between manager and managed increased. Blue-collar, even white-collar, workers began to be treated not as members of an entrepreneurial partnership but simply as an economic factor of production, labor. As unions then grew and ex-

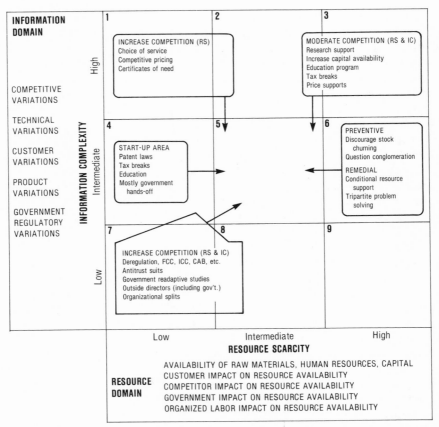

**Figure 10.6    Summary of Government Implications for Action**

panded in response to the frustrations of the work force, the antagonisms became institutionalized. Government gave a further, if unintentional, assist to the adversarial stance by forcing a sharp distinction between employees who are "exempt" and those who are "non-exempt." Finally, the gap has been increased as the potentially sound practice of recruiting college graduates with managerial potential developed into the system of dual entry points, dual career paths, and dual personnel practices.

Over the years serious, mutual antagonisms have also built up between business and government. At the end of the nineteenth century and into the twentieth, business excesses alternated with extremes in government reform. The formation of huge trusts led to a passion for trust-busting. Detailed government planning was the New Deal's answer to the unrestrained competition of the 1920s. Finally, in stereotype: government officials came to see managers as fast-buck artists set on ripping off the public, and businessmen to see government officials as closet socialists. Eventually this conflict, too, became institutionalized, particularly with the development of powerful lobbies by vested interests. When maturity leads to such relationships, is it surprising that the productive potential of American industry is in jeopardy?

As we have seen in the historical accounts in this book, however, industrial maturity clearly has not inevitably led to destructive antagonism and resulting low productivity. In agriculture and in housing, the split between management and labor has not been so wide, and sometimes something of a partnership has even evolved with government. Therefore, with history's lesson that it is not an immutable law that industrial maturity lead inevitably to antagonism and some degree or other of stagnation, there is every reason to believe that both the successes and failures in industrial development have something to teach us.

The pivotal lesson is certainly that all parties involved in renewing American industry, whether aware of it or not, have a fundamental stake, a shared goal. In our terms, the readaptive firm, where innovation and efficiency co-exist, is the healthy firm, the generator of continuing, real industrial wealth. Since history shows that innovation and efficiency are too often viewed as tradeoffs, all participants are challenged to seek solutions and courses of action that link the two goals rather than choose one over the other. History also reveals that readaptive organizations can be made simultaneously effective as social, learning, and production systems, all reflecting important American goals. As a learning system, an organization can pick up where formal schooling ends to help make education an on-going experience. As a social system, an organization can contribute significantly to people's needs for recognition and a sense of community. As a production system, an organization can meet every worker's need to demonstrate his or her competence and effectiveness.

Once management has opted for the path of readaptation, it needs carefully to define the organization's goals in terms of the continuing generation of real wealth. Along with this, management needs to make commitments to a strategy geared to achieving both efficiency and innovation and to a policy encouraging involvement of all members of the organization. Much more than a superficial, cosmetic endorsement of participation is needed if, in return, there is to be an equally genuine commitment by employees and union representatives. Having chosen the goal of readaptation, management needs, finally, to acknowledge government's legitimate concern with the conduct of businesses of any size and significance.

The skeptic can argue that moving American industry toward readaptation is an impossible dream, the odds against it overwhelming. From outside, foreign competition repeatedly demonstrates its superiority and, from the inside, many established forces inhibit change. Too many American firms, under pressure from capital markets, have for too long been going for short-term profits. Too many managers, at all levels, have been playing this short-term game, hoping to move up the ladder before all the results are in. Too many unions have been negligent in considering long-term benefits for their constituencies. Too many government officials have grown accustomed to using their power arbitrarily. Institutional policy, habits of thought, personal career stakes, and leadership commitment all reinforce and lock in these attitudes and practices. But in spite of these hazards, undertaking a course of readaptation is still a realistic and possible step for those who would work to renew and revitalize American industry. Nothing in the process makes individual effort inappropriate or fruitless. To the contrary: the theory of readaptation is built on the premise that independent effort, per se, carries no stigma or disadvantage. Regardless of the positions others are committed to, any firm, any union, any government agency — or any of their self-contained parts — can begin the process of renewal.

# Appendix

*THIS APPENDIX provides a more completely documented statement of our theory and indicates its relation to the existing literature on organizations.*

## TOWARD A THEORY OF ORGANIZATIONAL ADAPTATION AND READAPTATION

We believe our theory makes several contributions to current thinking about organizations. First, we attempt to synthesize two major interrelated controversies in organization theory: (1) the question of whether organizations are driven by environmental forces or by organizational choice; (2) the question of whether organizational forms depend primarily on resource availability or on information uncertainty. In making this attempt, we hope to enrich and extend contingency theory, by using dynamic as well as comparative analysis, and by adding normative, "one best way," implications. In particular, we have employed a single framework to explain a wide variety of organizational forms and to map their evolution. In addition, we hope that our effort will suggest a possible bridge between organization theory and industrial organization economics.

## CURRENT STATUS OF
## ORGANIZATION THEORY

In his recent book, *Organizations and Environments*, Aldrich* comments on the two major theoretical controversies in summarizing the
current state of organizational theory. His comments deserve to be
quoted at length:

> The significance of environmental selection and its effect on organiza-
> tional change are obscured by confusion and disagreement in the way the
> term environment is used. Two methods of dealing with this problem may
> be discerned in current theorizing and research on relations between or-
> ganizations and their environments. One approach relies heavily on theo-
> ries of perception, cognition, and decision-making, focusing on environ-
> ments as seen through the eyes of organizational members. The
> "environment" thus consists of information serving as raw material and
> acted on by sentient actors. Variation in information about the environ-
> ment, as filtered through members' perceptions, is the major factor ex-
> plaining organizational change. A special concern of investigators adopt-
> ing this perspective is the impact of uncertainty on the ability of
> organizational participants to make decisions, and on consequent organi-
> zational restructuring to cope with uncertainty.
>
> A second approach treats environments as consisting of resources for
> which organizations compete, with the level of resources and the terms
> under which they are made available the critical factors in organizational
> change. . . . The process through which information about environments
> is apprehended by decision makers is not given much attention. Pure en-
> vironmental selection arguments, such as the theory of the firm in micro-
> economics, assume resources are in the hands of a large number of actors
> whose individual decisions amount to a collective selection pressure
> against organizational inefficiency. Firms must sell to customers at a com-
> petitive price or go under. Modified environmental selection models take
> into account the concentration of resources in the hands of a few actors
> and analyze organizational attempts to avoid dependence on or achieve
> dominance over other organizations. . . .
>
> The two views are predicated on different assumptions about the au-
> tonomy of actors, on concern with different stages of the process of orga-
> nizational change, and ultimately on differences regarding the appropri-
> ate level of analysis in studying organizations (individuals or aggregates).
> Theorists leaning toward the rational selection model tend to view envi-
> ronments in terms of resources, but there is a continuum of positions be-
> tween the extremes on each of these two dichotomies. I have not forced
> the two distinctions—rational versus natural selection and information
> versus resource view—into one dichotomy, thus permitting the inchoate

*In this Appendix we will provide citations within the text and a bibliography at the
end.

nature of these competing conceptualizations to remain visible throughout. [pp. 110–111]

As Aldrich suggests, the long-standing opposition between information and resource perspectives is reflected in the several disciplines concerned with organization theory. Psychologists and social psychologists have written largely from the information perspective and have addressed issues such as conflict resolution (Sherif), leadership (Fiedler), environmental enactment (Weick), decision making (March and Olsen) and organizational learning (Argyris and Schön). The work of Burns and Stalker probably best exemplifies the thinking of sociologists favoring the information view. On the other hand, recent work in economics, especially in industrial organization economics (Caves), has been written mostly from the resource perspective. More recent sociological studies, including writings of Pfeffer and Salancik, Perrow, and Hannan and Freeman have taken the resource track.

As Aldrich indicates, the resource/information dichotomy is closely related to a persistent controversy in organization studies between researchers who argue that organizational behavior is determined by the environment and those who believe that organizations have choices and make decisions. This conflict is often more implicit than explicit in the literature. The most obvious split is again between economists and sociologists, who tend to take a deterministic approach to organizations, and psychologists and social psychologists, who see organizations in terms of critical choices. The former take organizations (and aggregates of organizations such as industries) as the prime unit of analysis, while the latter focus on individuals and groups.

Three earlier efforts to resolve these divisions are particularly relevant here. The first was March and Simon's development of the concept of "satisficing." They described satisficing (as opposed to optimizing) as the way decision makers in organizations actually process information given the limits of human cognitive capacity ("bounded rationality"). This represented a general solution to the problem, but it dealt only with cognitive resource constraints and failed to account adequately for the full variety of organizational forms.

Thompson went a step farther toward a useful synthesis. His key contribution lies in his well-known phrase, "norms of rationality." In effect, he argued that people in organizations operate under the shared ground rule that they should strive to be rational about resource allocations and other key decisions. Thompson showed how, given this norm, various organizational forms develop under various environmental circumstances. Thus he was able to explore and account for a wider variety of organizational experience. However, he ignored the linkage between the information and resource domains.

A third attempt appeared at about the same time as Thompson's. Lawrence and Lorsch proposed that two complementary organizational conditions, differentiation and integration, take different forms, depending on the degree and sources of environmental uncertainty. By *differentiation* they meant the variation between organizational units in individuals' cognitive and emotional orientations while *integration* referred to the quality of collaboration between organizational units. Lawrence and Lorsch recognized that environmental uncertainty promotes organizational differentiation, but failed to make clear what promotes integration. Was it a shared human tendency toward dissonance reduction (Festinger) or a shared norm of rationality (Thompson)? Or was it resource scarcity? The Lawrence and Lorsch model was better able to capture the impact of information uncertainty on organizational form than the effect of resource contingencies.

As Aldrich indicates, the theoretical split in organization studies has widened in recent years. Nonetheless, much valuable work has been done on both sides of the problem. Weick, March and Olsen, Miles and Snow, Ouchi, Mintzberg, Kotter, Williamson, and Child, for example, have worked on the information side; Pfeffer and Salancik, Hannan and Freeman, Campbell, and Caves, among others, have worked on the resource side. Any new attempt at a synthesis must take these contributions into account.

The concept that we believe links the information and the resource approaches is, of course, adaptation. While many writers — including most of those mentioned above — have considered organizational adaptation, none has made it central to their models. We shall argue that the key to synthesizing the information and resource perspectives is the inverted-U-curve relation between information complexity and innovation on one hand, and between resource scarcity and efficiency on the other. These two processes jointly affect the third, member involvement, and all three are central to our definition of adaptation and its form that is of particular normative interest, readaptation. Before directly moving to these ideas, however, we need first to spell out briefly a few premises as starting points for our analysis.

We believe we share with most of the authors we draw upon the definition of organizations, stated early and eloquently by Chester Barnard, as purposeful systems of coordinated action. As instruments of human purpose, organizations provide a means of establishing a relation between cause and effect, and between inputs and outputs. In a sense, rationality is their goal but its achievement is constrained by finite cognitive capacities; the limits of technical and other knowledge; the diversity of individual contributors' objectives; and physical resource constraints.

Also, following W. Ross Ashby, we see organizations both as systems of internal relations and as parts of a larger system encompassing the environment in which they operate. The environment sets conditions that help shape the organization even as the organization shapes and influences its environment. This interaction is seldom automatic. People feel, choose and decide as they work out various accommodations between organizations and their environment; and they make decisions with power, ideology, wealth, fame, and other individual and group considerations at stake. Moreover, many critical choices are made by a dominant coalition of people in an organization. We also see organizations as social institutions constrained by the choices and commitments of their past even as they continue to evolve. We believe that our statement of initial premises would be generally accepted by members of all the schools of thought we draw upon. In sum, we view organizations as learning, production, and social systems that, together with the environment in which they are embedded, function as a single larger system.

## DEFINING ORGANIZATIONAL ADAPTATION AND READAPTATION

We define *organizational adaptation* as the process by which an organization and its environment reach and maintain an equilibrium ensuring the survival of the system as a whole. *Readapation* is a form of organizational adaptation in which the organization and its relevant environment interact and  evolve toward exchanges that are more acceptable to the internal and external stakeholders as evidenced by continuing high levels of innovation, efficiency, and member involvement. Readaptation is distinct from adaptation in much the same way that research is distinct from search; it is a continuous and systematic process.*

Readaptation is a normative concept. We assume that innovation, efficiency, and member involvement are socially desirable, since in the long run each is necessary to the well-being of institutions and their members and, we believe, society at large. What makes readaptation problematic is that these three outcomes are very difficult to reconcile in the short run. Not surprisingly, therefore, one often finds adapta-

---

*What we mean by readaptation is similar to Selznick's concept of "dynamic adaptation" (as opposed to "static adaptation"), although he used these terms in a more psychological context.

tions that do not achieve these readaptative results. We shall consider such forms of adaptation at greater length below.

Our central concept of readaptation has been shaped by ideas from several disciplines: organizational behavior, business policy, evolutionary biology, economics, and psychology. For instance, "organizational learning," as developed by Duncan and Weiss, Jelinek, and Argyris and Schön, resembles our "readaptation." Duncan and Weiss defined learning as "the process within the organization by which knowledge about action-outcome relationships and the effect of the environment on these relationships is developed." Organizational learning differs from individual learning in that it arises in the course of social interaction and what is learned must to some degree be communicable, consensual, and integrated with other organizational knowledge. As Duncan and Weiss point out, however, organizational learning alone does not necessarily lead to innovation and adaptation. Organizational learning as they define it is thus only a part of readaptation.

A *strategy* links an organization's internal arrangements and its treatment of its environment. Andrews's definition of "corporate strategy" deserves a careful reading in this light. A corporate strategy, he says, is

> the pattern of decisions in a company that determines and reveals its objectives, purposes, or goals, produces the principal policies and plans for achieving those goals, and defines the range of business the company is to pursue, the kind of economic and human organization it is or intends to be and the nature of the economic and noneconomic contribution it intends to make to its shareholders, employees, customers, and communities. [p. 18]

Two phrases are particularly striking. "The range of business the company is to pursue" implies that in elaborating a corporate strategy a business selects the field in which it will seek its goals as well as the goals it will pursue. Andrews also notes that a corporate strategy "defines . . . the kind of economic and human organization it is or intends to be." In other words, a company gives itself an internal structure and a way of doing business appropriate to its goals and to the field in which it pursues them. Andrews's concept of corporate strategy is thus rather broad — certainly far broader than the "strategy" of everyday usage. It includes *all* the elements in the box diagrammed in Figure A.1.* We find this breadth appealing, since it defines a body of ideas that is at once a social product subject to change in the sense of

---

*It is roughly synonymous with several other phrases that have gained currency in the literature: Pfeffer's "organizational paradigm" and Lane, Beddows, and Lawrence's "institutional logics."

**Figure A.1    General Relationship of Organization Strategy, Relevant Environment and Organization Resources**

organizational learning, and a link (as Rosenbloom envisaged) between organizational realities and the environment. Organizational strategy is, so to speak, the internal regulator or governor of adaptation even as the relevant government policies are the external regulator of adaptation.

As biologists use the term, adaptation denotes an organism's accommodation to its environment. In our man-made world, however, organization and environment adapt to each other. This is especially true of large organizations. Furthermore, both the organization and its environment contain sentient actors who attach values to the outcomes of adaptational transactions (i.e., they judge the outputs of the organization in relation to its resource inputs). Dissatisfied customers respond, as Hirschman says, by exit (stop buying) or by voice (protest). The government or the public respond by conferring or withholding legitimacy. The primary internal stakeholders, owners and employees, measure the rewards they receive for their contributions in order to decide whether they will continue to contribute or will withdraw (March and Simon).

We shall call the outcome of these deliberations the *acceptability of exchanges*. It is an important concept in several ways. First, it describes a pattern of choices made by individuals, and thus helps us to avoid reifying either organizations or environments. Second, it provides a mechanism for describing change, since it takes into account the constant evaluations and reevaluations that supply motives for seeking "better" adaptive states. The primary motives — organizational "human nature," if you will — we see as desires to avoid resource deprivation and dependence; cognitive dissonance (Festinger) and irrationality (White); and a desire to seek a sense of competence (White, Lorsch and Morse). We shall elaborate on these motives later in discussing human resource issues. Over time these motives generally lead successful organizations to reduce both resource and information uncertainty, even as their relevant environments tend to generate new kinds of uncertainties.

To round out our discussion of the definition of readaptation we need to consider the *relevant environment*. As we define it, the relevant environment is much less than the total universe of all things external to the boundaries of the organization. Each organization has its own unique relevant environment defined by its strategy (which includes, as we indicated, the choice of domain in which it will do business). This selected environment for our purposes will include only those external elements with high importance to the organization: for example, relevant customers, suppliers, competitors, unions, technology generators, and government agencies.*

To sum up, then, *adaptation* is a process of accommodation between an organization and its relevant environment. An *organization* is a purposeful system of coordinated action. *Organizational strategy* is an organization's definition of its goals, the *relevant environment* in which it will pursue them, and its internal arrangements toward this end. *Acceptability of exchanges* is the calculation by those concerned with an organization's fate, the *stakeholders*, of their own commitment to the organization.

*Readaptation* is a special form of adaptation: the process by which an organization and its environment continue to evolve more mutually acceptable states. Readaptation is marked by the repeated discovery of ways to introduce innovations, while maintaining or enhancing efficiencies and member involvement.

The three outcomes that we take to be the indicators of readaptation require a brief comment.

*Efficiency* is the most straightforward. We follow economists in understanding efficiency to be the ratio of inputs to outputs. We assume, of course, that organizations must be effective in linking outputs to social utility. Thus the concept of efficiency encompasses product features of quality and delivery as well as price, and unintended as well as intended outputs.

*Innovations* are new ideas and more. We use the term as a kind of shorthand for "organizational innovations." Innovations are naturally closely related to the many sorts of information an organization has at its disposal. This information may stimulate new ideas, but novelty alone is not truly innovative in our sense. A new idea becomes an inno-

---

*In using the term *relevant environment* we are following the earlier Lawrence and Lorsch usage. This concept is similar to Thompson's "selected domain" and is to be distinguished from Weick's "enacted environment," which will be discussed later.

vation only after some set of people with a stake in the organization have found it appropriate to the organization's goals (satisficing), and only after it has been adopted for regular use. An innovation is a new idea that has been institutionalized.* Note that by definition innovations disturb the established order. They particularly threaten an organization's transformation of inputs into outputs — that is, its efficiency. Yet without a sustained willingness to adopt new ideas an organization cannot remain readaptive. Today's efficiency becomes tomorrow's inefficiency. Innovation and efficiency are at odds in the short run, but in the long run both are essential for readaptation.

*Member involvement* describes the extent to which all levels and categories of an organization's employees identify themselves with the organization and share a fate in it. A high degree of member involvement entails a rich and complex exchange between the individual and the organization. For example, if the exchange is simply trading time for money, the involvement is low. If there is an exchange of support, ideas, physical energy, career development, recognition, money, concern, involvement is high.† Note that high member involvement can be at odds with the other two readaptive outcomes. Innovation may threaten members' identification with the established order. Efficiency may become inhuman, and force members to see their work as "just a job." On the other hand, too much emphasis on involvement may promote inefficiency or discourage innovation. Readaptation thus creates a paradox in the social organization of a firm — a set of tensions it must repeatedly confront and resolve, and resolve again.

The next critical question for analysis is: What are the factors of the readaptive process that foster or impede readaptive results? Some companies are more readaptive than others in the same industry for considerable periods of time. An organization may be readaptive in some periods of its history but not in others. Some industries are more readaptive than others. To what extent can we explain these differences by identifying the critical environmental and internal conditions?

We must also add that, while our primary unit of analysis is the single business firm or strategic business units of multidivisional firms, we shall at times use the model to discuss an industry in terms of its characteristic firm, and sometimes even major functional departments of a single firm.

---

*Organizational ecologists refer to this as the retention stage of adaptation (Aldrich).

†Compare Walton's discussion of "high commitment work systems."

## ENVIRONMENTAL INFLUENCES ON
## ORGANIZATIONAL READAPTATION

We shall argue that *environmental* impacts on readaptation can be understood as a function of two different kinds of uncertainty, *resource scarcity* (RS) and *information complexity* (IC).

To survive, organizations must obtain essential resources and favorable resource exchanges; these resources may vary in their scarcity or abundance. We define resource scarcity as a composite measure of the availability to the organization of all of its essential resources. Problems arise, of course, in trying to measure RS in particular circumstances. The concept of RS suggests the need, for instance, to add such relatively incommensurable items as capital scarcity while subtracting for previously accumulated financial and manpower reserves. There is also the problem, to state the extreme case, of measuring RS when 99% of all essential resources are readily available and 1% are unobtainable. Although this list of measurement problems can easily be extended, we believe the RS concept is still useful if it is employed to characterize overall conditions during a significant time period — at least one year. In practical use the concept must be adapted to suit the circumstances of the particular research context using a selected set of indicators, such as historical gross margins and reserves in private organizations and the historical level and reliability of funding in public ones.

We define information complexity as the degree of competitive, product, market, technological, and regulatory variations in a firm's relevant environment. These variations represent the critical information uncertainties that must be analyzed by a firm trying to make rational choices about its environmental transactions. The concept information uncertainty has, of course, a long history in organization theory. It was used extensively in the work of March and Simon, Thompson, and Lawrence and Lorsch, to cite but a few who contributed to our current thinking. The concept has proven to be indispensable, even though it has always been difficult to define and use operationally. The key methodological problem is whether we can treat IC as a unitary dimension of the environment for the sake of parsimony or whether we must treat it as a set of related factors for the sake of accuracy. We believe that making IC an operational concept would require first identifying the important sources of variety and then determining the number of variations generated by each of these sources, while also taking into account the uncertainties associated with the interdependence among these variations, the degree of certitude about causal linkages, and the historical stability of these factors. While this way of proceeding promises more conceptual clarity it will remain difficult to measure IC. The use of multiple, approximate indicators tailored to the circumstances seems unavoidable.

Two lesser issues are raised by these definitions. First, are the two variables expected to be distinct? Our tentative answer is that it is highly useful to keep them conceptually independent but that they are certainly not empirically independent. A sudden increase in IC might well prompt an ill-equipped firm to make some strategic choices that lead directly to an increase in RS. Hypothetical examples of such cross effects are not difficult to generate. A simple example may clarify both the conceptual distinction and the empirical linkage. A customer in a restaurant can usefully distinguish between the IC created by a complex menu and his sense of RS created by the thickness of his wallet, even though the meal he orders is influenced by both.

A second awkward question is how to handle information that specifically concerns resource levels. As a matter of consistency and convenience, we treat the physical and energic transactions as moving across the horizontal axis and all information about these transactions as moving across the vertical axis. It should also be noted that competitors and customers will influence both the IC and the RS of a given organization.

To anticipate our argument somewhat, we can now offer the following hypotheses about the relationship between RS, IC, and readaptive outcomes:

H.1 Innovation has an inverted U-curve relation to information complexity in the organization's domain.

H.2 Efficiency has an inverted U-curve relation to resource scarcity in the organization's domain.

H.3 Member involvement has an inverted U-curve relation to environmental uncertainty generally.

Although they have not yet been thoroughly tested, we believe these hypotheses are plausible and can be supported by analogies drawn from cognitive psychology and, to a lesser extent, clinical psychology and personality theory, social psychology, and organization studies — as well as by the findings of our historical research.

Our hypotheses say that there can be either too much or too little IC to induce innovation, too much or too little RS to induce efficiency, and too much or too little of both to induce member involvement. When IC is very low, there is little external stimulus and variety to stir up the cognitive processes behind organizational learning and innovation. When too much IC surrounds strategic choices, information overload may inhibit innovation. On the resource side, when RS is very low and the living is easy, organizations have little incentive to strive for efficiency. At the other extreme, when a firm experiences very high RS, the firm's resource starvation causes the neglect of machine maintenance, inventories, the hiring of replacements, and so on. Thus efficiency is lost even in existing routine operations. Moreover, RS can be expected to have an important secondary effect on the rate of innovation, since resources are needed to carry on innovation. High RS, therefore, can be expected to depress innovation. Finally, we suggest, organization members get involved and stay involved in striving and learning when this kind of behavior is rewarded by, among other things, a sense of competence that flows from the achievement of efficiency and innovation.

We are now in a position to develop our three hypotheses in more detail. Figure A.2 illustrates our first hypothesis, that the rate of effective innovation (defined as the number of innovative trials in a given period that achieve the desired outcome) can be expected to increase, up to a point, in response to the stimulus of increasing complexity in the organization's information domain. Above a certain value of IC, however, the limits of human cognition and organizational integration become overwhelming and the rate of effective innovation drops. As we have already pointed out, the shape of this curve depends partly upon the amount of RS being experienced. In particular, high re-

**Figure A.2   Relationship Between Information Complexity and Effective Innovation**

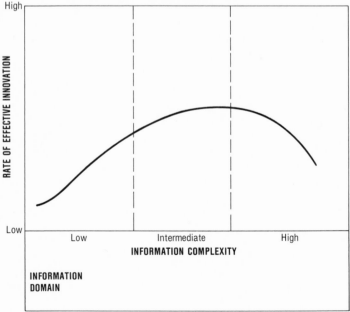

source pressures would attract attention and physical resources away from the innovative process.

Our second hypothesis is diagrammed in Figure A.3. Efficiency with existing methods can be expected to increase with RS until the point at which resource scarcity starves out the efficiency of even routine operations. The number of efficient innovations adopted will also initially increase with RS, because greater resource tension builds motivation for finding and using such innovations. At some point, however, the effect reverses, because with too much RS short-term efficiency becomes the overriding concern precluding innovation.

Our third hypothesis links the first two to member involvement, which we defined as the complexity and richness of the exchange between an individual and the organization. Increases in member striving and learning would both indicate increased involvement. When RS or IC are too high, members tend to look for ways to escape from the organization. When RS or IC are too low, members tend to be apathetic. (See Figure A.4.) At intermediate levels of RS and IC, we shall argue, member involvement is highest, springing from a sense of competence. We should stress, however, that member involvement is conditioned by internal organization features to be discussed later. This is

**Figure A.3    Relationship Between Resource Scarcity and Efficiency**

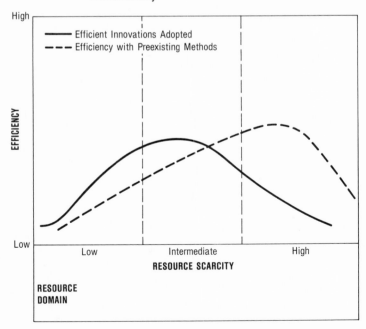

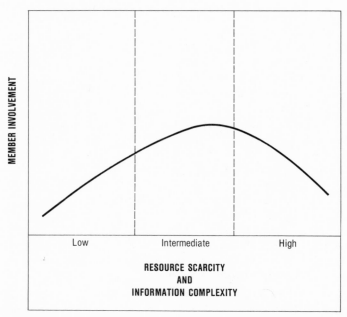

**Figure A.4    Relationship Between Member Involvement and
Resource and Information Uncertainty**

especially true in large organizations where environmental influences
are filtered through multiple organizational structures and practices.

By combining these three processes with our earlier definition of readaptation, we can state operationally that an adaptive organizational
act has taken place if an innovation: (1) has passed not only the preliminary test of effectiveness but also (2) the more rigorous efficiency test
in relation to other practical alternatives; (3) has been put in regular
use in ways that are compatible with existing efficient methods; and (4)
has enhanced rather than diminished the existing member involvement. We argue that IC and RS are the primary *environmental* forces
that foster or impede a continuing flow of adaptive organizational acts
(readaptation) and that they both function as inverted U-shaped
curves. The combined effect of these two influences on readaptation is
shown schematically in Figure A.5, which arrays three states of IC
against three states of RS to create a nine-area matrix. We have, of
course, used this familiar analytical framework repeatedly in illustrat-
ing different aspects of our readaptation theory; each cell of the matrix
represents an environmental niche that individual firms, or possibly all
firms in a given industry, may inhabit. In Figure A.6 we augment our
earlier model of organization strategy by tracking the exchanges between the organization and its environment through the flow of events

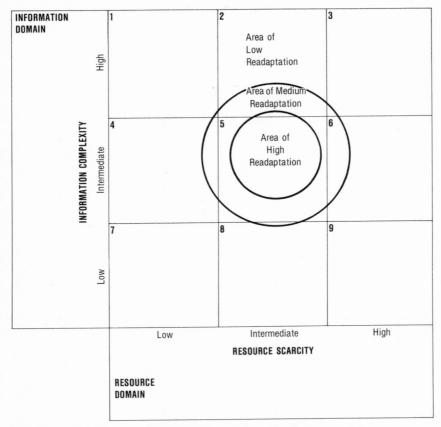

**Figure A.5  General Relationship Between Information Complexity, Resource Scarcity and Organizational Readaptation**

leading up to a discrete adaptive organizational act. The + or − notations indicate the direction of the effect (increase or decrease) of certain associations.

Our three hypotheses should not be interpreted as a statement that certain environmental conditions *cause* organizational readaptation. We would say instead that certain environmental conditions *favor* organizational readaptation; its actual achievement is an interactive process. As we shall argue later, readaptation can occur only when the organization has particular kinds of internal strategy and form.

An extensive literature in psychology lends support, by analogy, to our three hypotheses. Schroder, Driver, and Streufert have most thoroughly documented the existence of a general inverted U-curve relationship between environmental complexity and the creativity and

**Figure A.6  Flow Diagram of Organizational Readaptive Process**

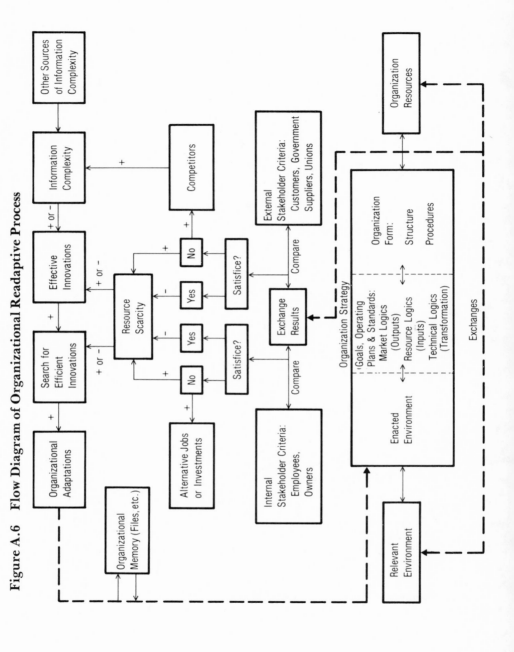

flexibility of human information processing. Their analysis rests primarily upon experimental methods and, as they say, "For any task, we can measure the number, the range, the rate of change, or the uncertainty involved in the units of information reaching the participants" (p. 33). Various laboratory experiments conducted and cited by Schroder et al. show that individuals process information in different ways under different experimental conditions. In summarizing these studies, however, the authors conclude, "In all experiments, the flexibility of integration (in both decisions and attitudes) increased as environmental complexity mounted from very low to optimal, then declined as complexity became stressfully superoptimal."

The Schroder et al. studies treat the costs and/or rewards experienced by individuals as secondary influences on information processing. Again, they hypothesize that "integrative complexity in information-processing structures will relate in a curvilinear fashion to both cost and reward dimensions, whether they act alone or in combination." And again they found substantial experimental support for this position. In particular, they found, "The results seem fairly clear: if there is too much or too little [cost] noxity, information-processing systems close and become simpler; that is, structure regresses from abstract to more concrete properties" (p. 93). We feel that a reasonable analogy can be made between Schroder and his co-authors' primary variable, environmental complexity, and our concept of IC and between their secondary variable, cost-reward, and our concept of RS. Finally, they see the level of information processing as central to the adaptive process. And even though most of their work focuses on individual information processing, they argue on the basis of some group studies that their findings are relevant to group behavior.

The clinical data of psychologists and psychoanalysts also lend support to our hypothesis. This work has best been summarized by Janis and Leventhal,* who are primarily interested in the influence of stress conditions on different types of cognitive efficiency. After reviewing the evidence from a wide variety of clinical studies they conclude that "an inverted U-shape function would be expected whenever the efficiency of any intellectual or motor performance is inspected in relation to the intensity of any type of emotional arousal" (p. 1051).

Finally, a social psychologist, Daniel J. Isenberg, has conducted a relevant study of group behavior. He found an inverted U-curve relationship between increasing time pressure (a scarce resource) and an

---

*As an indication that the studies of Schroder et al. and Janis and Leventhal represent relatively independent lines of research, it is notable that of the 341 references used in the two reports, only 3 are cited by both.

experimental group's performance of a task. Moderate time pressure resulted in higher performances than either high or low pressure.

To summarize, inverted U-curve relations have been found when the independent variable is noxity, stress, or time pressure (our analogy to RS) and the dependent variable is the efficiency or accuracy of cognitive and motor processes (our analogy to organizational efficiency). Similar relationships are observed when the independent variable is environmental complexity (our analogy to IC) and the dependent variable is the flexibility and creativity of cognitive processes (our analogy to innovation). We shall now turn to the psychological and organizational literature that supports our third hypothesis.

We believe that the positive psychological link between RS and IC and member involvement is forged by the competence, or "effectance," motive. This kind of motivation was originally identified by R. W. White, who drew on some of Freud's ideas. Karl Weick then applied White's ideas specifically to the workplace and argued that involved satisfaction with work depends on the extent to which an actor feels competent to remove equivocality (reduce uncertainty). Byrne and Clore described this "effectance" motive in the following way:

> Any situation which provides evidence of one's predictive accuracy, ability to understand, correctness, logicality, reality orientation, behavioral appropriateness — any information which permits or indicates effective functioning — would satisfy the effectance motive. [p. 4]

Lorsch and Morse have conducted the most extensive study of the effectance, or competence, motive of employees in organizations. They find that, when there is a match between the uncertainty of the task, the organization form, and the predisposed capacity of employees to handle uncertainty: (1) employees experience a sense of competence; (2) they find this rewarding; and (3) these events are associated with high performance. Lorsch and Morse observed this pattern both in high-performing industrial R&D laboratories and in routinized production operations. They also found that the pattern did not hold when there was a mismatch between the task characteristics and organizational form.

We believe that these findings provide a strong logical and empirical link between our model, motivation theory, and member involvement. We have argued that continuing organizational innovation and efficiency are most likely to occur under conditions of intermediate IC and RS. We now add that under these same conditions employees are most likely to experience a sense of competence at work, and as a result, a high level of involvement. In effect, the conditions necessary for achieving continuing organizational innovation and efficiency are the same conditions that are most likely to provide employees the greatest opportunity for feeling competent—a rewarding experience that leads to high involvement. It cannot, of course, be taken for granted that every employee at all levels from top to bottom in a large organization will have an opportunity to experience job competence even if the organization as a whole is readaptive. (Most current efforts to enlarge or enrich work assignments can be seen as efforts to spread a realistic sense of RS and IC throughout the organization so that all members can be challenged to contribute to the readaptive process and be rewarded by a sense of personal competence.) As shown in Figure A.7, competence and involvement are more likely to occur when RS is at low to intermediate levels, IC at an intermediate level.

As the next step toward refining our model, we turn to the field of evolutionary biology for ideas that help us explore the dynamics of adaptation.

**Figure A.7   Hypothesized Outputs in Terms of Member Involvement and Motivation**

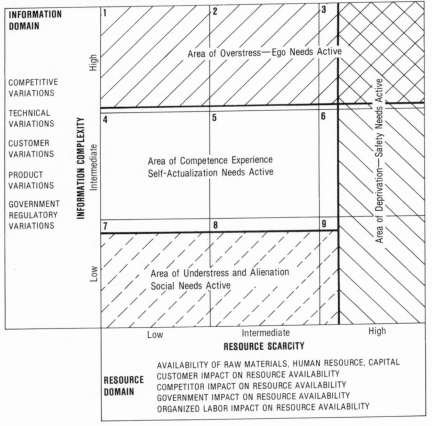

## DYNAMICS OF
## ORGANIZATIONAL ADAPTATION

In drawing upon evolutionary or population biology we are encouraged by the examples of Dunn, Campbell, Aldrich, Emery and Trist, McKelvey, and Hannan and Freeman who have demonstrated both the promise and the limitations of applying biological concepts to organization study. Key concepts used by population ecologists are environmental niches, species density, gene pool, resource limits, and the trait selection process. Current biological theorists such as Grime have derived a two-factor model of basic forces that guide the trait selection process toward a trio of "strategic" types.*

Grime's model draws on and extends the more widely accepted idea that plant evolution can be explained by two basic environmental forces or constraints: the interspecies competition stressed by Darwin and the amount of necessary resources in the environmental niche. Grime's model sets up a three-stage dynamic interplay between an environmental niche and a given set of species. If a set of plant species (gene pool) freshly encounters an uninhabited niche with ample resources, rapid growth of the total biomass could be expected. Eventually this biomass becomes dominated by species that develop features providing for fast and abundant reproduction ($r$, or ruderal strategy). This is the first stage. As the biomass approaches $K$, the size limit imposed by the amount of essential resources in the niche, the species with $r$ strategic features begin to give way to a second group of species of a different strategic type. These plants can be expected to have features that help them gain the scarcer resources from other plants. This interspecies competitive advantage may take such forms as height (to gain sunlight from other plants) or deeper roots (to obtain more water). Plants that develop combinations of such features are said to have $C$, or competitive strategies; they dominate the second stage.

Grime goes on to discuss a third strategic type of plant species, which develop features (such as moisture-retention devices) that aid survival in niches that are very limited in essential resources. These $S$ (stress toleration) strategic types appear in niches such as deserts or arctic areas. If the resource supply in a given physical niche moves from abundance to scarcity, Grime's theory predicts the successive dominance of $r$, $C$, and $S$ strategic types. The $S$ types do not out-compete the $C$ types but simply fill in the ranks as environmental scarcity wipes out the $C$s.

---

*It is interesting that biologists like Grime make frequent use of the language of business in describing biological phenomena. Clearly, the borrowing is not all one way.

By taking a number of theoretical liberties we can translate these ideas into organizational terms and add dynamics to our model of re-adaptation. To start this process, imagine a product market (ecological niche) where, because of some new technical or market development (a new strategic option), a producer faces a virtually unlimited demand and initially no competitors (low RS). This condition would not only foster the rapid growth of the initial entrant but would also soon at-tract a number of additional organizational start-ups and lateral en-trants (an increase in IC). The firms that dominate in this initial stage can be expected to be the ones with traits that foster the fastest growth in this lush environment ($r$ traits). Now imagine that resources gradu-ally become tight as this new market fills up. Under these new condi-tions biological theory suggests that the changed niche will start to se-lect for $C$, or competitive, traits. Concurrently, the number of different competitors in the niche will probably decline as some $r$ types are forced out of business (selected out). Finally, imagine that resource constraints in this product market become very severe. Biological the-ory suggests that this third set of conditions would select for stress-toler-ation traits; $S$ types would fill in the holes created by $C$ types failing to meet their resource needs.

In biological terms this entire process is constrained and influenced not only by the amount of resources in the niche but also by the variety in the gene pool of all the species in the niche. We would draw an anal-ogy between gene pool variety and the relevant environmental varia-tions (IC) that can stimulate an organization to be readaptive.* During each of the three stages of the resource reduction process sketched above, one would expect uncertainty in the information to increase and then, at some point of resource scarcity (RS), begin to decrease. Unlike plants, some organizations of each "type" will be able to learn and readapt — transform themselves from $r$ to $C$ to $S$ as needed to avoid being selected out.

The biological selection process with its two basic driving forces, provides an illuminating analogy to the mutual adaptation process be-tween organizations and their relevant environments. We must be wary, however, of pushing the analogy too far. Organizations can learn and change their strategies and forms. Plants cannot. To avoid the pit-falls of radical environmental determinism and enrich our thinking about adaptational dynamics in organizational terms, we shall next consider some of the relevant concepts developed by industrial organi-zation economists and by theorists who have focused on the life cycles of organizations.

---

*The number of variations is referred to by McKelvey as the "tech-pool."

## ADAPTATION AS A BRIDGE BETWEEN
## ORGANIZATION THEORY AND ECONOMICS

Industrial organization economists analyze the strategic dynamics of a set of firms forming an industrial cluster — often with special reference to the choices facing a particular organization in this set. These economists are concerned with barriers and opportunities for new entries into the set, market share and degrees of industry concentration, product life cycles, resource (cash) flows, the effects of new technology, and strategic moves such as capacity expansion, vertical and horizontal integration, and diversification (Caves, Porter). They categorize industries in terms of their competitive structure: perfect competition, oligopoly, and monopoly.

A growing body of work within organizational behavior reflects a complementary interest in organization life cycles. These theoretical and research efforts are most fully discussed in the recent volume edited by Kimberly and Miles. Interest centers on what goes on inside organizations at various stages of their development. This involves looking at such issues as organization start-up patterns, early transitions, growth, adversity and crisis management, maturity, decline, and demise. These studies show promise of enriching our understanding of internal organizational dynamics while paralleling the work of the industrial economists.

Our model of industrial adaptation bridges the perspectives of industrial economics and organization theory. Industrial economists study the structure of a given industry as it varies from monopoly to perfect competition. This variation maps onto our framework most dramatically along the NE-SW axis, as shown in Figure A.8. Organization theorists, on the other hand, tend to be more interested in the varieties of internal organizational forms. Burns and Stalker probably capture this variation best by the broad distinction between organic and mechanistic forms. These forms, as we shall discuss later, vary most dramatically along the NW-SE axis of our model.

Many of the concepts and concerns of industrial economists and life cycle theorists can be mapped on our Analytical Framework. Figure A.9, for example, shows two possible development trajectories that represent the characteristic firm of a newly developing industrial cluster. The degree of concentration or number of firms in an industry is roughly reflected on the vertical axis (high IC, indicating a fragmented industry with many firms). Ease of entry is indicated by the firm's starting point on the horizontal (RS) axis. Finally, a few features of individual firms forming a mature industrial cluster are represented schematically on Figure A.9 by W, X, Y, and Z, with each firm's size reflecting market share and its horizontal position reflecting its resource

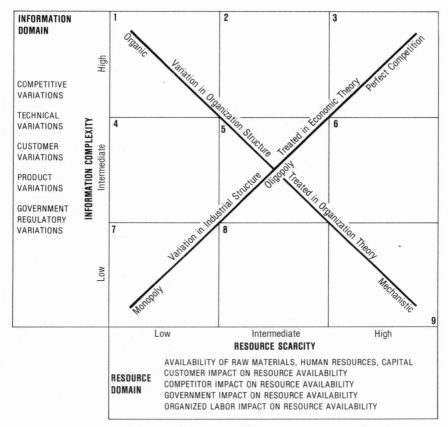

**Figure A.8    Schematic of Relationship Between Organization and Economic Theory**

strength. As indicated, all firms in a given industry cluster would experience roughly the same level of IC. The dispersion of these firms across our environmental field also serves to illustrate that different industries can be expected to vary in how tightly clustered or how scattered the firms in the industry are. These firms will, of course, be engaging in various kinds of competitive moves to influence their relative positions in the cluster and these tactics are of special interest to industrial organization economists (Porter).

Miles and Snow have conducted an important study of organizational adaptation that lends support to our biological analogy and also bridges industrial economics and the organization life cycle approach. This study warrants our special attention because it provides the useful typology for organizational strategies that we have employed in our research.

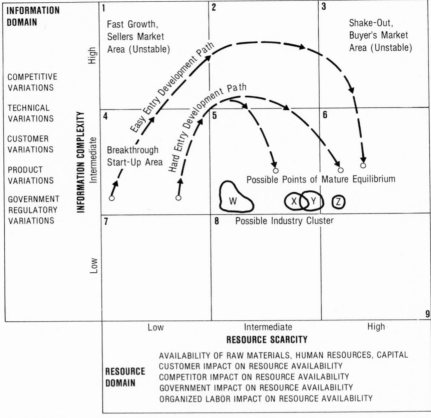

**Figure A.9    Potential Industry Development Paths**

Miles and Snow looked at clusters of firms in four different industries: textbook publishing, food processing, electronics, and voluntary hospitals. They found that firms in these industries typically follow one of four types of strategy as defined briefly below:

1. *Defenders* are organizations which have narrow product and market domains. Top managers in this type of organization are highly expert in their organization's limited area of operation but do not tend to search outside of their domains for new opportunities. As a result of this narrow focus, these organizations seldom need to make major adjustments in their technology, structure, or methods of operation. Instead, they devote primary attention to improving the efficiency of their existing operations.

2. *Prospectors* are organizations which almost continually search for market opportunities, and they regularly experiment with

potential responses to emerging environmental trends. Thus, these organizations often are the creators of change and uncertainty to which their competitors must respond. However, because of their strong concern for product and market innovation, these organizations usually are not completely efficient.

3. *Analyzers* are organizations which operate in two types of product-market domains, one relatively stable, the other changing. In their stable areas, these organizations operate routinely and efficiently through use of formalized structures and processes. In their more turbulent areas, top managers watch their competitors closely for new ideas, and then they rapidly adopt those which appear to be the most promising.

4. *Reactors* are organizations in which top managers frequently perceive change and uncertainty occurring in their organizational environments but are unable to respond effectively. Because this type of organization lacks a consistent strategy-relationship, it seldom makes adjustment of any sort until forced to do so by environmental pressures. [p. 29]

Miles and Snow illustrate the distinctive ways in which firms of each strategy type tend to determine their chosen domains, organizational structures, and procedures. Although they did not study the dynamics of their clusters of firms over time, their first three strategic types bear a strong similarity to the three strategic types described in plant biology by Grime. That is, prospectors are following the $r$ strategy, analyzers the $C$ strategy, and defenders the $S$ strategy. We suggest that prospectors are likely to predominate among firms moving through the early life cycle stage (expressed in Figure A.9 by movement from Area 4 through Area 1); that analyzers will predominate in firms that move through Area 2 and mature in Area 5; and that defenders will predominate in firms that evolve through Area 3 and mature in Area 6. We should also say that, while we would modify Miles and Snow's characterization of the analyzer strategy, this type comes close to the strategies that, in combination with appropriate forms, we found in firms that were readaptive. We shall return to this issue again.

The work of Oliver Williamson and that of William Ouchi provides a further link between organization theory and industrial economics. Williamson, an economist, has focused on simple transactions as the critical concept for understanding both interfirm and intrafirm activities. The most efficient ways of controlling or governing transactions, he argues, will vary according to the kind and amount of uncertainty a firm faces. Uncertainties may be generated by opportunistic behavior, by dependence on future events, and by bounded rationality. Some combinations of these circumstances favor the use of markets to govern transactions, while in other cases organizational heirarchies or bureaucracies are more efficient. Ouchi, an organization theorist, has extended Williamson's argument by explicating a third mechanism, which he calls clans. Clans provide for the governance of transactions by means of values that are shared among an interpersonally linked group of people. Shared values tend to generate faith in the long-term equity of the exchange process. Clans thus obviate the need to consider the equity of every transaction. We shall return later to the concepts of clans, markets, and bureaucracies in discussing human resource practices.

## ORGANIZATIONAL STRATEGY, FORMS, AND ADAPTATION

As we suggested earlier, our model sees organizational adaptation as a mutual, interactive process in which the organization's strategy and form play essential parts. Much of the literature of macro-organizational behavior or organization theory deals with issues of organizational form, i.e., organizational structure and process. A brief review of this literature, concentrating on newer contributions, will help test our model's capacity to order this knowledge and generate additional hypotheses. To organize these observations we shall discuss each of the ecological areas in our model, starting with Area 1 and proceeding clockwise to end at Area 5. In doing so, we will be paralleling the discussion in Chapter 9, but here we will emphasize the prior literature instead of our historical examples from seven industries.

Firms in Area 1 are exposed to high IC and low RS. Examples of organizations that have experienced these conditions for long periods of time are affluent universities. March and Olsen and their collaborators studied universities most extensively from the standpoint of organization theory. In their work, these authors found it necessary to depart from the customary ways of describing organizations in order to appreciate the unusual forms and especially the decision processes encountered there. They have variously referred to these forms as "organized anarchy," or "loosely coupled" organizations. They point out that there is no straightforward way to develop an integrated and coherent strategy in these organizations and that, when resources are abundant (as often has been the case since World War II), various departments and tenured faculty tend to act independently of the larger organization.

In these organizations, the occasions for making institutional choices often are used simply as receptacles for various, often unrelated, problems, solutions, and participations. March and Olsen point out that this "garbage can" decision process is not as illogical as it first appears, given the environment of these institutions. They understate the role of these special environmental conditions, however, believing that most organizations occasionally fit this model of the decision process. Significant differences among organizations make it unwise to generalize from their limited sample. We argue that our model helps to clarify the important but limited utility of their findings.

Other authors have studied organizations that probably exist in Area 1. Many hospitals (studied by Georgopoulos and Mann, and Perrow [1965] among others) are in this category. Mintzberg has reviewed some of this literature, calling less extreme versions of these organizations an "adhocracy."

Firms in young industries often pass through Area 2 as their markets begin to fill and mature. One type of firm that may reach an equilibrium in Area 2 is the so-called high-technology firm that contributes to or responds to one technical breakthrough after another, and thereby experiences a high level of IC while RS remains intermediate. Examples can be found in the semiconductor and integrated circuit industry. The most complete analysis of this kind of organization is Burns and Stalker's study of several advanced electronics firms in Britain, in which their well-known concept of the organic organization form was developed.

Organizations in Area 3 have received relatively little systematic study even though very many small organizations exist under these ecological conditions. This neglect is happily now being remedied by the population or evolutionary studies of organizations by such researchers as Campbell, Freeman, Hannan, and Aldrich. Examples of firms that sometimes fall into this area are restaurants and retail shops. Mintzberg has reviewed the literature on such organization forms, which he terms "simple" structures. In this highly resource-constrained area, a functional division of labor is generally observed and adaptation tends to proceed by selection or "survival of the fittest" rather than through learning. Area 3 conditions approach Adam Smith's vision of perfect competition, in which there is little room for error. Eccles recent study of home-building firms points to informal contracting networks or quasi-firms as one organizational device that helps firms in this area to move into Area 5. Other emerging forms that might also be described as quasi-firms are the loosely federated systems of the motel, restaurant, and soft drink businesses.

The organization forms characteristic of Areas 6 and 9 have been described by Mintzberg as "machine bureaucracy."* Here we expect to

---

*This treatment largely ignores the extreme southeast corner of Area 9 with its high RS and low IC. This area is characteristic of a very high risk monopoly and is probably not occupied for any significant periods of time. However, we would suggest that a strictly subsistence family farm on poor land might be thought of as an organization that, because it is not in the market economy, has a virtual monopoly position and could persist in this ecological area.

find the popular stereotype of industrial organizations. These "mechanistic" organizations, to use Burns and Stalker's term, emphasize strict lines of command and communication, rules and regulations, explicit and detailed role definitions, and the value of efficiency. This is the organizational world familiar to Frederick Taylor (steel) and Henri Fayol (coal). Another example of such an organization is the high -performing firm in the standard container industry that Lawrence and Lorsch studied. The organizational form to be expected in this area has been well documented.

In Areas 7 and 8 we expect to find what Mintzberg has called the "professional bureaucracy." Barnard supplied one classic description of this form based on his experience as a manager in the Bell System (which our model would place in Area 8 at that time). His emphasis on executive professionalism, cooperation, and on shared purpose (with more than a tinge of paternalism) makes sense in this context. The other classic study that we suggest applies to this area is Weber's famous analysis of government bureaucracies. Writers such as Crozier and Parkinson have spelled out the negative features of these organizations. Since the environment does not place heavy demands on them (especially in Area 7), internal politics becomes much more active, leadership styles have special weight, and the management of symbols is important to legitimate continuation in these areas. Pfeffer's paper on management as symbolic action draws many of its examples from organizations characteristic of Areas 7 and 8.

Area 4 has not been widely studied, perhaps because private organizations are unlikely to remain long in this area of fairly lush resources combined with only moderate IC. This is, of course, the start-up area for many new ventures, organizations created to take advantage of new technologies or new markets. These were organizations of special interest to Schumpeter but they have been the subject of more speculation that actual study. The fresh interest of researchers studying the beginning of the organization life cycle may remedy this situation. In any event, since such organizations are usually described as an informal group with a strong entrepreneurial leader, we have labeled the expected Area 4 form the "entrepreneurial group."

Our model focuses special attention on Area 5, since its conditions are most likely to foster readaptation. No generally accepted term has been developed for the organizational forms expected here, and only a limited effort has been made to describe them in the literature.

The earliest relevant work is Lawrence and Lorsch's description of the high-performing firms in the specialty plastic chemical industry. They found that these firms, faced with high environmental uncertainty (relative to food processing or container firms) adopted structures that combined high differentiation and high integration (high D and I). Lawrence and Lorsch considered the effect of resource differences among firms in each industry, but ignored the question of RS differences among industries. We would now reinterpret and add to their findings in the light of our adaptational model. Figure A.10 schematically compares the relatively high-performing specialty plastics firms they studied with the low-performing ones and with the relatively high-performing standard container firm. While the evidence available would support this positioning, any conclusions must be tempered by the small sample size and should be treated as merely suggestive.

**Figure A.10   Schematic of Functional Differentiation and Integration***

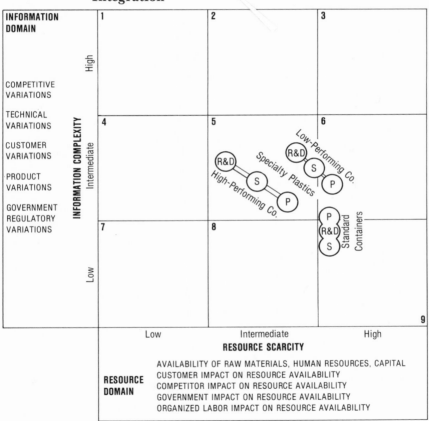

Key
R&D = research and development
S   = sales
P   = production

*The firms diagrammed are described in Paul Lawrence and Jay Lorsch, *Organization and Environment* (Cambridge, Mass: Harvard Business School, 1967).

We have diagrammed key functional units in the specialty plastics firms as separate circles connected by a diagonal line, to reflect the interview evidence that the R&D managers experienced both more IC and less RS than the sales (S) managers, and the production (P) managers. The distance between these functional groups is meant to reflect the degree of differentiation in orientation (time, formality, style, and goals) and the width of the connecting link the quality of integration achieved.

A second line of research dealing with organizational forms likely to appear in Area 5 is that of Ouchi and his associates characterizing the "Type Z" corporation. This form, a Japanese-American hybrid, features widespread use of informal "clan" control mechanisms with the simultaneous and integrated use of market and bureaucratic controls (discussed below). Finally, we would cite the literature on matrix structures (Davis and Lawrence, Sayles, Galbraith) as representing one way of achieving high integration among highly differentiated functional contributors to a product line when there are also significant advantages to maintaining pooled functional resources. Figure A.11 summarizes our discussion of the probable locus of the various organization strategies and forms.

It is always difficult for an organization to remain in Area 5, because its present form of adaptation, no matter how fitting today, must eventually be superseded by another and then another. The firm that locks onto a currently rewarding way of doing business will sooner or later drift into Area 6. Moreover, remaining in Area 5 requires the sustained reconciliation of opposing tendencies. We have already remarked on the difficulty of reconciling innovation, efficiency, and member involvement. Other polarities that must be balanced are short-term versus long-term orientations, internal competition versus cooperation, bureaucratic control versus entrepreneurship. Weick has stressed the necessity to preserve opposed tendencies in the interest of organization adaptation. He goes on to say:

> Both tendencies have survival relevance and if the organism and group are to survive, both must be retained. This means that alternate or simultaneous expression of these opposed tendencies will be more adaptive than will an intermediate or compromise expression.
>
> This point about compromise is important. Whenever a compromise response is fashioned, the adaptive value of the original opposed responses that were altered is destroyed. [pp. 219–220]

This position is consistent with the original Lawrence and Lorsch research, which found that conflict around polarities was a continuing element of organizational life in the high D and I firm. Particular issues were best resolved by problem solving rather than by compromise, smoothing, forcing, or avoidance. Zand's description of the alternation

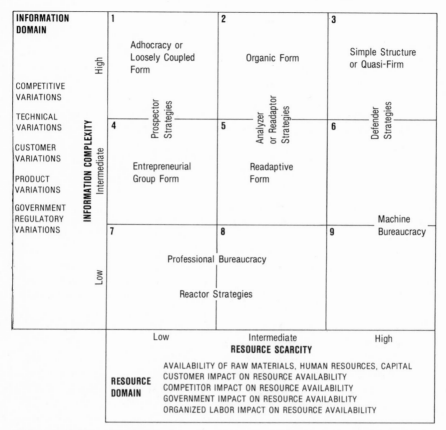

**Figure A.11    Probable Locus of Types of Institutional Strategies and Organizational Forms**

between executive and collegial decision modes, "the collateral process," provides another lead on this little-understood process. Carlson has developed his idea of the "parallel organization" in a similar vein.

Functional groups typically tend to pull the organization out of Area 5, each in its own direction. For example, the research division tends to foster more scientific inquiry, which in turn creates greater IC. Marketing tends to pull toward high margin products and new ventures. Finance is inclined toward acquisitions and other similar techniques to cut resource risks and IC. Production tends to emphasize costs per unit of production even if it may mean slimmer margins. These functional groups often exemplify and keep alive the more abstract polar tendencies that general management must constantly resolve. In Figure 10.3 we have already shown the directional tendencies associated with various functional groups that, in Weick's terms, must be preserved and dealt with rather than compromised.

This issue of functional orientation allows us to link our adaptation model to the literature on the power structure within organizations. Organization theorists generally accept that power tends to move toward those groups in the organization that have demonstrated a capacity to deal with critical uncertainties (Lawrence and Lorsch, Perrow, Hickson, Pettigrew). Building on this idea, we suggest that the distribution of power among the various business functions will depend on the ecological area the organization inhabits. For example, we would expect to find the research group given relatively more power and status in organizations that have persisted for some period of time under the conditions of Area 1. This hypothesis seems to be supported by studies indicating that the most prestigious and powerful groups are researchers in universities and academic medical centers. A similar line of analysis can be extended to each of the functional groups shown in Figure 10.3.

Like organization structure and power distribution, human resource practices affect adaptation significantly. For our purposes, the most useful classification of these practices is the one developed by Ouchi and his associates. The three-fold typology—markets, bureaucracies, and clans—is useful in examining both industry structure and organization form; it can help us understand both the most efficient placement of organizational boundaries and the regulation of human resource transactions inside the firm. Internal market mechanisms take the familiar forms of profit centers, transfer pricing, performance bonuses, and piecework wage payments. Bureaucratic mechanisms depend upon legitimate authorities who establish official role expectations, communication and decision channels, and operating rules. Clans develop through personal exchanges and through shared symbols, rituals, and myths.

It is a matter of common observation that every formal organization makes some use of all three of these mechanisms, but the mix varies considerably among companies. As shown earlier, Figure 10.2 arrays these three mechanisms across our model. We expect significant overlaps in the conditions that favor the dominance of particular mechanisms. We expect the larger firms found in the lower part of the framework will be concerned about order and tend to emphasize bureaucratic methods. The small firms in the northeast sector, in their concern for resources, would emphasize market mechanisms, while the firms in the northwest sector would express a concern for emotional commitment in their emphasis on clan mechanisms. Ouchi's research uses these categories to contrast the organizational patterns in typical Japanese and American firms, and then spotlight the hybrid Z-type practices found in some selected American firms. These firms have a balanced mix of clan, market, and bureaucratic methods that incorporates some traditional Japanese practices modified to suit American expectations. Ouchi's findings are summarized in Table A.1. He also found limited empirical evidence that supports our theoretical inferences in two matched firms he examined; the one using a balanced mix of clan/market/bureaucratic practices experienced higher employee involvement at all levels than the one using more typical American human resource practices emphasizing just market and bureaucratic methods.

The observant reader may have noticed that our model does not seem to provide a locus for the well-known multidivisional organizational form (which was also Mintzberg's final type).* As we see it, divisionalization occurs in such a wide variety of organizations that it is of limited utility for our analytical purposes. Undoubtedly, some divisionalized firms are high D and I organizations. These would be ones with fully integrated divisions, such as Chandler (1962) found in his classic study of Du Pont and General Motors. However, the term is also used to refer to highly diversified conglomerates that are loose federa-

**Table A.1   Three Types of Human Resources Practices**

|  | TYPICAL AMERICAN | JAPANESE/ AMERICAN | TYPICAL JAPANESE |
|---|---|---|---|
| 1. Employment | Short-term (M) | Long-term (C) | Lifetime (C) |
| 2. Responsibility | Individual (M) | Individual (M) | Collective (C) |
| 3. Decision Making | Individual By roles (B) | Consensual (C) | Consensual (C) |
| 4. Career Paths | Specialized (B) | Moderately specialized (B/C) | Nonspecialized (C) |
| 5. Evaluation and Promotion | Rapid (M) | Slow (C) | Slow (C) |
| 6. Financial Rewards | Tied to time & performance (M/B) | Performance & seniority (M/C) | Seniority (C) |
| 7. Control | Explicit, formalized (B) | Implicit and informal (C) and also explicit, with formalized measures (B) | Informal (C) |
| 8. Concern with the Personal Well-Being of Employees | Segmented concern with work-related aspects (M) | Holistic (including family) (C) | Holistic (C) |

SOURCE: Adapted from Ouchi, William G. and David B. Gibson, "Control and Commitment in Industrial Organizations," draft paper, October 1980.
We have added the Clan (C), Market (M) and Bureaucratic (B) symbols to link to our terminology.

*This type is similar to Scott's Type Three and Williamson's H and M forms.

tions of highly differentiated operations with only very modest levels of integration — seldom more than financial. Such firms frequently use the portfolio approach to corporate-level strategic planning. A variant of this approach might plot the position of each business unit on our nine-area adaptation model. The resulting scatter diagram of "strategic business units" could then be examined for central tendencies, balance, trends, capital flows, and congruence between strategy and form. Finally, a third type of divisionalized firm is so focused on a narrow domain that there is apt to be only a modest amount of differentiation although integration may well be high. We have in mind such organizations as standardized bottle firms, whose technology and markets are clearly defined and whose divisions have evolved only to provide geographic coverage. These would in all likelihood be Area 6 firms pursuing a defensive strategy. All in all, bearing in mind Rumelt's findings on the various kinds of diversification, we believe that the forms we have already discussed include the various ways divisionalization appears in practice.

Our analysis now enables us to frame hypotheses about the relation of strategic types, organizational forms, and organizational outcomes for each area of our model. As one example hypothesis 4 states this linkage for Area 1.

**H.4**    Firms in an industry cluster that centers on Area 1 will tend to manifest the organizational form of adhocracy, characterized by a prospector strategy, high differentiation, low integration, predominantly clan human resource practices, and higher relative power for research groups. Outcomes will tend to be high innovation, low efficiency, and moderate involvement.

We can now also complete our statement of the internal factors that contribute to the readaptive process in Area 5. The firm must pursue a readaptive strategy that commits it to the explicit, deliberate, and persistent pursuit of innovation, efficiency, and member involvement. The firm also needs to use: (1) a high D and I structure; (2) a balanced mix of clan/market/bureaucratic human resource practices; and (3) a reasonable balance of power, both horizontally among organizational functions and vertically between levels. These internal features, in combination with intermediate RS and IC lead to readaptive results. Figure A.12 summarizes our hypotheses not only for Areas 1 and 5 and for all other Areas based upon the findings of this research.

We do not mean to imply by these hypotheses that the environmental conditions of a given area *cause* the predicted organizational strategy and form. The environment strongly influences the organizational features, but the effects also run in the other direction. For instance, we expect that a firm pursuing a defender strategy and a machine bu-

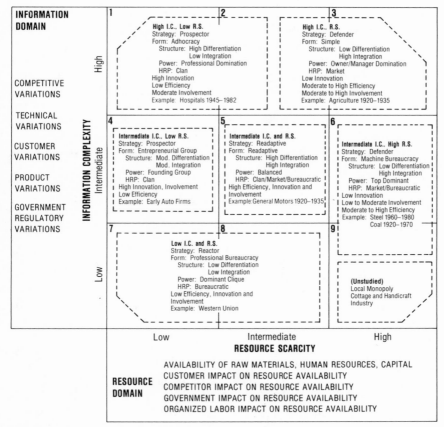

**Figure A.12 Summary of Findings by Areas**

reaucracy form will tend to move toward the environmental conditions of Area 6 regardless of its initial environmental conditions. Adaptive outcomes flow from the combination of internal and environmental conditions.

It now remains to test the extent to which our adaptation model can help make sense of a number of closely related topics in organization theory.

## ISSUES OF TECHNOLOGY AND SIZE

If organizational form is the most discussed issue in organization theory, the related topics of how technology and size affect organizational behavior are not far behind. Can our adaptation model throw light on these two thorny issues?

Over the years it has proved very difficult to find a typology of core technolgies that correlates strongly with organizational form and strategy. Woodward's work on the organizational consequences of batch, process, and mass production, while it has been rigorously challenged, still seems to hold insofar as it is limited to the manufacturing function. Thompson's threefold typology of "intensive," "long-linked," and "mediating" technologies is certainly more encompassing, but it has not been empirically tested or linked effectively to other key variables, such as environmental uncertainty. It does, however, offer a new approach to the problem in relation to our adaptational framework.

Technology can be seen as one of several influences that determine the probable equilibrium point of an industry on the adaptation framework. We suggest that intensive technologies, which Thompson defines as employing a variety of techniques, with feedback, to change some object, share the quality of geographical dispersion, usually in order to locate near the end users. They are user site-bound. He cites hospitals and schools as examples and we could add restaurants, motels, farms, consumer shops, and home construction. This "technological" feature clearly tends to multiply the numbers of firms in these industries and shrink the average firm size. Only in the form of quasi-firms and franchise systems do such organizations become very large. The great variety of firms and strategic approaches that this technology generates tends to locate these industries in the upper tier of our model with high IC. This placement tends to be consistent with the expected organizational forms, with transactions monitored primarily by internal markets and clans rather than by bureaucratic means, and with adaptation more by selection than by learning.

Thompson's second category (long-linked) pertains to the typical manufacturing firm that adds value primarily by transforming raw or semifinished materials into semifinished or finished states desired by consumers. These transforming firms have more choice about their sites and therefore about their size. To put it in economic terms, their technology offers opportunities for economies of scale. To the extent this technological influence is felt, it tends to concentrate an industry into an oligopoly and locate it in the middle tier of our model. Our projected organizational forms for this tier would not seem in conflict with this idea. It is in this tier, for example, that we expect to find the job shop, mass production, and process technologies stressed by Woodward.

For the third type, mediating (or, as we say, network) technologies, Thompson chose as examples such enterprises as telephone systems, railroads, and electric utilities. These industries are what economists call "natural" monopolies, because of a high level of technological interdependence and large capital requirements. It is relatively easy to assign these to the lower end of our IC scale and place them in the lower tier. Other mediating industries, including banks and insurance companies, are usually regulated—but not as heavily, because they mediate information rather than physical objects, and therefore have lower capital costs. Thus they have greater freedom in regard to industry structure. This also seems to be true of extractive technologies. They are site-bound by the location of their raw materials, but the tightness of their constraint varies greatly with the distribution of the raw materials in nature.

We have thus found a way to relate a typology of core technologies to our model (Figure A.13). We suggest that the level of IC a firm will experience in its mature stage can be roughly predicted on the basis of its industry and the associated technology. However, we by no means suggest a technological "imperative" but rather something closer to a

**Figure A.13     General Locus of Technological Types**

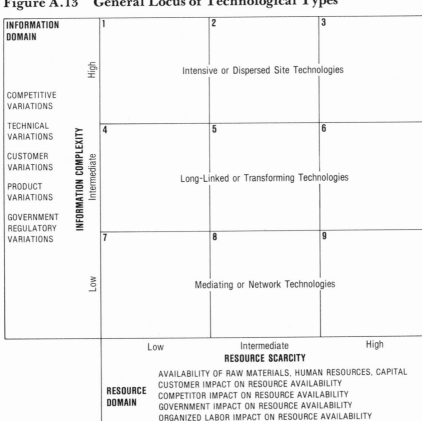

predisposition. We have already seen how firms in user site-bound industries can invent organizational forms that allow them to persist in Area 5.

We have only a few comments on the causes and effects of organization size. We have already pointed out that core technology influences organization size. Size also depends on the stage of the firm's life cycle: entrepreneurial groups are likely to be smaller than mature commodity firms. Size will also clearly increase when firms are managed into Area 7's monopoly condition in order to achieve monopoly profits. Largely by definition, the firms in the upper tier of our framework are smaller, on average, than those below. Finally we would add that, other things being equal, the literature suggests that larger firms are more formalized and bureaucratic than smaller ones (Pugh). They have much more difficulty securing member involvement. Thus it may be more difficult for larger firms to be readaptive and persist in Area 5. This is a question subject to empirical test.


## THE ENACTED ENVIRONMENT

All versions of contingency theory must eventually come to terms with the objective-subjective or the actual-perceived issue of how to treat the environment in which organizations exist. Weick has posed the issue most forcefully with his concept of the "enacted environment," which states that organizations generate a socially shared way of envisioning the complex world beyond their borders. This issue has been a methodological stumbling block for various researchers trying to define and measure the organizational environment.

We certainly agree that organizations enact their own environment (Figure A.1). Weick has presented a very useful model of how the enactment process proceeds, including tendencies of the process to develop cognitive distortions. No one to date, however, has searched for systematic relationships between these distortions and specific conditions in the organization's environment. While Weick is surely not unaware of this possibility, his emphasis on enactment has led others to treat such problems as insignificant. We are reminded of Winston Churchill's reply when he was asked whether the sun would really exist if no one perceived it. Whether it was perceived or not, he said, if you strayed too close, you would burn to a cinder. The accuracy of an enacted environment has survival consequences. Thus any adaptational model must not only take account of the enactment process but also be especially sensitive to any systematic tendencies toward distortion.

We know of no literature that directly addresses the systematic distortion tendencies in the enactment process. However, a very similar phenomenon has been studied extensively at the level of individual perception; these studies informed the work of both Schroder et al. and Janis and Leventhal, to which we have already referred. This research shows that people tend to focus tightly and overly simplify their perceptions when under stress. By analogy, we can state the following hypothesis:

**H.5.1**   Firms experiencing high levels of RS and/or IC will tend to overly simplify and minimize their environmental uncertainties.

This tendency in Area 3 firms leads us to doubt that they would develop the very high level of differentiation and integration necessary to cope best with their environment even if their resources were adequate.

While the evidence from psychology is not as clear, there seems to be a tendency for people to exaggerate environmental factors that, according to conventional wisdom, ought to be affecting them but, in fact, are not. Following this somewhat weaker lead, we hypothesize that:

**H.5.2**   Firms experiencing low levels of RS and/or IC will tend to exaggerate their environmental uncertainties.

## ORGANIZATION DOMINATION

Among the newest and oldest issues in the literature on organization are the questions of who controls the organization and the closely related question of who benefits from its activities. Perrow (1972) and Bell, among others, have persistently raised this issue of the relative power and the payoffs that flow to various kinds of stakeholders. The adaptation model provides an additional perspective on these questions. Figure A.14 summarizes the tendencies to be expected in the various ecological areas and requires only brief comment here.

The term we have used to characterize Area 1, "professional domination," was taken from the title of Freidson's book on doctors and health care. He (like others) argues that the key professionals who control such organizations as hospitals are also the chief beneficiaries. In Area 3 we would follow Adam Smith in saying that the "invisible hand" that controls the action is the consumer's. The consumer is also the chief beneficiary, although our model suggests that the long-term benefits that accrue to the consumer are constrained by the limited innovation that can be expected. No one controls or benefits in Area 9. The

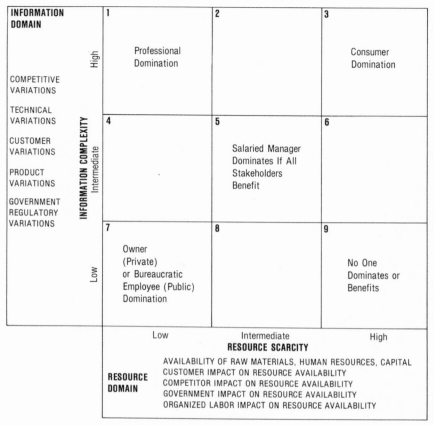

**Figure A.14    Organization Domination and Benefits**

primary controllers and beneficiaries of Area 7 are owners in the private sector and the senior bureaucratic officials in public sector organizations.

In Area 5 the salaried manager dominates the organization and, as noted in Chapter 9, managers can include all employees who are handling uncertainty. The rise of the salaried manager to a dominating position among stakeholders has been documented by Burnham and more recently and definitively by Chandler (1977). We would argue that a balanced distribution of benefits to all stakeholders is most likely in Area 5, since if the claims of any important group of stakeholders were long neglected, the firm would tend to slide into some other area.

Our discussion of domination leads next to the issue of organizational legitimacy. The broad social legitimacy of all types of organizations has been challenged at one time or another, on one ground or another. We expect that the issues on which a challenge to an organization's legitimacy is mounted would vary according to its ecological area. For instance, since many coal firms are found in Area 9, it is not surprising that employee exploitation in the mines has been an historical problem and source of challenge. Hospitals in Area 1 are challenged on grounds of efficiency. Perhaps the strongest questions about legitimacy can be expected in Area 7. When both IC and RS are low, we would be surprised to find much innovation or efficiency. Organizations in this area would be expected to expend considerable resources in efforts to establish and defend their broad social legitimacy. If, as we hypothesize, organizations in Area 5 do best in terms of innovation, efficiency, and involvement, they can be expected to enjoy the greatest social legitimacy. Such legitimacy is not guaranteed, however. For example, in the last two decades the cigarette industry has been experiencing intermediate levels of IC and RS but it clearly has also experienced a crisis of legitimacy because of the health hazard posed by smoking (Miles). The legitimacy issue, when it is salient, needs to be treated as a separate source of adaptational challenge.

## OVERVIEW OF THE ADAPTATION MODEL

We stated at the beginning of this appendix that our analytical model would attempt to synthesize the environmental determinism and organizational choice approaches, and the information and the resource perspectives of organization theory. Focusing on the fundamental theme of adaptation, with a particular emphasis on the readaptive process, we have shown how our model can help reconcile concepts and findings that have until now been seen as divergent. The basic notion of the inverted U-curve relations between the two environmental dimensions, IC and RS, and readaptation is simple and almost obvious, but that should be no handicap if it accounts reasonably well for the full range of organizational forms. It is the recent recognition of the great diversity of organizational forms that has created a sense of fragmentation in the whole field of organizational studies (Lorsch). Our model represents one attempt to rediscover the overall pattern.

We also said at the outset that we would attempt to build a bridge between organization theory and industrial organization economics. In this regard we can only claim to have shown that it is possible to work back and forth with the languages of both fields, and thereby establish conceptual linkages through our model. We hope our model will be a foundation for others to test and build upon.

Some weaknesses in our approach should be acknowledged. We have implied that the firms in a given industry will be clustered in a particular part of our Adaptational Framework. Other research, such as the Miles and Snow study of textbook publishing, indicates that firms in some industries may be widely dispersed across our framework. Similarly, the separate divisions of a conglomerate may be scattered across our framework although they are part of a single legal entity. Neither of these observations in itself supports or contradicts our theory—only fresh longitudinal research on the results existing under such conditions over time would serve this purpose.

Serious methodological questions can be raised about any theory that uses broad variables like IC and RS and posits an inverted U-curve relationship between them and other key variables. It is probably an understatement to say that researchers dislike inverted U-curve relationships, which are notoriously difficult to prove or disprove. Unlike straight lines, they come in many shapes. It is particularly hard to establish the apex beyond which a further increase in the independent variable will not increase but decrease the dependent variable. Yet this seems to be the point of greatest interest to most people. The only reason to put up with these very real methodological difficulties is if some important real world phenomenon happens to behave in an inverted U-curve manner. Our theory claims that it does and that it should be tested.

We have already noted the problems of measuring RS and IC. In this inquiry we have not invested any significant effort in trying systematically to resolve these problems. As the research was ending, however, we did take a first step in this direction. In the case of IC we started with the five most critical information sources that we have worked with all along: competitive, customer, technical, product, and government regulatory variations. For each of these information sources, over a particular time period, we judged the amount of variation experienced by the dominant or modal firms in each of the seven industries studied. The resulting scores are arrayed in Table A.2. Following a similar procedure, we scored RS for the same time periods. Here we first rated the availability of a type of resource—capital, raw materials and human resources—and then the adverse impact on availability of each of four major sources of constraint: customers, competitors, government, and organized labor. We used negative numbers as needed to indicate counterbalancing inputs such as government subsidies. This scoring is also recorded in Table A. 2.

The mental gymnastics we went through in assigning these scores were complex, and in the last analysis they represent a series of judgments. It is interesting, however, to compare ratings made in this manner with the broader judgments we had earlier made for each industry, as reflected in Figure 9.2. In Figure A.15 the scores of Table A.2 are arrayed on the adaptation grid, employing a nine-point scale. The correspondence to Figure 9.2 is fairly close and the deviations are interesting. Our latest calculations depict AT&T as having less RS for sixty

**Table A.2 Trial Scoring of IC and RS by Underlying Elements**

| | Auto | | Steel | | Hospitals | | Agric. | | Housing | | Coal | | Telecomm. | |
|---|---|---|---|---|---|---|---|---|---|---|---|---|---|---|
| Information Complexity | *1925 -70* | *1981* | *1901 -60* | *1981* | *1945 -75* | *1981* | *1920 -35* | *1981* | *Up Cycle* | *Down Cycle* | *1920 -70* | *1981* | *1913 -73* | *1981* |
| Competitive Variations | ½ | 1½ | ½ | 1½ | 2 | 1½ | 2 | 1 | 1½ | 1½ | ½ | 1½ | 0 | 1 |
| Technical Variations | 1 | 1½ | 1 | 1½ | 2 | 2 | 1½ | 1½ | 1½ | 1½ | ½ | 1½ | 1 | 1½ |
| Customer Variations | 1½ | 1 | ½ | 1 | 1 | 1 | 1 | ½ | 1½ | 1½ | ½ | ½ | ½ | 1 |
| Product Variations | 1 | 1½ | 1 | 1 | 2 | 2 | 1½ | 1½ | 1½ | 1½ | 0 | ½ | ½ | 1 |
| Gov't. Reg. Variations | ½ | 1½ | ¼ | 1½ | 1 | 1½ | ½ | ½ | 1 | 1 | ½ | 1½ | ½ | 1½ |
| IC Total | 4½ | 7 | 3¼ | 6½ | 8 | 8 | 6½ | 5 | 7 | 7 | 2 | 5½ | 2½ | 6 |
| Resource Scarcity | | | | | | | | | | | | | | |
| Availability of Resources | 0 | 1 | 0 | 1 | 0 | ½ | 2 | 1 | 1½ | 1½ | 2 | ½ | 0 | ½ |
| Customer Resource Impact | 1 | 1½ | ½ | 1½ | 0 | ½ | 2 | 1½ | 1 | 1½ | 2 | 1 | 0 | ½ |
| Competitor Resource Impact | ½ | 2 | 1 | 2 | 1½ | 1½ | 2 | 2 | 1½ | 1½ | 2 | 1 | 0 | ½ |
| Gov't. Resource Impact | – ½ | 1 | 0 | 1 | – 1 | – ½ | 1 | – ½ | 0 | 2 | 0 | 1 | 1½ | 1½ |
| Org. Labor Resource Impact | 1½ | 1½ | 1¼ | 1 | ½ | 1 | 0 | 0 | 1 | ½ | 2 | 1½ | ½ | ½ |
| R.S. Total | 2½ | 7 | 2¾ | 6½ | 1 | 3 | 7 | 4 | 5 | 7 | 8 | 5 | 2 | 3½ |

Source: The scale for each element in 0-2. We must stress again—as in the text—that we arrived at these values on the basis of our reading of history and informed judgment.

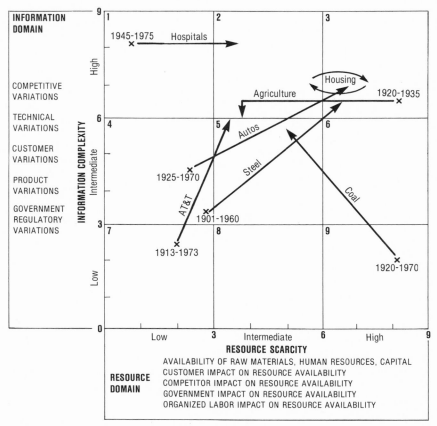

**Figure A.15    Map of Trial Scorings**

years than we thought initially, and as now moving to a higher IC. Perhaps our initial rating reflected the company's enacted environment, which could well be higher on RS than an objective reading. Autos and steel are also shown as recently moving to a higher IC than we had scored before. In general, however, the correspondence is strong enough to suggest that further measurement work in this direction is warranted.

Of course, unanswered questions still remain. Some we can identify and address here. Others will emerge only over time. We hope that our presentation of the readaptive theory will stimulate continuing questions and inquiry.

If over time, readaptation is most likely in Area 5, why do organizations in other ecological niches survive? First of all, the laws that apparently govern organizations are not so airtight that they prevent maladaptive organizations from surviving. As Cyert and March pointed out years ago, organizations are rather loosely coupled to their environment. We should expect to find exceptions to our hypotheses. Beyond that, we have seen that some simple structures organized around a site-bound technology are very unlikely to evolve the readaptive form. Likewise, it is difficult to organize network technologies without paying some readaptational costs implicit in regulated monopolies. In some industries, like hospitals, a combination of factors such as high public concern for health, the high status of physicians, and the third party payment system, permits a large set of organizations to exist for a surprising length of time under low RS and high IC. Organizational leaders may also be tempted to seek monopoly profits, if society permits, as it sometimes does. Finally, for various historical reasons, some industrial sectors seem not to have yet evolved a single readaptive firm that puts severe competitive pressure on its rivals. Our adaptational model reflects tendencies — it is not an iron law.

Can organizations deliberately move themselves from one environmental area to another? We maintain that organizations can, in some instances, influence their environment to this degree. More needs to be known about such cases that only focused longitudinal studies of industries and key firms can answer, but we saw one example in the history of AT&T (Chapter 8). After the expiration of Bell's patents, AT&T struggled with many competitors. Gradually, on the basis of its technological and managerial advantages (and by means of some rough and ready tactics), AT&T began to dominate. Theodore Vail clearly saw the technological justifications for a network monopoly. As such a monopoly position came within sight, but while the firm was still presumably operating in Area 5, Vail negotiated an agreement with the government subjecting AT&T to regulation in exchange for an unchallenged monopoly position in its operating territories. Vail thus moved his firm from Area 5 into Area 8. We also believe there may be a critical point in the early development of an organization when just a few managerial actions can determine whether the firm eventually moves into Area 5 or Area 6. At such a critical juncture, the firm moves toward a readaptive or a defender strategy, toward a high D and I structure or a machine bureaucracy, toward mixed or bureaucratic human resource practices.

What is the relationship between organizational survival and organizational readaptation? These are by no means identical concepts. We can imagine organizations existing indefinitely in every one of the nine ecological areas. Survival is possible in every area but we expect readaptation, as we define it, to occur only in and around Area 5. The version of contingency theory associated with the Lawrence and Lorsch work is known as a theory of "fit." Its simple normative implication is that managers should assess their environmental conditions and then employ the organization form that fits those conditions. In the terminology of our current adaptation model this would mean that a newly appointed chief executive of a firm located in Area 6 would be wise to install a defender strategy and a machine bureaucracy. This would improve the firm's survival chances, but it would not lead to readaptive results. That would require that the chief executive follow the somewhat riskier path of installing a readaptive form and strategy. Such a decision would mean investing additional resources in the face of high RS. It would clearly be judged successful if the firm achieved innovations and higher employee involvement without losing efficiency, and if it found its RS reduced. Survival and readaptation are different. The fit theory still holds but the concept of readaptation extends it and permits new normative interpretations.*

This discussion leads us to reiterate the important point that we see readaptation as a mutual interactive process between an organization and its relevant environment. In the most general terms, the environment tends to generate uncertainties that drive an organization toward Area 1 where the environment would be dominant. An organization tends to reduce uncertainties and move toward Area 7 where it would be dominant. Neither side of this ongoing exchange is simply passive. The challenge as well as the response can come from either side of the boundary. Readaptation comes from the tension between these forces, which are best balanced in Area 5, where neither side is in total control. In a similar way, the key organization members dominate the organization in Area 1 and the organization dominates its members in Area 9. The internal process by which readaptation occurs must come out of the creative tension between these forces, which again are best balanced in Area 5, where neither side dominates. The sustained reconciliation of innovation, efficiency, and member involvement, the process we call readaptation, will never be easy but we believe that our model provides guidelines for making it happen successfully.

## REFERENCES

ALDRICH, HOWARD E.
1979    *Organizations and Environments*. New York: Prentice-Hall.
ANDREWS, KENNETH
1980    *The Concept of Corporate Strategy*. Revised edition. Homewood, Ill: Jones-Irwin.

---

*Our model parallels the normative implications that Kotter's model of organizational dynamics has added to contingency theory's notion of fit.

ARGYRIS, CHRIS
1960    "Individual Actualization in Complex Organizations." *Mental Hygiene* 44:226–237.
ARGYRIS, CHRIS, and SCHÖN, DONALD A.
1978    *Organizational Learning: A Theory of Action Perspective*. Reading, Mass: Addison-Wesley.
ASHBY, W. ROSS
1970    *Design for a Brain*. London: Chapman and Hall.
BARNARD, CHESTER
1938    *The Functions of the Executive*. Cambridge, Mass.: Harvard University Press.
BELL, DANIEL
1970    "Quo Warranto? Notes on the Governance of Universities in the 1970s." *The Public Interest* 19: 53–68.
BOWER, JOSEPH L.
1970    *Managing the Resource Allocation Process*. Cambridge, Mass.: Harvard Business School.
BURNHAM, JAMES
1941    *The Managerial Revolution*. New York: John Day.
BURNS, TOM, and STALKER, G. M.
1961    *The Management of Innovation*. London: Tavistock Press.
BYRNE, D, and CLORE, G. L.
1967    "Effectance Arousal and Attraction." *Journal of Personality and Social Psychology* 6:no. 638.
CAMPBELL, D.T.
1965    "Variation and Selective Retention in Socio-cultural Evolution." In *Social Change in Developing Areas*, H. R. Barringer, G. I. Blanksten, and R. Mack, eds., pp. 19–49. Cambridge, Mass.: Schenkman.
CARLSON, HOWARD
1978    "The Parallel Organization Structure at General Motors . . . An Interview with Howard C. Carlson." *Personnel* (September-October): 64–69.
CAVES, RICHARD E.
1980    "Industrial Organization, Corporate Strategy and Structure." *Journal of Economic Literature* 18 (March): 64–92.
CHAKRAVARTHY, BALAJI S.
1981    *Managing Coal: A Challenge in Adaptation*. Albany: SUNY Press.
CHANDLER, ALFRED D., JR.
1962    *Strategy and Structure*. Cambridge, Mass.: The MIT Press.
CHANDLER, ALFRED, D., JR.
1977    *The Visible Hand: The Managerial Revolution in American Business*. Cambridge, Mass.: Harvard University Press.
CHILD, JOHN
1972    "Organizational Structure, Environment and Performance: The Role of Strategic Choice." *Sociology* no. 1 (January): 1–22.
CROZIER, MICHEL
1964    *The Bureaucratic Phenomenon*. Chicago: University of Chicago Press.

CYERT, RICHARD M, and MARCH, JAMES G.
1963    *A Behavioral Theory of the Firm.* Englewood Cliffs, N. J.: Prentice-Hall.
DAVIS, STANLEY, and LAWRENCE, PAUL
1977    *Matrix.* New York: Addison-Wesley.
DUNCAN, ROBERT, and WEISS, ANDREW
1978    "Organizational Learning: Implications for Organizational Design." In *Research in Organizational Behavior.* Barry Staw, ed., vol 1. Greenwich, Conn.: JAI Press.
DUNN, EDGAR S., JR.
1971    *Economic and Social Development.* Baltimore: Johns Hopkins Press.
ECCLES, ROBERT G.
1980    "Subcontracting and Management in the Homebuilding Industry: The Role of the Quasi-Firm." Draft Paper, Harvard Business School.
EMERY, F. E., and TRIST, E. L.
1973    *Towards a Social Ecology.* London and New York: Plenum Press.
FESTINGER, L.
1957    *A Theory of Cognitive Dissonance.* Evanston, Ill.: Row, Peterson.
FIEDLER, FRED E.
1967    *A Theory of Leadership Effectiveness.* New York: McGraw-Hill.
FREIDSON, ELIOT
1970    *Professional Dominance: The Social Structure of Medical Care.* Chicago: Aldine.
GALBRAITH, JAY
1973    *Designing Complex Organizations.* New York: Addison-Wesley.
GEORGOPOULOS, BASIL S., and MANN, FLOYD C.
1962    *The Community General Hospital.* New York: MacMillan.
GOULDNER, ALVIN W.
1954    *Patterns of Industrial Democracy.* Glencoe, Ill.: Free Press.
GRIME, J. P.
1974    "Vegetation Class by Reference to Strategies." *Nature* 250(7): 26-30.
HANNAN, M. T., and FREEMAN, J. H.
1977    "The Population Ecology of Organizations." *American Journal of Sociology* 82:929-964.
HICKSON, DAVID
1971    "A Strategic Contingencies Theory of Intra-Organizational Power." *Administrative Science Quarterly* 16 (June):216-229.
HIRSCHMAN, ALBERT O.
1970    *Exit, Voice and Loyalty.* Cambridge, Mass.: Harvard University Press.
ISENBERG, DANIEL J.
1981    "Some Effects of Time Pressure on Vertical Structure and Decision-Making Accuracy in Small Groups." *Organizational Behavior and Human Performance* 27:119-134.
JANIS, IRVING, and LEVENTHAL, HOWARD
1968    "Human Reaction to Stress." In *Handbook of Personality Theory,* Borgatta and Lamberts, eds., pp. 1041-1085. Chicago: Rand-McNally.

JELINEK, MARIANN
1979    *Institutionalizing Innovation*. New York: Praeger.
KIMBERLY, JOHN R., and MILES, ROBERT H.
1980    *The Organizational Life Cycle*. San Francisco, London: Jossey-Bass.
KOTTER, JOHN
1978    *Organizational Dynamics*. Reading, Mass.: Addison-Wesley.
LANE, HARRY, BEDDOWS, RODNEY, and LAWRENCE, PAUL
1981    *Managing Large Research and Development Programs*. Albany: SUNY Press.
LAWRENCE, PAUL, and LORSCH, JAY
1967    *Organization and Environment*. Cambridge, Mass.: Harvard Business School.
LORSCH, JAY W.
1975    "Managers, Behavioral Science, and The Tower of Babel." In *Man and Work in Society*. Eugene Cass and Frederick Zimmer, eds. New York: Van Nostrand.
LORSCH, JAY, and MORSE, JOHN
1974    *Organizations and Their Members: A Contingency Approach*. New York: Harper & Row.
MARCH, JAMES, and OLSEN, JOHAN
1976    *Ambiguity and Choice in Organizations*. Bergen, Norway: Universitetsforlaget.
MARCH, JAMES, and SIMON, HERBERT
1958    *Organizations*. New York: John Wiley
McKELVEY, BILL
1978    "Organizational Systematics: Taxonomic Lessons from Biology." *Management Science*, 24(13): 1428-1440.
MILES, RAYMOND, and SNOW, CHARLES
1978    *Organizational Strategy: Structures and Processes*. New York: McGraw-Hill.
MILES, ROBERT H.
1982    *Coffin Nails and Corporate Strategy*. Englewood Cliffs, N.J.: Prentice-Hall.
MINTZBERG, HENRY
1979    *The Structuring of Organizations*. New York: Prentice-Hall.
OUCHI, WILLIAM G.
1980a   "Efficient Boundaries." Working paper, UCLA.
OUCHI, WILLIAM G.
1980b   "A Framework for Understanding Organizational Failure." In *The Organizational Life Cycle,* Kimberly and Miles, pp. 395-429.
OUCHI, WILLIAM G., and GIBSON, DAVID B.
1980    "Control and Commitment in Industrial Organization." Unpublished Mimeo UCLA October.
OUCHI, WILLIAM G., and JAEGER, ALFRED
1978    "Type Z Organization: Stability in the Midst of Mobility." *The Academy of Management Review*. April:305-314.
PARKINSON, CYRIL NORTHCOTE
1957    *Parkinson's Law and Other Studies in Administration*. Boston: Houghton Mifflin.

PERROW, CHARLES
1979    *Complex Organizations: A Critical Essay.* 2nd ed. Glenville, Ill: Scott, Foresman.

PERROW, CHARLES
1972    *The Radical Attack on Business.* New York: Harcourt Brace Jovanovich.

PERROW, CHARLES
1965    "Hospitals: Technology, Structure and Goals." In *Handbook of Organizations,* Chicago: Rand McNally. James G. March, ed., 910–971.

PETTIGREW, ANDREW
1973    *The Politics of Organizational Decision-Making.* London: Tavistock.

PFEFFER, JEFFREY
1980    "Management as Symbolic Action: The Creation and Maintenance of Organizational Paradigms." In *Research in Organizational Behavior* Vol. 3. Cummings, Larry and Staw, Barry, eds. Greenwich, Conn: JAI Press.

PFEFFER, JEFFREY, and SALANCIK, GERALD
1978    *The External Control of Organizations: A Resource Dependence Perspective.* New York: Harper & Row.

PORTER, LYMAN W., and LAWLER, EDWARD E.
1968    *Managerial Attitudes and Performance.* Homewood, Ill: Richard D. Irwin.

PORTER, MICHAEL E.
1980    *Competitive Strategy.* New York: Free Press.

PUGH, DEREK S.
1981    "The Aston Program of Research: Retrospect & Prospect" in *Perspectives on Organization Design and Behavior,* Van de Ver and Tazel, eds., New York: John Wiley and Sons, pp. 135–166.

ROSENBLOOM, RICHARD S.
1978    "Technological Innovation in Firms and Industries: An Assessment of the State of the Art." In *Technological Innovation: A Critical Review of Current Knowledge,* P. Kelly and M. Kranzberg, eds. San Francisco: San Francisco Press.

RUMELT, RICHARD P.
1974    *Strategy, Structure, amd Economic Performance.* Cambridge, Mass.: Harvard Business School.

SAYLES, LEONARD R.
1976    "Matrix Management: The Structure with a Future." *Organizational Dynamics* (Autumn): 2–17.

SCHROEDER, HAROLD M., DRIVER, MICHAEL J., and STREUFERT, SIEGFRIED
1968    *Human Information Processing.* New York: John Wiley.

SCHUMPETER, JOSEPH A.
1961    *The Theory of Economic Development.* Cambridge, Mass.: Harvard University Press.

SCOTT, BRUCE
1973    "The Industrial State; Old Myths and New Realities." *Harvard Business Review* (March-April): 51, 133–148.

SELZNICK, PHILIP
1957 *Leadership in Administration*. New York: Harper & Row.

SHERIF, MUZAFER
1962 *Intergroup Relations and Leadership, Approaches and Research in Industrial, Ethnic, Cultural and Political Areas*. New York: John Wiley.

THOMPSON, JAMES
1967 *Organizations in Action*. New York: McGraw-Hill.

WALTON, RICHARD E.
1980 "Establishing and Maintaining High Commitment Work Systems." In *The Organizational Life Cycle*, Kimberly and Miles, 208–290.

WEBER, MAX
1964 *The Theory of Social and Economic Organization*. New York: The Free Press

WEICK, KARL
1980 *The Social Psychology of Organizing*. 2d ed. Reading, Mass.: Addison-Wesley.

WHITE, R. W.
1959 "Motivation Reconsidered: The Concept of Competence." *Psychological Review* 66:297–333

WILLIAMSON, OLIVER
1975 *Markets and Hierarchies: Analysis and Antitrust Implications*. New York: Free Press.

WOODWARD, JOAN
1965 *Industrial Organizations: Theory and Practice*. London: Oxford University.

ZAND, DALE E.
1974 "Collateral Organization: A New Change Strategy." *Journal of Applied Behavioral Science* 10:63–89.

# Notes

Chapter 1.  DILEMMAS
FACING AMERICAN INDUSTRY

1. William Ouchi, *Theory Z*, (Reading, Mass.: Addison-Wesley 1981).

Chapter 2.  AUTOS: ON THE THIN EDGE

1. "Detroit's Uphill Battle," *Time*, September 8, 1980, p. 48.
2. Joseph Kraft, "Annals of Industry: The Downsizing Decision," *The New Yorker*, May 5, 1980, pp. 134-162.
3. William Tucker, "The Wreck of the Auto Industry," *Harper's*, November 1980, pp. 45-60.
4. U.S. Department of Transportation, *The U.S. Automobile Industry, 1980*, (Washington, D.C.: Department of Transportation, January 1981), p. 64.
5. Ibid., p. 40. These figures are reported in William J. Abernathy, Kim B. Clark, and Alan M. Kantrow, "The New Industrial Competition," *Harvard Business Review* (September-October 1981): pp. 68-81.
6. Quoted in the *Wall Street Journal*, April 27, 1981.
7. U.S. Department of Transportation, *The U.S. Automobile Industry, 1980*, pp. 7-11.
8. John B. Rae, *The American Automobile* (Chicago: University of Chicago Press, 1965), p. 21.

9. John B. Rae, *American Automobile Manufacturers: The First Forty Years* (Philadelphia: Chilton, 1959), p. 10.

10. Robert Paul Thomas, *An Analysis of the Pattern of Growth of the Automobile Industry, 1895–1929* (New York: Arno Press, 1977), Table 1, p. 321.

11. John Brooks, *The Fate of the Edsel and Other Business Adventures* (New York: Harper & Row, 1963), pp. 21–22; Philip Hillyer Smith, *Wheels within Wheels: A Short History of American Motor Car Manufacturing* (New York: Funk & Wagnalls, 1968), pp. 191–275; and Reginald M. Cleveland and S. T. Williamson, *The Road Is Yours: The Story of the Automobile and the Men Behind It* (New York: Greystone Press, 1951), pp. 270–300.

12. U.S. Federal Trade Commission, *Report on the Motor Vehicle Industry*, (Washington, D.C., 1939), p. 22.

13. Harold Katz, *The Decline of Competition in the Automobile Industry, 1920–1940* (New York: Arno Press, 1977), pp. 28–29.

14. Quoted in Roger Burlingame, *Henry Ford* (Chicago: Quadrangle, 1970), p. 62.

15. William J. Abernathy, *The Productivity Dilemma: Roadblock to Innovation* (Baltimore: Johns Hopkins University Press, 1978), pp. 23–24.

16. Henry Ford, in collaboration with Samuel Crowther, *My Life and Work* (Garden City, N.Y.: Doubleday, Page, 1923), pp. 79–80.

17. U.S. Federal Trade Commission, *Report on the Motor Vehicle Industry*, pp. 632–633.

18. This part of Ford's success is usually forgotten, but it was absolutely critical for the company's growth: See Allan Nevins, *Ford: The Times, the Man, the Company* (New York: Scribner's, 1954), pp. 342–347; and Nevins and Frank Ernest Hill, *Ford: Expansion and Challenge, 1915–1933* (New York: Scribner's, 1957), pp. 257–261.

19. Rae, *American Automobile Manufacturers*, p. 88.

20. James J. Flink, *America Adopts the Automobile, 1895–1910* (Cambridge, Mass.: MIT Press, 1970), p. 312.

21. Alfred P. Sloan, Jr., *My Years with General Motors* (Garden City, Doubleday, N.Y.: Anchor Books, 1972), pp. 6–7, gives a slightly different interpretation.

22. The most thorough account of General Motors' formation and early years is Ronald Henry Wolf, "General Motors: A Study of the Firm's Growth, its External Relationships, and Internal Organization" (unpublished Vanderbilt University Ph.D. dissertation, 1962). A recent popular history of the company is Ed Cray, *Chrome Colossus: General Motors and Its Times* (New York: McGraw-Hill, 1980).

23. Ralph C. Epstein, *The Automobile Industry: Its Economic and Commercial Development* (Chicago: A. W. Shaw, 1928), pp. 257, 265. Time-series on profits and investment during this period are available in Lawrence H. Seltzer, *A Financial History of the American Automobile Industry* (Boston: Houghton Mifflin, 1928), p. 128 (Ford), p. 230 (General Motors), and chap. 5 (Studebaker, Dodge, Packard, Nash, Hudson, and Reo Motors).

24. U.S. Federal Trade Commission, *Report on the Motor Vehicle Industry*, p. 29.

25. The bald summary in this paragraph draws on Harold G. Vatter, "The Closure of Entry in the American Automobile Industry," *Oxford Economic Papers* 4 (1952): 213–234; Thomas, *An Analysis of the Pattern of Growth*, chap. 5; Katz, *The Decline of Competition*, passim; Seltzer, *Financial History*, pp. 56–69; Epstein, *Automobile Industry*, pp. 110–115, 162–192; and Abernathy, *Productivity Dilemma*, chap. 2, esp. pp. 18–19, 47.

    Sloan, in his assessment of the changing market in this period, added two other considerations, installment buying and improved roads. Sloan, *My Years with General Motors*, p. 172.

26. Quoted in Alfred D. Chandler, Jr., ed., *Giant Enterprise: Ford, General Motors, and the Automobile Industry* (New York: Harcourt, Brace & World, 1964), p. 153.

27. Sloan, *My Years with General Motors*, p. 74; cf. pp. 71, 76.

28. Ibid., p. 189. The term *emergent strategy* is Henry Mintzberg's. See Mintzberg, "Patterns in Strategy Formation," *Management Science*, 24 (May 1978): 934–948.

29. Sloan, *My Years with General Motors*, pp. 189–190 and chaps. 13 and 15.

30. U.S. Federal Trade Commission, *Report on the Motor Vehicle Industry*, p. 29.

31. Seltzer, *Financial History*, pp. 128, 230, and chap. 5.

32. Lawrence J. White, *The Automobile Industry since 1945* (Cambridge, Mass.: Harvard University Press, 1970), chap. 15, esp. pp. 272–275; and White, "The Automobile Industry," in Walter Adams, ed., *The Structure of American Industry*, 5th ed. (New York: Macmillan, 1975), pp. 165–220.

33. e.g. John B. Rae, *The Road and the Car in American Life* (Cambridge, Mass.: MIT Press, 1971).

34. U.S. Bureau of the Census, *Historical Statistics of the United States: Colonial Times to 1970* (Washington, D.C., 1976), series Q148.

35. White, *The Automobile Industry Since 1945*, p. 251.

36. AMC probably succeeded because it abandoned attempts to field a full line of automobiles and reverted to a "Fordist" strategy of concentrating on a single model in production, the Rambler. The best account of the fate of the independent producers is Charles E. Edwards, *Dynamics of the United States Automobile Industry* (Columbia, S.C.: University of South Carolina Press, 1965).

37. U.S. Federal Trade Commission, *Report on the Motor Vehicle Industry*, p. 29.

38. Chandler, ed., *Giant Enterprise*, part 2.

39. Ford, *My Life and Work*, pp. 91, 92.

40. Allan Nevins and Frank E. Hill, *Ford: Expansion and Challenge*, pp. 269–278.

41. Keith Sward, *The Legend of Henry Ford* (New York: Rinehart & Co.,

1948), pp. 188-194 gives a brief account of the burgeoning "Ford Alumni Association" in the 1920s. Sward described the company in 1920s as "a twentieth-century absolute monarchy" (p. 185).

42. Seltzer, *Financial History*, p. 57.
43. This famous story was first told by Alfred D. Chandler, Jr., in *Strategy and Structure: Chapters in the History of the American Industrial Enterprise* (Cambridge, Mass.: MIT Press, 1962), chap. 3, and in greater detail by Chandler and Stephen Salsbury, *Pierre S. Du Pont and the Making of the Modern Corporation* (New York: Harper & Row, 1971), part 4. Sloan himself gave two accounts of his achievements: the breezy *Adventures of a White-Collar Man*, in collaboration with Boyden Sparkes (New York: Doubleday, Doran, 1941), part 5, esp. pp. 131-137; and the more substantial *My Years with General Motors*.
44. Chandler, ed., *Giant Enterprise*, pp. 114-115, quoting from Sloan's "Organization Plan."
45. Quoted in Chandler, *Strategy and Structure*, p. 143.
46. Ibid., p. 2.
47. Sloan, *My Years with General Motors*, p. 505.
48. Donaldson Brown, "Centralized Control with Decentralized Responsibility," *American Management Association Annual Convention Series*, no. 57 (New York, 1927), p. 12. Reprinted in Alfred D. Chandler, Jr., ed., *Managerial Innovation at General Motors* (New York: Arno Press, 1979).
49. Chandler, *Strategy and Structure*, p. 373.
50. The full story of the postwar reorganization is told in Allan Nevins and Frank Ernest Hill, *Ford: Decline and Rebirth, 1933-1962* (New York: Scribner's, 1962), chaps. 12 and 13, esp. pp. 324-332. The Edsel story is in ibid., pp. 384-387 and 439-440 and Brooks, *Fate of the Edsel*, title essay.
51. "Behind the Conflict at Chrysler," *Fortune*, November 1960, p. 294.
52. "The Comer at Chrysler Tries a New Road," *Business Week*, July 14, 1974, p. 81; Michael Moritz and Barrett Seaman, *Going for Broke: The Chrysler Story* (Garden City, N.Y.: Doubleday, 1981), pp. 55, 223-226.
53. Sloan, *My Years with General Motors*, p. 477.
54. As of the spring of 1981, four of the top fifteen officers at General Motors, including President James McDonald, were graduates of GMI. See Shawn Tully, "The West Point of General Motors," *Fortune*, March 9, 1981, p. 53.
55. J. Patrick Wright, *On a Clear Day You Can See General Motors: John Z. DeLorean's Look Inside the Automotive Giant* (Grosse Point, Mich.: J. Patrick Wright Enterprises, 1979), pp. 8, 48.
56. Edmund Wilson, *The American Earthquake: A Documentary of the Twenties and Thirties* (Garden City, N.Y.: Doubleday Anchor Books, 1958), pp. 219-220.
57. Charles R. Walker and Robert H. Guest, *The Man on the Assembly Line* (Cambridge, Mass.: Harvard University Press, 1952), p. 51.
58. *General Motors and the United Auto Workers* (HBS Case Services 9-481-142), p. 2.

59. *Lordstown Plant of General Motors (A)* (HBS Case Services 9-475-700), p. 5.
60. White, "The Automobile Industry," p. 205; White, "The Motor Vehicle Industry," in Richard R. Nelson, ed., *Government and Technological Change: A Cross-Industry Analysis* (New York: New York University, Graduate School of Business Administration, Center for Science and Technology, 1982), chap. 8, p. 19.
61. Sloan, *My Years with General Motors*, p. 253.
62. Flink, *American Adopts the Automobile*, pp. 278–288; Abernathy, *The Productivity Dilemma*, passim; Richard Harry Fabris, "A Study of Product Innovation in the Automobile Industry during the Period 1900–1962" (unpublished Ph.D. dissertation, University of Illinois, 1966), passim.
63. For fuller treatments, see James J. Flink, *The Car Culture* (Cambridge, Mass.: MIT Press, 1975), esp. chap. 7, and Emma Rothschild, *Paradise Lost: The Decline of the Auto-Industrial Age* (New York: Random House, 1973), passim.
64. Tucker, "The Wreck of the Auto Industry," pp. 54–57.
65. Daniel Yankelovich, *New Rules: Searching for Self-Fulfillment in a World Turned Upside Down* (New York: Random House, 1981), pp. 41–42.
66. James Brian Quinn, *General Motors Corporation: The Downsizing Decision* (teaching case, The Amos Tuck School of Business Administration, Darthmouth College, Hanover, N.H., 1978), p. 3. General Motors did protest some regulations vigorously, including air bags and fuel emmissions standards.
67. The following discussion draws from ibid.; Kraft, "Annals of Industry"; and three articles by Charles G. Burck in *Fortune*: "How GM Turned Itself Around" (January 16, 1978); "What's Good for the World Should Be Good for General Motors" (May 7, 1979); and "How General Motors Stays Ahead" (March 9, 1981).
68. Quinn, *General Motors*, p. 10.
69. Burck, "How GM Turned Itself Around," p. 87.
70. Quoted in Quinn, *General Motors*, p. 11.
71. Burck, "How GM Turned Itself Around," p. 89.
72. Ibid., p. 96.
73. Quoted in Quinn, *General Motors*, p. 12; cf. pp. 23–24.
74. Burck, "How General Motors Stays Ahead," pp. 52, 53.
75. Quoted in *Business Week*, May 12, 1973, p. 142; see also *General Motors and the United Auto Workers* (HBS Case Services 9-481-142), p. 5.
76. Robert H. Guest, "Quality of Work Life — Learning from Tarrytown," *Harvard Business Review* (July-August, 1979): 85.
77. Quoted in *General Motors and the United Auto Workers*, p. 11.
78. Quoted in ibid., p. 14.
79. Rothschild, *Paradise Lost*, chap. 2. This terminology is not entirely new. In Europe in the 1920s the system of mass production was sometimes called "Fordism."

## Chapter 3.   STEEL: THE SLUMPING GIANT

1. William T. Hogan, *Economic History of the Iron and Steel Industry in the United States* (Lexington, Mass.: Lexington Books, 1971), vol. 1, p. 11; Peter Temin, *Iron and Steel in Nineteenth Century America: An Economic Inquiry* (Cambridge, Mass.: MIT Press, 1964), p. 109.
2. Temin, *Iron and Steel*, pp. 2–3.
3. Ibid., pp. 138–145; Hogan, *Economic History*, vol. 1, pp. 222–223.
4. Temin, *Iron and Steel*, p. 112.
5. Ibid., p. 8.
6. Harold C. Livesay, *Andrew Carnegie and the Rise of Big Business* (Boston: Little, Brown, 1975), p. 101.
7. Joseph Frazier Wall, *Andrew Carnegie* (New York: Oxford University Press, 1970), p. 505.
8. David Brody, *Steelworkers in America: The Nonunion Era* (Cambridge, Mass.: Harvard University Press, 1960), p. 24.
9. James Howard Bridge, *The Inside History of the Carnegie Steel Corporation: A Romance of Millions* (New York: Aldine, 1903), pp. 94–101. Wall, *Carnegie*, pp. 472, 635–636; Livesay, *Carnegie*, p. 166.
10. Temin, *Iron and Steel*, pp. 166–167.
11. Alfred D. Chandler, Jr., *The Visible Hand: The Managerial Revolution in American Business* (Cambridge, Mass.: Harvard University Press, 1977), chaps. 9, 10.
12. U.S. Bureau of Corporations, *Report of the Commissioner of Corporations on the Steel Industry* (Washington, D.C., 1911), vol. 1, pp. 109, 359.
13. Ibid., chap. 2.
14. Ida M. Tarbell, *The Life of Elbert H. Gary: The Story of Steel* (New York: Appleton, 1925), p. 212.
15. Gertrude G. Schroeder, *The Growth of Major Steel Companies, 1900–1950* (Baltimore: Johns Hopkins University Press, 1953), p. 216.
16. Robert Hessen, *Steel Titan: The Life of Charles M. Schwab* (New York: Oxford University Press, 1975), chap. 9, pp. 265–266.
17. Brody, *Steelworkers*, p. 58; cf. Katherine Stone, "The Origins of Job Structures in the Steel Industry," in Richard C. Edwards, Michael Reich, and David M. Gordon, eds., *Labor Market Segmentation* (Lexington, Mass.: Heath, 1975), pp. 27–84, esp. parts 1–3.
18. John A. Fitch, *The Steel Workers* (New York: Charities Publications Committee, 1910).
19. Brody, *Steelworkers*, p. 94; cf. Bridge, *Inside History*, pp. 194–197.
20. C. William Verity, *Faith in Man: The Story of Armco Steel Corporation*, (New York: The Newcomen Society, 1971), p. 18.
21. Hogan, *Economic History*, vol. 3, pp. 857, 834.
22. Schroeder, *Growth of the Major Steel Companies*, Appendix, Tables 1–12 (pp. 216–27).
23. "The Corporation," *Fortune*, March 1936, p. 61.
24. N.S.B. Gras and Henrietta M. Larson, *Casebook in American Business*

*History* (New York: Appleton-Century-Crofts, 1939), p. 607.

25. Walter Adams, "The Steel Industry," in *The Structure of American Industry*, Walter Adams, ed. (New York: MacMillan, 1975), pp. 110-112.

26. Alfred D. Chandler, Jr., *Strategy and Structure: Chapters in the History of the American Industrial Enterprise* (Cambridge, Mass.: MIT Press, 1962), p. 331.

27. Harry Richard Kuniansky, *A Business History of Atlantic Steel Company, 1901-1968* (New York: Arno Press, 1976), pp. 69-70; Chandler, *Strategy and Structure*, pp. 331-337.

28. Chandler, *Strategy and Structure*, pp. 336-337.

29. John N. Ingham, *The Iron Barons: A Social Analysis of an American Urban Elite* (Westport, Conn.: Greenwood Press, 1978), pp. 14-20, 79-82, 231.

30. Quoted in John Moody, *The Truth about Trusts* (New York: Moody, 1904), p. 195.

31. Chandler, *Strategy and Structure*, p. 334.

32. The foregoing description is based on Hogan, *Economic History*, esp. vol. 4, pp. 1677-1685 and information supplied by the U.S. Steel Corporation.

33. Eldon S. Hendriksen, *Capital Expenditures in the Steel Industry, 1900-1953* (New York: Arno Press, 1978), p. 184.

34. Ibid., chap. 5.

35. Hogan, *Economic History*, vol. 4, chap. 41. *Steel Industry Process Note* (HBS Case Services 9-677-145), pp. 14-16, 19-21.

36. "The Corporation," *Fortune*, March 1936, p. 170.

37. Adams, "Steel Industry," p. 118.

38. J. R. Meyer and G. Herregat, "The Basic Oxygen Steel Process," in L. Nasbeth and G. F. Ray, eds., *The Diffusion of New Industrial Processes: An International Study* (Cambridge: Cambridge University Press, 1974), p. 146.

39. Clinton S. Golden and Harold J. Ruttenberg, *The Dynamics of Industrial Democracy*, (New York: Harper and Brothers, 1942), p. xi; Robert R. R. Brooks, *As Steel Goes . . . Unionism in a Basic Industry*, (New Haven: Yale University Press, 1940), p. 190.

40. Golden and Ruttenberg, *Dynamics of Industrial Democracy*, p. xxvi.

41. Putnam, Hayes, and Bartlett, *The Economic Implications of Foreign Steel Pricing Practices in the U.S. Market* (n.p., American Iron and Steel Institute, August, 1978), pp. ii-iii. These figures have been challenged by the Japanese and others: Hans G. Mueller and Kiyoshi Kawahito, *Errors and Biases in the 1978 Putnam, Hayes and Bartlett Study on the Pricing of Imported Steel* (Middle Tennessee State University, Business and Economic Research Center, Monograph Series, no. 173, Murfreesboro, Tenn., January 1979).

42. *The Steel Industry and Imports (A) 1977* (HBS Case Services 9-379-041), p. 4.

43. David M. Roderick, "Business and Government: Removing the Roadblocks to Progress," address at the Harvard Business School, March 3, 1980.

44. American Iron and Steel Institute, *Steel at the Crossroads* (Washington, D.C., 1980), pp. 43, 69, 71–72.
45. *President John F. Kennedy Confronts the U.S. Steel Companies* (HBS Case Services 9-474-762), p. 3.
46. American Iron and Steel Institute, *Steel at the Crossroads*, pp. 73–74, 79–80.
47. Council on Wage and Price Stability, *Prices and Costs in the United States Steel Industry* (Washington, D.C., 1976), p. 4.
48. Quoted in *The U.S. Federal Government and the Steel Problem* (HBS Case Services 1-380-105), pp. 10, 8.
49. Ibid., p. 22.
50. *Business Week*, April 21, 1980, pp. 144–145.
51. Ibid.
52. Roderick "Business and Government."
53. Robert W. Crandall, *The Steel Industry in Recurrent Crisis* (Washington, D.C.: The Brookings Institution, 1981), p. 17; *The Steel Industry and Imports (C)* (HBS Case Services 9-379-043), pp. 3, 9; cf. American Iron and Steel Institute, *Steel at the Crossroads*, pp. 28–31.
54. Hogan, *Economic History*, vol. 5, pp. 1869, 1974.
55. Crandall, *Steel Industry in Recurrent Crisis*, pp. 20–21; Crandall, "The Roots of the Current 'Crisis' in the U.S. Steel Industry: An International Perspective," in Harold R. Williams, ed., *Free Trade, Fair Trade, and Protection: The Case of Steel* (Kent, Ohio: Kent State Steel Seminar, 1978), pp. 49, 53.
56. National Materials Advisory Board, Commission on Sociotechnical Systems, National Research Council, *Report of the Committee on the Steel Industry Study for the Office of Science and Technology Policy* (Washington, D.C.: National Academy of Sciences, 1978), p. 14.
57. Quoted in Luc Kiers, *The American Steel Industry: Problems, Challenges, Perspectives* (Boulder, Col.: Westview Press, 1980), p. 78.
58. Quoted in *U.S. Government and the Steel Problem* (HBS Case Services 1-380-105), p. 16.
59. Ingham, *Iron Barons*, pp. 14–20, 231.
60. Joseph V. Barks and Keith W. Bennett, "Why America Can't Afford to Overlook the Human Side of Productivity," *Chilton's Iron Age*, October 1, 1979, pp. 28–50.
61. American Iron and Steel Institute, *Steel at the Crossroads*, chap. 6.
62. Mayor George Vukovich, quoted in the *Boston Globe*, May 19, 1980, p. 3.
63. U.S. Steel Corporation, annual report (1979), p. 3.
64. Armco, Inc., annual report (1980), p. 4. Armco is running ahead of earlier projections in its race to diversify: see David Clutterbuck, "Armco Builds a Superior Company out of Steel," *International Management*, November 1979, and this volume, Chapter 7.
65. *Armco and the Bubble Policy (C)* (HBS Case Services 0-381-228), pp. 11–12.
66. *Inland Steel Corporation* (HBS Case Services 9-413-058), passim.
67. Inland Steel Corp., annual report (1979).

68. *U.S. Federal Government and the Steel Problem* (HBS Case Services 1-380-105), p. 17.
69. *Inland Steel Coal Company (A): The Sesser Coal Mine in 1977* and *Inland Steel Coal Company (B): The Sesser Mine and the 1978 Operations Task Force* (HBS Case Services 1-380-189 and -190).
70. Lydia Chavez, "The Rise of Steel Mini-Mills," *New York Times*, September 23, 1981, pp. D1 and D6; Douglas R. Sease, "Mini-Mill Steelmakers, No Longer Very Small, Outperform Big Ones," *Wall Street Journal*, January 12, 1981, pp. 1, 19.
71. Richard I. Kirkland, Jr., "Pilgrim's Profits at Nucor," *Fortune*, April 6, 1981, p. 43.
72. *Nucor Corporation* (HBS Case Services 9-676-078), p. 2; annual reports.
73. Quoted in *Chilton's Iron Age*, May 19, 1980, p. 13.
74. *Nucor Corporation* (HBS Case Services 9-676-078), p. 10.
75. Kirkland, "Pilgrim's Profits," p. 44.
76. Nucor Corporation, annual report (1980), p. 4.
77. Robert F. Huber, "Service Centers—Customers Talk It Out," *Production*, June 1977, pp. 74–78.
78. Ibid., p. 77.

## Chapter 4.   HOSPITALS:
## A VERY SPECIAL CASE

1. Eliot Freidson, *Professional Dominance: The Social Structure of Medical Care* (New York: Atherton Press, 1970), pp. 174–175.
2. Henry E. Sigerist, "An Outline of the Development of the Hospital," *Bulletin of the History of Medicine*, 4 (1936), 576–579; George Rosen, "The Hospital: Historical Sociology of a Community Institution," in Eliot Freidson, ed., *The Hospital in Modern Society* (New York: Free Press, 1963), p. 32.
3. Brian Abel-Smith, *The Hospitals in England and Wales, 1800–1948* (Cambridge, Mass.: Harvard University Press, 1964), pp. 6–7; see John D. Thompson and Grace Goldin, *The Hospital: A Social and Architectural History* (New Haven: Yale University Press, 1975), p. 84 for a description of a sixteenth-century London hospital, St. Thomas's.
4. William H. Williams, *America's First Hospital: The Pennsylvania General Hospital, 1751–1841* (Wayne, Pa.: Haverford House, 1976), p. 8 and chap. 2. Staff doctors at the Pennsylvania General Hospital were not salaried in the early years.
5. J. M. Toner, "Statistics of Regional Medical Associations and Hospitals of the United States," *Transactions of the American Medical Association*, 24 (1873): 314–315. These totals have been adjusted to omit mental hospitals by Morris J. Vogel, *The Invention of the Modern Hospital: Boston, 1870–1930* (Chicago: University of Chicago Press, 1980), p. 1.
6. David Rosner, *A Once Charitable Enterprise: Health Care in Brooklyn and New York* (New York: Cambridge University Press, forthcoming)

Paul Starr, "The Reconstitution of the Hospital," chap. 5 of *The Social Transformation of American Medicine*, (New York: Basic Books, forthcoming).

7. Vogel, *Invention of the Modern Hospital*, pp. 2–3; Vogel, "The Transformation of the American Hospital, 1850–1920," in Susan Reverby and David Rosner, eds., *Health Care in America: Historical Essays* (Philadelphia: Temple University Press, 1979), pp. 105–116; Rosner, *A Once Charitable Enterprise*, passim.

8. Milton I. Roemer and Jay W. Friedman, *Doctors in Hospitals: Medical Staff Organization and Hospital Performance* (Baltimore: Johns Hopkins Press, 1971), chap. 2; E. H. L. Corwin, *The American Hospital* (New York: The Commonwealth Fund, 1946), pp. 142–145.

9. Charles E. Rosenberg, "Inward Vision and Outward Glance: The Shaping of the American Hospital, 1880–1914," *Bulletin of the History of Medicine*, 53 (1979): 361–362; Rosner, *A Once Charitable Enterprise*, chap. 6.

10. Vogel, *Invention of the Modern Hospital*, pp. 67–68; E. H. Lewinski-Corwin, *The Hospital Situation in Greater New York* (New York: Putnam's, 1924), p. 122. This proportion appears to hold nationwide: Odin Anderson, *The Uneasy Equilibrium: Private and Public Financing of Health Services in the U.S., 1875–1965* (New Haven: College and University Press, 1968), p. 30.

11. Rosner, *A Once Charitable Enterprise*, chap. 3, table 2; cf. Vogel, *Invention of the Modern Hospital*, pp. 73–74.

12. Starr, "Reconstitution of the Hospital," and William A. Glaser, "American and Foreign Hospitals: Some Social Comparisons," in Freidson, *The Hospital in Modern Society*, pp. 37–72.

13. William Deakins White, "Occupational, Licensure and the Labor Market for Clinical Laboratory Personnel, 1900–1973" (unpublished Harvard University Ph.D. thesis, 1975), pp. 222–230.

14. Quoted in Starr, "Reconstitution of the Hospital."

15. C. Rufus Rorem, *The Public's Investment in Hospitals* (Chicago: University of Chicago Press, 1930), pp. 122–123.

16. Malcolm T. MacEachern and Carl Erickson, "Hospital Planning from the Days of Nickel Plate," *The Modern Hospital*, 51 (September 1938): 92.

17. U.S. Bureau of the Census, *Historical Statistics of the United States Colonial Times to 1970* (Washington, D.C., 1976), series B319-20, B329-30, B345, and B357. See also, Michael M. Davis and C. Rufus Rorem, *The Crisis in Hospital Finance and Other Studies in Hospital Economics* (Chicago: University of Chicago Press, 1932), pp. 3–15. Figures: total number of hospitals: 7,370 in 1924, 6,665 in 1929; number of proprietary hospitals: 2,397 in 1924, 1,939 in 1934; number of general hospitals in the total number of hospitals: 3,793 of 6,830, 56% in 1923; 4,268 of 6,665, 64% in 1929.

18. Ernst C. Meyer, *The Hospital Executive: His Functions, His Administrative Position, and His Training* (typescript report presented to the Rockefeller Foundation, August 4, 1920), p. 25.

19. Rorem, *Public's Investment*, p. 210.
20. Charlotte Aikens, ed., *Hospital Management* (Philadelphia: Saunders, 1911); Rorem, *Public's Investment*. Earlier books with titles including something about hospitals and organization tended to focus primarily on design and construction of the institutions.
21. Asa Bacon, "Operating Room Economics," *Trained Nurse and Hospital Review* (April 1913), pp. 202–204, quoted by Susan Reverby, chap. 6 of draft dissertation, pp. 6–13 to 6–15. We are grateful to Ms. Reverby for allowing us to see this material in draft form.
22. On the duties, powers, and significance of the superintendent, see George P. Ludlum, "The Superintendent," in Aikens, ed., *Hospital Management*, chap. 3, pp. 79–96; Rosenberg, "Inward Vision," 363–365. The quotation is from Meyer, *The Hospital Executive*, pp. 27, 48–49. Cf. Commission on Hospital Care, *Hospital Care in the United States* (New York: The Commonwealth Fund, 1947), p. 512. See also, Michael M. Davis, *Hospital Administration: A Career* (New York, 1929), pp. 5–7.
23. Daniel S. Hirschfield, *The Lost Reform: The Campaign for Compulsory Health Insurance in the United States from 1932 to 1943* (Cambridge, Mass: Harvard University Press, 1970); Anderson, *Uneasy Equilibrium*, chaps. 11, 12.
24. Frank Gilbreth, "Scientific Management in the Hospital," *Transactions of the American Hospital Association*, 1914, p. 492, quoted by Reverby, p. 6–27. See also, Reverby, " 'Borrowing a Volume from Industry:' A Study of Management Reform in American Hospitals, 1910–1945," unpublished paper, September 1975, pp. 17–20 and 27–31; and Rosenberg, "Inward Vision," pp. 380–383.
25. Rosemary Stevens, *American Medicine and the Public Interest* (New Haven: Yale University Press, 1971), pp. 66–68.
36. A copy of the American College of Surgeons' Minimum Standard (1918) is printed behind the frontispiece of Malcolm T. MacEachern, *Hospital Organization and Management* (Chicago: Physicians' Record Co., 1935).
27. Ibid., pp. 506–507; Stevens, *American Medicine*, part 2, and table A1, p. 542.
28. I. S. Falk, C. Rufus Rorem, and Martha D. Ring, *The Costs of Medical Care*, publication of the Committee on the Costs of Medical Care, no. 27 (Chicago: University of Chicago Press, 1933), p. 306. Between 1927 and 1933, the Committee on Costs of Medical Care, a group of prominent physicians, public health officials, and social scientists, published twenty-eight volumes documenting the inadequacies of the contemporary hospital system and called for modest administrative reforms.
29. James D. Thompson, *Organizations in Action* (New York: McGraw-Hill, 1967), p. 17. Cf. Jeffrey E. Harris, "The Internal Organization of Hospitals: Some Economic Implications," *Bell Journal of Economics*, 8 (Autumn, 1977), pp. 467–482, esp. pp. 469–470.
30. Quoted by Ivan L. Bennett, Jr., "Technology as a Shaping Force," in John H. Knowles, ed., *Doing Better and Feeling Worse: Health in the United States* (New York: Norton, 1977), p. 126. This book originally appeared as the winter 1977 issue of *Daedalus*.

31. Ibid., pp. 128-129.
32. Quoted in Anderson *The Uneasy Equilibrium*, p. 101.
33. Eliot Freidson, *Profession of Medicine* (New York: Dodd, Mead, 1970), pp. 183-184; Harris, "The Internal Organization of Hospitals," p. 475.
34. Commission on Hospital Care, *Hospital Care*, chap. 34; Corwin, *The American Hospital*, pp. 66-67.
35. Vogel, *Invention of the Modern Hospital*, p. 122.
36. Commission on Hospital Care, *Hospital Care*, pp. 498-499; U.S. Bureau of the Census, *Historical Statistics*, series B247.
37. See sources for Table 4.3 and Martin S. Feldstein and Amy Taylor, *The Rapid Rise of Hospital Costs*, staff report of the Council on Wage and Price Stability (Washington, D.C., January, 1977), p. 8.
38. Feldstein and Taylor, *The Rapid Rise of Hospital Costs*, p. 31.
39. Martin S. Feldstein, *The Rising Cost of Hospital Care*, (Washington, D.C.: Information Resources Press, 1971), p. 76.
40. Edward D. David, Jr., quoted by Bennett, "Technology as a Shaping Force," p. 127. Another indicator of information complexity is the sheer volume of published information about medical practice. The AMA's *Quarterly Cumulative Index Medicus* ceased publication in 1958 after cataloging some 60,000 articles. It was estimated that nearly a quarter million articles on medicine appeared annually in the mid-60s: David D. Rutstein, *The Coming Revolution in Medicine* (Cambridge, Mass.: MIT Press, 1967), p. 11.
41. J. Douglas Colman, late head of the Blue Cross program in New York, quoted in Victor S. Fuchs, *Who Shall Live? Health, Economics, and Social Choice* (New York: Basic Books, 1974), p. 81.
42. Ernest W. Saward and Scott Fleming, "Health Maintenance Organizations," *Scientific American*, 243 (October 1980): 47.
43. Quoted by Temple Burling, Edith M. Lentz, and Robert N. Wilson, *The Give and Take in Hospitals: A Study of Human Organization in Hospitals* (New York: Putnam's, 1956), p. 38.
44. Basil S. Georgopoulos and Floyd C. Mann, *The Community General Hospital* (New York: Macmillan, 1962), pp. 6-8. The first chapter of this volume, esp. pp. 5-15, provides an excellent introduction to hospital organization.
45. Ibid., p. 268.
46. Victor S. Fuchs, "The Economics of Health in a Post-Industrial Society," *The Public Interest*, 56 (1979): 3.
47. Freidson, *Professional Dominance*, passim.
48. Charles E. Rosenberg, "The Hospital in America: A Century's Perspective," in *Medicine and Society: Contemporary Medical Problems in Historical Perspective* (Philadelphia: American Philosophical Library, 1971), pub. no. 4, p. 193.
49. Ivan Illich, *Medical Nemesis: The Expropriation of Health* (New York: Pantheon, 1976), p. 3 and chap. 2. The list of recent books written for a popular audience that criticizes American health care is a long one. See for example: Fuchs, *Who Shall Live?*; Knowles, ed., *Doing Better and Feeling Worse* (more moderate than most); Barbara and John

Ehrenreich, eds., *The American Health Empire: Power, Profits, and Politics* (New York: Vintage Books, 1971); Rick J. Carlson, *The End of Medicine* (New York: John Wiley, 1975); and David Kotelchuck, ed., *Prognosis Negative: Crisis in the Health Care System* (New York: Vintage Books, 1976).

50. *Note on Federal Regulation of the Hospital Industry* (HBS Case Services 1-381-068), p. 12. The next several paragraphs are based on information provided in this *Note*.

51. There is evidence that such rate-setting programs have been effective in controlling costs: See Brian Biles, Carl J. Schramm, and J. Graham Atkinson, "Hospital Cost Inflation under State Rate-Setting Programs," *New England Journal of Medicine*, 303 (September 12, 1980): 664–668. For a contrasting view, however, see: Alain C. Enthoven, *Health Plan: The Only Practical Solution to the Soaring Cost of Medical Care* (Reading, Mass.: Addison-Wesley, 1980), pp. 95–101.

52. Congress raised this figure to $150,000 in 1979.

53. James F. Blumstein, "The Role of PSROs in Hospital Cost Containment," in Michael Zubkoff, Ira E. Raskin, and Ruth S. Hanft, eds., *Hospital Cost Containment: Selected Notes for Future Policy* (New York: Published for the Milbank Memorial Fund by PRODIST, 1978), pp. 462, 467. It should be noted, as Blumstein does, that PSROs have not been uniformly effective in reducing costs while they have created tension between local and national physicians' groups.

54. Enthoven, *Health Plan*, chaps. 5, 6.

55. Duncan Neuhauser, "The Hospital as a Matrix Organization," in Jonathon S. Rakich and Kurt Darr, eds., *Hospital Organization and Management* (New York: SP Medical & Scientific Books, 1978), pp. 36–37. cf. Alan Sheldon, *Organizational Issues in Health Care Management* (New York: SP Medical & Scientific Books, 1975), pp. 72–74 and 92–105; and Sheldon, *Managing Change and Collaboration in the Health System* (Cambridge, Mass.: Oelgeschlager, Gunn & Hain, 1979), pp. 164–165.

56. *Note on the Hospital Management Industry* (HBS Case Services 9-377-169), p. 22. 1978 total computed from information in *Statistical Abstract of the United States, 1980*.

57. Thomas A. Barocci, *Non-Profit Hospitals: Their Structure, Human Resources, and Economic Importance* (Boston: Auburn House, 1981), p. 89. David G. Williamson, Jr., "The Investor Owned Approach," in B. Jon Jaeger, ed., *A Decade of Implementation: The Multiple Hospital Management Concept Revisited*, a report of the 1975 National Forum on Hospital and Health Affairs, (Durham, N.C., 1975), p. 47.

58. *Hospital Affiliates International, Inc. (A)* (HBS Case Services 9-377-170), p. 28. In August, 1981, Hospital Affiliates International was acquired by Hospital Corporation of America.

59. Hospital Corporation of America, 1970 stock prospectus, quoted by Lynda Diane Baydin and Alan Sheldon, "Corporate Models in Health Care Delivery," in Rakich and Darr, eds., *Hospital Organization and Management*, p. 71.

60. *Hospital Affiliates International, Inc. (A)*, p. 26; *Note on the Hospital Management Industry*, pp. 12, 25; Hospital Corporation of America, Annual Report (1981), pp. 1, 22; Jeff C. Goldsmith, "Outlook for Hospitals: Systems are the Solution," *Harvard Business Review* (September–October, 1981), pp. 130–136, esp. p. 133.

61. *Note on the Hospital Management Industry*, p. 11.

62. Ibid., p. 2.

63. Scott A. Mason, ed., *Multihospital Arrangements: Public Policy Implications* (Chicago: American Hospital Association, 1979), p. 4; cf. a similar chart in Sheldon, *Managing Change and Collaboration*, p. 38.

64. Diana Barrett, *Multihospital Systems: The Process of Development* (Cambridge, Mass.: Oelgeschlager, Gunn & Hain, 1980), p. 1.

65. Ibid., p. 4. Slightly lower estimates appear in Montague Brown and Howard L. Lewis, *Hospital Management Systems: Multi-Unit Organization and Delivery of Health Care* (Germantown, Md.: Aspen Systems Corporation, 1976), pp. 30–31. Brown and Lewis provide brief descriptions of each MHS by region.

66. Mason, ed., *Multihospital Arrangements*, p. 2.

67. Montague Brown, "An Overview," in Mason, ed., *Multihospital Arrangements*, pp. 17–18, 20.

68. Brown and Lewis, *Hospital Management Systems*, pp. 66, 69–70.

69. James P. Cooney, Jr. and Thomas L. Alexander, *Multihospital Systems: An Evaluation*, part 1, *An Overview* (Chicago: Health Services Research Center, Hospital Research and Educational Trust, and Northwestern University, 1975), p. 48. These advantages were most notable in older systems; indeed, the two youngest MHSs in the study were found to be less effective than the independent hospitals. Cooney and Alexander suggest that there may be a period of adjustment of two to three years after the establishment of a MHS before it begins to pay off. This finding is corroborated by Barrett, *Multihospital Systems*, pp. 144–150.

70. Robert Duncan, David P. Gilfallan, William H. Money, and Harold P. Welsch, *Organizational Studies* (part 2 of Cooney and Alexander, eds., *Multihospital Systems*), pp. 92–94, 143–150; Dan L. Dearden, "Comprehensiveness, Availability, and Quality of Care in a Multihospital System," in ibid., part 4, pp. 20–24. Brown and Lewis, *Hospital Management Systems*, pp. 288–291, argue that while MHSs increase the power of administrators, they also offer advantages to doctors such as more attention to specialized needs, a wider range of services, more flexibility to permit different types of private practice, and better teaching facilities.

71. Brown, "An Overview," in Mason, ed., *Multihospital Arrangements*, pp. 16–17.

72. Stanley Joel Reiser, *Medicine and the Reign of Technology* (New York: Cambridge University Press, 1978), p. 154.

73. Ibid., pp. 156–157.

74. The general notion of ambulatory care with emphasis on preventive medicine dates back to the emergence of "dispensaries" in the eighteenth and nineteenth centuries, and "neighborhood health centers" in the early twentieth century. See George Rosen, "The First Neighborhood Health

Center Movement—Its Rise and Fall," *American Journal of Public Health*, 61 (1971): 1620–1637; and Charles Rosenberg, "Social Class and Medical Care in Nineteenth-Century America: The Rise and Fall of the Dispensary," *Journal of the History of Medicine & Allied Sciences*, 29 (1974): 32–54.

75. Saward and Fleming, "Health Maintenance Organizations," p. 47; Roger W. Birnbaum, *Health Maintenance Organizations: A Guide to Planning and Development* (New York: SP Books, 1976), p. 5; Harold S. Luft, "Health Maintenance Organizations, Competition, Cost Containment, and National Health Insurance," in Mark V. Pauly, ed., *National Health Insurance: What Now, What Later, What Never?* (Washington, D.C.: American Enterprise Institute for Public Policy Research, 1980), p. 284.

76. Luft, "Health Maintenance Organizations," pp. 285–286.

77. Saward and Fleming, "Health Maintenance Organizations," p. 51. The HMO statute, PL 93-222, is printed in Birnbaum, *Health Maintenance Organizations*, pp. 105–127.

78. Ibid., pp. 287, 290; Saward and Fleming, "Health Maintenance Organizations," p. 50.

79. Luft, "Health Maintenance Organizations," p. 292.

80. The intensive study of Duncan, et al., *Organizational Studies* (part II of Cooney and Alexander, eds., *Multihospital Systems*), pp. 242–244 shows mixed results on this point. They found that doctors and corporate staff in the larger, more prestigious hospitals in one MHS generally disapproved of the merger and new methods but that personnel in the less wealthy, rural hospitals were more positive about the changes. These results may be vitiated by the comparative youth of the MHS concept, however.

81. Ibid., pp. 147–148, 288–305.

## Chapter 5.   AGRICULTURE:
## THE AMERICAN MIRACLE

1. Willard W. Cochrane, *The Development of American Agriculture: A Historical Analysis* (Minneapolis: University of Minnesota Press, 1979), p. 110. Chapters 5 and 6 of this volume provide a good survey of farming between the Civil War and the Great Depression.

2. David E. Conrad, *Forgotten Farmers: The Story of Sharecroppers in the New Deal* (Urbana: University of Illinois Press, 1965), pp. 1–2. Trend data from U.S. Bureau of the Census, *Historical Statistics of the United States, Colonial Times to 1970* (Washington, D.C., 1976), series K113 and K124.

3. Lawrence A. Jones and David Durand, *Mortgage Lending Experience in Agriculture* (Princeton: Princeton University Press, 1954), p. 8.

4. Willard W. Cochrane, *Farm Prices: Myth and Reality*, (Minneapolis: University of Minneapolis Press, 1958), p. 15; James H. Shideler, *Farm Crisis 1919–1923* (Berkeley: University of California Press, 1957), chaps. 2, 7, 8.

5. Jones and Durand, *Mortgage Lending*, p. 10. Cf. Van L. Perkins, *Crisis in Agriculture: The Agricultural Adjustment Administration and the New Deal* (Berkeley: University of California Press, 1969), pp. 11, 18–19.
6. Jones and Durand, *Mortgage Lending*, p. 10; William E. Leuchtenberg, *Franklin D. Roosevelt and the New Deal, 1932–1940* (New York: Harper & Row, 1963), pp. 23–24.
7. The report is excerpted in Wayne D. Rasmussen, ed., *Agriculture in the United States: A Documentary History* (New York: Random House, 1975), pp. 2,102–2,120, esp. p. 2,108.
8. See Theodore Saloutos and John D. Hicks, *Agricultural Discontent in the Middle West, 1900–1939* (Madison: University of Wisconsin Press, 1951) for a survey, and John L. Shover, *Cornbelt Rebellion: The Farmers' Holiday Association* (Urbana: University of Illinois Press, 1965), esp. pp. 80–81, for the troubles in Iowa.
9. Farmer Harry Terrell quoted in Studs Terkel, ed., *Hard Times: An Oral History of the Great Depression* (New York: Pantheon, 1970), pp. 214–215.
10. Quoted in Berton Roueché, *The River World and Other Explorations* (New York: Harper & Row, 1978), p. 171.
11. Murray R. Benedict, *Farm Policies of the United States, 1790–1950: A Study of Their Origins and Development* (New York: The Twentieth Century Fund, 1953), p. 235.
12. Perkins, *Crisis in Agriculture*, p. 21.
13. Benedict, *Farm Policies*, p. 267.
14. Wayne D. Rasmussen, Gladys L. Baker, and James S. Ward, *A Short History of Agricultural Adjustment, 1933–75* (Washington, D.C.: U.S. Department of Agriculture, Economic Research Service, Agriculture Information Bulletin 39, 1976), pp. 5–6.
15. Paul E. Mertz, *New Deal Politics and Southern Rural Poverty* (Baton Rouge: Louisiana State University Press, 1978), pp. 28–29. The Federal Emergency Relief Administration had been concerned with rural poverty before 1935.
16. Richard S. Kirkendall, *Social Scientists and Farm Politics in the Age of Roosevelt* (Columbia, Mo.: University of Missouri Press, 1966), pp. 109–119, 128–129; Paul K. Conkin, *Tomorrow a New World: The New Deal Community Program* (Ithaca: Cornell University Press, 1959), chap. 7, esp. pp. 153 ff.
17. Rasmussen, Baker, and Ward, *Short History of Agricultural Adjustment*, p. 39.
18. Ibid., p. 42.
19. Benedict, *Farm Policies*, p. 312; Theodore Saloutos, "New Deal Agricultural Policy: An Evaluation," *Journal of American History* 61 (1974): 394–416.
20. Edward D. Eddy, Jr., *Colleges for Our Land and Time: The Land-Grant Idea in American Education* (New York: Harper and Brothers, 1957), p. 176.
21. Ibid., p. 158.
22. Saloutos, "New Deal Agricultural Policy," p. 399.

23. John T. Schlebecker, *Whereby We Thrive: A History of American Farming, 1607–1972* (Ames, Iowa: Iowa State University Press, 1975), pp. 226–230.

24. Cf. Cochrane, *Development of American Agriculture*, pp. 124–125.

25. John L. Shover, *First Majority Last Minority: The Transforming of Rural Life in America* (DeKalb, Ill.: Northern Illinois University Press, 1976), p. 4.

26. It is difficult to make more than the most general statements about rural outmigration since there is little objective research to go on. Most studies are flavored by opinions as to whether the quality of life in the northern industrial cities represented an improvement over rural poverty. Conrad, the historian of the southern sharecroppers, concludes that the effects of the New Deal were harsh on tenants, but that they probably went on to better lives away from farming. Conrad, *Forgotten Farmers*, p. 209.

27. U.S. Bureau of the Census, *Historical Statistics*, series K109 and K113; and *Statistical Abstract, 1980*, p. 689.

28. Ed Edwin, *Feast or Famine: Food, Farming, and Farm Politics in America* (New York: Charterhouse, 1974), pp. 288–289.

29. Mark Kramer, *Three Farms: Making Milk, Meat and Money from the American Soil* (Boston: Little, Brown, 1980), p. 104,; cf. pp. 161–162.

30. Lowry Nelson, *American Farm Life* (Cambridge, Mass.: Harvard University Press, 1954), p. 69.

31. Wayne D. Rasmussen, "The Impact of Technological Change on American Agriculture, 1862–1962," *Journal of Economic History*, 22 (1962); 578–591, esp. 588–590.

32. Schlebecker, *Whereby We Thrive*, chap. 22.

33. Ibid., p. 249.

34. Statistics derived from charts in U.S. Department of Agriculture, *Agricultural Handbook*, no. 318 (1966).

35. Wendell Berry, *The Unsettling of America: Culture and Agriculture* (San Francisco: The Sierra Club, 1977), p. 33.

36. *Business Week*, June 1, 1981, p. 71.

37. U.S. Department of Agriculture, *Status of the Family Farm*, second annual report to the Congress (Washington, D.C.: 1979), pp. 7–8; Lyle P. Schertz et al., *Another Revolution in U.S. Farming?* (Washington, D.C.: U.S. Department of Agriculture, 1979), p. 23.

   For a contrasting analysis to the one presented here, see the more pessimistic views in: U.S. General Accounting Office, *Changing Character and Structure of American Agriculture: An Overview* (Washington, D.C., 1978), and Ingolf Vogeler, *The Myth of the Family Farm: Agribusiness Dominance of U.S. Agriculture* (Boulder: Westview Press, 1981), chap. 7.

38. Philip M. Raup, "Corporate Farming in the United States," *Journal of Economic History*, 33 (1973): 280–281.

39. Edwin, *Feast or Famine*, p. 284; U.S. Congressional Budget Office, *Public Policy and the Changing Situation of American Agriculture* (Washington, D.C., 1978), p. 20.

40. Lynda Schuster, "Farming Did In Many, but some Corporations Are Making a Go of It," *Wall Street Journal*, August 31, 1981, p. 1.

41. Raup, "Corporate Farming," p. 282.
42. Logic paraphrased and quotations taken from Kramer, *Three Farms*, pp. 249–251.
43. John H. Davis and Ray A. Goldberg, *A Concept of Agribusiness* (Boston, Mass.: Division of Research, Graduate School of Business Administration, Harvard University, 1957), p. 2.
44. U.S. Department of Agriculture, *Status of the Family Farm*, pp. 10–11.
45. Ibid., pp. 14–15. Some economists worry that farmers who submit to agribusiness contracts may sacrifice their entrepreneurial interests. To date, however, evidence on this point is inconclusive. See Marshall Harris, *Entrepreneurial Control in Farming* (Washington, D.C.: U.S. Department of Agriculture, Economic Research Service, 1974), no. 542, pp. 4–6.
46. U.S. Congressional Budget Office, *Public Policy*, pp. 11–14.
47. Ibid., pp. 3–5.
48. Glenn V. Fuguitt, "The Places Left Behind: Population Trends and Policy for Rural America," *Rural Sociology*, 36 (1971): 449–469.
49. Shover, *First Majority*, pp. 75–76.
50. Quoted in Roueché, *The River World*, p. 178.
51. U.S. Bureau of the Census, *Statistical Abstract, 1980*, p. 698.
52. U.S. Department of Agriculture, *Status of the Family Farm*, p. 6.
53. Quoted in Maisie Conrat and Richard Conrat, *The American Farm: A Photographic History* (Boston: Houghton Mifflin, 1977), p. 228.
54. Jim Hightower, *A Summary of Hard Tomatoes, Hard Times* (Washington, D.C.: Agribusiness Accountability Project, 1972), p. 15.
55. Dan Morgan, *Merchants of Grain* (New York: Viking Press, 1979), p. 158.
56. Yao-chi Lu, *Prospects for Productivity Growth in U.S. Agriculture* (Washington, D.C.: U.S. Department of Agriculture, Economics, Statistics, and Cooperatives Service, 1979), pp. 1–3.
57. William Lin, George Coffman, and J.B. Penn, *U.S. Farm Numbers, Sizes, and Related Structural Dimensions: Projections to the Year 2000*, (Washington, D.C.: U.S. Department of Agriculture, Economics, Statistics, and Cooperatives Service, July 1980), pp. iii–iv.
58. Harris, *Entrepreneurial Control*, pp. 13–17.
59. Quoted in Roueché, *The River World*, p. 184.

## Chapter 6.  RESIDENTIAL CONSTRUCTION: A HIDDEN RESOURCE

1. Robert Gibson Eccles, Jr., "Organization and Market Structure in the Construction Industry" (unpublished Ph.D. dissertation, Harvard University, 1979), App. C and Eccles, "Subcontracting and Management in the Homebuilding Industry: The Role of the Quasi-Firm," unpublished paper, Harvard Business School, July, 1980.
2. Eccles, "Organization and Market Structure," Historical App. B; Clinton C. Bourdon and Raymond E. Levitt, *Union and Open-Shop Construction* (Lexington, Mass.: Lexington Books, 1979), pp. 23–27.

3. Much of the following discussion draws on Miles L. Colean, *American Housing: Problems and Prospects* (New York: The Twentieth Century Fund, 1947); and Sherman J. Maisel, *Housebuilding in Transition* (Berkeley: University of California Press, 1953).

4. James D. Thompson, *Organizations in Action* (New York: McGraw-Hill, 1967), pp. 17–18.

5. Kenneth T. Rosen, *Seasonal Cycles in the Housing Market: Patterns, Costs, and Policies* (Cambridge, Mass.: MIT Press, 1979), esp. chap. 2–3.

6. Kenneth T. Rosen, "Cyclical Fluctuations in Residential Construction and Financing," in Julian E. Lange and Daniel Quinn Mills, eds., *The Construction Industry: Balance Wheel of the Economy* (Lexington, Mass.: Lexington Books, 1979), pp. 115–146.

7. Arthur P. Solomon, "The Cost of Housing: An Analysis of Trends, Incidence, and Causes," in Federal Home Loan Bank of San Francisco, *The Cost of Housing*, (San Francisco, 1977), p. 20.

8. Another indicator that confirms the same cyclical pattern is the failure rate of homebuilding firms. See Franklin E. Williams, "Failures in the Construction Industry, 1967–1976," *Construction Review* (September-October, 1977), pp. 4–20.

9. U.S. Department of Commerce, Bureau of the Census, *1977 Census of Construction Industries*, Industry Series, *General Contractors—Single-Family Houses*, SIC Code 1521, p. 1–7.

10. Eccles, "Organization and Market Structure," p. 436 ff.; Eccles, "Bureaucratic versus Craft Administration: The Relationship of Market Structure to the Construction Firm," *Administrative Sciences Quarterly*, 26 (1981): 451–453; Bourdon and Levitt, *Union and Open-Shop Construction*, pp. 23–27.

11. See "Conclusion" at end of this chapter.

12. In the nineteenth century craftsmen formed trade societies and unions and established work rules to protect against the erosion of their skills. They have successfully maintained their independence ever since. See William Haber, *Industrial Relations in the Building Industry* (New York: Arno Press, 1971; orig. 1930), chap. 10 also pp. 78, 510–511.

13. Eccles, "Organization and Market Structure," chap. 7.

14. This terminology draws from Oliver E. Williamson, *Markets and Hierarchies: Analysis and Antitrust Implications*, (New York: Free Press, 1975).

15. Alfred D. Chandler, Jr., *The Visible Hand: The Managerial Revolution in American Business* (Cambridge, Mass.: Harvard University Press, 1977).

16. Maisel, *Housebuilding in Transition*, p. 59.

17. Eccles, "Organization and Market Structure," App. C; and Eccles, "Subcontracting and Management," pp. 31–49.

18. Daniel Quinn Mills, *Industrial Relations and Manpower in Construction* (Cambridge, Mass.: MIT Press, 1972), p. 262.

19. *Professional Builder*, especially annual surveys of large-scale housing firms in July issues. Latest figures taken from the July, 1981 issue, p. 116.

20. Leo Grebler, *Large Scale Housing and Real Estate Firms* (New York: Praeger, 1973), chap. 3.

21. Arthur L. Stinchcombe, "Bureaucratic and Craft Administration of Production: A Comparative Study," *Administrative Science Quarterly*, 4 (1959-60), p. 181.
22. U.S. Home Corp., Form 10-K (1974), p. 26.
23. U.S. Home Corp., annual report (1978), p. 14.
24. U.S. Department of Housing and Urban Development, *Housing in the Seventies: A Report of the National Housing Policy Review* (Washington, D.C., 1974), pp. 187-194.
25. Alexander Stuart, "U.S. Home's Management Religion," *Fortune*, December 4, 1978, p. 66.
26. *Professional Builder*, July 1981, p. 34.
27. U.S. Home Corp., annual reports.
28. Stuart, "U.S. Home's Management Religion," pp. 66, 68.
29. Michael Sumichrast, Gopal Ahluwalia, and Robert J. Sheehan, *Profile of the Builder* (Washington, D.C.: National Association of Homebuilders, 1979), p. 138.
30. *Professional Builder*, July 1979, p. 123; the 1980 survey shows that larger firms tend to subcontract greater amounts of finish and rough carpentry. Issue of July 1980, p. 77.
31. U.S. Home Corp., annual report (1974), p. 12.
32. Eccles, "Organization and Market Structure," pp. 421-424, 442-445.
33. Grebler, *Large-Scale Housing*, pp. 135-150.
34. The company's own analysis stresses environmentalist opposition to its recreational developments and litigation stemming from alleged unfair sales practices in California as the principal causes of the troubles. Boise Cascade Corp., annual report (1972), pp. 23-24.
35. John Fery, quoted in the *Wall Street Journal*, December 29, 1971.
36. Quoted in Martin Mayer, *The Builders: Houses, People, Neighborhoods, Governments, Money* (New York: Norton, 1978), p. 214.
37. Ibid., chap. 10; and Howard Rudnitsky, "The Centex Story," *Forbes*, February 6, 1978, pp. 64-66.
38. Karl G. Pearson, *Industrialized Housing* (Ann Arbor: Industrial Development Division, Institute of Science and Technology, University of Michigan, 1972), p. 5.
39. U.S. Department of Housing and Urban Development, *Final Report of the Task Force on Housing Costs* (Washington, D.C., May, 1978), p. 1.
40. Steven Rosefielde and Daniel Quinn Mills, "Is Construction Technologically Stagnant?" in Lange and Mills, eds., *The Construction Industry*, pp. 83-114.
41. For a convenient survey of economic studies on productivity in homebuilding, see John M. Quigley, "Residential Construction and Public Policy: A Progress Report," in Richard R. Nelson, ed., *Government and Technical Change: A Cross-Industry Analysis* (New York: New York University, Graduate School of Business Administration, Center for Science and Technology, 1982), chap. 7, esp. table 1. *Professional Builder*'s 1980 survey shows annual growth proceeding at about 2% per year between 1968 and 1980. Issue of July, 1980, p. 96.
42. Albert Rees, "Measuring Productivity in Construction: An Overview," in National Commission on Productivity and Work Quality, *Measuring*

*Productivity in the Construction Industry* (Washington, D.C., 1972), p. 8.

43. Solomon, "Cost of Housing," p. 9.

44. Rosefielde and Mills, "Is Construction Technically Stagnant?" in Lange and Mills, *The Construction Industry*, p. 95.

45. Ibid., p. 91, Quigley, "Residential Construction," is less sanguine.

46. Michael Sumichrast's study (1977) reported in Solomon, "The Cost of Housing," p. 17; cf. U.S. Department of Housing and Urban Development, *Final Report of the Task Force*, pp. 46–47.

47. Solomon, "The Cost of Housing," p. 17; and U.S. Department of Housing and Urban Development, *Final Report of the Task Force*, p. 4 and chaps. 2 and 4.

48. U.S. Department of Housing and Urban Development, *Housing in the Seventies* (Washington, D.C.: A Report of the National Housing Policy Review, 1974), pp. 198–203; Richard Bender, *A Crack in the Rear-view Mirror: A View of Industrialized Building* (New York: Van Nostrand, 1973), pp. 20–57; Quigley, "Residential Construction."

49. James W. Myrtle, "Characteristics of New Housing," *Construction Reports*, April 1979, pp. 4–9.

50. *Professional Builder*, July 1980, pp. 80–83. This survey is not based on a scientific sample.

51. Mayer, *The Builders*, pp. 248–251. Mayer, on the basis of other impressionistic evidence, believes that the business is changing enough that such satisfactions may disappear, however.

## Chapter 7.   COAL:
## THE BORN-AGAIN INDUSTRY

1. U.S. Congress, Office of Technology Assessment, *The Direct Use of Coal: Prospects and Problems of Production and Combustion* (Washington, D.C., 1979), p. 60; Richard A. Schmidt, *Coal in America: An Encyclopedia of Reserves, Production, and Use* (New York: McGraw-Hill, 1979), chap. 3.

2. Hans H. Landsberg, chairman, *Energy: The Next Twenty Years* (Cambridge, Mass.: Ballinger, 1979), p. 278.

3. T. T. Tomimatsu and Robert E. Johnson, *The State of the U.S. Coal Industry: A Financial Analysis of Selected Coal-Producing Companies with Observations on Industry Structure* (Washington, D.C.: U.S. Bureau of Mines, 1976), pp. 25–27.

4. Molly Selvin and Lenore Barkan, *Productivity in the Underground Coal Industry: A Historical Perspective on the Current Decline*, report for the U.S. Department of Energy, Division of Solid Fuels, Mining and Preparation, Budget Activity no. AA-01-01-00 (Seattle: Battelle Memorial Institute, 1979), pp. 17–21.

5. James H. Thompson, *Significant Trends in the West Virginia Coal Industry, 1900–1957* (Morgantown, W.Va.: West Virginia University Press, 1958), pp. 3, 11. William Graebner, "Great Expectations: The Search

for Order in Bituminous Coal, 1890–1917," *Business History Review*, 48 (1974): 49–72.

6. U.S. Federal Trade Commission, *Report of the Federal Trade Commission on the Structure of the Nation's Coal Industry, 1964–1974* (Washington, D.C., 1978), chap. 6; U.S. General Accounting Office, *The State of Competition in the Coal Industry* (Washington, D.C., December 1977), pp. V-1; U.S. Department of Justice, *Competition in the Coal Industry* (Washington, D.C., May 1979), pp. 26, 67.

7. Harold Barger and Sam H. Schurr, *The Mining Industries, 1899–1939: A Study of Output, Employment, and Productivity* (New York: National Bureau of Economic Research, 1944), pp. 120, 123–124.

8. Ibid., pp. 137–141 and Table 7.2.

9. The organization of traditional coal companies shares much in common with the organization of copper firms: see Alfred D. Chandler, Jr., *Strategy and Structure: Chapters in the History of the American Industrial Enterprise* (Cambridge, Mass.: MIT Press, 1962), p. 328.

10. Selvin and Barkan, *Productivity*, pp. 96–97.

11. Carter Goodrich, *The Miner's Freedom: A Study of the Working Life in a Changing Industry* (Boston: Marshall Jones, 1925), pp. 30, 99, 182; cf. Eric L. Trist et al., *Organizational Choice: Capabilities of Groups at the Coal Face under Changing Technologies* (London: Tavistock, 1963) for a view of this process in England.

12. Keith Dix, *Work Relations in the Coal Industry: The Hand-Loading Era, 1880–1930* (Morgantown, W.Va.: University Institute for Labor Studies, 1977), pp. 67–69; cf. Thompson, *Significant Trends*, pp. 33–39.

13. Joseph E. Finley, *The Corrupt Kingdom: The Rise and Fall of the United Mine Workers* (New York: Simon & Schuster, 1972), chap. 5; Saul D. Alinsky, *John L. Lewis: An Unauthorized Biography* (1949, reprinted New York: Vintage Books, 1970), chap. 3. For miners' own recollections of some of these incidents, see Anne Lawrence et al., *On Dark and Bloody Ground: An Oral History of the U.M.W.A. in Central Appalachia, 1920–1935* (n.p., A National Endownment for the Humanities Youthgrant Report, n.d.).

14. The biggest and most authoritative biography of Lewis is by Melvyn Dubovsky and Warren Van Tine, *John L. Lewis: A Biography* (New York: Quadrangle, 1977) but Alinsky's *Lewis: An Unauthorized Biography* is well-written and full of insight.

15. Quoted in Finley, *Corrupt Kingdom*, p. 61.

16. Selvin and Barkan, *Productivity*, pp. 36–37.

17. Finley, *Corrupt Kingdom*, p. 171.

18. Quoted in Finley, *Corrupt Kingdom*, pp. 171–172.

19. In addition to studies already cited, see Mel Horwitch, "Coal: Constrained Abundance," in Robert Stobaugh and Daniel Yergin, eds., *Energy Future: Report of the Energy Project at the Harvard Business School* (New York: Ballantine, 1980), chap. 4; Martin B. Zimmerman, *The U.S. Coal Industry: The Economics of Policy Choice* (Cambridge, Mass.: MIT Press, 1981); Congressional Research Service, *The Coal Industry: Problems and Prospects—A Background Study* (Washington, D.C., 1978);

World Coal Study (WOCOL), *Coal—Bridge to the Future* and *Future Coal Prospects: Country and Regional Assessments* (Cambridge, Mass.: Ballinger, 1980); and the President's Commission on Coal, *Recommendations and Summary Findings* (Washington, D.C., March 1980); Balaji S. Chakravarthy, *Managing Coal: A Challenge in Adaptation* (Albany: State University of New York Press, 1981), chap. 3.

20. U.S. Congress, Office of Technology Assessment, *Direct Use of Coal*, p. 116. The evidence presented by Chakravarthy, *Managing Coal*, p. 185, can be interpreted to support this view, although Chakravarthy does not do so.

21. See Edward J. Mitchell, ed., *Horizontal Divestiture in the Oil Industry* (Washington, D.C.: American Enterprise Institute for Public Policy Research, 1977), for a general discussion of this topic. Papers by Walter Adams and Jesse W. Markham argue the two sides of the question cogently. The National Coal Association (NCA), the industry's major trade association, endorses the new entrants: NCA, *Implications of Investments in the Coal Industry by Firms from Other Energy Industries* (Washington, D.C., September 1977), p. 21.

22. U.S. Congress, Office of Technology Assessment, *Direct Use of Coal*, p. 261.

23. Ibid., p. 147.

24. *Note on the U.S. Coal Industry* (HBS Case Services 9-676-057), pp. 6–7.

25. This discussion draws on Congressional Research Service, *Coal Industry*, pp. 52–57.

26. Ibid., p. 53.

27. *1981 Keystone Coal Industry Manual* (New York: McGraw-Hill, 1981), p. 713; Ann M. Reilly, "A Second Coming for Old King Coal," *Dun's Review*, September 1980, pp. 47, 52.

28. Horwitch, "Coal: Constrained Abundance," p. 104.

29. Chakravarthy, *Managing Coal*, p. 55.

30. Congressional Research Service, *Coal Industry*, p. 27.

31. Charles Simeons, *Coal: Its Role in Tomorrow's Technology. A Sourcebook on Global Coal Resources* (New York: Pergamon Press, 1978), pp. 131–135.

32. Selvin and Barkan, *Productivity*, pp. 8–11; U.S. Congress, Office of Technology Assessment, *Direct Use of Coal*, chap. 4.

33. Selvin and Barkan, *Productivity*, passim.

34. Finley, *Corrupt Kingdom*, chaps. 9–11.

35. National Coal Association, *Implications of Investments*, p. 9; U.S. Congress, Office of Technology Assessment, *Direct Use of Coal*, pp. 135–136.

36. Congressional Research Service, *Coal Industry*, p. 115.

37. Chakravarthy, *Managing Coal*, p. 58.

38. National Coal Association, *Implications of Investments*, pp. 20–21; Chakravarthy, *Managing Coal*, pp. 58–61.

39. Chakravarthy, *Managing Coal*, chaps. 4–7.

40. This section is based on Chakravarthy, *Managing Coal*, chap. 7 and public documents filed by the Exxon Corporation.

41. This section is based on public documents and interview and materials provided by PP&L and NERCO officers. We are grateful to Don C. Fris-

bee, chairman of PP&L, and Gerard K. Drummond, president of NERCO, for their cooperation.

42. These experiences are described most fully in Paul S. Goodman, *Assessing Organizational Change: The Rushton Quality of Work Experiment* (New York: John Wiley, 1979).

43. Quoted in Ted Mills, "Altering the Social Structure in Coal Mining: A Case Study," *Monthly Labor Review*, October 1976, p. 6.

44. This section is adapted from Chakravarthy, *Managing Coal*, chap. 6 and public documents.

45. Chakravarthy, *Managing Coal*, p. 115.

46. Ibid.

47. This discussion draws from company reports, *Coal Age*, March and October, 1979; David Clutterbuck, "Armco Builds a Superior Company out of Steel," *International Management*, November 1979, pp. 41–43; and the *1981 Keystone Coal Industry Manual.*

48. This section is based on Chakravarthy, *Managing Coal*, chap. 5 and public documents.

49. This section draws on Chakravarthy, *Managing Coal*, chap. 4; public documents; *1981 Keystone Coal Industry Manual*, p. 714; and U.S. Congress, Office of Technology Assessment, *Direct Use of Coal*, pp. 120–121.

50. Chakravarthy, *Managing Coal*, p. 71.

51. Ibid., pp. 77–84, 196–198.

52. Ibid., pp. 186–194. As of 1980 NERCO had two senior vice-presidents (resource evaluation, construction and operations) and six vice-presidents (project development and regulatory affairs, business development, finance, marketing, personnel and administration, western mining) reporting to the president. The company also used temporary project teams for certain purposes such as new ventures. Though this evidence is less complete than Chakravarthy's, it appears that NERCO is more highly differentiated than most traditional coal companies and perhaps more highly integrated as well.

## Chapter 8.   TELECOMMUNICATIONS: NEW RULES FOR THE BELL SYSTEM

1. There is a vast and trendy literature on this topic but the following works bear particularly on our theme: Daniel Bell, "Communications Technology—for Better or for Worse," *Harvard Business Review*, May-June 1979; and Ithiel de Sola Pool, ed., *The Social Impact of the Telephone* (Cambridge, Mass.: MIT Press, 1977).

2. Alfred D. Chandler, Jr., *The Visible Hand: The Managerial Revolution in American Business* (Cambridge, Mass.: Harvard University Press, 1977), part 2, esp. chap. 6, pp. 195–203.

3. James H. Madison, "Communications," in Glenn Porter, ed., *Encyclopedia of American Economic History* (New York: Scribner's, 1980), vol. 1, pp. 335–336; Alvin F. Harlow, *Old Wires and New Waves* (New York: Appleton-Century, 1936), chap. 2, esp. p. 23; Robert Luther Thompson,

*Wiring a Continent: The History of the Telegraph Industry in the United States, 1832–1866* (Princeton: Princeton University Press, 1947), p. 11.

4. Thompson, *Wiring a Continent*, chap. 2, esp. pp. 27–34.

5. Harlow, *Old Wires*, p. 116.

6. Richard B. Du Boff, "Business Demand and the Development of the Telegraph in the United States, 1844–1860," *Business History Review*, 54 (Winter 1980): 461.

7. The foregoing discussion draws on Harlow, *Old Wires*; Thompson, *Wiring a Continent*; James D. Reid, *The Telegraph in America* (New York: John Polhemus, 1886); A. R. Brewer, *Western Union Telegraph Company: A Retrospect* (New York: James Kempster, 1901); and Gerald W. Brock, *The Telecommunications Industry: The Dynamics of Market Structure* (Cambridge, Mass.: Harvard University Press, 1981), chap. 3.

8. The Western Union Telegraph Company, *Annual Report of the Directors* (1869), p. 33.

9. Reid, *Telegraph*, p. 140; Western Union, *Statement of the Directors* (October 1, 1865), p. 4.

10. E. B. Grant, *The Western Union Telegraph Company: Its Past, Present, and Future* (New York: Hotchkiss, Burnham, 1883), p. 7; Thompson, *Wiring a Continent*, p. 426.

11. This paragraph draws on Thompson, *Wiring a Continent*, chaps. XVI, XVII and Reid, *Telegraph*, chaps. 35–37 and 41. Western Union's attempt to reach Europe through Alaska, the Bering Straits, and Russia collapsed in 1866 when a British company succeeded in opening a line across the Atlantic. This venture was Sibley's only notable failure.

12. Chandler, *Visible Hand*, p. 198; Du Boff, "Business Demand," p. 461.

13. Western Union's New York headquarters are described in *The Telegrapher*, July 15, 1867, pp. 249–250. See also, Western Union, annual reports of 1869 and 1873; Chandler, *Visible Hand*, pp. 197–198; Reid, *Telegraph*, pp. 485–486. The best account of the early history of Western Electric is George David Smith, "The Anatomy of a Business Decision: The Acquisition of Western Electric and the Origins of the Vertical Structure of the Bell Telephone System" (unpublished manuscript, 1981). We are grateful to Dr. Smith for permission to see his manuscript prior to publication.

14. Western Union, annual report (1869), pp. 17–19.

15. Chandler, *Visible Hand*, p. 197.

16. Harlow, *Old Wires*, pp. 338–339, points out that Congress considered postal telegraph bills in 1845, 1869, 1870, 1872, 1874, 1875, 1881, 1883, 1884, 1890, and 1896.

17. *The Telegrapher*, April 15, 1867, p. 180; Frank Parsons, *The Telegraph Monopoly* (Philadelphia: C. F. Taylor, 1899), esp. chaps. 4 and 5. Parsons' book is highly critical of Western Union but some of his charges are well documented.

18. Smith, *Anatomy of a Business Decision*, App. A.

19. "Deposition of Theodore N. Vail," in Circuit Court of the U.S. District of Massachusetts, in equity, *Western Union Telegraph Company, et al. vs. American Bell Telephone Company* (1899), *Record on Exceptions to*

*Master's Report*, vol. 1, p. 252; Sidney H. Aronson, "Bell's Electrical Toy: What's the Use? The Sociology of Early Telephone Usage," in Pool, ed., *Social Impact*, pp. 19-20.

20. U.S. Federal Communications Commission (FCC), *Investigation of the Telephone Industry in the United States* (Washington, D.C., 1939), p. 149.

21. The appellation is Watson's: Thomas A. Watson, *The Birth and Babyhood of the Telephone* (n.p., AT&T Information Department, n.d.), p. 41.

22. Donald T. Jenkins, "A Schumpeterian Analysis of the Origins of the American Telephone Industry," unpublished Harvard University seminar paper, 1974, p. 29. We wish to thank Professor Alfred D. Chandler, Jr. for making a copy of this paper available to us.

23. Ibid., p. 20.

24. FCC, *Investigation*, p. 150; Jenkins, "Schumpeterian Analysis," p. 17.

25. "Deposition of Vail," pp. 234, 248; FCC, *Investigation*, staff report, exhibit 1360A, pp. 203-210, 218; Jenkins, "Schumpeterian Analysis," pp. 18-19.

26. These functions were gathered into the "mechanical department" in 1884. See Leonard S. Reich, "Industrial Research and the Pursuit of Corporate Security: The Early Years of Bell Labs," *Business History Review*, 54 (Winter 1980), esp. p. 507. See also, FCC, *Investigation*, pp. 181-182; M. D. Fagen, ed., *A History of Engineering and Science in the Bell System: The Early Years (1875-1925)* (n.p., Bell Telephone Laboratories, Inc., 1975), pp. 37-38.

27. Horace Coon, *American Tel. & Tel. The Story of a Great Monopoly* (New York: Longmans, Green, 1939), p. 60; FCC, *Investigation*, exhibit 1360A, pp. 206, 217.

28. This agreement is printed in FCC, *Investigation*, exhibit 1360C, app. 7.

29. Smith, *Anatomy of a Business Decision*, chap. 2, sec. 6; cf. Rosario J. Tosiello, "The Birth and Early Years of the Bell Telephone System, 1876-1880" (unpublished Ph.D. dissertation, Boston University, 1971), chap. 14; Aronson, "Bell's Electrical Toy," pp. 15-19.

30. Smith, *Anatomy of a Business Decision*, chap. 2, sec. 6; Brock, *Telecommunications Industry*, pp. 89-99; Fagen, *History of Engineering*, pp. 473-475.

31. Quoted in Albert Bigelow Paine, *In One Man's Life. Being Chapters from the Personal and Business Career of Theodore N. Vail* (New York: Harper & Brothers, 1921), p. 126.

32. Smith, *Anatomy of a Business Decision*, passim.

33. FCC, *Investigation*, exhibit 1360A, p. 25.

34. J. Warren Stehman, *The Financial History of the American Telephone and Telegraphy Company* (Boston: Houghton Mifflin, 1925), pp. 26-27; Coon, *American Tel. & Tel.*, p. 72.

35. Harry B. MacMeal, *The Story of Independent Telephony* (Chicago: Independent Pioneer Telephone Association, 1934), pp. 40-41, 116, 155.

36. Ibid., passim.

37. Coon, *American Tel. & Tel.*, p. 80.

38. FCC, *Investigation*, pp. 133–134; exhibit 1360A, p. 30.

39. FCC, *Investigation*, exhibit 1360A, p. 36 features a chart showing the growth of the long-distance company's revenues. Cf. table 19, p. 81 in ibid. for figures on the combined income of AT&T and American Bell in the same period.

40. FCC, *Investigation*, p. 30.

41. The Kingsbury Commitment, named after AT&T vice-president N.C. Kingsbury, is printed in FCC, *Investigation*, exhibit 1360C, app. 18, sheets 2–3. The commitment was later embodied in federal legislation in the Willis-Graham Act (1921).

42. Reich, "Industrial Research," pp. 513–514; FCC, *Investigation*, chap. 7. As an illustration, the Bell System eagerly bought the rights to DeForest's vacuum tube in 1913. The 1907 Lab is described briefly in H. W. Bode, *Synergy: Technical Integration and Technological Innovation in the Bell System* (Murray Hill, N.J.: Bell Laboratories, 1971), pp. 63, 77, 99ff.

43. Manley R. Irwin, "The Telephone Industry," in Walter Adams, ed., *The Structure of American Industry*, 5th ed. (New York: MacMillan, 1975), p. 315.

44. Paine, *In One Man's Life*, p. 166; Theodore Newton Vail, *Views on Public Questions: A Collection of Papers and Addresses* (n.p., privately published, 1917), p. 24, from the annual report of 1910; ibid., p. 129, from an article in the *Atlantic Monthly* in 1913.

45. John Books, *Telephone: The First Hundred Years* (New York: Harper & Row, 1976), p. 173.

46. AT&T, *Words We Live By* (n.p., 1978), sec. 2.

47. Vail, *Views on Public Questions*, p. 13.

48. This account of OTC organization is based on American Telephone & Telegraph Company, *Application of Some Principles of Organization* (n.p., 1909).

49. As an illustration of how little things changed over the decades, Figure 8.6 can be compared with an organizational chart of New York Telephone in the 1930s (FCC, *Investigation*, exhibit 1360A, p. 167). The later structure is virtually identical except for the addition of a directory department and the separation of the commercial and sales departments.

50. FCC, *Investigation*, exhibit 1360A, p. 169.

51. FCC, *Investigation*, p. 35.

52. Reich, "Industrial Research," 525–529.

53. J. Brooks, *Telephone*, pp. 250–251.

54. Ibid., pp. 27–28.

55. FCC, *Investigation*, exhibit 1360A, p. 56; J. Brooks, *Telephone*, p. 6.

56. N. R. Danielian, *A.T.&T. The Story of an Industrial Conquest* (New York: Vanguard Press, 1939), chap. 9, esp. pp. 232, 227.

57. Thomas R. Brooks, *Communication Workers of America: The Story of a Union* (New York: Mason/Charter, 1977), pp. 3–9, 78–80, 166–168.

58. See, for example, Elinor Langer, "The Women of the Telephone Company," *New York Review of Books*, issues of March 12 and March 26, 1970.

59. Danielian, *A.T.&T.*, pp. 216–217.

60. Brooks, *Telephone*, p. 191.
61. Ibid., p. 167.
62. AT&T has been the testing ground or field site for several other impor-
    tant studies: Chester A. Barnard, *The Functions of the Executive* (Cam-
    bridge, Mass.: Harvard University Press, 1939); Robert N. Ford, *Motiva-
    tion through the Work Itself* (New York: American Management
    Association, 1969); and some current quality of work life experiments.
63. T. Brooks, *Communications Workers*, chaps. 8, 10.
64. Irwin, "Telephone Industry," p. 317.
65. See M. D. Fagen, *Impact: A Compilation of Bell System Innovations in
    Science and Engineering Which Have Helped Create New Industries and
    Products* (n.p., Bell Laboratories, 1971), for a catalog and brief descrip-
    tion of innovations at Bell Labs.
66. John W. Kendrick and Elliot S. Grossman, *Productivity in the United
    States: Trends and Cycles* (Baltimore: Johns Hopkins University Press,
    1980), pp. 6, 38, 69–70; cf. Laurits Christensen, Diane Cummings, and
    Philip Schoech, "Productivity in the Bell System, 1947–1977," paper de-
    livered at the 8th Annual Telecommunications Policy Research Confer-
    ence, Annapolis, Md., April 29, 1980.
67. See, for example, Bode, *Synergy*, chap. 5, for a brief statement of
    AT&T's position.
68. John Sheahan, "Integration and Exclusion in the Telephone Equipment
    Industry," *Quarterly Journal of Economics* 70 (1956): 263–265. See also,
    Alfred E. Kahn, *The Economics of Regulation*, vol. 2, *Institutions* (New
    York: John Wiley, 1971), pp. 290–305 for an excellent economic analysis
    of vertical integration in the Bell System.
69. This section closely follows a similar section in *AT&T: Adaptation in
    Progress (A)* (HBS Case Services 9-481-074), pp. 15–18. For an extended
    analysis of emerging changes in this industry see Brock, *Telecommunica-
    tions Industry*, chap. 8–10.
70. Albert D. Wheelon, "Telecommunications Satellites: Their Future Con-
    tribution," *Computers & People*, January-February 1980, p. 14.
71. J. Brooks, *Telephone*, p. 9.
72. John R. Meyer, Robert W. Wilson, M. Alan Baughcum, Ellen Burton,
    and Louis Caouette, *The Economics of Competition in the Telecom-
    munications Industry* (Boston: Charles River Associates, August 1979),
    p. 67.
73. Ibid., p. 71.
74. The most complete discussion of the FCC decisions is Thomas Joseph Ke-
    hoe, "Federal Communications Commission Regulation of the American
    Telephone and Telegraph Company, 1965–1974" (unpublished Ph.D.
    dissertation, New York University, 1978), esp. chap. 2.
75. FCC, *In the Matter of Amendment of Section 64.702 of the Commission's
    Rules and Regulations (Second Computer Inquiry)*, docket 20828, *Final
    Decision* (Washington, D.C., May, 1980).
76. This section draws heavily on the case series *AT&T: Adaptation in Pro-
    gress* (see footnote at beginning of chap. 8, this volume).
77. Irwin, "Telephone Industry," pp. 328–329.

## Chapter 9.　THE READAPTIVE
## PROCESS: FITTING IT TOGETHER

1. Henry Mintzberg, *The Structuring of Organizations*, (New York: Prentice-Hall, 1979).
2. This again is Mintzberg's term.
3. We are again borrowing this term from Mintzberg.
4. Raymond Miles, and Charles Snow, *Organizational Strategy, Structure, and Process* (New York: McGraw Hill, 1978), p. 29.
5. William Ouchi, *Theory Z* (Addison-Wesley, 1981).
6. James March, and Herbert Simon, *Organizations* (New York: Wiley, 1958).

## Chapter 10.　THE READAPTIVE PROCESS:
## PUTTING IT TO WORK

1. Ezra F. Vogel, "Guided Free Enterprise In Japan," *Harvard Business Review*, (May-June 1978):

# Index

**J**

**K**

**L**